Random Events Tend To Cluster

Published by Lisa Hagan Books 2017

www.lisahaganbooks.com

Powered by

SHADOW TEAMS

Copyright © Judy Wieder 2017.

ISBN: 9781945962097

All Rights Reserved. No part of this publication may be reproduced, stored in a retrieval system, or transmitted in any form, or by any means, electronic, mechanical, photocopying, recording or otherwise without the prior permission in writing of the copyright holders, nor be otherwise circulated in any form or binding or cover other than in which it is published and without a similar condition being imposed on the subsequent publisher.

Interior formatting by Simon Hartshorne

[Author's Note: Some names have been changed to protect a person's privacy. Some characters are a composite of several real people. This memoir is written in the present tense. Everyone changes over time. For the "FURTHER READING" list that educated and inspired the author, please go to IntuitionsMedia.com.]

Random Events Tend To Cluster

a memoir

Judy Wieder

Contents

	Preface	9
1	Judy & The Lost Boys In The 'Hood	12
2	Swimming In The River Jordan	33
3	Greenwich and My Lai: A Tale of Two Villages	88
4	On A Gender Bender	173
5	When Rhythm Gets The Blues	225
6	A Mother of A Meltdown	283
7	Between Rock And A Hard Place	320
8	"Judy Wieder—*Lesbian!*"	356
9	Matthew and Nicole	403
10	Aloha Technology!	442
	Afterword	473
	Acknowledgments	480

Judy Wieder is an extraordinary person who has lived an astonishing life in which she has made rich and enduring contributions. From a child musician, Judy went on to win an R & B Grammy, tour as a heavy metal journalist, and launch the first national black-teen magazine. She was an exceptional first female Editor-in-Chief of *The Advocate*, the largest gay newsmagazine at the height of the LGBT movement for equality in America.

I had a front row seat to Judy's profound ability to lead. In a movement often marked by division and strife, Judy was the unifying wise voice in the storm. She brought a brand of talent, integrity and intelligence to her work that rivals the very highest standards of global journalism. And now she brings us the gift of this book.

– Elizabeth Birch, former Executive Director, Human Rights Foundation

Judy was the first woman Editor-in-Chief of *The Advocate*. She turned the brand into the "magazine of record" for the LGBT community. She rose in the ranks to become the Corporate Editorial Director of the company where she oversaw the purchase and redesign of the *Out* brand, the launch of *The Out Traveler* brand, and the revitalization of Alyson Books. Her passion, creativity, ingenuity, and drive inspired me on a daily basis. I find her memoir absolutely enthralling!

– Joe Landry, Executive Vice President, Here Media

For Suzanne

Preface

Many years ago, three unfortunate things happened to me within the space of a single week: First, my apartment was robbed after I dashed out the front door calling for my dog, who'd scurried into the night. Apparently, an opportunistic thief passing me on the sidewalk as I screamed my dog's name, figured I'd be gone for a bit; so he ran in the apartment and grabbed my purse and a few other things. I found the dog.

Then, the very next day, I got a call from one of my oldest and closest female friends. She told me some screwball she was nice to while showing an apartment in the building she managed, had started stalking her. The police said there was nothing they could do unless he attacked her, so she moved out of the neighborhood.

And finally, worst of all, my first and best gay male friend, an author and enthusiastic fan of my own writing, committed suicide. I was a basket case.

Why had all these dire things happened at once, one right after the other? Frantic with grief and dread, I felt very small and vulnerable. I wanted the comfort of nurturing grown-ups, perhaps even my own parents, though in truth, they weren't always up to the task of solace when it came to me.

I drove to their home and found only my Dad in that evening. When I unloaded the distressing week on him, he stared at me with his deep sienna eyes. Dad was a scientist, a mathematician, and an aeronautical engineer. He didn't know what to do with his own emotions, let alone mine. Things had to have logic to him, a rule, a rationale—even in poetry and literature. Feelings were messy.

I thought he'd begin with, "Calm down, Judy," but he didn't. Instead he said something I will never forget: "Sometimes, for no reason, 'Random events tend to cluster.' It's a physics principle, if I remember correctly."

I think I must have just glared at him, frustrated. "What?" I finally managed to whisper.

"For instance," he continued, undeterred, "if you flip a coin many times, you will get enough heads in a row to surprise most people. Normally, people think of random as being something more 'uniformly distributed' in heads and tails. Like first heads, then tails, then tails again, then perhaps heads again. Instead, the coin flips will actually turn up heads more often; they will cluster…

"*Stop! Dad!* What are you talking about? What has this got to do with me? The world is clobbering me from all sides! I'm sorry I came over. I know it's difficult for you when I'm upset…"

But he pushed back. "Judy, I know it feels like the end of the world, or at least the end of *your* world," he persisted. "But it's not. No one is out to get you. Luck has not turned against you. It just happened this way. All these things coming at you in rapid succession? There's no special evil behind it. Sometimes things cluster randomly for no reason. Just the way good things cluster too. This will pass. You will be fine."

Suddenly I understood. He was comforting me in his way—using a formula of all things! But odder still, it was working. I felt something dark leaving my body. I was going to get over this. I wasn't alone. He was there. My father had his own—decidedly unique—way of opening my eyes to a bigger picture. And squinting like a beginner on that memorable evening, I could almost glimpse it.

Preface

My life has been, and continues to be, a piñata of implausible and sometimes fabulous surprises. There is no way to have planned the path it's taken and no one is more stupefied and pleased than I am.

But lucky and full as it is, my life coexists with many vital and revolutionary events that have occurred during the past half-century. Are they random, really? Do they cluster with meaning or arbitrariness? Perhaps we alone must decide.

As a classical child musician, working songwriter, creator and editor of the first national black-teen magazine, touring journalist for music magazines, first female editor-in-chief of the gay & lesbian newsmagazine of record during the height of the gay-rights movement, and editorial director of a multi-million-dollar media company, I've had the privilege—and uncommon good fortune—of being exactly where history is happening.

Yet, like all of us in the heat of our own lives, I was too caught up in the work in front of me to see the jaw-dropping, "clusters" going on in the world around me. But *now* I can see them. Looking back, I've had 20/20 hindsight into the rich backstories quietly informing my own experiences. And being able to observe them with the advantage of distance, I can clearly see how certain events taking place at the same time undeniably influence each other.

Awakening to these "random historical events" bumping against my life has been profound; the experience has landed on me like a wild animal and blown open the boundaries of my own story. So, I want to expand my father's physics principle by attaching another theory to it, a Buddhist proverb:

"You cannot touch a flower without disturbing a star."

People, entities, events, feelings, circumstances, matter, and all that matters, not only cluster, they affect each other. Thank you for the bigger picture, Dad, and behold:

1

Judy & The Lost Boys In The 'Hood

I am six-years-old and Grandville Avenue is the street I rule. My two-year-old brother, Jonathan, is running out the front door and into the street with his diaper falling off. Thank God for me, 'cause I can scream so frighteningly loud, the sounds of screeching car brakes are drowned out completely. Traffic on our pleasant street is at a complete standstill when my mother comes racing out the front door of our little tract house. Wearing a red and white gingham blouse—which nicely frames the blush of horror on her face—she stops on our front lawn, standing warrior-like amid the splashing sprinklers, waiting for her next cue.

I wail harder to get her focused: "*Maaahhhh-meeee!* He's loose again." I point to Jonathan getting ready to put an unsteady leg further into the street.

"*Stop!*" she gives one of her nuclear power-shouts, way louder than I ever could. Screaming is one of Mom's specialties. I know I get my volume from her, but her yelling scares me. She does it a lot, and mostly I don't know why.

For a split second, my brother freezes. Cars now pull as far away as they can from Jonny. Giving him the kind of generous latitude granted the village newborn, they stop cold, even try backing up, as he wobbles hell-bent towards his murky destiny. Mom continues to wave her arms threateningly as she

1 Judy & The Lost Boys In The 'Hood

follows him into the abyss. Suddenly, it's very quiet, as if the sun is holding its breath. Then scooping up her surprised son, she races back to me on the curb.

"Why didn't you stop him?" she yells at me, as she rushes by toward the house. "You could have done something!"

Like what? If I had run into the street after him, we both could have been hood ornaments! Better to scream for her to scream.

This kind of stuff happens all the time. I'm always busy. I run the neighborhood. It's my job. Being a girl doesn't hold me back from leading many super-smart guys (two of whom got the highest IQ scores in Los Angeles) into constant trouble. Over the next years, I officialize this fact by becoming founder and chief of "The Mischief Club." More on that later.

We live in Mar Vista, a part of Los Angeles, as the troubled '30s and '40s finally give way to the incomprehensible '50s. It's 1950 exactly, and our home is directly next door to The Mar Vista Grammar School. We actually moved here before they built the school, so I feel like I have the upper hand. It's very exciting. Bells ring all day long. Balls fly over the fence and people beg you to throw them back. There are busloads of kids that could be my friends even though they're not. I can go home for lunch everyday even though I don't.

Our backyard has a swing, a crib that my brother breaks out of whenever he's in it, and a fence with a gate. The gate leads to another backyard and the home of my parents' best friends, the Demings. They live on Stoner Avenue. *That's* the early 50s for you. You could name a street "Stoner" and not guffaw. At first there was only Margaret and Fred Deming—both dancers in movies—and their son, Michael, whose birthday is the same day as his mother's. I bring this up because this proved incredibly confusing to both Michael and me when my brother was born. You see, since I'm born on my father's birthday and

Random Events Tend To Cluster

Michael's born on his mother's birthday, we wisely concluded that you simply couldn't arrive here without being born on one of your parent's birthdays. My brother Jonathan's birth on no parent's birthday, and a year later, Michael's sister Jenny's birth on any old day, really disgusted us. It was one of those early *What's the point of figuring stuff out?* — disappointments.

Michael's mother, Margaret—we call her Maggie—is a terrific seamstress. She makes sleeping bags and fabulous little cowboy outfits for us with fringed vests, little denim jeans, and a real holster for our toy guns. Apparently, we spend a good part of our lives driving all sorts of bad characters out of the neighborhood, and developing rather officious personalities along the way.

Maggie told me about a time when she, Fred, and Michael were traveling through Mexico, and a traffic patrolman pulled them over. Fred decided the reason was altogether bogus, so he reached for his wallet to bribe the policeman. This didn't go over well, and the officer asked Fred to step out of the car. Just then, Michael—always impressed with authority figures—bolted out the back, yelling, "Judy hit me with a stick! Judy hit me with a stick!" Somehow this weirdness did the trick. The cop waved them on, which doesn't bode well for law enforcement in Mexico because I wasn't even in the car.

Mom says whenever she used to cross the border from Mexico back to San Diego, where Dad was stationed in the Army for some time, the border patrol thought she was smuggling a little Mexican girl into the States. My naturally tan skin and curly hair flagged their attention, so Mom took to bringing my birth certificate along just to make things easier. I guess she was lucky that they didn't say, "Oh, so *that's* Judy—didn't she hit some kid with a stick?"

But for me, the innocent joy of clasping Michael's hands in mine, leaning back, and spinning round and round in my backyard, shouting in unison "We're both five! We're both five!" was bliss beyond ice cream. Then I turned six the very next week and Michael didn't. We decided we could still be friends, though maybe we'd branch out a little, for in our neighborhood, the yard really does go on forever.

You can walk to the end of Grandville Avenue, where it intersects with Woodbine Street, and a bevy of families with children my age, await. My folks found everybody at the same time. Honestly, it's an embarrassment of early-childhood riches! After the Demings, we met the Mitchells: Mina and Bob (Bob works at Mattel Toys), and their twin sons Ralph and David. They're the boys who scored the highest I.Q. tests—a fact that agitates the neighborhood parents so much they bring it up constantly, torturing the rest of us kids ("The Mitchell boys have the top L.A. IQ scores." "Did you hear about the Mitchell boys' IQ scores?"), like Tourette's Syndrome.

Big deal! So, the twins are geniuses. But they're still dupes and pushovers. I manage to trick them into putting on their heaviest shoes and sliding down a freshly painted car (that was stored in Dad's garage) until the new paint is ruined. How bright can that be? I told them, "Go on! Put on your heaviest shoes and come slide down Horace's car." And they did! Was I being mean? No, I was just making a point about being "smart." Intelligence isn't all that useful if you're not also "on the ball"—a favorite expression of Mom's—though the "ball" part confuses me.

But honestly, I'm crazy about the twins. My only problem is telling them apart. It's their biggest problem too. See, it's very disturbing to be a person whom nobody's sure is really you. Maybe you are your brother!

For instance: Last week I was riding in the front seat of the Mitchell's car while Mina was driving and the boys were in the back seat. Suddenly I wanted to tell Ralph something; but when I turned to tell him, I wasn't sure which twin was Ralph.

As usual, I asked Mina. "Who is Ralph?"

She looked at me a little sad. "Why don't you ask them?"

I was bewildered. "Do they know?"

"Judy," Mina said, using her low-register-I'm-trying-to-be-patient-with-you voice, "Are you Judy or are you Jonny?"

WOW. That hit me like flying food. I turned around and looked in the back seat. The twins were waiting and smiling.

"I'm Ralph," one announced.

"I'm David," said the other. You'd think they'd just aced another I.Q. test the way they were vibrating back there. In fact, Ralph looked so happy, just basking in the glory of being able to distill himself from David, I wish I could have guessed right then and there, that being able to continue doing this in years to come, would become the struggle of both their lives. As identical twins—who look exactly alike at first glance—with similar tastes and interests, they will fight their attachment in an ultimately futile struggle to be separate and to find lasting individuality: They will live in different cities, go to different schools, and insist on different friends. Finally, gratefully, they will accept their deep bond, attend Harvard Grad School together, and become highly respected scientists involved in important research—only to have their lives shattered in their mid-40s, when they're both ensnared in the early years of an unforgiving epidemic, and die within a year of each other.

But thank God, none of that happens today while we're still kids and working on solving one of the twin's most pressing childhood questions: "Which would you rather eat: throw-up or doo-doo?"

"Wanna see what Juno can do?" David asks me; with that demonic grin he and his brother can whip their faces into right before sharing some of the worst tommyrot. Juno is the Mitchell's German Shepherd. We are all in the Mitchell's living room—Mom, Dad, Jon, and I—about to have dinner with the twin's family. The boys are nuts about Juno and play obsessively with her. Well, they do everything obsessively. I think they prefer Juno to anyone, and tonight I find out why.

"Watch this," Ralph instructs everyone. Dave is so excited he is shaking. "Hurry up!" he yells at the swinging kitchen door, behind which he knows his mother is still fussing over the meal.

At this point, they're literally swaying back and forth in place they're so wired. So, I quickly sit down next to my parents and brother and try to get them to act interested in the twins. Mina and Bob take their seats as well.

"Thanks," David says sweetly, surveying his captive audience. All at once he starts running around the couch as fast as he can. After a few seconds, Juno begins to chase David. We all sit there stupidly as he continues circling the couch over and over again, with poor Juno panting away behind him. Just as my mother says, "OK, Davy, enough!" Ralph takes David's place and starts racing around the couch while David dives behind a nearby chair. Juno doesn't notice at first, and continues chasing Ralph as if he was David.

Then, like a cartoon dog coming to a screeching halt, Juno sticks her front legs out and skids to a stop. Ralph follows suit. Juno walks up to Ralph, smells him, steps back, and barks. Then she turns, sniffs a few times until she picks ups David's scent, walks over to the chair he's hiding behind, and barks triumphantly.

Applause, applause! "Good dog, Juno. You can tell the twins apart!" But it will take me years to understand the magnitude of well-being this "trick" brings to Ralph and David. It's the joy of having someone, anyone, even a dog, know without a doubt—exactly who you are.

What is it about smart boys? Their frantic energy is so undiluted, so incisive and ferocious, and so different from us girls—though I don't really know this now. I keep thinking

I'm one of them. And yet, I can sense something. Right in the midst of a tumultuous game of hide and go seek, some space, some shadow, some margin opens up in which I exist without them. And in that space, I can observe things. I see how easily they go bonkers when something thwarts their game. They're lost, spinning like feral animals in their own fur. It seems to me they suffer because they never expect anyone but them to control the narrative—even at six! And, I know I'm here to poke a big hole in that notion. I can't explain why. I just know it's my job to make their toy box explode!

Yesterday, for example, I watched the simultaneous crack-ups of "Chicky" (Michael) Brustin, Michael Deming, and Ralph and David Mitchell just because I poured a bottle of milk into a neighbor's mail box, and blamed it on them. (This is the Mischief Club stuff I mentioned). What a pathetic sight. I was embarrassed for them. I tried not to look at the lot of them blubbering and spitting baby teeth at the neighbor about their innocence in the prank.

Then Ralph threw my bike into the street, and said they were all going to beat-up Jonathan as payback. Okay, wow, that freaked me. I've never understood the word "consequences" when Mother yells it at me; but in that moment, I think I glimpsed the concept.

* * *

Piliki is six too. At this moment, there are two thuggish men standing on the front steps of her Honolulu home. The frightened girl is trying her best to understand why her mother would leave her there to greet them alone. Worse yet, from the other room, Piliki can hear her mother crying. "It's *them*," she's wailing. "How is it possible it's happening again? The bounty hunters are back!"

1 Judy & The Lost Boys In The 'Hood

Bounty hunters? Is this about my father? Piliki wonders, still holding the front door open. Although her father died suddenly of a heart attack last year when Piliki was still living in Kaua'i, the six-year-old remembers hearing her mother say, "bounty hunters" often before he died. And lately Piliki has heard her rambling more and more about her father, as well as her dead grandfather. Why?

"Is your *makuahine* [mother] home?" one of the somber officials snaps at her, annoyed that they are being kept outside. "We must speak to your makuahine."

Piliki turns to retrieve her only parent. "Wait," the other officer orders "We need you to stay here. Just call out for her, he instructs, while clutching a worn briefcase full of papers. "Don't you leave!"

Piliki calls for her again loudly, feeling a wave of heat rush to her burning cheeks. Somehow instinct tells her not to ask the men in. Finally, her makuahine, head bowed, shuffles up beside her. The men address her sharply with words Piliki does not understand. Then, despite her makuahine's objections, they push by the two of them and enter the small living room.

Oddly there is silence. No one speaks for a minute; Piliki takes it as a good sign and asks her mother if she can go outside to play. Just as her mother says, "yes," both men grunt, "no!" and instruct them to be seated together. Piliki sits on the couch next to her quivering makuahine. Across from them, one sitting, one standing, the two officials from Hawaii's Health Department begin their well-rehearsed rap. Rearranging some papers with Piliki's name on each of them, they spread the sheets out. With great care, they hide one sheet containing Piliki's father's information at the top. Then they begin speaking:

"You have several small water blisters on your body," one envoy addresses Piliki.

"No, no," her makuahine interrupts frantically. "They've gone away. She's better!"

"I am sorry," the other official says in a weary tone. After all their years doing this, both men have seen and heard every possible reaction so often, they no longer feel a thing. Besides, there's $10 in it for each for them if they bring Piliki to the hospital before she runs away.

"Your daughter's cheeks are rosy, and have been that way for weeks. She has complained of stomachaches. I can see a discolored spot on her hand from where I am standing," he says, pointing at Piliki's left hand, which she quickly pulls behind her back.

"Piliki was examined by the school doctor who called the health department," the other officer continues briskly when he sees Piliki's mother try to speak. "We are very familiar with these marks and what they mean."

"They don't hurt, Sir," Piliki offers, but feels her makuahine's hand grab her arm to stop her.

"Yes, we know they don't, Piliki. Numbness is one of the signs. The school doctor took a cutting from your skin, and we have preliminary results…"

"But I didn't even feel it when he cut me!" Piliki tries again, still not understanding. This time her mother doesn't even try to shush her; instead she merely drops her head in her hands and sobs.

"We need you to come with us," the older official says.

"No! She is too young!" Makuahine blurts, unafraid suddenly.

"Madam, be still. This will do you no good."

"Where will you take her?" she cries out, undeterred. "She's only a child. She can't go there, where you took her… her…" Makuahine catches herself quickly, but her resolve melts into tears.

The men ignore the disintegration going on in front of them, and concentrate instead on the terrified child. To Piliki, they explain that more cuttings are necessary to "confirm the diagnosis."

"What?'" Piliki whimpers defeated, finally caving into her mother's clutching arms. Makuahine cuddles and rocks her daughter helplessly as one agent attempts to pull Piliki free.

"No!" Makuahine screams, when Piliki is abruptly wrenched away from her.

Ignoring her protests he says simply, "Enough! We are taking her to Kalihi Hospital in Honolulu. We are doing this because we must finish testing her. As you know yourself, these are all symptoms of Leprosy!"

"No! No! Don't say that!"

* * *

Emptying a bottle of milk into the neighbor's front door mail slot, turns into a real parental nightmare for me. It's hard to get all the information when people are screaming at you, but I definitely heard about "desecrated carpets" and "sour furniture smells." I just don't know what it all means, other than "no television for a week"—one of mother's "consequences?"

It's clear all this "Judy and the lost boys" just isn't doing it for Mom anymore. She decides what will fix things is me making a friend who isn't a boy.

"It's time for Judy to play with girls," I hear her telling my father, one evening after I broke a lamp trying to be Tarzan. "She doesn't have the slightest idea what girls do or how they play," she goes on.

"What do you mean?" Dad asks.

"I bought her two Mattel dolls…." Mom says.

"Well, that's good, right?"

"No, not if she ripped off their arms and legs and rolled their heads down the street with the twins! That's not how girls play with dolls!" she says.

Who can say why boys seem to match my rambunctious personality and fill my days with the perfect commotion? I just have a lot of screwy energy. Does it really matter that I roll doll parts up and down streets with the Mitchell twins and play baseball using Chatty Cathy's head with Chicky and Michael?

Apparently. One day Mom sees a neighborhood girl, Anne Beth, sitting quietly on our backyard swing. And it begins:

"Judy, come in here quickly!" she yells to me from the kitchen where she's doing dishes.

Ugh, chores?

"Look at that lovely girl on your swing. Go out there and make yourself a friend," she coos, as if she hasn't set up the whole thing.

I look out the window. Anne Beth looks very girly to me. She's roundish, freckled, wearing a little yellow dress and, honest to God, has ribbons in her hair. This isn't going to work. I don't like her.

I explain my feelings very carefully to Mom. I don't whine. I smile. She does not meet me halfway. She's not interested. She frowns, sighs, and says my reasons are the exact reasons that she wants me out there with this girl. "You need a 'girly' friend too. You can't just horse around in the mud with boys all the time."

Now that's so typical. I do not see my life that way at all. The nifty contraptions we build, like the space panel. The big rocks we find, the things we collect and roll down the street—fantastic.

And really, what am I going to do with this silly thing on the swing?

* * *

"Why is my daughter cursed with this *too?!*" Piliki's mother persists in her futile arguing.

The word "too" springs across their island living room like a tiny gecko, catching Piliki's attention.

"It can't be happening again in this family! *Oh, Analu!*" the distressed woman rails on between bouts of sobbing.

Piliki runs to her makuahine, astonished. Why is she calling out her papa's name? Where is he? Although she only knew her father for five short years, he was everything to Piliki. Before he died, every evening, she and her older sister, Malakia, waited for him to return from the sugar plantation in Kaua'i, where he worked. After his death, her makuahine moved Piliki and her sister to Honolulu, though the girls never understood why. Makuahine said she "felt closer" to their father in Honolulu than on Kaua'i. But that made no sense. The island of O'ahu was never Analu's home.

"You can wait for Piliki while she has further tests at Kalihi Hospital, in Honolulu," Piliki overhears the officer assuring her weeping mother. Finally, one of them literally lifts Piliki's makuahine upright off the couch, and shakes her hard.

"You have to stop this!" he hisses at her. "Your daughter needs you! You must help her gather her things."

"I will. I will. If you would only come back tomorrow, please," makuahine begs.

"*You* of all people know we can't do that!" the officer insists. "We will not give you the opportunity to run away with Piliki, or attempt to hide your daughter with someone. We know all the tricks. And *you* know all the tricks. You have seen how this works"

"We must take her now," the unshaven *haole* [Caucasian] officer says; and with that, he grabs Piliki by the wrist with his leather-gloved hand. She lets out a shriek that nearly stops her makuahine's heart cold. No one else cares. Without further interruption, the health officer leads Piliki out the front door to their official health van.

The younger officer holds makuahine back gently. "You can visit her. You know that. It won't be so bad," he advises her, offering unusual comfort. "She will meet others like herself, make new friends. She may even get to see her…"

"No, shhhh! Don't say it!" Makuahine whispers. "Piliki doesn't know her father is alive!"

✳   ✳   ✳

"I'm Anne Beth," the sweet package of good-behavior announces to me at the backdoor. "Your mother told my mother I should come over and wait on the swing for you to find me. Then I guess we…become friends."

"OK," I say, not wanting to be rude in case she tells her mother who will tell my mother. "What do you want to do? Would you like to swing?"

"Do you have any dolls?" she asks pleasantly.

"Dolls! No, I don't have dolls."

Anne Beth stares at me with pity. She thinks I am suffering because I have no dolls to play with. "That's ok," she says, waving me to follow her. "I do."

I walk into my backyard with her, despondent. I glance toward the Deming's backyard gate, hoping some miracle might cause Michael to pop out and invite me to visit the moon with him.

"I have lots of dolls we can play with," she continues, oblivious to my despair. "I have a whole collection…"

"I hate dolls. *I kill dolls!*" I blurt cruelly, hoping to scare her off. This stops her cold.

1 Judy & The Lost Boys In The 'Hood

"Why?" she asks incredulously, her large cocoa brown eyes tearing up.

"Don't cry!" I say, aghast. "I just don't like playing with them. Little tiny people? I don't understand what to do with them. I get bored."

Now I've done it. I feel out of control. I feel like this a lot of the time. "I…I don't want a new friend. I already have friends and they don't like dolls either—unless we take them apart and roll their heads downhill or hit them with bats…"

"*What?!*" Anne Beth sobs. She looks so freaked, I start crying too.

Mother Paula is staring at us from the kitchen window as we cry and sputter at each other. A very dark look crosses her face, which makes me cry harder. I know she doesn't like how this new girl thing is going, at all.

"Judy! Really, what in…?" she says, making one of her authoritative entrances through the kitchen door into the yard. I should mention here that I'm used to Mom's tempestuous temperament, but the neighborhood boys usually vault at least 12 feet back when she arrives like this. However, I notice that this little Anne Beth girlie person isn't fazed at all.

Why doesn't this scary-ass adult frighten the ribbons out of her hair?

※ ※ ※

Piliki is standing on a large wooden lazy-susan platform. She is completely naked except for a sheet that has been wrapped around her, leaving her back exposed. There are three band aids on her, where, a few hours earlier, a hospital doctor took a razor and snipped her hand, ear lobe, and upper back. The samples from Piliki's body are being analyzed as the humiliating examination continues.

Three male doctors from the Board of Examining Doctors enter the room. They have been told that they are dealing with a petrified six-year-old, so they've assumed freakish grinning facial expressions. Piliki is not comforted.

A nurse removes the six-year-old's sheet, and begins turning the platform clockwise. The three doctors, positioned like opposite points of a triangle, slowly inspect the child's shivering body as she passes round and round them. When Piliki tries to cover her left hand or thighs, the nurse moves in quickly and stops her.

"It's all right," one of the younger doctors smiles. "You have such lovely eyes, Piliki," he addresses the girl as she turns past him.

Piliki begins to cry. "No, no, I am bad. Something wrong with me! *Makuahine!*" she weeps, calling for her mother. The other doctors continue their note-taking, numb to all the frightened children they probe. After 20 minutes, the examination ends, and the nurse brings Piliki back to the small cubicle where she had been stripped earlier. "Wait here for a minute," she instructs. "I will get you some infirmary pajamas."

In the main office of the hospital, Piliki's mother and sister sit frozen. There's been a mix up and they did not get to say goodbye to Piliki. One of the doctors from the board comes by and confirms what Piliki's mother knew long before any snippings were taken: Piliki has the active leprosy bacilli, mercifully renamed "Hansen's Disease" after the Norwegian physician, Gerhard Hansen, who identified the germs causing the illness. He also discovered that only 5% of the human population has the genetics to get Hansen's Disease, even if exposed to it.

Unfortunately, despite such forward movement in medicine and science, the cultural attitudes remain backwards and cruel through the 40s, 50s, and 60s. Most continue to use the word "leprosy" for the illness, and "lepers" for the patients. Worse yet, this ignorance is accompanied by a cruel behavior known as "blaming the victim," or insisting the patient brought the sickness on him or herself with "dirty, sinful behavior:" "This is God's punishment for your depraved actions!" Out of this destructive presumption springs the equally injurious consequence of punishing those who are ill with total isolation.

Sadly, without enlightenment, human error tends to repeat itself—and in this case, it does: During the height of an epidemic 30 years in the future, the U.S. Surgeon General will hear from terrified and "concerned citizens" that all AIDS patients should be isolated and sent away, perhaps to Kalaupapa, on the Hawaiian island of Moloka'i, where many Hansen's Disease patients still live. In fact, the Surgeon General will actually make a trip to Kalaupapa to inspect "The Colony" before deciding it's not a good idea; though he does concede, "AIDS is the new Leprosy!"

"Hello?" Piliki calls out softly from her cubicle. "Please, somebody, I want my makuahine. *Papa...?*" She whispers, tentatively. The ailing child has never felt so alone in her life.

※ ※ ※

Mom remains on the back porch, hands on hips, eyes flaming.

"What is going on?" she hisses, making it clear it's all my fault. "She's been here 20 minutes and you've got her crying," she points to Anne Beth. Then, to me, she asks, "How did you manage that?"

"Mrs. Wieder, Judy didn't make me cry," Anne Beth says with considerable self-assurance.

Mom's head almost falls off from whipping it back around to face this polite little girl. "W-what?" she stammers, truly confused.

Anne Beth respectfully repeats herself. "This isn't Judy's fault. She didn't make me cry. I just cry a lot."

"She didn't?" Mom says. Now if mom's surprised about this tiny iron soul in front of her, I'm stupefied. This has never happened to me before. All my boys pretty much run for the hills when we're in trouble.

"No, no. We were just talking about dolls, and I, well, I kept talking and talking about my dolls and it made Judy upset and that made me cry and that made her cry. It's my fault."

Her fault? Oh, I like this Anne Beth girlie person.

"Show me your dolls," I blurt out.

"Really?" Anne Beth says.

"Really?" my mother echoes.

"Sure. Let's go," I say, pointing the way to the gate in the fence.

Mom takes hold of my arm for a second and yanks me to her: "Don't tear her doll's head off!" she hiss-whispers to me. Then she lets me go.

"Bye," I say and wave. She smiles and waves back at me. But her face doesn't look right, like she's slipped and fallen into the land of the bewildered. Like: *Yes, isn't my daughter wonderful? There she goes. Off to play with dolls! HUH?*

"Nice to meet you, Mrs. Wieder," the unexpected-but-getting-more-interesting Anne Beth calls back to her as we leave. I look at her silly ribbons bobbing up and down as we walk down the street, and feel really happy; my first girl friend. Not so awful at all.

* * *

Piliki looks at her small suitcase. There's almost nothing of her Honolulu life in it. "She won't need much," the nurses told her mother. Clothes and small items can be bought at the hospital.

1 Judy & The Lost Boys In The 'Hood

Her makuahine tried to pack Piliki's favorite doll, but was told it was best to burn all her possessions and clothes. The hospital may provide a new doll for her in time. But for now, only photos can accompany her from her old home.

At Kalihi Hospital, where officials brought her last week, Piliki will share sleeping quarters with one other young girl, also being examined and treated for early stages of Hansen's Disease. There is a small research laboratory on the premises funded by the National Institute of Health, but by the end of the 1940s, most experimentation on patients stopped.

"Why can't my makuahine come inside here with me?" Piliki asks over and over to the nurses. Patiently they explain the same thing. "People who come from the islands, like you, Piliki, cannot fight off this sickness alone. You need a lot of medicine. And, it is very easy to make other Hawaiians sick with this illness. So, our government must isolate—keep apart—anyone with this illness. Your makuahine and sister are not sick. So, they cannot be in here with you. Do you understand?"

Piliki sobs. How much she understands, no one knows. Only that in one week all her friends are gone and she can only see her mother briefly across a chain-link fence that keeps visitors on one side and patients on another.

"There are new, very good drugs we can use on you," the main hospital doctor explains to Piliki, now sitting on a chilly steel examination table trying her best to be 'brave and good,' as her mother asked of her. "The sulfones we now have are making patients better."

Perhaps if she listens and doesn't cry too much, they will let her go home? Instead the doctors and nurses continue to lecture her as if piling on scientific explanations of what's happening to her small body will do something other than drive her deeper into despair: "For you, my dear girl, there is such hope," one doctor says with genuine enthusiasm. As he talks,

Piliki tries to cope with another bout of tears. "Your life will not be like those who came before. With sulfur drugs and the miraculous Dapsone drug to boost your immune system against PCP..." he rambles on.

"What is pee pee...?" Piliki asks, her chattering teeth slowing down the doctor's patter for a moment.

"Pneumonia Carinii or Pneumocystis," he explains, as if he's lecturing to a forum of specialists. "It is a very bad illness that can happen if your immune system does not work any longer."

"My system doesn't work?" Piliki whimpers.

"Doctor, please!" a nurse moves in to rescue Piliki, who looks more and more battered by the doctor's words. But he is stubborn and insists on finishing his ineffectual attempt to make the little girl smile over his complicated "good news."

"Piliki! Listen, there are many medications and treatments, and in time we can make sure that you are not contagious. You may never have to go to The Colony on Kalaupapa. You may even be able to return to your family—if you and they want that."

Piliki stares at the doctor. She mayn't understand the medical talk, but his last sentence grabs her like a hook: Of course her makuahine wants her home with her.

"Yes, I want to go home. When?"

He sighs, frustrated. "This is what I am telling you, Piliki. We will give you medicines here. We must try to see what will work on you. Then, in time, we will test you to see if you are... safe. You don't want to make anyone sick, do you?"

"I don't want to make my makuahine sick," Piliki cries, appearing to understand some small piece of this new nightmare. The nurse nudges the exhausted physician aside. She lifts the despondent six-year-old off the table. "Of course not! You will never make anyone ill. That is why you are here. And now you will find a new friend here. There are several girls just like you. Tomorrow you will meet one. Things will get better. I promise you. And guess what? I have a brand new doll, only for you to play with tonight. Do you like dolls?"

"Yes," Piliki sighs, burying her tearstained face in the nurse's uniform.

* * *

I'm sitting with Anne Beth in her stuffy pink bedroom. She's right. She has a lot of dolls, and she's dragging them out by the millions as if this makes her the best hostess ever. I wonder how long I have to sit here before I can suggest that we put all her carefully finished puzzles—neatly stored around the room—on our heads, *upside down.* Then we can run through the house and watch all the pieces fall out and onto the floor. I love doing that.

But just then there is a very loud crash. It's a slamming door, and it scares the wits out of me. Anne Beth stands up immediately. I notice she looks different. Her face is a little wet and pink.

"It's my father," she whispers.

"Anne Beth? Jimmy?" an ill-tempered male voice bellows through the house. "Where is everyone?" Anne Beth's door flings open. A stocky, muscular man with dark, greasy oil stains on his clothes and hands, stands in the room staring at us. He never asks who I am or how his daughter is. He doesn't hug or kiss her.

Then, he orders, "Both of you come here. I need help unloading the barrels off of my truck. *Now!*" he adds, seeing us both frozen.

Anne Beth runs out of the room and disappears—I assume to his truck. I don't like this bully one bit, so I'm moving like a blur to the front door when he comes 'round through the kitchen and plants himself directly in my path.

"Where do you think you're going?" he grunts.

"Home," I say, trying to sound logical.

"I said I need help unloading the barrels from my truck. I don't see my son anywhere." He pauses to howl his name again. No response. "Yeah, you're gonna have to help me and Anne.

"But I'm only six," I say like the spoiled brat I apparently am.

He grabs my arm and hauls me outside where I join my not-so-girly-after-all new friend and her way-scarier-than-mom father to roll huge oil barrels off an old truck and into his filthy garage.

I don't want to be here I shudder to myself. *I want my mother.*

* * *

I don't want to be here, Piliki cries herself to sleep. *I want my makuahine.*

* * *

2

Swimming In The River Jordan

"ברוכים הבאים האמריקאים"

"What? What did the pilot say?"

We'd been flying for an eternity since landing in London sometime in the dim past. But where did we start? Not in New York, where I'd been visiting my aunt and uncle with my college roommate, Ann, who's accompanying me on this great adventure to the Promised Land. No, I think we actually packed in Berkeley, where I am two-years over my head but on my way to a Bachelor's Degree nevertheless.

At the University of California, I have my doubts about so much, I literally can't hold still. When I am in class, my mind's wanderlust defeats my ability to do well in most subjects I take. In fact, the only thing I see clearly when I gaze out my classroom window is how pregnant the world seems with my future. Well, there is one other thing I see: my reflection puzzling back at me, *What are you doing in the only California climate you hate?* Fog and drizzle are inevitably the forecast of both the weather and my mood in Northern California.

So, at the beginning of this year, feeling again like I was walking around campus in the wrong life and ready to follow the first face I saw, a series of things came together to propel me to the Middle East: First, being a Theatre Arts major, I directed a scene from *The Diary of Anne Frank*; simultaneously, I read

Leon Uris' *Exodus* and attended a lecture on campus about Zionism. At the lecture, I found a pamphlet for a program inviting U.C. students to descend on a number of kibbutzim around Israel in order to sample the life there—*if* we could physically work six-hour days of hard labor! There was also the matter of a $1,500 fee to get there and back.

"Jack," my mother needled my father when I asked for the money to go. "You know they have 'free love' over there. Young people all sleep together."

"Free love!" Dad shot back. "*$1,500 is not free!*"

It's 1964, a mere 16 years since Israel officially became a country—or more accurately since the United Nations voted to partition Palestine into two independent nations: one Jewish, one Arab. It seemed like a good idea at the time; a little something for everyone. But after the British gave up their control and pulled out, every single Arab nation declared war on Israel. When I look at a map of the Middle East, my eyes are engulfed in the ginormous landscapes of the Arab nations surrounding infinitesimal Israel. *They've got to be kidding!* It feels like a bunch of Montana ranchers insisting on farming in some poor New Yorker's little apartment. They don't have enough land where they are? Apparently, it's more complicated.

So now the land of milk and honey is looking to expand its population, drawing from the West in particular. By encouraging college age Americans to spend time on settlements literally blooming across the length and breadth of Israel, from the Galilee to Judea and the Negev, they hope to introduce us to everything there is to know about kibbutz life. Then, the expectation is that we will want to become Israeli citizens ourselves. That's their unspoken objective; but I'm ignoring all that, and taking a break from university life.

Naturally, if I had any introspective talent at this point in my life, I'd be aware of an acutely traumatic incident six months earlier that is surely a part of my urge for going. Like so many my age, November 22, 1963 marked the crushing death of innocence. I guess every generation gets at least one scarring event that changes everything. For mine it's the assassination of President John Kennedy. Idealism and a sense of permanence have been fragmented, just as it was two decades ago under the dark skies of Hiroshima, and will be again two decades on when Three Mile Island nearly burns to the Earth's core, and two decades still further on as the Twin Towers fall.

When the shot heard round my world rang out in Dallas, and all the amazing civil rights progress—that Kennedy at least gave us the illusion we were having— exploded along with his fragile head, the devastation left me spouting the final words of Henrik Ibsen's *Hedda Gabler* at my fellow drama majors: "People don't do such things!" In the same way that childhood seems such a limitless realm, the collapse of innocence shuts your heart down profoundly. Thus, Berkeley feels claustrophobic and impossibly narrow, releasing endless restlessness in everyone around me.

Some students are heading South where the "Mississippi Freedom Summer" is in full swing. They're joining students from around the country currently pouring into rural Southern towns to help register the "Negro" vote for President Lyndon Johnson's first real election. I considered going myself; but after monitoring a few sign-up sheets for the "Berkeley to Birmingham" drive last year—a noble effort that no doubt helped to provoke the Ku Klux Klan into bombing a Baptist Church in which four young Negro girls were killed—I reconsidered. I just don't have that kind of courage.

Of course, running off to a country at war with every nation around it, doesn't faze me at all. But, I'm 20, a dangerous age. I'm an ignoramus and I don't know it. Even a year ago I was smarter when I knew I didn't know enough. Now I've dropped the "teen" from my age and think that makes me an adult when actually it makes me an arrogant ditz. People in their early 20s should be watched as closely as children. Maybe even closer because we're allowed to do things no child can do. I know many, for example, who are having children when they shouldn't even have plants.

Well, I have no plants or children, but I do have a marked-up paperback entitled *Israel on $5 A Day*. And being the know-it-all that I am, I have few doubts I'll need anything more. So, when the pilot repeats, "Welcome, Americans," in Hebrew *(Oh, that's what he said?),* and the plane touches down in Lod Airport on the northern coast of Tel Aviv, I feel ready to meet my destiny. Then all the passengers suddenly begin weeping.

"What's wrong?" Ann asks, looking scared. "Are we being hijacked?"

An elderly couple sitting a few rows forward begins clapping. Soon more follow suit until the entire plane is applauding and crying. Now we can see their tears are tears of joy.

"We are home! We are here in the only place where we are the majority! We are home! *L'chaim!*" wails my seatmate to the left, who reaches out for me with rambunctious enthusiasm.

"Oh, wow, yeah," I mumble, buried in her embrace.

Then the singing starts. A beautiful melody in minor that I've heard before, with words I don't understand, floats across the crowded aircraft: *"Kol-'od balevav penimah/ Nefesh yehudi homiyah/ Ul (e) fa'atei mizrach kadimah/ Ayin letziyon tzofiyah..."*

"That's pretty," Ann mouths and smiles. Ann is a sweetheart who is more accepting than I am. But we can barely hear each other with all the emotion spilling around us.

"Yeah, but what is it?"

"What?" she shouts in my face.

2 Swimming In The River Jordan

"What is it?" I yell at her over all the crying, singing, and clapping permeating our sweaty plane as it crawls toward a gate.

There's a surprising drop in volume as two rows of "joyous Jews" turn toward me and answer," It's 'Hatikvah,' Israel's national anthem. Come, sing, *sing!*"

I am ashamed and immediately begin faking the words to this mournful and haunting melody that will become the first of many I will learn over the next months as my fellow kibbutzniks alternate "Come, sing! Sing!" with another favorite, "Come, eat! *Eat!*"

When I glance sideways at Ann, she too is singing along but about to start giggling. That pretty much punches a hole in my exhaustion balloon. I burst out laughing with her. This is an unimaginably bad habit we've developed over our high school and college years. It's evolved into a tradition that we ultimately carry all the way to her wedding, when to the dismay of her future ex-husband, we lose total control, starting when the priest says, "Do you promise to obey your husband always..." It probably should have been an omen for Ann.

And now, here we are laughing together on the other side of the world—heading off to different kibbutzim—stranded on a steaming runway in an airless plane swollen with exultation. What have we done? Ann isn't even Jewish. And me? Am I here to explore my discontent, a bewildered young woman stalking her roots in a country that is itself engaged in a search for identity and normalcy?

If somebody said straight out to me, "You are running away from the intellectual pressures of college, a future profession, and adulthood in general," I'd say, *"That's it!"* I feel the force of these next steps coming at me fast and furious. And I'm just not meeting them with the appropriate grace and strength. Does anyone in his or her 20s? We're too young! No one I know addresses these things at Berkeley. And honestly—although this may be the outsider in me talking—I find the academic world at U.C. Berkeley uncomfortable. Too often I sit at tables with scholars, writers, and teachers all smoking cigarettes, drinking coffee, and discussing…their own opinions. And even if they accidentally meander over to the real world or academic subject matter, it's usually to club one another to death with their astounding smartness (which is kinda unpleasant, really).

So, what's my truth? Maybe I'm fighting the American dream. In the States, the appropriate arc is for a farm kid to become a doctor or lawyer. But on a kibbutz, the opposite is happening. Former lawyers, doctors and architects have come (or escaped) to Israel, and now find themselves needing to become farmers and soldiers. Many who arrive on their kibbutzim have no background in physical labor. They come from families like mine where the goal is to get as much education as possible, better yourself, and get a lucrative career. To adjust to Israel's way of life, a person must literally create a new criterion of achievement around the idea of manual labor. It's as if physical work itself is elevated to a holy, mystical, ideal. But for me, at the halfway mark in climbing higher education's slippery slope, it sounds like an astonishing, if grueling, camping trip. All this promised physical activity and purpose, genderless and modern, is hugely attractive to me.

So, yes, I find myself longing for something that makes me as excited as my college peers feel when they are exchanging cerebral critiques of each other. And when I hear about a kibbutz—a little community run on economic equality and collective responsibility—I'm in. I have a vision of human existence where brave, useful people impose order on a land full of troubling ambiguities and disorder. What's more, I like the way I can dress on this new frontier.

Of course, like anyone who's struggled through her teens with her parents, I'm fascinated by the idea of these settlements having their children live with their own age groups, not their families. How brilliant and efficient. The arrangement frees the parents to perform whatever their special skills are for the kibbutz, and, if the time comes, allows them to run into the night with a gun without leaving their children unprotected. It's the great experiment, but very different from the communes so many hippies are joining today to dabble in social democracy. For Israelis, necessity is the mother of this invention: the kibbutz is conceived in war and tailored to conquer the inhospitable land and people around it.

Israel is very different in 1964 from the country it will be in just three short years. The 1967 war will change Israel's boundaries, towns, feelings of safety, and perceptions of how both the nation and the world view it. We, Americans aboard this plane heading for different kibbutzim, are accidental pioneers. After the '67 war, Westerners will pour into Israel, full of excitement and celebratory feelings, no longer in constant fear over the continuous shelling from Arab border patrols. The war's outcome will be such a massive transformation that the experiences I speak of here are truly from a different era.

When the plane doors open, and we file out into the late afternoon heat, another kind of panic hits. Ann is in front of me, so I see her red face before I feel it myself: *Oh, my God, it's hot!* It's after 5, and still so hot? Surely after it gets dark, some of this heat will dissipate? Finally, we tumble down a rickety metal ladder that's been wheeled out to the plane, and touch Israeli soil for the first time.

Entering Lod Airport (later renamed Ben Gurion Airport to honor Israel's first Prime Minister), we are immediately submerged in something else foreign: Signs that mean absolutely nothing to us. Who comes to Israel with no knowledge of how to read, write, or speak Hebrew? Let me introduce myself. The sight of so many angular symbols (Hebrew looks and acts like no Romance Language) lined up together creating words pointing to places that you know are crucial for you to find, is the final knockout thrust to my brain. I am so weary, I finally join the other criers who have staggered off our plane. No one notices my tears anyway; our faces are so sopping wet from the heat, who could sort out which part of the streaky mess are tears? I will cry for joy at other times in this indescribable place, but not this evening. In the distance, I vaguely see Ann, who has gone in search of orange juice— *good luck with that!*

* * *

For Leroy Jeffries, the deciding incident occurred during the last election. That's when he made the decision to face the ugliness going on around him. It's not as if he hasn't been aware. He listens and he sees plenty. He just wasn't ready to get involved. But when his mother came home from the voting polls in tears because new Mississippi voting procedures required her to fill out a 21-question registration form to the satisfaction of a *white* registrar, Leroy thought she must be confused, so he gently sat her down in the blistering Meridian County heat. There, he listened to her story, and for the first time, confronted what he'd been ever so carefully avoiding.

"I couldn't explain any of the 285 sections of the state's constitution," Adelaide Jeffries wept, ashamed and embarrassed.

"*What?*" her son cried. "What sections of the constitution?"

Leroy decided the only way to get to the bottom of this, was to go register; so, the next day, he went to the polls and was horrified: The test was preposterous. Average citizens cannot be expected to talk intelligently about the hundreds of sections that make up their state constitution. Even more insulting, when Leroy asked the registrar if *he* knew any of the answers, the man laughed in his face:

"Don't have to, son! Ain't no nigger." he said, matter-of-factly. For as a white man, he didn't have to take a literacy test. His voting rights were automatic.

That's when Leroy decided he couldn't stand outside his life any longer. Fear about the consequences of doing something had finally fallen into second place behind his anger over doing nothing. Yeah, he was still afraid. You'd have to be crazy not to fear what was going on in this part of the country. Local Negro organizers have been going missing for years. The KKK has been beating "trouble makers" half to death; and although there've been a couple of trials, there've been no convictions. Only a year ago this week, fellow Mississippian, Medgar Evers, stepped out of his car after listening to President Kennedy's rousing Civil Rights speech, and was shot dead on his driveway by a hidden rifleman. Yes, being afraid made a lot of sense down here. But it wasn't going to stop him any longer.

For Leroy's childhood friend, James Earl Chaney, Medgar's murder was the final blow. The slight but eager activist told Leroy he was joining the Congress of Racial Equality (CORE) because he knew he had to do something. Chaney felt he could help to acclimate the white students arriving in droves from Yale and Stanford. "They're coming to study voter registration in Mississippi, but there are places they won't be safe, and I can go to places white CORE members shouldn't go," Chaney explained to Leroy. What's more he found he enjoyed working with the college kids; it was a good marriage.

Then, in January '64, CORE asked New Yorker Michael ("Mickey") Schwerner to be the first white civil rights worker stationed outside the capitol of Mississippi. When Schwerner opened a field office in Meridian, Chaney became his number one go-to person. "For the first time, I really feel useful." Chaney told his friend. "These volunteers and students are naïve, but they're coming here! They're coming to *our* problems from their fancy homes and colleges. It takes guts to do this with us."

Although Leroy agrees, he knows that last summer's practice voter drives were just that: practice. They were mock elections designed to teach the students and locals how to read the ballots and get around the preposterous test. Most of the training was done in secret, purposely executed under the radar. The idea was to show students the Southern landscape without calling attention to what they were up to. No one wanted any publicity. No one tried to stir up the local law enforcement.

But now everything will be different. This summer it's the real thing. If all goes as planned, everyone will be watching—and the politicians and law enforcement in 'ol MS won't like that one bit.

"This summer, we hope to send upwards of 1000 teachers, ministers, lawyers, and students from all around the country into Mississippi," CORE director Dave Dennis tells the press on a muggy June evening. Squeezed together in a wooden barn with other CORE members who've gathered to hear Dennis' speech, Leroy's body shivers with anticipation despite the fierce heat.

"They'll engage in a program designed to open up Mississippi to the country," Dennis continues, as if opening Mississippi to the world's scrutiny won't provoke Mississippians into a fury. "We feel that by bringing in these particular people (white), the attention of their parents and relatives from across the country will be on Mississippi." Then Dennis adds for emphasis: "And by having a large group of white people here, the American public and the press will be much more concerned than if just a bunch of Negroes were here."

Everyone in the sweltering barn nods and mumbles approvingly. Leroy looks around until he catches Chaney's eye. *Oh, Lord! This could be big.*

* * *

By the time Ann comes back holding a small, waxy container of icky orange fluid, I've had time to review my life and decide this whole Israel thing is a bad idea. Maybe I should have gotten on one of those buses going to Mississippi for the Freedom Summer? To think I was concerned about the mugginess of the South! Like I'm not sitting here in a pool of my own sweat. Or, why not forget these character-building adventures altogether; I could be water skiing at Lake Arrowhead or something else refreshing like…

I am startled to feel a firm hand on my shoulder pulling me out of what must have been a long stupor. I turn and look at the man attached to the arm. He squints at me slightly, as if he's inspecting someone a couple of bubbles off the beam.

"My name is Motle," he says, his heavily accented English humming with more than Hebrew in it. He turns my sweaty face to meet his. I'd say that Motle is in his 30s, nice looking, and seriously concerned about me for reasons I don't yet understand.

"You are being with the American group going to Kibbutz Amir?" he asks.

My mind begins to clear. *Where is Ann?* I look around and find large sections of my plane's passengers gone. "What? Yes, I'm going to Amir. But, what happened to the others?"

"They have gone with their buses," Motle says.

"What buses? Where is Ann?"

"Who is Ann?"

"My friend"

"Is she being at Amir too?"

"No, Ann is going to kibbutz Kfar Blum," I answer.

"Then her bus has left."

"She left?"

I feel sick. Motle picks up my suitcase and walks ahead of me through the crowded airport hallways.

"I'm going in there," I abruptly announce, and duck though a door with Hebrew letters and the universal cutout of a lady. I don't know if Motle heard me but for now I don't care. I need a moment. After throwing water on my bright pink face and wrists, I realize that I don't want to be left in an Israeli airport bathroom so I race back out to find Motle. Mercifully, he hasn't drifted far; he is circling around and round wearing a very dour face.

"I'm sorry," I begin, as I approach him, but his face turns so happy with relief when he sees me, I feel a little happy myself. This time he takes hold of me and steers me through the rest of the airport and out an exit where the air is still baking hot.

"These are others going to Kibbutz Amir," Motle says quickly.

Lined up near two old dented buses is a ragtag crew of once bright and shining young American adventurists. One look at the 11 girls and 8 boys staring back at me with woozy, unsteady eyes and I know I'm not the only one undone by the 12-hour haul from New York—not to mention the 3-day bus ride to Manhattan from Berkeley.

Motle shoves me gently into the others while he opens the bus door and goes inside to talk with the driver. No one smiles at me. No one smiles at anyone. After a few awkward seconds, we all give up and focus on our feet.

Finally, the doors reopen and we're allowed to file onto our buses. Our suitcases have been shoved somewhere beyond our vision, and other supplies suggested by the kibbutz were sent ahead to Israel months earlier (a pair of work boots, towels, a sleeping bag, etc.). I drop down on a hard tin seat next to another sweaty girl; we both stare straight ahead, mouths shut, hands folded, eyes forward, like well-bred misplaced mops.

"The bus ride from Tel Aviv to Amir will be five hours, maybe more," Motle announces from the front, leaning against the bus driver whose back is to us. "Shimon is the driver," he continues. "He knows the roads very good, and you will be safe."

Safe? "What do you mean: 'safe?'" I ask, sticking my hand in the air as if I was waiting to be called on in a classroom. Motle confers with Shimon for a minute. Then he says, "From Arab terrorists."

Terrorists? As we will learn from the Israelis—who were among the first to use it successfully—terrorism is "a small group of people who attack you—but you don't know *where* and you don't know *when*. And if you don't know where or when, you don't need armies to wreak chaos and bring down nations.

After we've been on the bumpy road for some time, Motle says, over the grating of the motor, "we have a special surprise to give to you from the kibbutz." Everyone looks up at him relieved.

"Plums," he says with great pride.

The word "plums" is so out of context, it ricochets around the bus, from mouth to mouth as one person after another tries to figure out if that's what he really said or if it's a Hebrew word for something else—like, God willing, water?

But this pleasant interlude ends rudely when Shimon pummels the gas pedal and our giant tin can pitches left on the road. The sudden movement throws everyone sitting in an aisle seat (that would be me) onto the grubby floor.

"Ouch!" I bellow, along with five or six others now on the floor. I try to stand up, but can't find a thing to hold onto. My seatmate is still pretending she's not here, so I search other faces sitting near where I've fallen. A "nice Jewish boy" holds out a hand to help me up, but the bus reels again, and my gentleman hero joins me on the floor instead. I'm not sure the bus has tires, because rather than roll, it just jerks forward in quick guttural thrusts.

Then I hear laughter—not just chuckling, but full-blown, knee-slapping laughter. Motle and Shimon are doubled up in tears howling at us. I'd say they were rolling in the aisles, but that would be my part in the merriment.

"You silly Americans!" Motle mocks. "You cannot even sit in bus seats? What will be happening to you at the kibbutz?" Now *that* makes me want to go home. I have torn the light-weight pedal pushers I'm wearing, scraped my arms and knees, knocked heads with at least two cursing strangers, and the only person who's been kind to me, Motle, is ridiculing me. The arrogance of these people!

Without warning, the bus abruptly stops lurching from side to side. We all sense we might be momentarily chugging forward and use the time to vault off the floor and onto our seats. I look out the bus windows and distract myself with thoughts of the 1940s settlers who lived on farm communities, in tents, got malaria, and fought off Arab attacks in order to cultivate the lush Galilee foliage I'm now looking at. But if the land has come a long way, many of the human sights going by me don't look like they've changed much since Biblical times. Tall veiled women take water from wells and walk slowly alongside the road with large jugs on their heads. Shepherd boys in black robes herd flocks of white goats out of our way and onto the hillsides where they can graze. I fumble for my Nikon—a rare camera that few Americans have yet; I acquired mine when a family friend working in Japan brought it back for me. Focusing the lens on a long-gowned Arab sitting atop a dozing donkey, it's clear the character of his life has stayed untouched for 2000 years. But when I switch to my telephoto lens, I see that's not entirely true: this Arab is nodding and singing along to a transistor radio he has pressed to his ear. (In years to come it will be a cellphone.)

The bus falls quiet as night begins to cover everything and we bump our way North toward Haifa. The Mediterranean looks ink black with only a candle of moonlight to find it. Our bus windows are down and the warm desert air is finally growing easier on the skin. I doze for an hour or two, but am awakened by a new attempt to flip the bus by Shimon. I throw both feet into the aisle to stop another painful plummet, and collide with an Israeli who is trying not to drop the basket of large plums she's handing out. I grab one feverishly.

This is my first experience with the fruits and vegetables grown on Israeli kibbutzim. They are huge and delicious. In fact, at first sight, the size can worry you. A tomato fight could be lethal. Maybe it's the weather, the farmers, the techniques, or the respect that the damaged soil has for anyone conquering it. I don't know. But I will never get over the super-sized veggies and fruits that come out of Amir's kitchen. There are murmurs of delight throughout the bus as the plums, along with figs, dates, cheeses, olives, bread, cakes, apples, and other goodies make their way around.

As we close in on Haifa, we turn away from the Mediterranean, and begin to travel East toward the small village of Kyriat Shmona. Soon we can barely make out a famous body of water known both as Lake Tiberias and the Sea of Galilee. For now, though I strain my eyes, the lightless sky has stolen the blue from the sea, leaving only a pale gunmetal wash behind. So, again, I let the battering of the bus against the road rock me to sleep.

"אנחנו כאן !Wake Up! האמריקאים".

My silent seatmate shoves me rudely awake.

"What? What?" I sputter at her. "Are we being attacked?"

She points, stone faced, to Motle, who is repeating in both Hebrew and English: "Americans! Wake up! We are here!" over and over like a mantra.

I look through the open windows into a dimly lit area near a bungalow that looks like an old army barrack. Nearby a small group of men and women dressed in shorts, rolled up shirts, and odd looking blue hats are gathered. They are talking fervently, then abruptly stopping to stare at us. Motle has now joined them. After a short time, he gets back on the bus with a woman.

"We have still another bus coming here to us with Americans," he says. "Some had to come on another bus to make room on this one." Someone asks how many Americans there are in total.

Motle looks in the direction of the question, smiles, and says, "This is Miriam. She speaks good English too, and will help me to help you while you are with us at Amir."

"But isn't this an English-speaking Kibbutz?" I ask, as a sense of foreboding breaks through my burnout. They both stare at me with pity on their faces. "I mean, we were told Amir is an English-speaking Kibbutz," I plead.

"No, Amir is a Hebrew-speaking Kibbutz," Miriam says in clear, precise English. "Motle and me, and a few others, speak some English because we have family in America, but the people on Amir speak Hebrew."

Well, that's the ballgame. The entire bus goes crackers! Everyone begins babbling and shouting and complaining at the same time. Miriam and Motle look frightened and exit, rushing straight to the blue-hat people. There's another pow-wow, followed by more staring at us. Finally, Motle and Miriam come back.

"Please take your things. We are going out the bus now," Motle says.

I strap whatever I can find of my belongings onto myself and follow the person in front of me out of the bus and down a winding dirt path. I have no more questions. Like everyone else, I don't like the answers we're getting. We've all stopped complaining. What's the point? They don't understand us anyway. Instead, I sigh loudly and throw my head back. That's when I see the Israeli sky!

There have been times in my life when I've looked up at the sky and been stone cold frightened—literally stopped breathing with a mixture of reverence and fear. It's so big and absolute and we're so piddling. My father once tried to comfort me with the theory that many of the stars we see actually blew up millions of years ago, but we're still getting their light because that's how far away they are. I gave him a look of acute frustration. I mean, really, where was the comfort in that? It just added another layer of heebie-jeebies for me: The universe is that big? It takes millions of years for the last ray of a dead star to reach us—and, of course Dad went on to point out that light travels faster than anything we know? That's just too damn big! So, during these times, when the sky is bursting with the full picture of who we are, I shut my eyes, tell myself *it's only the ceiling,* and follow the person in front of me.

That's exactly what I'm doing when a door opens and we file into a large dining room. The tables have been pulled off to the side, and men and women of all ages are dancing in a circle. A phonograph is playing hora dance music and everyone is wearing white shirts. I've tried the hora at one Jewish Center or another, but this is like watching Zorba The Greek fly by in a rapturous blur. At first, they don't notice us they're so engrossed. There's another group off to the side clapping loudly with the rhythmic stomping of the dancers. Everyone looks incredibly happy, laughing and singing along as they dance. Then a few notice us gaping at them. One by one they begin bumping into each other as they stop dancing and stare back. The hand-clappers soon follow their eyes, see us, and gawk too. In a few seconds only the jubilant singers and musicians on the well-worn record can be heard.

Miriam breaks this interminable trance, claps her hands in a more "snap out of it" cadence, and signals us to follow her into the kitchen. I do, but turn once to watch the Israelis reassemble their dance circle and begin again, seemingly unaffected by this digression.

When we enter the large kitchen, it looks like an army mess hall. There are huge pots and pans, bowls, platters, and serving utensils hanging everywhere. Too bad we're still so stuffed from the all the food they fed us on the plane and bus.

"You must be hungry!" Miriam announces. At least 10 Americans politely answer, "Oh, no, thank you so much—we're so full from our trip." Miriam gasps. There are other women Miriam's age in the kitchen cleaning up. They whirl around with looks of suspicion—definitely a Greek Chorus to Miriam's unhappiness. We must have answered wrong. Either we eat something, anything, or we're headed back to the dancing stare-down in the other room. Someone in our group tries for a light snack, as a compromise, but that doesn't seem to translate into anything in Hebrew (or anything they want to hear). While we believe we are still negotiating a solution, the kibbutz women usher us to a large dining table that the staff uses when it's their turn for kitchen duty. Places have already been set for us and, God help me, they are beginning to pour matzo ball soup into our bowls.

I ask for and finally get a glass of water. But when I lift it to my lips, Miriam swoops down and whisks it out of my hand before I get a single drop. Then an eruption of Hebrew follows and we all freeze where we are. *What?!* Arms whirling with half-familiar gestures, heads whipping back and forth between the women and our table, we deduce the cooks of Amir are blaming each other for some near calamity involving me.

Miriam eventually breaks away, head shaking, and comes to the table. There is a sheen on her forehead that she wipes away before speaking: "You will have your water, yes," she begins. "But you must always boil it first here. Do not drink any water unless it is boiled or in a bottle. Yes?" She gives me an extra stare.

"Yes, thank you, yes," I say.

"We are now boiling water for everyone," she continues. "Eat your soup!"

I eat the soup. Slurping and spoon clanking fills our area. We begin to talk amongst ourselves for the first time, envisioning the Israelis busy making up our rooms for our long, much needed sleep after so much grueling travel. To finally stretch out on something comfortable after all these hours of hard tin seats, is what we crave. Then—we all agree—we'll be up for anything. The soup is, not surprisingly, scrumptious. So what if we've already had three bowls of it on the plane? Warm fluid before bedtime is always a good idea.

Then the full chicken dinner arrives! Everyone gets plates loaded with gefilte fish, chicken, potatoes, kreplach, and giant mixed vegetables all grown on Amir. I want to cry again. This can't be happening. We all look at each other, then up at Miriam and her accomplices. They're beaming with pride: *Just look what we've cobbled together for you!* I hear forks being picked up all around me, napkins slipping onto laps, and I realize I am doing the same.

"Eat! Eat!" "לאכול! לאכול!" Miriam says these words as if they've never been spoken before—the battle cry of every Jewish mother worth her salt and pepper. "So why don't you eat?" she continues in this, the Judean nucleus of the universe. Her words break into our ancient gene pools and stun us into obedience. Soon we're plowing through our plates like loopy gobblers, all determined to get this nightmare over with so we can go to sleep and wake up to find that in the Middle East you eat only once a week like a camel.

※ ※ ※

Samuel Holloway Bowers Jr., of Laurel Mississippi, was 39 years old this past February when he officially became the Imperial Wizard of the White Knights Of the Mississippi KKK. It's a position he holds with enormous pride and full conviction in all that it represents. For Bowers, Klansmen are nothing short of sacred Christian militants dedicated to opposing the forces of Satan on this earth. And if this means getting rid of the Jew-communists, the civil rights activists, the liberal media whores, the pagan academics, the atheists, and homosexual heretics—all coming to get the good Christians of this state, then by God, he is more than up for the task. Which is why when the dreaded "Mississippi Freedom Summer" begins in full force, and Bowers comes to understand that these pagan academics are headed for his beloved home, he kick-starts the most aggressive and violent policy imaginable to meet these evil forces head on.

Bowers sees one CORE volunteer, "Jewboy Goatee Schwerner," as a singularly agitating manifestation of the Antichrist, Satan. This, Bowers comes to because Schwerner has earned much Klan hatred already by organizing a Negro boycott of white-owned Meridian businesses, as well as aggressively registering Negro voters in and around the area. Additionally, "Goatee"—as the Klan refers to Schwerner because he sports a "satanic" goatee—has earned himself an eternal burning cross because of his friendship with someone the Klan has long wanted dead, the "CORE nigger" Chaney.

And so, Bowers issues what is known in Klan lore as a "Number 4 Order" (i.e. "elimination") to the entire Lauderdale-Neshoba Klavern. They are told to kill the activist Schwerner. It will be one of at least nine Number 4 Orders Bowers issues from 1964 to 1967 in his role as Imperial Wizard.

There are few who doubt that Sam Bowers would be successful without the zealous support of Preacher Edgar Ray Killen. Despite statements to the contrary, it is Preacher Killen's home that serves as Klan headquarters for the Neshoba County area. Like Bowers, Killen has a near evangelical mission to plunge as many stakes as possible through the hearts of all godless communists out to end what he so cherishes: segregation of the races. Killen's mind is so steeped in decades of closed Southern thinking about skin color, he's half-crazy with it. When Martin Luther King is assassinated in 1968, it's Killen who pushes his way into FBI headquarters in Memphis, begging the authorities to tell him who shot the "commie nigger, so I can shake his hand!"

Not surprisingly, it is Killen who receives the Number 4 Order from Bowers. The target, just as he'd hoped, is Schwerner. And that will be easy. The sheriff and his deputy are both Klan members, though they don't brag on it publicly. Together they'll all think up something smart, a plan to waylay "Goatee" when he gets here. Already the word is he's coming early to visit that nearby Negro church again. So, Killen is preparing to meet with fellow Klansmen at his house this very evening. It will be gratifying, he thinks, to sit together in the well-appointed accommodations of his home, have some fine rye whiskey, then, finally, get the murderous plan nailed down.

* * *

About our lovely kibbutz accommodations: I don't know what I was expecting. I can, however, tell you what I was not expecting: rusted steel cot frames holding decrepit, stained, lumpy mattresses; one long pole for all our clothes to hang on, but no closets or drawers—"Use your suitcases, very good for that!" One light bulb dangling from the ceiling in the middle of the room with a useless lampshade; cracked peeling walls, long dusty curtains covering two layers of windows, one glass and one thick screen to keep out the bugs and bats. Right! Huge bugs and real bats that—after an unpleasant chorus of shrieks—two Israeli soldiers chase out of our lodgings and into an outside shared bathroom where they will enjoy hanging upside down and swooping down on us at the worst possible moments.

I have two roommates: Marilyn and Nancy. I immediately decide I have nothing in common with either of them; I can just tell. In fact, I'm sure I don't like them. I just want to go home. Already there have been several announcements and each of them has driven me deeper into a depression. To begin with, we've been given our first two-week work assignment, and for me, the news is grim. Instead of being asked to work the fishponds, grape vines, dairy barn, or apple groves—I got laundry duty! How am I going to get a tan doing that? Worse, we were originally told we'd be getting two 10-day vacations, and I have it all worked out with Ann that we're going to meet and take a plane to Greece. Well, there must be some small print somewhere in Hebrew because they just told us that our first 10-day vacation is divided into two parts: one 3-day and one 7-day vacation. And the 7-day vacation starts next week! How am I going to get a hold of Ann so fast? I don't even know if she made it to her kibbutz. My decomposing wits quickly race to our second vacation as a better Greece getaway plan but, lo, more dismal news. Our second 10-day vacation doesn't really belong to us at all. It turns out members of the kibbutz are going to take us by bus *(Oh no)* to different places of interest throughout Israel. Places they think are interesting.

I climb into my sleeping bag with no sheet—how did I know they didn't provide sheets?—and try to drift off, composing a letter to my parents asking for help getting out of here. Around midnight all three of us find ourselves awake and staring at a man standing outside our door. Before we can say a word, he begins walking back and forth across our porch. We can see that he is carrying a rifle slung across his shoulder. His shadow moves past one curtained window and soon appears in the next, as he circles our barracks, round and round, guarding us the entire night, protecting us from the dangers ("Terrorists!") that lurk somewhere out there. I follow his shadow for a few minutes like counting sheep, then fall sound asleep.

※ ※ ※

While most folks are safely asleep inside their homes, on June 16th, in the rural Neshoba County community of Longdale, 30 Klansmen line up in imitation military fashion. With their rifles and shotguns held tightly in their trigger-happy grips, they wait impatiently. Facing them is the old wood-framed Mount Zion Church, a local Negro congregation.

Working with secret information, the Klansmen have learned that the much-despised civil rights heretic, "Goatee," visited Lauderdale's Mount Zion this past May on Memorial Day. He was right here, under their collective noses, meeting with the church deacons to ask permission to use their site for one of the Mississippi "Freedom Schools"—or as Preacher Killen put it: "…more devil's work from Commie-Northern-Jew-agitators filling the heads of our neighborhood niggers with uppity learning."

Acting on a tip from County Sheriff Lawrence Rainey and his deputy, Cicil Price, the men learned that a special "Mississippi Freedom" business meeting would be going down inside the church tonight; and "Jew-Boy" Schwerner will be attending. The exhilaration over this information has been downright uncontainable. No one has slept. All at once, the Klansmen sense movement from inside. Giving each other a knowing nod, they lift their rifles. The church doors open slowly and seven men and three women, all Negroes, walk out. None of them sense any danger and continue talking to each other until, ultimately, someone looks up and into the dark. They stop cold.

A Klansman shouts roughly to them: "Where is 'Jew-Boy?'"

The terrified ten freeze. One calls back, "No one here called that."

"Where is 'Jew-Boy?'" the Klan demands over and over, surrounding them like hunters. Then the Klan group leader signals for other Klansmen to forage through the Mount Zion church itself. But it's clear after a long and destructive search that Schwerner isn't here. What happened? Could their information be wrong? Frustrated, they continue interrogating the Mount Zion churchgoers relentlessly.

When they can get no information at all, several of the Klansmen start beating the Negroes. They hit them with clubs, fists, and the butts of their rifles. Still they learn nothing about Schwerner. Either the church goers don't know or they won't say.

Furious now, the Klan pulls a truck into the clearing and from the back they begin unloading diesel fuel. Within minutes, ten gallons of fuel are splashed recklessly inside and around the church. As the bloodied and beaten captives try to run or crawl away into the surrounding woods, they feel an enormous heat at their backs. They don't need to turn around to know their place of worship is now engulfed in flames.

* * *

It's 4 a.m. and Marilyn is shaking me awake. I knew I didn't like her.

"We have to get up and get fitted for work boots," she says tentatively.

"What? Now? Wait…" Somehow, even in my predawn food and travel hangover, I manage to get a hold of an important detail: we sent work boots to Amir. They mailed us instructions to ship them before our arrival.

Marilyn, turns out to be far brighter than I have any hope for at this point: "I know, I know…" she pats my shoulder sweetly as I attempt to sit up in my sleeping bag. "I tried to say that to them when they woke me about the boot thing, but, well, they're fitting us for work boots anyway, so you might as well get up."

Another spirit-slaughtering announcement that went by last night was our work hours at Amir: 4 a.m. to 12 noon. *That's* the usual 8-hour day here, dictated by the excruciating heat. People simply can't work in the fields after 12 noon or they melt. At 8 a.m. we take an hour break for breakfast, then back to work until noon. The "good news" is that any time before *(before?)* or after those hours, belongs to us. However, we quickly discover that what we really want to do the most after work is dive face first onto (what we've come to perceive as) our beautiful cots until about 4 p.m. That's when the salt pills we've taken earlier usually kick in enough to let us stagger around the kibbutz meeting Israelis.

Meanwhile at the boot-fitting gibberish fest, where we lose the battle with Hebrew and get fitted for work boots anyway, we're handed a sheet of paper that freely translates to "your need lists." We can check things we need on this list once a week and get them shortly after. Well, sorta. The lists are in Hebrew so you can only imagine. I thought I was asking for a sheet and got a blanket (which should be on the "not ever needed list!"), but at least the thought is nice. We get free aerogramme paper to write home for help, and the stamps are courtesy of the kibbutz. Everyone gets one of the funny blue hats, which, it turns out we absolutely must wear during the day because of the heat, as well as blue shorts. I ask about wearing sandals instead of boots, since I drew the poop card and got laundry duty, and some garbled translation gets back to me about snakes—or maybe he said spiders—that roam the distance between the laundromat and the mess hall. Either way, it's definitely work boots for Judy! So, hi ho, hi ho, it's off to the laundry room I go. *So humiliating.*

One hour into folding diapers in the morning heat, and I'm dripping sweat all over them. It's sweltering in this laundromat, and though the windows are wide open and fans are blowing the fiendish air around, I feel a little faint. So I sit down with my basket of warm clothes and watch the other girls and women move at a slow but steady pace, never complaining, and only pausing to wave to their children or a friend walking by outside. Since its mandatory that women join the army here, one of my fantasies about men and women in Israel is that there's some sort of gender equality regarding work duties. However, I see no men folding or washing clothes anywhere around me. This makes me even less tolerant of my work assignment.

At breakfast, I seek out Motle and plop down next to him as he's trying to enjoy his meal. He does his best to be pleasant but as soon as it becomes clear I'm on a mission to get out of the laundry room, his English takes a powder and suddenly he can only speak Hebrew. So, I look around for Miriam. Thankfully I'm still full from last night because it takes me the entire breakfast hour to trap Miriam into giving me hope that something can be changed. If I just fold clothes for two more days, she thinks I can be transferred to the apple orchards. She also wants me to meet my family tomorrow.

"Every American is assigned to a kibbutz family," she explains.

"But you don't live as families," I respond—the authority on *her* life!

"No, but husbands and wives live together, and after work and on the Sabbath, children and parents eat together; yes? It is different for each kibbutz."

"Oh." I sigh, realizing how little I know, again.

"We have a nice family for you with a nice sister your age. No, maybe younger. But perfect. You will meet soon and see," she concludes.

"Fine," I agree easily, "but you'll get me out of the laundry room this week?"

She walks away from me quickly, waving a hand in the air. "I work on it, shalom."

※ ※ ※

Schwerner was heading down a different road in life in 1963 when four young girls, attending a Sunday school class in their Birmingham, Alabama Baptist Church, were murdered. Cynthia Wesley, Addie Mae Collins, Carol Robertson, and Denise McNair were merely singing and clapping hands when firebombs thrown by Klansmen abruptly ended everything for them at the ages of 11 and 14.

After news of the bombing reached New York, the young social worker made a life-changing—and ultimately life-terminating—decision. Along with his wife of one year, Rita, Schwerner asked the CORE national office to give him a post in the South. They were hesitant, but Schwerner spoke to them from the heart: "My profession has not become directly involved in the most devastating social disease of the present time: discrimination." Helping the Negro in the North was one thing, according to Schwerner. But what they're going through in the South is a "more bitter fight...and I wish to be a part of that fight."

Rita also petitioned the main office, asking to be near her husband and their shared crusade, so that "someday [we can] pass on to the children we may have, a world containing more respect for the dignity and worth of all men, than that world which was willed to us."

Their words proved convincing, and in November of 1963, shortly after Lee Harvey Oswald shot President Kennedy, they were assigned to open the Meridian, Mississippi field office. There was something about Schwerner that the local Negroes picked up on right away. He didn't see them as less or more or special or different. They were just other people. Right away the center became a place where Negro and white volunteers could congregate. Training sessions to help prepare for the atrocious literacy tests were in full session all the time; but that wasn't the truly groundbreaking part. It was the atmosphere of the place. The Meridian field office felt safe and welcoming—something new and unfamiliar for this part of the country. The Schwerners often looked around the center and felt that the co-mingling of the races was the real accomplishment, far more than any of the learning activities going on.

Unfortunately, what they didn't notice as they gazed around, was the one or two Negroes drifting through that were moles—informants—hired by the Klan. In fact, the minute Schwerner arrived in Meridian, the Lauderdale and Neshoba County Klansmen put him under rigorous surveillance. Did he suspect at all? Some say yes, but Schwerner refused to show concern. After all, what would these moles report anyway?

2 Swimming In The River Jordan

Everything was on the up and up and out in the open. At least it was on Schwerner's end.

But, alas, the moles were quite dangerous. Unbeknownst to the Schwerners, they were feeding the Mississippi Klan the names of every single volunteer arriving in the state, along with the license plate numbers of their cars, and every place each volunteer would be traveling during his or her stay. This private information then made its way from the Klan to the local sheriffs, so that they, in turn, could run "night clinics." In these clinics, law enforcement officers were given the ammunition they'd need for the upcoming summer. With this information, they'd be able to single out and arrest the "invading enemy" with trumped-up charges from a long list of criminal codes. If only Schwerner could have been monitoring the big picture, he might have seen two righteous and opposing forces perfectly poised for a tragic collision.

Now with the Freedom Summer finally in high gear, Schwerner's Center is overwhelmed with so much activity, he not only can't take notice of possible moles, he finds himself writing to CORE's headquarters requesting additional money to fund eight more staff members. Among them is his favorite volunteer, Chaney. Ever since Memorial Day, when Chaney facilitated a meeting with the deacons of the Mount Zion Church in Longdale, Schwerner has felt Chaney's usefulness to CORE has gone past volunteerism and needs to be rewarded. At this point, Schwerner almost never goes anywhere without him—a fact destined to seal Chaney's fate along with his own in less than two weeks.

※ ※ ※

The very next afternoon, following a nap, I am escorted to the small home of Shulamit and Pinchas. They have a 17-year-old daughter, Ora ("light") and son Shmuel. Although Ora and Shmuel live, play, eat, and sleep with kids their age, the first thing I notice is the passionate connection they have with their parents. Perhaps the enforced separation that communal living demands enhances their desire to belong to their nuclear family? I am certainly seeing it from both sides: Today a mother in the laundry room nearly fell out the window when she leaned over it to swoop up her little boy as he went running by with his living group. Her euphoria—and his—was palatable, just as Ora's is when her father finally joins us at the dinner table for their weekly family meal.

How perfect, then, that Ora (who becomes a friend and sister to me), will grow up to be a recognized authority and professor of Child Development at the University of Haifa, where she will publish widely read papers questioning the effects of kibbutz communal sleeping arrangements on the mental health of Israeli children. The attachment problems they incur later in life, as a probable result of this profound sacrifice for their young country, is simply uncharted now. Yet here we are, eating Shulamit's home cooked meal, surrounded by clues. But these tiny observations that scatter like desert sand over my kibbutz-life fantasies, mean nothing to me now. I'm young and naive. I have no gray hair or gray areas—everything is either black or white. And right now, this arrangement is utterly perfect and heroic to me. By the end of the day with Ora, something has changed in me. I can't explain it. I just suddenly, really arrive in Israel.

The next morning, I get a new assignment: the apple orchard. I'm so happy I wake before 4 a.m., dress and stride down to the kitchen for their version of coffee, "botz" *(mud)*, a rich, black Turkish bean that can wake you up for weeks. I hitch a ride on a flatbed truck with a bunch of Americans working in the fields, and within an hour I'm on a ladder with a large mailbag-like contraption around my neck that opens on the bottom. The idea is to climb around the trees, pick apples, and drop them into the bag. Naturally, the bag gets heavier and heavier. When your bag is full, you climb down the ladder and open the bottom of your bag by unhooking the buckle, which allows the apples to drop out and into large baskets on the truck below. That's the idea anyway. Here's what I learn rather quickly: a lot can go wrong.

Chava Shur, a classmate of Ora's, is in a tree with me. She is quite beautiful, strong, and very graceful. I feel thousands of miles from any of those qualities as I wobble ludicrously in the branches. Each time I snap an apple away from its stem, a surprising amount of dust flies up my nose and into my eyes causing me to cough and sneeze. At first this silliness is quite a knee slapper for the Israelis and other Americans in nearby trees.

"Stop! Stop! It's hard enough to get into a good pace." someone yells, laughing. Regardless, I continue plucking and sneezing. Then, not surprisingly, I lose my balance, half tumbling off the ladder from the weight of the apples and my sneezing. Chava calls to me in Hebrew, and though I don't understand her, the tone of her voice offers a lot of information. She is working in some branches below me, and she begins miming how I should come down and immediately unhook the bottom of my bag to release the apples into the baskets. Then she yells something I don't understand—later I find out it means "wait"—and looks around for somewhere to stand clear.

Understanding neither her words nor thoughts, I reach for one last apple, snap it off, inhale more dust up my sinus, sneeze abruptly, slam the bag against the tree trunk, catch the release buckle on a branch, and drop all the apples on Chava.

"Oh, my God! Chava!" I scream, watching her cover her head as my apples clobber her one by one. All those beautiful apples that took me half our workday to capture are out of the bag and bruising both Chava and themselves. Watching Chava discard one battered apple after another, I imagine I'm the only bad apple she wants out of the orchard.

* * *

While the Klan is burning down the Mount Zion Baptist Church in a fury over failing to find and kill "Goatee," Schwerner himself is in Oxford, Ohio, at the Western College for Women. Along with 300 of the more than 800 volunteers who ultimately serve in Mississippi, he's learning lots of last minute hard lessons about the lack of protection he and his fellow participants will be getting from the local and federal government during the summer. President Johnson is not enamored with the Freedom Summer idea, and J. Edgar Hoover is dead set against it. So, the trainees soon discover that the FBI will only "investigate" incidents, but have no power to protect them from the harm they will surely incur.

It's a horrible week, with even the strongest civil rights veterans weighing the risks and reconsidering their decisions. Fear is rampant. Training sessions, group gatherings, and even casual chats instantly turn into explosive arguments. Volunteers are told by speaker after speaker they should be prepared to be hurt and even killed. Many pack up and leave after long phone calls with parents who urge them not to stay.

At the end of the week, someone brings Schwerner a write up from a Louisiana newspaper about the beatings and burning at Mount Zion Church. Although the story is finally in the news, the tragedy is several days old. Nobody's heard anything because all the local Mississippi papers were told not to cover it.

2 Swimming In The River Jordan

Naturally Schwerner is devastated. Although he has no idea the Klan had been looking for him that night, he feels guilty for what happened to the congregation because he suspects it has something to do with his visit there last month. Telling his wife he can't possibly stay in Ohio with her, Schwerner asks Chaney and Andy Goodman, a young white, Jewish volunteer he'd talked into coming South: "Will you ride back to visit Longdale with me and take a look at what they've done to the church?"

Of course, Chaney is an eager passenger. In fact, he volunteers to drive when it gets dark so the others can hide and rest. Twenty-year-old Goodman is the son of an affluent, Upper West Side Manhattan family. His mother, Carolyn Goodman, a well-known anti-fascist and human rights activist in the New York area, influenced Andy's deep sense of justice. Though he is the junior in the trio, the young anthropology student has been "feeling the suffering of those less fortunate" since his first civil rights protest at 14.

And so, piling into Schwerner's old blue wagon, the three brave but naïve protestors wave goodbye to Oxford, and take off for the magnolia state.

* * *

A few weeks after the apple debacle, I say "shalom" to Amir, catch a plane, and meet Ann in Greece. It took a lot of doing. Most of the Americans at Amir had misunderstood the small print as well, so together we sob-storied our way into trading some kibbutz travel days for free travel days.

Ann and I manage to rent an amazing 2-room suite overlooking the Aegean Sea in Athens for $25 a night. This is the place and these are the days for great deals. As we sit eating candy bars on our beds, I lay out my work failures so far on Amir.

"I've got to find a way to pull myself together or they're going to vote me off the kibbutz," I exaggerate.

"Can they do that?" Ann asks, gullibly.

"No, no, I doubt it, but really, Ann, you have no idea! I bitched for days about being assigned to the laundry room, so they moved me to the apple orchards, where I instantly developed an allergy to apple tree dust, or something. I feel very embarrassed about how it's going."

"Oh, so what?" Ann shrugs, supportively. "It's only been a few weeks."

"God, is that right? It feels like a year. Oh! And another thing," I begin working myself up, "Yesterday I noticed all the American boys were missing from the Kibbutz. I asked where they were and found out they'd been taken for a swim in the River Jordan."

"Cool."

"No, not cool! What about the girls? What about me? I could've used a swim in the River Jordan. I mean, what was that all about?"

"Oh…I don't know," Ann murmurs, stuffing the rest of her candy bar in her mouth. "I'm sorry."

"For what? It wasn't your fault. Do they separate you guys at Kfar Blum? The boys from the girls?"

"No, no…and everyone goes swimming in our pool," she adds adamantly.

"Well, let me just say this: I intend to go swimming in the River Jordan, Ann. Even if I have to sneak off to do it."

"*Oh, no*, don't do that!" she says, alarmed.

"Why?"

"What about the Arabs across your border who kidnapped those Amir kids last Spring!"

"Oh, yeah, *that*." I agree, angrily. "Well, there has to be a way…"

"I'm sure you'll find it—but not alone, and not now, please. We should do something here. Let's go see the Acropolis, Judy! Forget about swimming in that river. We're in Athens, for heaven's sake!"

* * *

Carolyn Goodman's phone rings on the morning of June 19th. It's her son, Andrew, with news of a change in his plans. A good son in the habit of keeping his family up to date with all his activities, Andy tells his mother that his mentor, Schwerner, has asked that he accompany him and another volunteer back to Lauderdale County. Carolyn is a little surprised, as Andy is supposed to depart for Canton, Mississippi in a few days, where he's scheduled to carry out his Freedom Summer work. But, a civil rights warhorse herself, she understands the need for flexibility in responding to evolving situations. So, wishing him a good and safe trip, Carolyn hangs up the phone with her usual mixed feelings: "Here is our son, wanting to go into the belly of the beast," she tells everyone with pride and a healthy dose of trepidation.

The 163-mile drive lasts a full day and night as the trio hurries along without taking any unnecessary breaks. Ultimately, Schwerner decides to stop off in Meridian to briefly freshen up before heading out to face the destruction in Lauderdale. While he and Chaney race around the office, Goodman steals time to sight see along the streets of Meridian, a quaint town he finds heartwarming.

By the time they arrive at the still smoking ashes of the church, it's Sunday, June 21, Father's Day. Walking around the rubble, a crushing sadness engulfs Schwerner. He speaks with one or two of the congregation elders, apologizing to them for bringing the Klan to their door during last summer's scouting trip. Obviously, no Freedom School will ever take place at this site now. Still, he and Chaney try to show some hope by talking of ways CORE might eventually help in the rebuilding of their beloved church. As the morning rolls into early afternoon, everyone grows anxious. Neshoba County is a known high-risk area for civil rights workers and anyone seen with them.

Schwerner decides it might be safer if the trio goes to the homes of the Negroes who suffered the worst beatings in the attack, rather than chance a meeting with them here. So, he uses a nearby phone to call his Meridian CORE office to let them know of their change in plans. Speaking with co-worker Sue Brown, he checks in about the Lauderdale situation, tells her where they will be going, and that his plan is to be back at the Center by 4 p.m. "If we're not back there by 4:30," he tells Sue, "Start making phone calls!"

In the impoverished but welcoming home of one of the church members, Chaney and Schwerner coax their host into talking about what happened the night of the burning so they can understand why the Klan so brutally attacked them. When Schwerner hears about "Jew Boy," his body literally spasms over the chilling revelation that the Klan plans to dispose of him. *At least it's just me*, he mutters to himself. But that isn't true.

Pointing to each of his guests slowly, the more-determined-than-frightened host warns: "There's a group of white men looking for you! *None of you are safe.* The Klan has orders to kill you, Mr. Mickey. But they will kill all of you if they can catch you together. They surely will."

Goodman reaches out for Mickey's arm, and turns it so he can read the time on his watch. It's 3 p.m. All three Freedom workers stand up at once, say their goodbyes, and walk outside to where their blue wagon is parked. It should be an easy ride back to the relative safety of the Meridian office; and despite the usual sticky afternoon heat, the trio is eager to embrace the sense of relief they know will be theirs as soon as Neshoba is in their rearview mirror.

Huddled together, they make quick plans:

"I'll drive," Chaney suggests.

"Fine," Schwerner agrees, and pulls out the blankets he and Goodman will use to cover themselves while they lie on the floorboards, making it seem as if only Chaney is in the car. As they take their places, a discussion ensues over the best route back.

"There's two ways to go," Chaney offers. "The fastest is to use the same road we came on, Highway 491."

Schwerner pops up from under his blanket, "Wait, no, it's too narrow. All those dirt roads intersect with it. We could be easily ambushed."

Chaney agrees. "Then let's take Highway 19. It looks longer cause it's not as direct, but at least it's a blacktop highway! We might even make better time."

Goodman likes this idea. He enjoyed his brief time in Meridian yesterday; he even sent his mom a postcard from there. "If we take Highway 19," he says, "we go through Philadelphia, MS, the county seat, and I'd kinda like to see it." Schwerner and Chaney break out laughing at their sightseeing cohort. Soon all three are howling, releasing a carload of tension.

"Great," Chaney says, finally. "Okay, we're outta here!"

"Thank God!" Goodman says, and covers his head.

* * *

"Marilyn! Thank God!" I rush her as she strolls—in an unexpectedly aimless fashion—into our barracks after her Tel Aviv vacation. "I have so much to tell you." By the end of our first month, nothing happens without a shred-it-to-ribbons recap between the two of us. The girl I thought I had nothing in common with, has exactly my world views and gets through most things the same way I do—laughing 'til it doesn't bother us anymore.

Marilyn stands in the middle of the room dreamily. Before I can go any further, she smiles and says, "I met someone."

"What?" I ask, puzzled.

"I met someone in Tel Aviv."

"What do you mean? A guy?"

"Yeah," she blushes. "I went with one of our groups to Tel Aviv, and then we went our separate ways; so, I was walking by myself and I met Joseph on the streets of Tel Aviv…"

"Wait! You met someone on the street?"

"Um huh," she grins, glowing. "He offered to show me the city, and…"

"Wow, you are gutsy, girl. You coulda' disappeared!"

"Oh, no, it doesn't seem that risky here at all. Strangers are always befriending me and inviting me into their homes. There have been such incredible instances of hospitality…"

"Obviously!" I tease her. "But that's great, really! Is he American?"

"No, he's an Arab-Jew who lives in Israel," she says matter-of-factly, as if *that* won't be any problem whatsoever. We continue talking for some time about the unforeseen dawning of what will become a long and passionate relationship, soaring and plummeting many times over the next decade, before it finally releases them both to calmer, happier lives.

We chat until the sun drops below the sizzling soil, and the cooler dusk liberates new energy in us both to do evening things; we take out clean white cotton for supper and dancing, get dressed, and admire our glowing skin in a tiny wall mirror. "Wait," Marilyn suddenly remembers. "How was Greece?"

"Oh, Greece was beautiful—except for all the men pinching our bottoms everywhere. You'd be about to sit down in a restaurant or a bus, and before your butt hit the chair, in that split second, some guy would manage to get two fingers around the flesh of your tushy. It's freaky! I mean, do women like that in Greece?"

"Now see, that didn't happen to me in Tel Aviv," Marilyn grins.

Later that evening after supper, I'm alone in the room, lying on my cot writing a letter to my family and telling them how I've been all wrong about Amir and Israel. I love it here. Every day is better than the last. The more I learn about the kibbutz and how it was founded, the more inspired I am. Like, I never knew Amir is the only kibbutz established during World War II. Or that the land was purchased from the nearby Arab village of Khiyam al-Walid. Originally, the founders were immigrants from Lithuania, Poland, Germany and Yugoslavia, and they suffered from outbreaks of malaria, but somehow managed to establish a sophisticated farm despite that. In fact, instead of being ruined by the disease, it became a catalyst for the kibbutz to open a successful clinic for malaria and eye diseases, and until the recent Arab-Israeli conflicts, treatment at Amir for neighboring Arab villagers was free.

So, yes, I feel a definite sense of pride about Israel, Amir, and even me—for hanging in.

* * *

The Southern sun feels like a brush fire to Schwerner and Goodman, lying under their blankets on the back-seat floorboards. Chaney turns the old blue wagon onto Highway 19 and starts down the long road to Meridian. To the local cops, they appear just like they hope to: an "old junk wagon with some nigger driving it down a dusty dirt road." In fact, that's just what Deputy Sheriff Price reports when he spots the vaguely familiar wagon heading in his direction outside of Philadelphia.

Grabbing his car radio, Price can barely contain his excitement. "I've got a good one!" he bellows. Apparently, he has mistaken Chaney for another hated Negro civil rights worker. "I think I got George Raymond!" Deputy Price puffs proudly. Executing a U-turn that nearly flips his car, Price positions himself and begins to stalk his prey. When he finally pulls Chaney over and realizes his mistake, his disappointment is only temporary. Looking into the back seat, Price pokes at the blankets piled on the floor. That's when he immediately understands that he's hit the mother lode, and caught the biggest fish of all.

With a straight face, Price arrests Chaney, Schwerner, and Goodman for "suspicion of having been involved with the arson of the Lauderdale Mount Zion Church." He forces the three civil rights workers to drive all the way back to the Neshoba County Jail, where he deposits them under lock and key. After leaving strict instructions to give out no information about the prisoners no matter who calls, Price races off to Klan kleagle Killen to announce his amazing catch. Now, at last, their lethal plans can swing into action. The trap has slammed tight.

* * *

Having tried a number of work assignments by now, I find myself standing in Amir's fields with six other Americans at 11:30 AM, waiting to be picked up and taken back to the kibbutz mess hall for lunch. Our 8-hour day is almost done, and tomorrow we leave for our much-anticipated tour of Israel that will include the divided city of Jerusalem, Tel Aviv, the Negev Desert, and the Dead Sea. So, as hot and tired as we may feel now, we're also totally psyched about seeing more of this enthralling country. Looking up, my spirits feel like a perfect match for the sun's radiance. I stare into the shimmering distance for that welcome sign of relief we usually see by now; but I'm straining my eyes for nothing.

By 12:10 we begin to panic. Where's the truck? Usually we follow its tiny outline for 20 minutes in the distance as it makes its way towards us. Today there's no sign of any Israelis heading our way. Is this a joke? A test?

"What are we going to do?" I ask the others who stare at me blankly. There's absolutely no shade anywhere. We are standing in Amir's farming fields where all work must be over by the time the sun is standing exactly where it is now. I cup my forehead with my blue hat and pull it down low enough to steal a glimpse at the flaming sky. We have no water, food, phones, horses, bikes, nothing. Walking back is impossible. It's too far. Salt is pouring out of our bodies and any suntan lotion we used has long ago left our skin to deep-fry on its own. Our only hope is that someone somewhere will realize we're missing and come get us…fast.

For another five minutes, we stand there with no activity whatsoever going on in our heads. Then forest-fire heat from the outside and rising panic from within spark me to drag an idea—any idea—into our situation:

"I have a suggestion," I say. "What if four or five of us line up and cast a shadow over one or two of us?"

The group turns and looks at me like we're not only shipwrecked, but one of the survivors just went batty-bonkers at a crucial time. I try again: "I mean, we could try shading each other, using our bodies to block the sun. We have to create some shade, *somehow!*"

"But what about the ones standing in the sun, shading the other ones?" Gary, an easily confused American asks.

"No! No one stands up the whole time," I answer, trying not to get unpleasant. "We will take turns standing. It's just a way to give one another a break for a minute or two."

"What if they don't remember us at all?" Gary continues down Death Boulevard.

"Don't even think that!" I moan, elbowing the same grim thought aside.

"Okay, let's do it!" someone says optimistically. "It could work. And at least it gives us something to do until they come or we die."

So, two of us lie down on the scorched earth, while the others stand over us, bending slightly at creative angles to stop the worst of the sun's rays.

"It...it isn't bad," I say with more enthusiasm than I feel. Now you guys try it," I urge, pointing at two others.

With astonishing tenacity, we keep this up for 10 minutes until someone suddenly points towards the horizon and yells, "Look! It's the Amir truck! They're coming. *They remembered us.*"

Hoping this isn't a hallucination, I pop up from the ground and begin waving to the truck. The others jump up and down waving too, until someone abruptly throws up. Nothing like vomit to bring you to your senses. We're all too dehydrated and dizzy to be dancing the hora in an inferno, so we lay our barfing coworker down gently, and resume our shadow-blocking until the truck is no more than seconds away.

"Let's not say a word to them," the upchucker on the ground whispers, wiping his face. "Let's not bitch or complain. Since they ridicule us incessantly about being spoiled Americans, let's just get on the truck without a word."

His suggestion is met with a unanimous thumbs-up. When the Amir truck roars up to us and both cab doors fling open with Hebrew-speaking sabras jumping out carrying

2 Swimming In The River Jordan

first-aid kits, canteens, fruit, towels, and apologetic faces, the six of us step around them and pull each other up and onto the flatbed of the truck. We lie down, straight back and happy, smiling as the kibbutzniks stare down at us, flummoxed.

"You do not need anything from us?" one asks, holding the canteen up to me. I look at his tarnished face and bronzed hair for a minute, then back at my sweating American mates.

"Yes, actually," I say, and hand the canteen to a boy who is already falling asleep. "We girls would like to go swimming in the River Jordan. Would you drive us there, please!"

And, so it comes to pass that my female field workers and I find ourselves cannon balling off the slippery rocks that splinter the currents of the Jordan River's east bank. Snacking on grapes and yogurt, our elated screeches shaking up the Hula Valley, nearby Amir, and the Syrian border patrol. Hell, it's good for these people to hear a different kind of noise, a joyful one.

※　※　※

"I need to make a phone call," Schwerner says firmly, keeping panic out of his voice as best he can. "It's my right." He raps hard against the Neshoba County jail bars hoping to get someone's attention. Nothing happens. Chaney and Goodman stand on either side of him, steadying themselves with white-knuckle grips on the grungy bars. The prison smells of fear and years of dank injustice. Still, Schwerner persists:

"Everyone has a right to have one phone call!" he shouts again, trying not to sound antagonizing. Still nothing happens. He sits down in the dark humid cell and rubs his face with his T-shirt, trying to think.

"When you made that call to your CORE office," Goodman asks, "what did you tell them?"

Schwerner sits ups. "To call around for us if we didn't return by 4:30!" he says, feeling a small surge of hope. He quickly checks his watch and sees that it is 5:30 p.m. "Oh, my God! They must be panicked. I bet they're calling everywhere."

In fact, Minnie Herring, who is in the other room answering phones for Neshoba County Jail, is receiving a call this very minute from CORE's Sue Brown. Unfortunately, when Sue enquires if anyone there has seen or heard of three men answering the descriptions of Chaney, Goodman, or Schwerner, Minnie tells her they have not. It's not that she's confused. It's not that she doesn't know. And it's not that she came on duty after their arrest. She's just lying, exactly the way Preacher Killen told her to.

After more hours pass, the three incarcerated rights workers hear cars circling the jail outside. Goodman gives Chaney a leg up so he can reach a small barred window too high to see out otherwise. Schwerner helps steady them both.

"What do you see?" Schwerner asks, a little more than concerned now that darkness is falling along with his hopes of getting out of Neshoba.

"Oh, no…" Chaney moans.

"What?" both Schwerner and Goodman gasp.

"I can't be real sure," Chaney says, "but it looks like a bunch of Klan guys in different cars. Wait, they're coming 'round again. Yeah, fo' sure, it's the Klan circling the jail."

"Oh, my God," Goodman sighs to Schwerner who throws a free arm around him, giving Goodman support so he can continue holding up Chaney

"Oh, hey!" Chaney calls out again. "They're leavin'! They're going. That's it! They've left." They ease Chaney down and nearly collapse in a pool of their own clammy fright right there on the cell floor.

"What were they doing?" Goodman hisses. "Were they trying to scare us?"

"Maybe, maybe…" Schwerner mutters, his eyes drifting out of focus as his mind whirls through all the possible scenarios in store for them. He checks his watch: 8:30 p.m. How much longer until something happens?

Two hours later, at 10:30 p.m., Deputy Sheriff Price finally returns to the Neshoba jail. When Price walks back to the holding cell containing the three anxious prisoners, he quickly side lines Schwerner's legal rights questions with elaborate excuses about how he had to find a local magistrate for Chaney's speeding ticket. *Speeding ticket? What speeding ticket? Another b.s. charge?*

But the three know better than to argue with Southern lawmen. It was drilled into them during their training at Oxford boot camp. Instead they suggest that Chaney pay the insignificant fine, which Price mysteriously allows before leading them outside to their parked car.

"I would like to make that one phone call now," Schwerner says, trying to conceal his despair. He knows it's probably hopeless, but the call is their only chance of letting CORE know where they are.

Price glares at Schwerner for a second. "I want you to get back on Highway 19 and head outta town, back to where you came from," he says. Then he adds menacingly, "And I'm gonna tail you to be sure you do it."

Inside the ol' blue wagon, Chaney whispers hoarsely, "It's a trap."

✳   ✳   ✳

How awful. The Wailing Wall is off-limits for Jews. From the Western side of divided Jerusalem, where I am literally standing on my tiptoes, it's not possible for me to even catch a glimpse of the Holy Wall. What does it say about my life and sense of timing that I will stand in two carved-up cities—this one, and in twenty years, Berlin—both only short breaths away from seeing their subdivisions plowed into the future?

Suddenly, someone taps my shoulder and indicates I should look over at an Arab guard tower with massive barbwire covering its base. There are dozens of these intimidating sights in this city, and since we're standing right in front of this one, I'm unsure what it is I am supposed to see—until I take one more step and find myself staring down the long, pointed rifle of an Arab guard. He is standing in his station, hidden in the dark of the stone window that frames him perfectly and keeps most passing tourists from noticing his exceedingly close presence. His job is to aim menacingly from his border post, and my mistake is stepping into his sight line and freezing. His gun is now literally trained point-blank at my face. One of his eyes is squinted like a hunter focused on a distant prey; except I'm no more than five feet away, so close he surely hears my heart pounding.

Everything around me fades away. The music and chatter of tourists and Israelis, abruptly ends. For the longest minute of my life, I experience what it's like to lose your past, present, and future. I'm nowhere. If I could think, I'd wonder how this menace suddenly got a spot on my life's path. But I can't think. I'm frozen, as if his gun is a camera and I'm his photograph. Even Jerusalem's golden sunlight has now blackened into the dark side of the moon, making the sky fold tight around me. Deep inside this shrinking time capsule, it's just him and me. My breath is gone. What takes the space of your breathing right before you die? I'm about to know. Inside I'm flying past the ends of my life to find the nearest faraway star.

Then I hear Marilyn calling my name from another world. Where can she be? Where am I? Marilyn's words rise up out of the darkness like anti-matter: "What are you doing? *Judy!*"

Still I remain paralyzed in his magnetic field until finally the invisible shell encircling us cracks, and I manage to take that one crucial step out of his view. Then everything snaps back on again.

"Come on!" Marilyn is waving at me from atop some large stone stairs. Sounds and smells are returning so fast, I have to cover my ears. I'm dizzy and my sleeveless top is completely drenched with a raunchy mixture of heat and fear. Am I leaving behind breadcrumbs of perspiration, a path of panic for him to find me again? I walk zombie-like towards Marilyn and our American group.

"What were you doing—watching telly?" She jokes. "That's what it looked like from here. I couldn't see what you were staring at."

She doesn't really wait for an answer because her attention, like everyone's, is on the view from the stairs. There, in the distance, is our history and our destiny. We can see the other side of the Wailing Wall, where pilgrims and sightseers crowd the cobblestone streets of old Jerusalem, wandering its churches, mosques, and synagogues just as they've done since Israel's story began.

And that's the problem, isn't it? Finding a beginning to Israel's "story?" Do you explain Israel from the perspective of having a gun barrel between your eyes, or from three years in the future when Moshe Dayan leads his troops into the old city and changes its boundaries yet again? You're never really at the right starting point, are you? Did Israel's narrative have its "big bang" three-thousand years ago, when a boy named Abraham gave up clay idols and decided to worship one god. If so, that's a lot of dots to connect, *especially in this heat*. Because, in my mind, there's no question that the climate in the Middle East has a lot to do with the spirit and burden of all its religions—Jewish, Muslim, Christian, Druze, and Baha'i.

After all, the harsh weather alone can drive anyone to near-fanatical beliefs; life is too damn hard under this scorching sky. Surely the constant uprisings and wars across this parched side of our planet, have a climate correlation? And wouldn't the misery of such difficult lives make religions and governments more vulnerable to extremists? Perhaps I will one day reach out for Buddhism and Hinduism—both originating in Asia and the South Pacific—because their climates are milder and their influence less dogmatic...

"Want some leben with a falafel?" Marilyn fractures my mind-babble again. When she gets a better look at my drenched top she asks, "Are you all right?"

"I thought he was going to shoot me," I tell her.

She looks at me thoughtfully. "Well, then, what about a Maccabi Beer?"

*　*　*

When Chaney looks in his rearview mirror and sees Deputy Price turn off the road behind them, his lungs fill with undiluted relief.

"Price just turned his Chevy around!" Chaney says, breathlessly.

"Really?" asks Goodman, who's in the back seat. He turns around to check. "You're right. He's gone. Maybe we're okay."

Schwerner is cautious. He glances around the eerily quiet night outside their slow-moving wagon. "Just keep driving," he says. "Don't go fast. Don't go slow. Just go." For at least fifteen minutes they bump down Highway 19 without seeing a single car.

"Where is everyone?" Chaney wonders aloud. "I mean, isn't this strange?"

Then, when they're less than 10 miles from the county line, it happens. Deputy Price's souped-up guzzler sprints out of the dark, lights on, siren shrieking. Chaney panics. Sensing it's not going to end well, he hits the gas as hard as he can, and makes a run for it. The high-speed chase takes them swerving and screeching onto Highway 492, with Price gaining on them quickly. Then, for reasons no one will ever know, Chaney brakes the wagon, and abruptly pulls over. The three surrender without further incident.

"I thought you said you would go back to Meridian if we let you out of jail," Price bellows into their car.

Chaney sticks his head out and answers, "Yes, Sir, that's where we're headed."

"Well, you sure were taking the long way around." Then, as if savoring the moment, Price steps out of his car and walks up to theirs. He bangs his billy club on the wagon door, and orders: "Get out of the car!"

Chaney, Schwerner, and Goodman freeze for a beat, look at each other, then each open separate doors and leave the vehicle. Price uses his club to bang on the side of their wagon again for attention: "Now, get into the backseat of my police car," he commands authoritatively. Chaney hesitates, then thinks better of it, and gets in with his soul mates.

As Price ferries them back to Philadelphia, near Neshoba, the trio in the back seat slowly begin to realize the car is no longer alone on the road. Two other vehicles, with their headlights off, have rolled up beside them filled with Klan members. Decked out in white hoods and wearing rubber gloves, they're an evil sight that the civil rights workers are blessed not to be able to see, thanks to their darkened cars.

Then Price turns off the Highway onto an unmarked dirt path called Rock Cut Road. The three cars continue traveling in a procession for another mile or so. Inside, fear has created a new and suspended eternity for Goodman, Schwerner, and Chaney. There they've been left to experience the last minutes of their extraordinary lives. No longer speaking to each other, Goodman is thinking of his family, his mother, and how beautiful the South is. Schwerner is worrying that Rita is as frightened as he is now. And Chaney is plotting where he will run when he finally gets a chance to bolt.

Then the cars stop. The motors all turn off at once. Only the familiar Southern sounds of bugs and frogs scratch at the silence. Price sighs heavily in the front seat, then steps out of the car and raps on the back-seat window. "Get out!" is all he says, before turning to disappear into the woods.

Chaney erupts out of the backseat. Before anyone can do or say anything he escapes the car and is running as fast as he can. More car doors fling open dispersing the eager Klansmen after him carrying chains and rifles.

Twenty-six-year-old, dishonorably discharged Marine, Wayne Roberts, yanks open the other back seat door to Price's car. "You didn't hear the Deputy?" he growls at the terrified Schwerner and Goodman. "Get out now!"

When they get out, the two can hear screaming in the distance.

"What are they doing to him?" Goodman asks, tears running down his handsome face.

"Shut up!" Roberts barks, his voice slashing through his white KKK mask.

"Look, I understand what you guys must feel," Schwerner begins, reaching for old lessons of compassion that have always served him in the past.

"I said shut up!" Roberts screams, and fires his gun point-blank into Schwerner, killing him mid-sentence.

"Oh, no!" Goodman sobs. But his words, too, are punctuated by a bullet shot straight into his virtuous heart.

Chaney's fate is not so merciful. Concealed for 36 years, it takes one tenacious journalist until the year 2000 to uncover an autopsy report that reveals that unlike his Caucasian brothers, whose bodies show no definitive damage from beatings, Chaney's remains are so badly mutilated, only a few bones remain unbroken.

All three bodies are tossed into the Klansmen's cars, and part two of "the plan" begins: With their headlights dimmed, the unmarked vehicles drive to the 253-acre Old Jolly Farm. There, work's been going on for days as busy Klansmen use equipment to dig a deep dam in preparation for the burial. Olen Burrage, Old Jolly's owner, made it clear he'd be proud to use his farm to bury all the civil rights activists headed for Mississippi. Every single one of them.

And so, while CORE workers in Meridian frantically try to locate their three missing brothers, Schwerner, Chaney, and Goodman are placed together in a make-shift grave at the dam site. Then a ton of dirt is dropped on them from a Caterpillar D-4. When the last ounce of soil has fallen, the younger Klan members responsible for the hands-on dirty work, stand around the finished grave, high-fiving and congratulating each other for a job well done.

Next, the familiar blue wagon is driven to North East Neshoba County and set on fire. *This is a mistake.* It is the first in a chain of mistakes that will take half a century to unravel, and ultimately expose hard evidence of America's dirty little holocaust. For finding justice for "those three," will literally unearth hundreds and hundreds of missing African-Americans whose murdered, broken bodies are dug up and pulled out of rivers and graves for years to come.

* * *

Wow! For the first time since landing in Israel, I am pleasantly cool. My body temperature is normal, and I am not sweating.

We are only an hour away from the steamy Jerusalem streets, but we could be in the darkened cave of a long-forgotten forest. Actually, we are in near darkness, and it does feel a little cave-like. This is the Hall of Remembrance at Yad Vashem, a 45-acre complex devoted to the six million Jews who perished in the European Holocaust.

Although I've noticed many men and women on our kibbutz with numbers tattooed on their arms, I am still completely unprepared for this imposing structure, with its walls made from boulders hauled in from the Sea of Galilee, and its tall, angular roof pointing tent-like to the stars. The large eternal flame burning in the center offers us our only light; and the smoke from the flame rises to an opening in the ceiling, like an endless stream of questions: how could this have happened? What is going on in the mind of people doing such cruel things to others? Certainly, this grim brutality and hatred could never happen in America?

In front of the Eternal Flame, someone shows me a stone crypt holding the ashes of holocaust victims taken from each concentration camp's ovens, and brought to Israel after the war. Engraved on the mosaic floor that my sandals now seem glued to, are the names of the 22 most infamous Nazi death camps. They are written in Hebrew and German. Suddenly it becomes essential that I read every single death camp name out-loud to myself. It's the least I can do.

This gets overwhelming very quickly. Some of us can only stay in the hall a few moments. "It's as if they want us to feel what waiting for the gas inside the ovens was like," a frightened woman cries and pushes past us, heading for the exit. "No!" Motle whispers to me, saddened. "This is a peaceful, safe place! A place made for honoring their suffering."

I take his arm and lean on him for several minutes. But soon I too want to leave the great room I'll never forget. We walk out of the dark through a wooden door and into the blazing sunlight that leaves my eyes unable to see anything for several minutes. It's a fair transition. Everyone needs a moment. Then we stroll into a garden lined with small trees, each one planted for a non-Jewish person who risked his or her life to save a Jew during the Nazi occupation. In Poland alone, if someone in a gentile family was caught giving a Jew a glass of water or slice of bread, the entire family was put to death. Most people aren't brave enough to save their own lives after living in fear too long. The idea of risking yours or your family's for "an outsider" is astonishing. And yet, here I am, turning round and round in this magical grove, looking at all the trees that are standing in for people who did just that.

In a few short years these young trees will become so big and the garden so crowded, Yad Vashem will need to come up with a different way to honor the bravery of these uncommon heroes. And they will: "The Righteous Among Nations" is the name of the medal presented to all non-Jews who stepped in harm's way to save Jews from Nazi extermination. Using special criteria and documentation that evaluates the risk each rescuer went through, a committee headed by a justice of the Supreme Court of Israel, bestows the awards.

I walk among the thin trees for some time on my own, listening to their rustling branches, and reading the dedication plaques near each one. Such commanding redemption greeting you after such unfathomable savagery. Yad Vashem is the gift of balance. Only humans can repair inhuman acts.

* * *

At Chaney's funeral, his 12-year-old brother, Ben, sobs uncontrollably as the gathering sings "We Shall Overcome." Cameras catch the agony of his loss so well, the televised moment is compared to John John's salute when his father's casket passed him nine months earlier. Leroy Jeffries watches Ben in despair. He wants to touch his old friend's sibling, but his own hands won't stop shaking. "Your brother was the bravest man I ever knew," he finally whispers to the tiny boy who never hears him.

Then Chaney's mother, Fannie Lee, stands; and with bold words meant to throw a healing shroud around every one of every color, she says to the mourners, "These white boys came down here to help us. They didn't have to do that. They died helping *us*." Then Fannie Lee then steps back beside her heart-broken son, and holds him with all her might.

* * *

Sitting on a hill outside Amir, my Israeli sister, Ora, and I are talking about why I'm not going to stay on the kibbutz, why I'm returning to the United States.

"I'm too spoiled," I say truthfully. "I've already had a taste of too many possibilities. I can study anything, be an artist, be a musician, a writer, travel the world, make a choice, not make a choice, indulge myself."

Ora looks at me with wonder. What can America possibly be like that its people can do such things? Her face is so full of amazement, I just want to grab her up and warn her that I don't know what on earth I'm talking about, or what I really want out of life. We are both so naive despite the harsh realities in her world and the higher education in mine.

"I am going to miss you and this kibbutz life," I say as we walk. Her head is down; I think she is crying. "Maybe it's a mistake," I tell us both. "And maybe I will come to know that. But I'm not finished. I have to finish school. I believe that when I don't know what to do next, I should just finish what I'm doing."

"I know." Ora says softly. Then she looks up at me and announces, "Judy, I will go to college too…after the Army. We all must go into the Army. But then I go to college like you."

Though I'm not sure why, that makes me feel very proud. "Do that. Then I too will finish college. But, Ora, please be careful in the army. Please…"

"Yes, yes…" she waves my concern away.

We reach out and hug each other in the midday sun, long and hard. It is a good thing too, for with the exception of one unsatisfying letter exchange, it will be 47 years before we re-connect our richly different lives.

After a long time, Ora lets go of me, and slowly walks away. I watch her disappear for several minutes; then I realize I can't go back to the barracks yet. Instead, I decide to walk to the other side of Amir and sit on a wood fence by myself. Could I really come back here to live? Give up "my elitist American life?" Except for the heat, parts of the upper Galilee look like Southern California, thanks to all the agricultural work the Israelis have done. But, underneath, what about this feral place? Though no different than anywhere on earth, the Middle East embellishes, with sad eloquence, the history of humanity's need to divide up, bracket, organize, and categorize as better, higher, lower, wiser, stronger, and weaker—absolutely everything. Whose skin color is the best? Who has wandered the desert longer? Whose land is my land? Whose land is your land? I know only one thing: there are no answers in these measurements.

Shalom, Ora, little kibbutz sister. In America, I can still put my head down for a few more years and ignore the turmoil tearing at the edges of my life. But something of me will return in my own way and find my own cause worth fighting for. Please don't die for yours! Stay alive. And don't forget to splash and swim in the River Jordan for us both.

3

Greenwich and My Lai: A Tale of Two Villages

I did it. I graduated college and left California. I boxed up my "important things," and sent them to friends and family who live in New York City; then I bought a one-way ticket to Manhattan and arrived last week. Now I'm at my first residence, the midtown YWCA, where my friend Bonnie says, "When you turn the lights on, it gets darker."

I absolutely don't care. It's the fall of 1966, and I've barreled through a quagmire of emotions to get here, the city of my birth; the luminous and cockamamie place I'm hell bent on offering my music, writing, and singing, in exchange for madcap happiness and a profound sense of purpose. No high-anxiety expectations from this 22-year-old! No, I've been focused on Manhattan since I visited my aunt and uncle in Great Neck when I was 16. That was the summer I spent my days taking the Long Island Railroad to 42nd Street, sneaking into rehearsals and matinees, and falling madly in love with the theater.

So now I'm finally here, undeterred by the barrage of "you can always come back home if it doesn't work out," sermons I received from my parents and their well-meaning friends. Of course, I also secured a few introductions from them like, for example, Alan Arkin's and Milt Okun's telephone numbers. I don't know what to do with Mr. Arkin's number, but Milt

3 Greenwich and My Lai: A Tale of Two Villages

Okun...! Oh yeah, he could be most helpful. Milt produces and publishes Peter, Paul, and Mary's music; and right now, except for the great god [Bob] Dylan, PP&M seem like the perfect guides to lead me into the rapture.

I actually make my very first call to Milt Okun from a hallway pay phone at the Y. The experience is just as twisted and humiliating as you would imagine. The incessant people-parade, amplified by the cement walls surrounding the phone booth, inspire a desperate, "What was *that*?" every few seconds from Milt. When he finally asks me where I'm staying so he can give me directions to his apartment, I freak and lie. Thus, I jot down directions to Milt's apartment from the Chelsea Hotel (where I've never been, but heard Bob Dylan often stays in room 205). Of course, with my harrowing sense of direction, this is a very bad lie. How am I going to get from one place I don't know to another place I don't know in a city I don't know? Regardless, we make a date in two weeks for me to bring my guitar and come to his place to sing my songs. "We'll see what to do with you after that," he concludes.

Fortunately, I am only staying at the YWCA until my friend Ann (remember our Israel trip?) arrives and we can share an apartment. Between us we have $100 a month to spend on rent, and given the liberating power of my fantasy life, I believe the world of New York dwellings will open its doors wide. After all, I'm only speaking of the world below 14th Street. No one with an ounce of coolness lives outside the Village. Only about a square mile in total, the West Village has a history so rich and imaginative, it pulls on my dreams like a magnet. All the creative rebels on the planet have made art here.

I'm just sorry to have missed the beatniks. Sometimes I see a few leftovers haunting the narrow Village streets. With books tucked under their arms and cigarettes dangling from their goateed lips, they still hold court in the corners of coffee houses I frequent. But mostly they have taken off their turtleneck sweaters, shaved their facial hair, and grown their coifs long. The thoughtful, poetic vitality the beat generation once infused the Village with, is slowly losing its influence to a new and raunchier kind of maverick. Harsher times create sharper dissenters. America's civil rights movement has morphed into an angry revolt against an incomprehensible war in the Asian jungles. Vietnam is a cancer we didn't treat immediately or wisely, and now the country is very ill. How perfect that Ann is leaving Berkeley, one hotbed of conscientious objectors, for another; heading straight into Greenwich Village, while her future husband marches blindly into the moral morass of Vietnam's own civil war.

Well, I can't fix that, so let me at least find us a cool place to live. But my bout with real estate optimism loses its zip the minute I begin looking, and a severely grim cavalcade of two-bedrooms present themselves. I fear it's verifiable: you can only live in certain places when you're young; that's when you're impulsive and harebrained. If you're mature and sensible, you wouldn't dare, which is probably why some of our most memorable memories are gathered when we're emotionally and intellectually a wee bit wobbly. For example, my first apartment in the Village, on the ground floor of 521 Hudson Street:

Indeed, it is a bargain: exactly $100 a month. It sorta has two bedrooms, if you convert the living room into a bedroom; it has okay views, if you stain all the windows so you can't see out and into the inner courtyard that houses the building's dumpsters; it has two bathroom "areas," meaning the toilet and sink are near the bedroom and the shower is in the...kitchen! Yes, there is actually a full shower with a wraparound curtain standing right next to the stove. The walls are

3 Greenwich and My Lai: A Tale of Two Villages

very entertaining all by themselves, as you can not only hear everything your neighbors do and say, but at night you can hear mice running through them at break-neck speed looking for food. This will keep Ann up until dawn, which is a shame because she's in New York to do graduate work at Banks Street School of Education.

But worse than any of this is the fact that by the time Ann actually arrives—after I pay first and last month's rent plus a cleaning fee (what a joke!)—we discover something truly abysmal about the place: an assortment of "bums" have been crashing and drinking *in* our apartment for years:

"What's that?" Ann bursts into the "toilet room" where I just planted myself on our first Hudson Street evening. I start to ask her what she's talking about, but then I too hear it: great thundering thrusts plowing into our front door. We creep, terrified on hands and knees into the kitchen, and watch the door reverberating violently in its frame as someone or something slams—with gladiatorial force— against it, screaming viciously, "Lemme in! Damn it. I sleep here!"

Ann and I crawl under a card table we found on the street to use as our kitchen table, and huddle together to think. The "tramp" on the other side is blotto drunk, furious, clueless about us, and hell bent on getting in. Without the slightest sense of my own silliness, I decide the best thing to do is to speak honestly with him through the door about our situation. After all, wouldn't I be overwrought if I was locked out of my home and didn't know why? Shaking Ann's grip off my ankle, as she hisses, "No, don't go near the door!" I stand up, and knock loudly from the inside several times until my sharp taps cut through his racket and he goes silent.

"I'm sorry, sir, please go away," I coo. "We have rented this apartment now. So, you have to sleep somewhere else in the future, okay? Sorry and thank you so much."

Everything goes quiet for 10 seconds, then we hear him talking to someone. *There are others out there?* At least three inebriated male voices grunt to each other using barely audible terms of vulgarity. Then like a five-minute drum solo that goes absolutely nowhere, they bombard the door with another tumultuous assault. This goes on all night, for three nights, until they give up and find another dilapidated apartment in our tenement building to crash in.

And yet, despite this, I still feel like I've found home. Maybe we have to buy four more deadbolts for the front door, so? Nothing deters me, not the poor bums, not even the broken light bulbs we trip over in the hallway leading to our front door—ostensibly smashed by thieves so no one will see them trying to steal things at night. And I certainly do my best not to dwell for any length of time on the 80-year-old lady whose front door is across the hall from ours, because I have some grave concerns about what she eats. Wrapped in layers of ratty blankets, she never leaves the building, only pokes her head out her door when she hears us coming or going. Her large tabby cat is obviously everything in the world to her, as she is never seen without him wrapped tightly in her arms. Once, after Ann and I catch several mice with traps in our apartment, we are too freaked out to kill them, so we put them in bags outside our front door until the morning, when our plan is to turn them loose in a vacant field between condemned buildings. But when we open the door the next morning, the bags are gone. Later when I run into the old lady hugging her cat in the hallway, she thanks me for the mice. Honestly, I'm too alarmed to ask who ate them; I fear it was a joint meal.

Ann tells me that she needs a desk for her early-childhood studies, and since our apartment is only big enough for one card table, I find a couple of shelf brackets and purchase a long, wide board for 5 cents. I screw the brackets into her bedroom wall and lay the board across them to create a make-shift shelf she can use for a desktop. The problem is I attach everything too high; our folding chairs are too low. So, after a lengthy hunt, Ann finds a tall stool in a Hoboken, N.J. dumpster, which she brings home on the subway despite numerous calamities with commuters. I score some semi-fresh paint lying outside our building and even though the colors make you light-headed and are so unsuitable for indoor walls they actually glow in the dark, I paint every visible surface in the apartment.

My uncle says the place looks like a brothel; hipper friends think we should open a psychedelic head shop. I push on valiantly, un-boxing each photograph and poster I created for the UC Berkeley drama department as their official photographer. I buy a can of glue and use it to wallpaper the artwork to whatever surfaces haven't been painted: the side of the stove, the back of the doors, a room divider, and the front of the refrigerator. Behind the frig, by the way, Ann and I find a pile of used condoms the day we pull everything out for a thorough cleaning. Unfortunately, this marathon clean-up collides with a surprise visit from my Aunt Estelle and Uncle Arnie. While Estelle "screams bloody murder," my uncle drolls, "What? Doesn't everyone screw on the top of a refrigerator?"

After several weeks of scrounging around for food and apartment essentials, both Ann and I are pretty worn out by our poverty. So, I decide to send my resume (with absolutely no previous work experience on it!) to an agency. Within hours they call me with a job offer: The Winstin Lester Music Company in Gramercy Park needs a copywriter. "Have you ever written copy?"

"Well, of course I have."

I run out our front door, stumbling over the broken light bulbs, slipping onto the filthy snow, and rush off towards the Eighth Street Bookshop, hoping to find a dictionary or style manual that might explain what a copywriter does. I already know what Lester Music does: they make guitars. That's a good match, right? I play guitar, well, folk guitar. Regardless, Lester is introducing a line of electric guitars under their own Destiny brand name. At this point I have no idea that my life working for New York companies that make money knocking off cheaper versions of already established and successful brands, is about to begin.

Finally, after thumbing through several publishing reference books, I learn that a copywriter is someone who writes interesting stuff about stuff. Hey, I can do that. So, I drag out my one suitable winter skirt and call my friend Bonnie who lives in Gramercy Park to help me find 20 Irving Place, where my interview is scheduled to take place tomorrow. Bonnie, whom I met two summers ago doing summer stock theater at the New London Players in New Hampshire, is a fearsome mixture of alpha princess and New York intelligence with racing cross-currents of kookiness. A ball of fire with more opinions than there are ingredients in Julia Childs' cook books, Bonnie has her own complex childhood secrets to break free from. Unfortunately, because she can make a real meal of people I thought she liked, I never quite feel safe with her. What does she really think and say about me when I'm not around? Still, I'm crazy about her because she's absolutely fascinating and able to command my attention like a compelling thriller. The truth is, now and forever, I cannot look at Manhattan without seeing Bonnie there.

"Sounds like you'll get this job if you can just make it to the interview. Why don't I share a cab with you from your dive to their offices, then let you off, and take the taxi home. I think Lester Music is very close to my place. Really, I just want to be sure you actually get there. The other night was inexcusable…!" she continues, in a tone eerily close to my mother's when she's getting mad.

3 Greenwich and My Lai: A Tale of Two Villages

"*Oh, Gawd,* don't bring that up," I plead.

"This is New York City, Judy!" she drills on anyway. "You are not at Berkeley anymore. You are not going home with guys you met on campus. You're going home with men from the city that you know nothing about. You can't have one-night stands with some man you met in a coffee house..."

"We've been over this, 'Mommy!'"

"I'm just warning you! You didn't know him and then you didn't even know where you were when you woke up with him the next morning," she flings this last bit at me triumphantly, weaving together two blunders I made in one night. "All you could tell me was that he had model airplanes and plastic war ships all over his apartment."

[Pause] "Okay, Bonnie, I am never calling you again when I'm in trouble," I pout.

"That's not my point, she softens. "Some guy at a club..."

"He wasn't some guy. *He was the headliner...*" I brag, "...at the Tin Angel."

"Has he called you since that night?"

"No."

"See!" *[Triumphantly]*

"See? What is your point? That I should have held out on him? It's the 60s, Bonnie!"

"No, that wasn't my point! I'm just glad you're not dead. We don't go home with guys we don't know a thing about *here*. It's not safe. We *vet* them first."

"*Vet them?*" With that, we break into hysterics.

* * *

Warrant Officer Hugh ("Buck") Thompson, Jr. pulls on his controls, lifting the little reconnaissance helicopter up high until it literally sweeps across the tree tops that surround

Landing Zone Dottie, about 12 miles northwest of Son My Village. There are days Vietnam is truly the prettiest place on earth. The morning fog burns off by noon, revealing an idyllic painting below: farmlands, old men and women boiling water by their huts, cows and roosters, young children playing while their parents head into the rice fields for the day's work.

Buck Thompson's presence in Vietnam with Charlie Company is about to change the course of history for the embattled citizens below, his fellow soldiers and the entire United States military. Embodying absolutely everything the armed services says it cherishes, the handsome 24-year-old Thompson has been called out for being exactly the kind of soldier you want on your team. And God knows, teamwork is the holiest of grails for the military.

Raised by strict parents in Stone Mountain, Georgia, Buck and his older brother, Tommie—also on duty in Nam—learned early and well the rules of a life that you can be proud of: "Don't lie; do your chores; don't run away from a whipping; and do unto others as you would have them do unto you." Their teacher was their father, Hugh Sr., who spent four years in the service during World War II and another 30 in the Navy reserves.

The military's way of structuring life came in handy when Hugh Sr. became the town's scoutmaster and drilled the sky-high standards of "trustworthy, loyal, helpful, friendly, courteous, kind, obedient, cheerful, thrifty, brave, clean, and reverent" into his sons as if they were the mighty commandments themselves. But even if Buck hadn't been a Boy Scout, there's one lesson he would have learned just from being his father's son: always, always stand up for the underdog. After all, Hugh Sr. is half Cherokee. All Buck's life he's been told stories about the plight of the Cherokees; how they were forced off their North Carolina land by the U.S. Government, and how,

3 Greenwich and My Lai: A Tale of Two Villages

by the mid-1800s, many of them resettled on Georgia farms. Sometimes things are unfair and you just have to find some way to make it better.

Breathing in the delicious moisture that flows off the South China Sea bordering the tiny Nam villages below, Buck scopes out Son My Village—an area made up of three hamlets: My Lai, My Khe, and Co Luy. According to reports they've received, the civilians below have been harboring the Viet Cong—supporters of the communist National Liberation Front who are fighting against South Vietnam and the U.S. For the last months, too many Americans have been killed or maimed in surprise Viet Cong attacks, booby traps, mine explosions, hidden bombs, and sniper fire. U.S. troops aren't used to this kind of enemy. They're accustomed to fighting wars where you can clearly identify the other side, where battles are planned and carried out in plain sight.

Recently a very popular sergeant in Charlie Company was killed in one of these booby traps, and Buck can feel how pissed off and hungry for revenge the men are. The problem is, the jungles are so damn thick that half the time they can't find the Viet Cong—which is exactly why Buck's flying around up here.

With two door gunners aboard, Buck's job is to fly his small Observation Helicopter [OH]-23 Raven close to the ground, spraying machine gun fire haphazardly from the treetops, hoping the enemy will shoot back and reveal their positions. When they do, Buck pulls his little helicopter up and out of the way, allowing the big Huey gunships flying protectively above him, along with the troops on the ground, to take over.

The information Charlie Co. receives about their targets must be absolutely accurate. And that can be a problem because this information—which comes from "higher ups" on the chain of command—often isn't right. For example, Buck has some concerns about the directives received by Charlie Co. four days ago from their Commanding Officer, Ernest Medina:

The Viet Cong's crack 48th Battalion is in the vicinity of a village known as My Lai. Charlie Company's mission is to engage them and destroy the village of My Lai. By 7 am, the women and children will be out of the hamlet, and all you can expect to encounter is the enemy. You are to explode brick homes, set fire to thatch homes, shoot livestock, poison wells, and destroy the enemy.

How can they be so sure every single Vietnamese citizen will be out of My Lai by 7 am? Buck wonders. According to the briefing Charlie Co. got with these orders, "All the good guys in My Lai will be gone; so, if you see anyone, assume they're the enemy, and—kill them!" Hopefully the leaflets they've been dropping over the My Lai village will warn residents to prepare in advance and get the hell out.

Buck pulls his aircraft up and flies above the River Diem, taking the long way back to Landing Zone Dottie. OH-23 needs to refuel again, and truthfully, he needs a break from his own relentless thoughts. Some days he sees things very differently from his vantage point. For one thing, he can see the little guy down there, scrambling for safety. Inside his head, if he listens closely, he can hear questions the other soldiers don't hear—or at least never talk about: *How many years have these poor souls had to run for cover, war after war, while foreign nations (France? Japan? England? China? America?) fight to control their exquisite countryside?* One after the other, the cunning wolves come. Buck wagers most of the farmers running for safety through their rice fields don't know or care what Communism, Socialism, or Capitalism means. They just want the ugly killing machines in the sky to stop sabotaging their simple lives, day after day, year after year.

3 Greenwich and My Lai: A Tale of Two Villages

※ ※ ※

Amazing things are happening this week! First, I'm going to meet Milt at his Manhattan apartment on Saturday; second, I got a very cool job that begins today. Winstin Lester's son, Rick, is my boss. He's the head of the company's newly formed advertising department which basically consists of Rick, an artist, and me. Since Lester Music is launching a line of electric guitars, including a knock-off of a successful Vox guitar, under their Destiny brand, the heat is on to cook up a bunch of smart ads that will run in *Downbeat* magazine over the year.

The odd thing is, *Downbeat* is a highbrow jazz musician's magazine, and from what I've studied over the weekend about Destiny's new Impulse guitar, it's a little trashy. I mean, it looks fabulous, especially in photographs, but practically everything about it is either replicated from other brands or synthetic. Still, I study every scrap of literature I can hunt down on electric guitars in order to seem as knowledgeable as possible; then I enter the Gramercy offices prepared to make an impact:

"So, we'll go with the Impulse's great looks, I imagine," I announce with faux authority at our first morning meeting. I've never been to a real meeting in my life, but I sip coffee and smile steadfastly at my two teammates nevertheless.

"What are you talking about?" Rick asks me.

I realize I have to be careful. I know nothing about him; he may think he's selling a Fender Electric XII, the guitar Jeff Beck and Pete Townsend play, worth hundreds of dollars!

"Oh! I mean, well, how much are you selling the Impulse for?" I dodge, trying to get more information.

"Seventy-five dollars."

"Ohhhhh, wow!" I reel. "I see. So, it's a guitar for beginners?"

"And pros; it's an amazing deal," he boasts. Then ignoring the other person in the room completely, he pulls his seat closer to me and says, "And I have a great idea about how I want to sell it. So, I'd like you to come over for dinner tonight."

At first, I'm not sure he said that. "What?"

"I said I want you to have dinner with me tonight at my apartment," he repeats, oblivious to my recoiling, "and I'll tell you about my idea. I think you're gonna like it a lot."

I suggest that he tells me about it right now. The artist, a slight, shy, black man named Jed, agrees. If nothing else, he's curious.

"Naw," Rick says, strutting over to his desk as if it contains a bazillion urgent things for him to do instead of talking to us. "If tonight is too short notice, then let me know tomorrow what evening this week is good for you."

"Uh…wait," I say, desperately. "I have an idea, too. I was actually thinking about it this weekend. Why don't we use the name of the guitar, the 'Impulse,' and create ads about having fun in different locations, like…"

"Exactly!" Rick says, pointing at me.

"Really?" I say, pleased.

"That fits perfectly with my idea. We'll talk about it at dinner."

When he finally leaves the room, I turn to find Jed staring at me.

"What am I going to do?" I whisper to him.

"Run!" he hisses back.

On the way home that evening, I stop at Macy's department store to look for a new work outfit. One skirt isn't going to do it—unless the whole job goes away over this freakish dinner meeting. At one point, I get so lost in the hugeness of Macy's, I wind up in the linens department, where I finally find someone who can direct me to the women's clothes.

3 Greenwich and My Lai: A Tale of Two Villages

Unfortunately, the saleswoman gets as far as instructions to the escalator before she covers her mouth, squawks, and points. When I turn to find the reason for her conduct, I see him too: dark and stunning, toweringly tall, in a perfectly tailored dark suit, with a posse of gorgeous black women encircling him; Cassius Clay, newly dubbed Muhammad Ali. His voice booms across the sheets and comforters to several stunned shoppers:

"Oh, hello there, how's everybody tonight?" he remarks graciously, nodding in various directions.

Someone standing on a display mattress and box springs calls out loudly, "Thank you, brother, for refusing to be drafted to Vietnam. You're doing what I only wish my own son could do."

Ali whirls around to find him. When he does, he waves a warm greeting in the air, then lets his hand turn into a fist and addresses the man loudly. "No Viet Cong ever called me 'nigger,' brother!" His words are greeted with cheers and applause from the mainly black crowd now flocking towards his famous voice. "I have no quarrel with the Viet Cong."

Another voice calls out to Ali, but we can't hear the question from where we're standing. His response, however, is bell-like: "Then I'll go to jail! I said it before: I am not going no 10,000 miles to be murderin' and burnin' brown people just to help the domination of white slave masters over dark people!"

Oh my God! I gotta get outta here! I search out the bewildered sales lady who is still covering her mouth, and ask her how to get all the way out of the store. "Please, just tell me where the exits are! I want to go home."

Later that evening, when I tell Ann about Mr. Ali yelling in the linens department of Macy's, I find myself actually thinking about his point. Ann says she's seen flyers circulating Banks Street which make the same argument: the U.S. is sending a disproportionately large number of black soldiers to Vietnam because so many of them don't have the money or education to get out of the draft; and yet these guys are over there shooting down people who aren't white!

Knowing that Ann's boyfriend is in Nam now, I'm not sure I should launch into my "why are we there at all?" pitch, so I slide over to the other thing that's making me nuts tonight—my dinner invitation from Rick. Ann's very clear: "Yuk! Don't go!" Even after I share my hunch that if I don't do this dinner thing, I'll lose my job, she's firm: "Too icky, don't go."

Bonnie is more considered: "Do you have pepper spray?"

Pepper spray? I've never carried pepper spray in my life. If I thought I needed pepper spray, I'd just quit and be done with it. Finally, after two more workdays of trying everything I can think of to steer the meeting onto office hours *in* the office, I give up and agree to meet Rick at his apartment near work on Friday evening.

When he opens the door, his brow and face are gleaming with sweat. As he steps aside to let me enter his apartment, now swimming with the smells of dinner, I notice he has a dish towel thrown over his shoulder, and looks like I've pulled him out of a very creative endeavor.

"You cook!" I say with some relief and pleasure.

"No, no, I order in," he responds matter-of-factly. The table is set for two, no candles, thank goodness, but a bottle of red wine already opened and one glass half full. I hardly have my coat off and he fills my glass to the brim. Then raising his for a toast, he disappears into the kitchen. While surveying the dining-living room, I see my resume—the one with no work experience on it—sitting next to several drawings of the Impulse. What is he up to?

I wander into the kitchen, which has a chaotic you-are-there *verite* about it, with unwashed pots, pans, dishes, and food strewn about. (And he *didn't* cook tonight?) Even though

3 Greenwich and My Lai: A Tale of Two Villages

the wine tastes bitter, one gulp has me loose enough to blurt out, "Why did you hire me?" straight at Rick, who's portioning out our spaghetti with such severe concentration, he jumps. He glances up for a second, then belly laughs. My heart sinks. I must be a total idiot. Isn't it obvious? He hired me so he could use his authority to bully me into having sex with him. I'm now part of an old cliché, and the dawning of that realization makes me madder than the thought of having sex with him. I glare in his direction with all the pissed-off-ness I can muster, but he just turns away indifferently and goes back to concentrating on our plates with the solemn expression of a man working through an impenetrable math problem. Finally, he decides the portions look right, and begins talking:

"You're a musician," he says unexpectedly. "You were classically trained on the piano, then you took up the cello and then the guitar…"

Did I put that on my resume? I can't remember.

"I'm a musician too," he goes on. "I'm doing this 'cause it's an opportunity to approach music differently, and to make money working for my dad; but I intend to do more with music."

"Me too!" I say, taken off guard.

"I know," he says, gesturing for me to sit down at the table.

We eat in silence for quite a while, me feeling better about him and much lighter than before. Then he pushes his empty plate aside and moves to the couch, where the guitar photos and papers are stacked on the nearby end table. I don't budge, pretending I'm still engrossed in my meal, which I've been done with for some time. He pats a space next to him on the couch.

"Come here," he directs. "I wanna tell you my idea for an ad.

"I can hear you," I say pleasantly, and continue to chew.

He waits. And waits. Obviously, he wants me to finish eating and get over there. After an excruciating few minutes, I give up and throw my napkin on the table. Making a show of it, I walk over and take a seat at the other end of the couch.

"You can't see," he points to the guitar photos under the lamp on the end table near him. I still don't move. "Come here," he barks. This time his command has a grim cock-of-the-walk tone to it. *Ugh.* I scoot next to him.

As soon as I do, he throws a meaty arm around me as if we're on a movie date sharing popcorn. Then he casually starts talking about his idea to run a contest for the Impulse guitar, featuring *me* as one of the winners.

"Of course, there won't be any other contestants or winners," he smirks and squeezes me knowingly. "We'll make the whole thing up to sell the guitar and to collect contact information—from the kids who enter—to use for our Destiny Guitars catalogue mailing list. We'll photograph you playing the Impulse with your band, and say it's your guitar, like 'Judy's guitar is a blah blah blah…' Then we'll run the whole thing as an ad," he concludes, still holding me too close.

"What?" I finally cry, shaking my brain free of this maniacal plan as it pirouettes around the bend in my head. But you know how you sometimes pick the oddest detail to latch onto when, really, the whole thing is a staggering pile of feces?

"Wa-wait," I stutter, "I don't have a band!"

"Oh, come on, Judy, who cares! I'll be your band; me and other guys I know," he huffs, clearly annoyed that I'm not beside myself with gratitude over this big break he's offering. "You're going to be in *Downbeat* magazine! You're going to be in *Hit Parader* and *Hullabaloo* too."

Because I don't know what else to do, I make him take me through the whole tacky farce again, and notice that whenever I ask a question involving details about the scheme, he

3 Greenwich and My Lai: A Tale of Two Villages

answers with, "Oh, *you'll* work that out. *You're* the copywriter." For instance: Who are the judges? What's the contest called? Are you pretending to give guitars away? Is this legal?

Finally, I understand that he's said all he knows. And in that moment, I realize that I will have to pay more than a modicum of attention to this whorey idea starring me, or I will surely become someone who can't believe the shit she's gotten herself into. But first I need to power past this prolonged mating dance he's concocted, and get the hell out of here. So, I look around for my purse and begin making noises about how late it's gotten, how nice dinner was, and what a privilege it's been spending quality time with my boss; but for now, "see you tomorrow *at work*." Naturally this only sparks his next, nefarious move.

"Aw, it's only 10," he whines, flushed and uncomfortable from the steam pouring out of his living room heater and the rubbish pouring out of his mouth. "Aren't you turned on by my idea?" He actually winks at me as if I'm something spectacularly stupid and can't see through his transparent maneuvers.

"Judy, this could be your big break in music. I was hoping…"

"What? What were you hoping?" I snap back, twisting around in his grasp to face him. The question is too direct and his eyes flee from mine. Suddenly, I'm actually embarrassed for him. His shallow scheme never transcends the obvious for a second. Maybe if I can soften the rejection, I can get us through this? Is he a bad guy or a doofus? I'm really confused. Maybe we're just two lost souls meeting at precisely the wrong moment. (A sudden vision of Bonnie giving a roof-raising shriek shatters this line of analysis pronto.) Okay, he's clunky and pushy, but maybe not a total turd. I'll go with that. After all, I don't want to lose a job I just got.

"Look, the idea sounds fun," I lie. "But I definitely think you should talk to your dad about it before you go any further.

There are lots of issues about the ad that concern me and he might…"

This snaps him out of his syrupy wine haze like I had slapped him. "*My dad?* Forget my dad! This is my department. I'm in charge!"

"Oh, good! No problem then!" I shake off his restrictive arm and pop up, launching myself from the couch to the chair he'd dropped my coat on earlier. As Rick watches his evening veer off its inappropriate course, he slouches back on the couch, resolved and sulky. His features droop three inches when I turn to say goodbye. Although I really know nothing about him, I suddenly get the feeling that I'm watching a childhood of disappointments tugging his face into a whopping pout:

"We could've at least watched TV together," he grouches, then slumps back further and scratches his crotch pathetically.

That's it for me! I close the front door and try to balance brooding about the safety of my job with how proud Bonnie's going to be over what she'll consider excellent vetting on my part.

* * *

Lawrence (Larry) Colburn has the entire right-hand side of Warrant Officer Buck Thompson's helicopter to protect. Glancing over at the pilot he respects and enjoys more than he can say, Larry knows the parameters of his assignment: the aircraft, the pilot, and the men on the ground. Next to him is an M-60 belt-fed machine gun that hangs from a bungee cord. Since its not mounted, if he must, Larry can take the gun with him out of the helicopter.

Growing up a long way from Vietnam, in Mount Vernon, Washington, Larry's upbringing was not unlike Buck's, in that it was fairly strict and he was taught a strong moral code early on, especially from his mother. Just like his command pilot,

3 Greenwich and My Lai: A Tale of Two Villages

Larry's father is a veteran contractor from WWII, so for him as well, the military has always been a part of the family's conversation.

After joining the army in 1966, Larry earned his GED while stationed in Hawaii. By then everyone in the armed services understood that sooner rather than later they'd be deployed to South Vietnam. After talking with several of his army buddies, Larry learned that his chances of coming back alive would be much higher if he could join an aerial unit. So once in Vietnam, 18-year-old Larry began aircraft training, and was assigned shortly after to an Assault Helicopter Company with the rank of Specialist Four.

When he first met Buck, Larry was instantly relieved on several scores. "Mr. Thompson"—as he and the others call him—has a great sense of humor with lots of Southern charm and swagger. Unlike most of the aloof officers Larry's served with, Buck has authentic personal magnetism to go with his very unusual communication skills. Refusing to let his men address him as "Sir," Buck isn't afraid to horse around with the enlisted men even though officers aren't supposed to fraternize. Buck actually insists that they get to know each other inside and out. What they're up against every single day is a matter of life and death. Being able to anticipate one another's moves—because they've really bonded—will put them ahead of the game. And Buck believes the game in Vietnam is very, very close.

While most war pilots are thrill-seekers by definition, Buck is a little different. He certainly has the daredevil gene, but he has something extra. Putting aside Buck's infamous John Wayne swagger and Cherokee "blood of a warrior" heritage, when Buck takes the pilot's seat, Larry knows that there's another, even more powerful influence at work in this officer. He's seen for himself that Buck has the *honor code* of a warrior as well.

Once, during what's known as "snatch operations"—when the air units are searching the ground for draft-age Viet Cong males to kidnap in the field—Buck's aircraft spotted one who just wouldn't stop running. Larry kept firing his gun all around the guy in order to make him stop, but the kid would just turn around, laugh at them, and keep running as if it was a game. They chased him for 15 minutes, until the helicopter started to get overheated. While another team would have given up and shot the kid down, Buck worried he might be mentally challenged in some way and unable to understand what was happening.

Finally, Larry recalls, Buck turned to him and said, "You want to take him out?" Surprised, Larry pointed his weapon at the kid, only to have Buck scream: *"No, no, no. Take your seatbelt off; get out on the skids, and I'll get close to him. Then you just tackle him. Bulldog him!"*

Larry was more than willing, and later told fellow crew chiefs, "When we finally got this crazy kid into the helicopter, guess what we found in his pocket? A card that said: 'Don't take me in for interrogation. I've been interrogated 15 times. I'm challenged.'" *Yeah, Buck called that one perfectly,* Larry remembers. He just has this special sense of humanity!

As for how successful Buck's unprecedented tackle technique has become, the maneuver is something many gunners have started using whenever they're not taking on gunfire. It works better; it's clearly more humane; and, hell, sometimes it's fun!

※ ※ ※

I find Milt Okun's apartment without a hitch! Riding up in the elevator, I lean my guitar—with a collage of black & white photographs glued to the rapidly deteriorating cardboard

3 Greenwich and My Lai: A Tale of Two Villages

case—against a wall, and straighten my skirt. I wish I could have worn jeans, but all the girls I see performing in coffee houses around here wear skirts. My eyes sting from the heavy eyeliner and dark shadow I've anointed myself with. I have a light headache as well. It could be nerves, but more than likely it's due to these hulking earrings I've clipped on. They're pinching too tightly. And actually it's not the skirt that's bothering me. I did something I've never done before and it wasn't a good impulse: I bought self-tanning lotion and smeared it all over my legs so I didn't have to wear stockings. What a screw up. The lotion did not dry evenly. Nothing on the bottle warned me about this possibility. Thank God I didn't rub it on my face too. Oh, well, no one's going to look at my legs. I'm here to sing my songs!

Milt is a friendly man who welcomes me into his living room, where I think I hear music and voices somewhere deeper in his apartment. After offering me a glass of water, he sits down in a chair, motions to my guitar and says simply, "Play."

I begin running through a few of the songs I've written recently, songs about leaving home and living in the city; one called "You'll Forget" about some Vietnam horror stories Ann's passed along; and one sort of amusing one about my apartment. In the middle of the last song, I finally get the courage to open my eyes and look at Milt. To my complete horror, he is staring at my legs. Only inches away from me, he is sitting straight-backed in his chair, expressionless except for his wide eyes which are glued to my painted legs. I don't know how, but I finish the song.

I feel so mortified, naked, and ugly. Not only because of the asinine tanning disaster; that's just the final coat on this phony presentation I've wrapped myself in. Who am I dressed as? Not me. I don't look or feel attractive this way. I feel like I'm in a costume. I thought I had to appear as feminine as possible to be heard, which may be true, but I don't know how to do that. What's more, I'd wager after staring at my streaky finger painting below, nothing I sang made it to his ears.

The silence now inhaling our entire meeting is mercifully violated by a howling city siren outside. Although I still can't look at him, I hear Milt say, "Do you want to meet Peter Yarrow?" Unable to face him, I'm unsure I heard right. He reaches out and taps my guitar a couple of times until I look at him. His smile disarms and rescues me from a complete breakdown. "Leave your guitar here," he says quietly. "Peter is inside, with the others."

It's obvious he feels sorry for me, so he has to do something. Holding out his hand, as if to escort me, he walks me down a hallway, chatting easily, "Peter and Paul and Mary are working on harmonies for an arrangement to Peter's song." These last words are intoxicating enough to wrench me out of the pity party I'm currently throwing:

"I'm going to meet Peter, Paul, & Mary?" I ask, disbelieving another arrow of hope could possibly be heading for me after the muck I've made of this opportunity. Milt opens a door to a large study, and there on the floor, with sheet music and hand-written notes strewn around them, lie the three biggest hit makers of the moment. Then I remember that the first thing they're going to see are my legs!

After several aggressive attempts, Milt finally breaks through their ironclad concentration—or at least it looks that way at first. When they do glance up, it's as if we are Martians. Honestly, I could have no legs and they wouldn't notice. The trio is struggling with Peter's masterpiece, "The Great Mandala," and want only one thing: to be left alone so they can continue. They're deep in the creative process and have lost all other connecting skills. Finally, Milt tells Peter he will give him my telephone number and we leave the room.

3 Greenwich and My Lai: A Tale of Two Villages

"She has nice songs," Milt says over his shoulder to the closing door. In the living room, I pack up as fast as I can while Milt assures me he will pass my number onto Peter. "He's good fun and a great writer. It will be nice for you to meet him," he continues, ushering me back into the hallway outside his apartment. He waves goodbye.

When I'm finally alone in the elevator, I burst into tears. I'd give anything for a re-do; but all I can do is learn from what I did do. Better to be rejected for myself than whomever I tried to be back there.

* * *

Glenn Andreotta is another high school drop out who has enlisted in the army to discover his destiny, which turns out to be flying around the unfriendly skies of Vietnam. Unlike his two comrades aboard OH-23 Raven, this isn't Glenn's first Nam tour of duty. He's already spent a year here as a radio repairman. And while it's true his family is absolutely heartbroken that he signed up for another year, they also know their restless 20-year-old doesn't do that well in civilian life.

Unfortunately, Glenn's mother can't seem to shake a bad feeling she has about his return to combat. She's been overcompensating by smiling and taking pictures of Glenn and his brother horsing around in the family backyard before his deployment. Trying her best to keep her fears to herself, when Glenn hugs her goodbye for the last time, it nearly breaks her.

Glenn, like his OH-23 partner, door gunner Larry Colburn, has heard the reports indicating that Charlie Company may soon be caught in a number of missions with a 50/50 chance of survival. Thus, he too has developed an enthusiastic respect for aircraft commander, Buck Thompson. It's just nice to know that whatever calamity comes at them, they're in the sky with the best.

And on those occasions when all hell is breaking loose and real danger fills the copter with panic, out of nowhere, Buck will lob a joke, injecting levity the very moment Larry and Glenn are thinking "it's over." Glenn particularly loves it when Buck opens his mic, and connects the three men through an intercom in their flight helmet headsets. Just hearing his mates breathe, can synchronize Glenn's heartbeat and flood him with indescribable comfort. If a man's gotta live in fear every day, Glenn believes he's scored the best possible ammunition against it with Mr. Thompson.

※ ※ ※

What can I possibly say? I am completely astonished when our Hudson Street phone rings and a man sounding just like Peter Yarrow asks for me.

"Yes, this is Judy," I manage.

"Yes, this is Peter Yarrow, *really*."

After a few enquiries, Peter asks if I'd like to get together. *How fantastic is this?* I knew he hadn't registered my suntan lotion fiasco or anything else that day; and how fortuitous that Milt didn't enlighten him.

Naturally, for this second chance, I think long and hard about my outfit. I have never seen Mary Travers—of P, P, and M—in pants. Even in Milt's apartment, she was wearing a skirt. But I'm not Mary. Nothing about me looks like Mary. I'm thinking about Mary because I imagine Peter is used to looking at women who look like Mary.

Oh my God! I'm doing it again.

I've been all over this with myself. After dying my legs 10 shades of mahogany, I thought I was okay looking like me from now on. And I am. But will Peter be? Well, if he isn't, there's nothing I can do. I've already proven that. I've also established how badly it sucks to be a victim of your own desperation trying to be something other than who you are. My problem is I'm just a little lost about who that is. So, in an effort to distinguish between illusion and reality, I unload all my favorite jeans and sweaters from the cardboard boxes that are standing in for a chest of drawers; then I begin trying on combinations. After some time, I hit on one I like enough to add shoes: sneakers? boots? suede moccasins? Okay, the boots. Plus, of course, my second-hand Navy peacoat that I scored in a Village Army-Navy Surplus store. And my guitar. That's it. This is how I'm going. I can only pray I embody what it means when something amounts to more than the sum of its parts.

Since our meeting isn't until this coming Saturday, I spend every waking moment—that I'm not dodging the daily barrage of Lester pandemonium too weird to mention here—practicing my songs. I stand in front of our full-length mirror—another alley-hunting score with something of a fun-zone wobble to it—and critique how I look making music. Eyes open, eyes closed, smiling, serious, I'm relentless. By Saturday I'm also really ready.

I take several deep breaths when I get to Peter's building. I can't believe this is really happening. When I arrive and the doorman calls Peter, I keep thinking he'll turn to me and say, "Peter is not expecting anyone, especially *you*." But instead he gives me the apartment and floor number, walks me to the elevator, and tells me which way to turn when I get off.

I lift an old fashioned doorknocker and knock three times. I hear movement inside and get a surge of anticipation so fierce it gushes through every part of my body hitting my bladder the hardest.

"Hello?" I hear a man's voice say behind the door. The little door window thingamajig opens and an eyeball stares out at me. "Is that you, Judy?"

"Yes, yes. It's me."

The door opens and I blink. Peter is standing in the doorway completely naked. I was prepared for all kinds of shenanigans today, but this incongruous sight was not on my list.

"P-P-Peter?"

"That's me," he says, dripping wet with no sign of a towel. Neither of us move for what seems like two years. Being way too bashful to look anywhere but his face, I'm forced to instantly clock that he's disappointed in what he's seeing: me. Apparently I'm not the adorable groupie he's used to receiving, and my heart aches watching his face fall.

"Come in," he mumbles distractedly. "I'll dry off and get dressed."

He leaves me still standing in the hallway like a delivery boy. After a few deep breaths to stop myself from fleeing, I step into his foyer and close his front door. His living room is airy with several large windows that let the sun light flood across his high ceilings, walls, bookcases, musical instruments, and artwork. I've heard about places like this, but never expected to be in one so soon after arriving in NYC. I wonder where his bathroom is, but realize I can't use it because he's in it. Then I ponder sitting down. Two of the biggest chairs that face a fireplace have guitars on them, and the couch is covered with papers, magazines and books. I'm not sure where I would sit even if…

"Why did you bring your guitar?" Peter asks, appearing suddenly from somewhere.

"What? Why did I bring my guitar?" I repeat back confused. "Aren't we going to… I mean, Milt told you I write songs, right?"

"Yeah," Peter shrugs, pushing things off a corner of the

3 Greenwich and My Lai: A Tale of Two Villages

couch and sitting down. "But I've got plenty of guitars here." He points to at least six guitars lying about the room in and out of expensive cases.

"Oh," I shake my head, "but I didn't know."

"You didn't know I'd have a guitar?" he snaps at me unpleasantly.

"No, no," I protest, rattled. "It's just that I would never assume I could play one of *your* guitars."

He stares long and hard at me for several uncomfortable minutes. I feel like I've definitely done something that just isn't allowed in the better bistros. I'm so antsy I could happily jump out one of his picture windows. Instead we both begin speaking at the same time:

Peter: "Take your coat off. That thing looks like someone got shot in it. What?"

Me: "Can I use your bathroom? What?"

Peter: "It's down the hallway. Huh?"

Me: "It's possible someone got shot in it, I guess. Where?"

I take off my hulking Navy peacoat and drape it and my suddenly sorry looking guitar case against one of the chairs and flee to the bathroom. Rubbing his still steamy mirrors so I can assess myself, I give up and pee out a quart of anxieties. By now, I'm reaching the outer limits of my paranoia. Am I colliding with this swirl of gasbag characters to get them all over with at once? Peter Yarrow is a larger than life folk-singing star, a major godhead in his set. He's in his salad days and fancies himself quite the young buck, that's obvious. So being able to spend even a few minutes with him should feel flat-out amazing—not harrowing. Let me focus; I'm here to share my music. Let's get back to that. "Why did you bring your guitar?" *Really?*

I regain some confidence in the bathroom; however, when I reach the living room, Peter is putting on a coat and searching the apartment for his keys.

"What's going on?" I ask, worried.

"Oh, I just got a call from a friend who needs money from the 'Fuck-Up Fund.'" he says, as if I know what he's talking about. When I say nothing, he actually explains: "It's a fund several of us—performers—put together for when one of us gets into trouble and needs money. Y'know, bail money, travel funds, Nam protests, marches?"

"Oh, how cool," I say, still not understanding why he looks like he's leaving.

"Hey, how would you like to run some errands with me?" he says, cheerfully, like he's used to girls swooning over this kind of invitation. "It's Mary's birthday next week, and I need to get her a present."

"Oh?"

"Yeah, she loves antiques, really loves antiques," he continues, holding up his apartment keys triumphantly. "You live in the West Village, right?"

I'm thunderstruck that he's held onto that piece of information. "Right, but aren't we going to…?" I motion to my guitar. "I could just run through a couple of songs quickly."

"Actually, I've got to get to the bank right away," he insists. "Get your bullet-ridden coat," he chuckles, "and you can take your guitar too. Maybe you can play me some songs somewhere. But I've gotta get to the bank before it closes. The Fuck-Up Fund calls."

And so, before I can fully register what's happening, I'm standing outside on the curb, trying for an agreeably daft "go-with-it" attitude, while Peter hails a taxi for us and talks nonstop about everything that's troubling him. Once inside the cab, he gives the driver directions to several of "Mary's favorite antique shops," and turns to me with sudden seriousness:

"You heard about Bob, right?"

"Bob?" I say, spinning through every Bob I've ever known.

3 Greenwich and My Lai: A Tale of Two Villages

He exhales, piqued at my lack of plugged-in-ness. "Dylan!"

"What about Bob Dylan?" I gasp, displaying the appropriate reaction.

"He almost died!"

"*What?*" I scream, as if my brother had been hurt.

"Yeah, he and *[his wife]* Sara were on their way home from *[Dylan and PP&M's manager]* Grossman's house, and Bob lost control of his bike."

"His bike?" I interrupt, imagining a bicycle.

"His *motorcycle!*" Peter tells me that Sara was driving their car behind Bob and was able to get him to a hospital immediately. He cracked a lot of vertebra and had some serious road rash. There've been rumors circulating that he's brain damaged. "But thank God, that's not true."

"Wow, yeah!" I echo. My mind is flooded with thoughts of Dylan—my favorite artist ever. But words can't express my thoughts. They immediately go silent the minute I open my mouth. Then just as I get close enough to try, Peter hollers to the driver:

"Stop! Stop here. Let us off at this corner. *[Then to me]* Let's try that store."

For the next four hours, without so much as a cup of coffee, Peter drags me in and out of every antique store in the Village. I have no idea what he's looking for, what Mary's taste's are, what things are worth, or—given all this—why he keeps asking me what I think. For now and forever, the experience sours me on antiques. They only conjure up the bait-and-switch experience I had with Peter: endless smelly old things taking the place of sharing one note of music with him.

"Good luck, Judy! And thanks for your help!" he calls to me, holding up some aging piece of porcelain for Mary, as the cab pulls away. I stand motionless, still clutching my guitar in the evening chill outside my Hudson Street tenement.

Stepping inside, I can smell everyone's dinner at once. A gloomy sensation floods the hallway to my front door. Shuffling along slowly in the near dark, I pare down what's bothering me: So what if Peter didn't hear my songs? At least he didn't hear them and hate them. Besides, it's not his job. He's a busy celebrity doing important things in the world—protesting wars and financing Fuck-Up funds. There are girls everywhere who would give anything to have spent my day with him. So why am I depressed? Why did I want to cry when he looked me over like that in his apartment? And if we weren't going to share music, why do I have this blurry feeling I would've rather spent today running around with Mary? Actually, why does the very thought of Mary spark my interest more than Peter?

Sometimes, I swear, I feel like those fractured Picasso paintings. Maybe years on, in the cold light of hindsight, my mind will reassemble all my puzzle pieces and show me the obvious picture I should have seen all along.

✳   ✳   ✳

After a particularly troubling night of interrupted sleep and ominous pep talks about the need to destroy entire hamlets known to be aiding the Viet Cong, Buck lifts OH-23 up and into the dawn like a balloon someone suddenly cut free. Crew chief Glenn on the left and door gunner Larry on the right check their M-60 machine guns and bungee cords, while happily breathing in the temperature change. Yesterday was one of those monsoon weather days, when the climate alone feels like it can take you out of the sky. And yet, somehow the crazy Nam rains managed to bounce off their tiny silver bubble and return them to the evening unharmed and ready for another day. And, dear God, have they ever seen a more beautiful morning in Vietnam?

3 Greenwich and My Lai: A Tale of Two Villages

Over Buck's radio, a stream of chatter persists like white noise. Then they hear that familiar word, "gook" jump out at them. Buck swoops down for a look, but they don't see anyone.

"Where did that come from?" Glenn asks.

"What?" Buck says.

"That word? 'Gook?' Why do we use that word for *both* the Viet Cong and Vietnamese civilians? I mean, isn't it confusing enough for us? It's not like we can tell the difference by looking at them anyway."

Buck smiles to himself. He asked his father the very same question months ago. "It's an acronym, or it used to be," he says.

"What is?" Larry joins in.

Never taking their eyes off the soft green and yellow rice fields below, the conversation settles in on Buck's information:

"When the British were here, there used to be signs above certain doors that read: 'Gentlemen of Other Colors,' or 'G.O.O.C.' The acronym became associated with any indigenous, non-British person; and now, I guess, it's a derogatory term for any non-white enemy around here."

Glenn thinks about this for a few minutes. "Really? That's kinda small-minded considering *they* aren't the foreigners," he says, cross.

"Well, that's true," Buck answers. "Still, we've always used demeaning labels for our enemies. In WWII, the Germans were 'Krauts' and the Japanese 'Japs.' The Italians were 'Dagos.' I guess it's considered human nature to denigrate your opponent so he seems less powerful and…"

"…easier to blow away?" Glenn finishes.

"I guess," Buck says, glancing back toward Glenn. "But look, I'm sure our enemies have equally unflattering names for us." Then Buck shuts the conversation down with a sudden drop in altitude.

"What's that, *down there?*"

Random Events Tend To Cluster

* * *

Lester's Impulse guitar ad, "The Spotlight of Musical Achievement Contest" goes into action like the campy, wreck-on-the-side-of-the-highway I feared. If Rick had lived in medieval times, he'd be the buffoon burning down villages to get the girl's attention. He's relentless. He's also tasteless and the very last person in Manhattan who should be producing advertising.

Instead of hiring a real photographer or real musicians to pull off my "Judy and her band" photo shoot, we are all locked up in Lester's offices for an entire Saturday as Rick takes laugh-out-loud snapshots of us making the worst music ever. While I fight off despair, my batty boss flings himself at drums, bass guitars, keyboards, and me—creating what he calls "a cool rock sensibility" and I call the dorkiness of a polka convention. Still I hold out hope for a last minute, save-the-day, intrusion from Rick's father. Surely he isn't going to let this adolescent madness go public?

But whenever I pass Winstin Lester in the hallway, he literally sneers at me. It's as if the man secretly blames me for the mayhem his son is creating. I suspect that's easier for him. When I ask Rick what his father thinks about the ad that Jed has managed to cut and paste together from the schlock-gothic photo shoot, he can't even hear the question.

"It's fantastic. It's fantastic! Stop worrying. We're going to run the first one in next month's *Downbeat*," he gallops past the point. "And you better get ready for a lot of attention."

God forbid. Really, what am I going to do? Jed tries everything he can think of to help me—burying the poorly lit snapshots inside a filmstrip layout, and sticking as many pictures of the Impulse guitar onto the page as he can. But there's nothing he can do about the copy I'm directed to write:

3 Greenwich and My Lai: A Tale of Two Villages

"Winner #13: Judith Wieder" followed by a crackpot list of my past sins and the whopper: "Her Guitar: The all new Impulse."

Naturally with Lester's ad budget, things like grammar and fact-checking are expendable; so, with a speed that defies clocks, the ad is signed off on (by whom?) and out the door. Okay, well, surely *Downbeat* has certain standards for the kind of ads it accepts, and certainly this won't cut it. But, surprise, the game isn't about quality; it's about money. So, the abysmal thing not only appears in the March and April (1967) issues of *Downbeat*, but true to Rick's word, soon you can see me wailing away with "my band," while shredding "my favorite solid body electric guitar" on the pages of the June *Hullabaloo* and July *Hit Parader*.

But wait—there's more: at the end of the year, Rick announces that he's ordered several thousand print-outs of the ad—with "As Seen in *Downbeat*" stamped on them—to be passed out at the upcoming National Association of Music Merchants [NAMM] trade show. With this news, the controlled catatonic state my spirit's been floating in, bursts. *This is ridiculous.*

In the eight or nine months I've been at Lester, I've written copy for at least seven different ads. All of them have appeared in major music publications. Even if I disappear the contest ad, I've certainly got enough samples of "my work" to retool my resume and try again. There's no way things are going to get better here. Pushing out another trite medley of rock 'n bull for Destiny guitars isn't going to get me a better job, and could cost me my wits. I'm already collapsing under the weight of this mumbo-jumbo. So, on a whim, in the middle of the day, I pack up my desk and prepare to tell Rick, "I'm leaving."

The irony is, walking up and down the hallways looking for Rick, I realize the rancorous clamor I hear is Winstin himself wailing away behind his closed office door. That's never happened before. One of his product managers passes me in the hall and whispers, "He's had it with Rick!" When I stop in my tracks and turn to him, he warns: "I'd think about getting another job if I were you. Winstin is gonna dismantle the in-house ad department, and hire a legit ad agency. He believes the stuff coming out of here is amateurish."

You think?

Hallelujah! I had my epiphany just in time. How much better to leave when *you* want than when *they* want! I return to the office I share with Rick and Jed. Jed must be at lunch, and now I know Rick is in with his angry father. Picking up my box of desk things, I wait a few minutes, but Jed never returns; so I take one last look at my first real office, and close the door.

✴ ✴ ✴

It's 7:30 in the morning, and everything is crystal clear beneath Buck, Glenn, and Larry, allowing any movement to catch their attention. On the ground, the My Lai invasion has begun, with Charlie Co. marching down the roads that begin at the village parameters and lead inward. Flying at a low level, the first thing OH-23 sees is a draft age Viet Cong soldier tearing as fast as he can across a rice paddy in between two My Lai tree lines. Buck ducks the copter down, repeating, "There! See? What's that?"

"We caught him in the open!" Larry whoops, excitedly.

"I'm gonna take him on the right," Buck responds, meaning its Larry's job to start firing at him since he's obviously VC and carrying a carbine and a pack. The idea is to get him to stop before he gets to the safety of the trees at the end of the rice paddy.

"Aww, man!" Glenn yells, watching the young VC make it to a tree line and vanish. Frustrated, Buck calls down a gunship above him just in case it has better luck finding the VC.

3 Greenwich and My Lai: A Tale of Two Villages

"Do you see anything else?" Buck yells to Glenn, whose eyes are often sharper than his copter mates.

"No, nothing, nothing anywhere."

"No more VC?" Buck asks, bewildered. "I thought we were told they'd be crawling all over the place down there."

"Mr. Thompson, I don't see anyone either," Larry adds.

On the other hand, there is a great deal of movement on the roads leading out of the village's interior where many residents live. After re-checking the perimeters of My Lai—where Lt. William Calley and Charlie Co. are now marching in—Buck points to all the older My Lai citizens walking out of town on foot.

"Look at all the old men and women leaving My Lai," he says into his mic. *"That's good.* That's real good. They'll be out of the way. That's what's supposed to happen. We musta dropped leaflets to warn the civilian population—including these older villagers and children. They gotta get out of there in case there's gunfire."

"Yeah…" Glenn agrees. "It's Saturday morning, so they could be going to market."

"I guess," Buck says.

"Look at em." Larry repeats, overwhelmed at the sight of so many women, children, and elders moving along the roadways of the vulnerable hamlet. "There are hundreds and hundreds of them," he marvels.

* * *

I decide it's important to connect with a new job and a new music opportunity as quickly as possible. Otherwise I'll start to perseverate about Peter and Rick, as if they have anything to do with my happiness. So, stepping into the firing range again, I buy an issue of a music and theater trade paper called *Show*

Business, and write up an ad for their Classified department: "FEMALE SINGER/COMPOSER seeks professional music venture. Please call blah blah blah."

Well, I simply had no idea how many narcissists with gaping holes in their morals live in New York City! It's as if I wrote, "For a good time, call Judy!" Clearly you can make a lotta dough here selling your body in a music trade paper.

Then several days on, when the sex trade calls cease, someone actually phones about music. He has a publishing company with his own recording studios where songwriters can make demos, and he's very eager to discover more good songwriters. After the cautionary tale of this past week, I find my spirits black with paranoia soot. Is this guy, Wayne, going to be the protagonist of my story, or another malfunctioning appliance?

"If I like your songs," he offers, sensing my reticence "I have the equipment to cut some acetates (instantaneous discs, ready to play on a phonograph), right here. The worst thing that can happen is you'll have demo recordings of your tunes to shop around. Or I'll shop them around, and we'll see what develops from there."

Well, how bad can *that* be? After all, I don't want to be one of those people who turns skeptical and quits just because of a jerk or two. It's going to take several tries to find the right match for my songwriting, and I need to get a few songs down on acetates to take around. So, the obvious answer is to say "yes," right?

Wrong!

Perhaps the first alarm bell should have been him asking me to meet him at 10:30 pm the following evening. But, hey, it's the music business and people have crazy hours that don't fit the 9 to 5 formula. Since I'm not one of his signed songwriters, I decide he's sticking me into his schedule any way he can; so, by the time I get off the elevator in his busy 221 West 57th office building, I'm comfortable with our meeting time.

3 Greenwich and My Lai: A Tale of Two Villages

The second alarm bell I ignore is that there is no receptionist at the front desk. Okay, it's late, and she doesn't have to stay. But there is absolutely no one around. And the place is kinda dark, as if most of the lights have been turned off for the night. Standing in the dim reception room, I look around to see if I can make out any legitimate music business paraphernalia. Straining my eyes, I barely see a coffee table that has a couple of *Billboard* and *Cashbox* issues on it. Good sign. As I make my way towards the table, a bright light blasts on along with a gregarious voice:

"Great, you made it," Wayne says, entering the waiting room from the same outside front door I used. "Everyone's gone so we can go back there and use one of the offices." *(Doesn't he have an office?)* He's younger than I had imagined. More my age, 22, than the gravitas in his phone voice suggested. I follow him obediently down an ill-lit hallway past four or five offices. I can see one door that says "Studio," and feel my heart leap over all the red flags so far.

"Let's use this office," he announces and stands back to let me walk in first. I hesitate for a second, but when Wayne flips on the light, I can see the office is a prestigious one, full of tapes, acetates, and sheet music. There are three gold records on the wall and two other trophies on the desk that I don't recognize.

"Is this your office?" I ask Wayne, who takes his seat with an exuberant sense of ownership. He dodges my question with one of his own:

"So, what is it you ultimately see yourself doing in music, Judy?"

"I, I…what? What do you mean?"

"Do you want to be a songwriter? A singer-songwriter? An artist who sings other writer's songs? What's your dream?"

"Oh, well, I want to be a singer-songwriter," I say, trying to feel confident.

"Are you a good singer?" he shoots back.

"Um, not like Streisand, but like singers who sing their own songs today, like Tim Hardin or Dylan or…I don't know if I'm a good singer. Maybe you'll tell me when I sing you some songs." I smile hopefully and glance at my guitar.

"Okay, okay, good idea," Wayne agrees affably, to my relief. Finally, someone wants to listen.

* * *

After 15 minutes of checking all the perimeters of My Lai, OH-23 swoops back over the same region they were in when they watched the elders, women, and children leave the village. To their astonishment, they can still see them, all the same people—but something's wrong. Now they're all lying in the roads. Some are moving slightly, crawling, but most are lying still, dead still.

"I don't understand!" Buck calls out to Glenn and Larry. "Do you see this?"

"What happened? Are they dead?" Glenn yells through the propeller noise.

"Mr. Thompson!" Larry shouts to Buck, "I…I think these people…are dead or badly injured. What could have happened while we were gone? Did the VC attack them?"

Buck immediately begins spinning scenarios; but nothing makes any sense: "Well, we weren't gone that long. Could it be these *aren't* the same people? Or maybe these people below ran out of their houses when the artillery came in, when our troops marched through, you know, and maybe they got excited and ran out in the open and got killed."

"Really?" Glenn questions.

"No, no, that can't be," Buck regroups. "Every house in My Lai has a bomb shelter in it. Why would they run out into

3 Greenwich and My Lai: A Tale of Two Villages

the open? No, that didn't happen. Oh, God," Buck moans, his despair and reality-barometer sharpening with every second.

Buck alerts the gunships above him as to what he's seeing. His hope is that by making a fuss over the airways, his observations will be passed along to someone who can do something about what's happening below.

"It looks to me like there's an awful lot of unnecessary killing going on down there!" he bellows into the radio "Something's way off about this. There's bodies everywhere. There's a ditch full of bodies that we can see from here." Then to Larry and Glenn, he says: "Let's start marking the wounded below by dropping smokers near them. Then the Charlie Co. medics on the ground can find and help them."

With that Larry and Glenn begin dropping green smoke grenades near any bodies they spot below them that appear to be wounded but still alive. They mark at least a dozen My Lai citizens on the roads or lying injured in rice fields. After another 15 minutes they're forced to leave the area again to fly to Landing Zone Dottie for a refuel.

* * *

My voice doesn't sound good to me. It sounds stressed when I play "I Stained All My Windows" for Wayne. Something about the place or him has me off my game. But, when I finish, to my utter surprise, he applauds and immediately asks me to play another. I decide to try my Vietnam protest song, "You'll Forget," to test his politics, and again, Wayne comes through with flying colors, thumping and hooting, giving me the thumbs-up, and asking for another. This goes on for at least an hour: me playing and singing, and Wayne tapping his feet, clapping, complimenting, and asking for more. Finally, he stands up from behind the desk, and announces:

"Let's go into the studio and cut acetates on three of these songs for starters!"

I can hardly believe it. *So this is how it happens!* I've been in New York nearly a year, and finally: contact. But, glancing at my watch, I wonder out loud if it might be better to come back another time when we're both fresher.

"No, no," Wayne nixes, "let's take advantage of the fact that no one is using the demo studio tonight. It's hard to book time in there. This company's always using it for its writers and their new material."

For a fraction of a second, my mind notices—then ignores—that he didn't say "our" company, he said "this" company.

The little studio is adorable, at least by my naive standards. There's a small control board for Wayne to operate and a little soundproof cubicle for me, complete with a stool and microphones. Wayne quickly sets me up and explains that we won't be doing anything fancy—"just getting the bare bones of your tunes down."

Despite the now late hour, we record three songs directly onto acetates. I keep asking to re-record things; but Wayne insists they're just demos and people will either get the gist of the songs or they won't. I argue that I've seen the opposite occur in L.A., where people who responded well to me singing a song live, didn't care for the song at all when they heard it again on a funky demo. Without the energy of the live performance, little mistakes on a demo stand out for them to hear over and over.

"Look, Judy," Wayne interrupts in a tone that's suddenly lost its airbrushed charm, "This is the best we're gonna do. And..." glancing up at a clock on the wall that says midnight, "we're done."

Getting the message, I go into pack-up gear while Wayne gathers up the three acetates, puts them into envelopes, and

3 Greenwich and My Lai: A Tale of Two Villages

labels everything. I notice he does not put the publishing company's name on anything.

"So what's next?" I ask expectantly, noticing that Wayne has taken a seat in a chair next to the control board. "Do you want to shop these songs for me and..."

"No, I don't think so," he says abruptly.

"Oh." I choke. "I thought...I mean, you were acting as if you liked my songs. So, now you don't?"

"I needed to hear them a few more times, and I just did. I'm not sure what I can do for you right now; you're better off taking them around yourself," he says, but offers no sign of handing me the acetates that sit on the control board.

"Okay. Fine," I swallow my disappointment. "Well, now I have something to leave with publishers to listen to," I say with false cheeriness. "So, thank you so much for making these for me." I gesture towards the acetates.

"Well, yeah," Wayne grouses, "but what do I get out of this?"

Seriously? "What?"

"You didn't have any demos and I just made three for you," he says matter-of-factly.

"But on the phone, you said... Okay...so how much do I owe you for them?"

Wayne stares at me in defiance. "It's your call, Judy." Then, without a trace of discomfort, he unzips his fly. "You want the acetates or you don't."

Just like every young girl who's heard anything about the "sinful entertainment business," nothing that's happening is a surprise to me. What is heart-breaking, and will always be deeply disappointing to me, is my own desperation, and what for six or seven minutes I think is necessary to do to move forward. All I know for sure as I get into a cab on 57th with the acetates tucked safely into my guitar case, is this: in the sad, sad music of remembrance, this memory will never go away. I will carry it with me forever, rumbling around the depths of my privacy. It will help me stand against bullies without blinking. For I know I'm not alone. Close by, I have a guide, a warning, my secret companion: the scars of this very wrong decision.

* * *

Approaching the Village of My Lai again after a brief refuel, Buck has a sick feeling in his gut. He's tried and tried over the last hour to come up with something, anything that would make sense of the tragic vision spreading out beneath them. As his ideas diminish, his rage escalates beyond anything he's ever felt.

"Mr. Thompson," Larry shouts, "Look!"

Buck immediately sees it too. All the green smoke bombs marking injured My Lai citizens are now marking dead citizens. Everyone they left alive, everyone they identified for Charlie Co. to find and aid, is dead. If what they suspect is true, then they've accidentally helped Charlie Co. kill all the innocent villagers below.

Somehow, though they don't have final proof yet, gliding over this potentially terrifying indictment of American war values, the men aboard OH-23 sense that if they take the next step, if they push further into the truth, they will be risking life and limb to halt the most appalling military screw up ever.

There is only one way to know for sure. Listening to each other nervously gasp for breath in their headsets, wordlessly, Buck, Glenn, and Larry agree. With immense concentration, they begin to scout the bloody ground below for wounded My Lai inhabitants. After several passes they spot a woman, a young female with a bad chest wound. She has her coolie hat lying next to her, and Glenn can see she's moving a little. The green smoke they left earlier is still floating up into the

3 Greenwich and My Lai: A Tale of Two Villages

wind. Larry motions to her from the helicopter to stay down. Then to her left they spot a Captain with a squad of Charlie Co. soldiers approaching her. Is help—or certain death—on the way? Buck does not fly off. This time he pulls OH-23 just high enough to hover and watch.

From their perfect vantage point, the three men watch as Captain Ernest Medina (Lt. William Calley's direct commander), walks up to the injured woman. He looks down at her briefly, kicks her with his boot, steps back, and blows her away with his M-16 automatic.

"You son of a bitch!" Buck, Larry, and Glenn scream in unison at the top of their lungs. Now they know for sure. Now they can't pretend they don't know who's been doing the killing. Now their world has changed forever.

"She was no threat! We're supposed to be looking for Viet Cong." Buck can't stop yelling into the sky. "We don't indiscriminately kill civilians. That's not what we do! What have you done?" Looking around at all the death below him, he bellows again, "Oh, Jesus! What have you done?"

Oh my God, Glenn thinks, burying his face in his trembling hands. There is no other scenario. *They killed them all. American soldiers murdered these sweet, helpless people.*

* * *

Ann has to leave New York. It's clear she needs to be with her future husband, who, on the surface, has survived his year in Vietnam. The life crushing post-traumatic stress he will suffer is temporarily buried alive, awaiting the right moment to lay claim on him, his wife, and his future children. Ann's visit with him during a furlough last December was a harbinger of unstable times to come. And his god-awful war experiences—sometimes notated in letters to her—have poured considerable gasoline on a smoldering psyche, long ago cast from the stress of his "military brat" childhood.

Although his letters upset her, Ann can't get her fiancé to talk further about his Nam experiences. Never the less, without questioning if they're still the right people for each other, she packs up her New York life and moves to a small apartment in San Clemente, California. There she can be close to her invisibly impaired soldier at Camp Pendleton.

Since there's no way I see myself living alone on Hudson Street—just a few doors down from the White Horse Tavern, where Dylan Thomas drank himself to death—I decide Ann's leaving should be a catalyst for my own geographic adjustment. Thus, I begin a new apartment search and soon find an amazing studio at 97 MacDougal Street in the heart of the West Village. The cross street is Bleecker, so half the time when I go to turn on my $75 black 'n white TV that sits between my two front windows overlooking MacDougal, I never actually get the damn thing on because the street action is far more entertaining! There's always someone yelling, protesting the war, overdosing, singing for their supper, running for office, or practicing new dance steps—usually all at the same time. I live at the center of the 60s.

The Cafe Wha? is just up the street, where the uncle of David Lee Roth—the future lead singer for the rock band Van Halen—Manny Roth, books the best folk artists in the country. From Bob Dylan and Woody Guthrie to Dave Van Ronk and Fred Neil, the club is a riptide of cool people listening to and looking for other cool people. Right next door and still right on MacDougal is The Gaslight Cafe, actually located in a basement. The audience experience there is a little strange because when you listen to performers like Ramblin' Jack Elliott or Tim Hardin in The Gaslight, you can't applaud. You have to snap your fingers or the neighbors living above the cafe

3 Greenwich and My Lai: A Tale of Two Villages

complain. The club's air shafts reach up to the apartment windows and apparently disturb the residents who take turns calling the police. Interestingly, they don't mind the free music, just the audience clapping.

Most important of all for me on MacDougal Street is Izzy Young's Folklore Center. The heart of the folk scene, Izzy opened his Folklore Center in the late '50s and filled it with books, records, instruments, sheet music, and everything else related to folk music. Photographs and acoustic instruments hang on the walls while folk music fans and stars mill about continuously. Izzy gave Dylan his first small Manhattan gig, and keeps an old typewriter in the back room in case the legend wants to stop by and write lyrics.

I spend many quiet evenings by myself amidst Izzy's gallery of musical characters, soaking up their deep respect for authentic folk music—those grand old songs we've all heard varnished over and over by the celebrities of this oral history. Since the Village clubs only pay performers in tips, most of the folkies floating around the Folklore Center are pretty much sleeping on each other's couches and living hand to mouth. Taking guitars, banjos, and dulcimers off the wall, they teach one another new songs and strums, or huddle over a new album they've pooled their cash to buy to study a song they've been dying to learn. The dedication of these mainstream music refugees makes me swoon. Although I often feel like I could fold myself into music, I know I cannot hang with others worshipping it. Something about that makes me feel like I'm marching in place.

One snowy December evening, Izzy breaks into my anonymity. As I begin my exit out the main door of the Folklore Center where Izzy keeps his desk and often sits chatting with friends, he calls out to me. A Lower East Side toughness pervades his kind words, "Hey, quiet lady, tell me about yourself."

So I do, and quickly discover that the warmth and well-honed supportive skills of this 40-year-old folk guru are just what I need. When he takes down one of the store's guitars and asks me to play a song for him in the back room, he listens, responds, and gives me some honest feedback. The next evening, after taking his critique to heart and coming up with a more adhesive melody line as well as re-writing a few lyrics to make the sentiment clearer, Izzy asks me to play more songs for him. I literally perform everything I've ever written for him, and when I finish, he asks how I'd feel about doing a small recital of my original songs in his store.

"Like you did for Dylan?" I blurt.

Izzy, who is used to being identified as the man who gave Bob Dylan his first concert, just pushes his chair back on two legs and balances there with great dexterity, smiling at me.

"When?" I manage to recover. We hit on a night the following week, and to my total bliss, he asks for a photograph of me to hang on the Folklore Center's wall of fame, announcing my concert date.

The next morning, I bring in a recent picture, then return in the evening for the pleasure of seeing where Izzy placed it. When Izzy spots me cruising his wall of today's great minstrels—from Tom Paxton and Janis Ian, to Judy Collins and Phil Ochs—he comes up from behind and gently turns my head up toward the far right where my photo hangs next to a hot new artist named Tim Buckley.

"Tim's from Venice, California," Izzy says. "He was in the store last month and told me there's a cool new music and art community happening there. I just thought I'd put you next to him since you're both from California."

"Venice?" I say. "I'll have to check it out on my next visit to my parents."

3 Greenwich and My Lai: A Tale of Two Villages

※ ※ ※

The emotions pounding through OH-23 are intensifying with every blood-red sight that looms up from the once peaceful countryside below. And yet, with all the grim chaos unfolding at every turn, there's one thing they never see; one thing the men can't find no matter where they look: There are no weapons anywhere on the ground—aside from those belonging to Charlie Co. Are there no weapons because there are no Viet Cong, no resistance of any kind? Will the draft-age VC they chased hours ago be the only "enemy" they'll see all day?

"Oh no, there's another ditch!" Buck calls across to his gunner:

Below them is a ditch full of bodies. Some are dead. Some are moving. Buck looks at Glenn and Larry. "We can't get any radio information, so, I'm going to land," he tells them sharply. After setting the copter down near the ditch, Buck calls to a lieutenant who appears to be guarding it. The lieutenant is sitting next to another soldier and they're both eating lunch, undisturbed by the death and suffering in front of them.

"Hey, there's some civilians in this ditch and they're still alive. Can you help them out?" Buck screams from the copter. Lt. William Calley stands up and walks closer.

"This is my business," Lt. Calley barks at Buck. "I'm in charge here."

Buck raises his voice and says again, "What is this? Who are these people?"

"Just following orders," Calley grins.

"Whose orders? These are human beings, unarmed civilians, sir," Buck gags on "sir."

Calley plants his feet and shouts, "Look Thompson, this is my show. I'm in charge here. It ain't your concern."

"Yeah, great job!" Buck starts to lose it. Then, remembering his objective is to help the victims, tries again: "Look, you need to help them out."

"Yeah, I can help them out of their misery," Calley indicates he'll throw a grenade into the ditch.

"Come on," Buck snarls, "stop joking around. Help them!"

After a bitter exchange, the lieutenant sighs and appears to agree. "Sure, okay, Chief, we'll take care of it."

Buck leans back into the aircraft and starts the process of taking off. But just as they break over the ditch, Glenn hears machine gun fire and turns to look. Realizing what's happening, he jumps on the intercom screaming, "My God! *He's firing into the ditch.*"

* * *

Riding a cab to 222 Park Avenue South, I find myself soaking up yet another of Manhattan's infinite personalities. Definitely not the Village, not Gramercy Park, not the Flatiron District, and not quite Union Square. But somehow just perfect for a publishing company that's not quite on the level. Let me explain:

I got a call from the same job agency that found the Lester Company for me the first time around, with a very interesting offer: "A magazine publishing house called Nationwide Publications is looking for an assistant editor to work on their movie magazines," said the pithy voice of an employment agent. "They liked your resume, so you need to come in and meet with the editorial director of all their movie magazines."

This time I told the truth. "But I've never been an editor before."

"Well, you've written. You wrote all that copy for ads. I think this job is going to be more about writing than editing

3 Greenwich and My Lai: A Tale of Two Villages

other writers. Just go in and meet the editorial director for an interview."

And so, after hearing a very nasal New York voice announce my name into Nationwide's public address system, a great looking man named Roy enters the waiting room and brings me back to his office. His space is brimming with stacks of papers and magazines, photographs and schedules, supplies and books—all well organized, all in use. While I examine the fascinating room surrounding Roy, he studies my resume. After several minutes, he looks over the top of the resume, lifts his eyebrows dramatically, and gives a low whistle: "Berkeley? Theater Arts? Hmm…" Then, he stands and asks me to come with him to another office. There I take a seat in front of a typewriter and a stack of blank paper. While I start worrying that I'm going to be asked to take a speed test, Roy says, pleasantly:

"I give all our candidates an assignment and ask you to begin it here, so I can be sure it's you—and not someone else in your home—who is writing it." Although I look at him confused, he goes right on with instructions that get even stranger:

"Connie Stevens and Eddie Fisher may be getting a divorce," he says out of the clear blue.

"What?"

"Connie Stevens and Eddie Fisher may be getting a divorce," he says again, as if the second time clarifies the first. "I want you to start a story right here and now about their situation. Just begin it, and after twenty minutes, I'll come in and see what you've written. If it's okay, I'll send you home to finish the story tonight. You will bring it back in tomorrow for me to go over. That's all." He turns quickly and heads for the door.

Everything I want to say to him, I censor. I know absolutely nothing about these people—Connie Stevens? I think Eddie Fisher is some crooner who dumped Debbie Reynolds for Elizabeth Taylor who dumped him. But I assume my ignorance about Stevens and Fisher will emerge from whatever shadowy place it resides as soon as I try to write this. So, I sit dazed in front of the typewriter, unable to tap out one word. Although less than the allotted time goes by, Roy sticks his head in the room to see how I'm doing; and when he sees the blank page still in the typewriter, he rushes to my side:

"Oh, my god! What are you doing? This isn't a college paper! You are giving it too much thought. Just write. Go!"

And with that, I swear, something inside my brain snaps free like an alien fabrication devil, making up staggering amounts of nonsense that could easily apply to anyone going through a break-up. The first sentence I fire into the opening paragraph comes out like magic:

"Connie Stevens lit her last cigarette and drew a deep, melancholy breath." And then, without hesitation, I go right on: "It's not like these past days have been a surprise to her. She and Eddie haven't been getting along for months. The jealousy, the competition, the children—*do they have children?*—it's all gotten too much for two famous people with demanding careers…."

"That's it! That's great! Just great!" Roy cheers over my shoulder. Take it home. Finish it. Bring it back in tomorrow.

"How long should it be?" I ask, kinda thrilled with myself.

"A page and a half, double spaced. No more; no less."

When I call my friend Marilyn (from our Israel adventure), who is now living in Newark, New Jersey, and tell her about Nationwide Publications' screwy editorial test, she remarks, "Wait—it's all a lie, then? Everything we read in movie magazines is really made up? I have heard that."

"Um, maybe not all movie magazines," I wonder out loud, then decide, "Yeah, probably they're all crap. I don't know. I also don't have the job yet. But it's kind of fun just writing whatever comes into your head. I mean, why do people want

3 Greenwich and My Lai: A Tale of Two Villages

to read about movie stars anyway? Aren't they just making movies? I mean, who cares about Eddie Fisher with everything else that's going on in the world? And they do! These magazines sell like hotcakes."

Marilyn exhales thoughtfully. "Well, I guess it's just more fun to read about Liz and Dick and Eddie and Debbie than to read President Johnson dropped another 110,000 tons of bombs on Vietnam…"

"Connie Stevens…" I correct.

"What?!"

"…Eddie and Connie Stevens, not Debbie…"

"Oh, good God, Judy!" Marilyn gasps.

I completely ignore her warning that I could lose my way in this infectious drivel, and go right on: "And, wait, listen to this: Roy told me that the publisher is trying something radical. He's including other kinds of celebrities in his fan magazine business. He just put Jackie Onassis on the cover of one of his movie magazines!"

"W-H-A-T?"

We have a great laugh over that. Who on earth wants to read about Jackie O. in a fan magazine? The American people aren't that vapid, right?

* * *

"Is this what we've become?" Buck keeps pounding his fist against the bubble window and sobbing. "*Where was the leadership?* Why didn't someone stop this?"

After watching Calley fire into the ditch, the men know they are on their own. Maybe every soldier in Charlie Co. hasn't lost his mind, but so far there's no evidence to the contrary. At this moment, they're flying over sights they've only seen in Nazi concentration camp photographs. How could

U.S. soldiers have machine-gunned, violated, and disfigured babies, women, and the elderly?

Suddenly Glenn's ace vision spots an earthen bunker with terrified Vietnamese faces peering out of it. Not far from it, he also sees an approaching Charlie Co. squad.

"Mr. Thompson!" Glenn cries, pointing.

Buck sees the bunker and approaching U.S. soldiers. "Okay, guys," he replies, pulling himself together as best he can. "This is it! If we don't do something within the next 30 seconds, these people will die."

Without even speaking, there's no question what they're going to do. Within seconds Buck lands his aircraft strategically—as only he can—between the advancing American troops and the bunker. When the aircraft is on the ground, Buck purposely leaves the propellers spinning to give Charlie Co. the impression that the OH-23 is bigger than it actually is. Then he jumps out, taking no guns with him, and plants himself close to the bunker. Larry and Glenn are uncertain what to do, so they take their machine guns off their bungee cords and step outside the aircraft, careful not to point their weapons directly at their fellow soldiers. Tipping their guns toward the ground, the two men assume body language that communicates their determination and consummate support of Officer Thompson.

Once again, Buck finds himself confronting a lieutenant who outranks him. He finds his voice: "Say, how can we get these people out of the bunker? They're obviously civilians."

The lieutenant gives him a Calley-like response, suggesting he can get the Vietnamese out with hand grenades.

Buck says simply, "I have a better idea."

And with that, he walks over to Glenn and Larry and says something they'll never get over hearing: "If those soldiers shoot at me or these civilians, fire on them!"

3 Greenwich and My Lai: A Tale of Two Villages

Then, approaching the lieutenant, Buck says the same thing: "If you fire on these people when I'm getting them out of the bunker, my people will fire on you."

Turning away from the stunned soldiers of Charlie Co., knowing full well they could mow him down in a heartbeat, Buck walks over to the bunker, where, for all he knows, there could be Viet Cong hiding and ready to take him out. Using his most gentle voice, he cautiously coaxes the terrified people into trusting him and leaving their hiding place. It takes several minutes for the first peasant to believe Buck, but soon they all begin stumbling into the daylight, unsure and confused.

While Buck's relieved that they aren't Viet Cong, his reassurance quickly turns to alarm when not two or three, but eleven or twelve civilians crawl out. "Oh, geez," he calls to Glenn and Larry. "I didn't think this through! The helicopter only seats three, and all the seats are occupied. How are we going to get them to safety?"

Fortunately, the stand-off between Charlie Co. and OH-23 is beginning to take on a calmer atmosphere; in fact, two or three of the soldiers have dropped their guns, squatted down, and started devouring their lunches. Glenn makes eye contact with one of the soldiers, and the two wave, sending a clear message that neither one of them want to die this way. Larry keeps thinking of his mother: *Oh my God, Mom, get me outta here!* He knows the real reason she's in his head right now is that she'd want Larry to do exactly what Mr. Thompson is doing—the moral thing.

Once everyone is out of the bunker, Buck takes advantage of the break in tension and gets on the radio to call a friend of his, Dan Millians, who's one of the gunship pilots above them.

"Danny, I need a favor," Buck says, excited and unsure he can pull this off. "Will you come down, actually land, and be a medic for these civilians? Maybe you can fly them down the road and leave them a few miles away where they'll be safe, and then come back and do it again?"

Miraculously, Buck convinces the bigger gunship to land and ferry this handful of survivors to safety. It takes a few trips, but every single villager hiding in the bunker is flown to a safe spot. Less than an hour later, standing in a windy locale outside My Lai, a frightened woman who was dropped off there with her daughter, runs toward the gunship as it lifts off. She waves both arms and calls out in Vietnamese to pilot Millians:

"I am relieved. I was sure you were going to drop us in the sea to die. But, I see we are safe. Thank you and the man who came to get us."

* * *

I don't know whether to be pleased or horrified, but I got the job! I'm a movie magazine editor. I decide to walk to work my first day, just to get a physical sense of the new landscape. Although I leave quite early, it's no surprise that I get turned around and wind up back in the Village, hailing a cab—but not before passing a large newsstand where I rubberneck at a cover of *Movie TV Secrets*—one of the magazines I now edit. There, for the world to see, is a poorly spliced together two-shot of Jackie Onassis and Elvis Presley with the cover line: "Jackie dumps Ari for Elvis the Pelvis!"

Please, no! It's one thing to make crud up, but shouldn't it be based on true crud? I decide to take this up with Roy first thing, but never get a chance. Bewitched by a myriad of introduction activities the minute I arrive, I'm whisked into a large room with several desks, no surrounding cubicles, five or six male editors, and no windows. Roy points to one set up,

3 Greenwich and My Lai: A Tale of Two Villages

and announces, "That's yours." On one side of me sits Stephen Lewis, a 20-year-old escapee of Springfield, Mass., and my very first openly gay friend. He knows a little bit about absolutely everything from fashion to entertainment; and our wayward souls bond the moment we meet.

Across the room from my desk is Al Goldstein, who in the very near future will create and launch the first blatantly pornographic newspaper in America, *Screw*. Right now, he's the editor-in-chief of Nationwide's Men's magazines, including such garish girlie feasts as *Brutish, Swashbuckler, Jaguar Male*, and *Virile*.

All Nationwide magazines are "look-alike publications," or mags you (accidentally) grab off the newsstand thinking they're another more well known magazine. Pulp publisher, Maurice Gassman, who owns Nationwide, puts out up to 50 magazines a month, covering absolutely anything that Gassman thinks will sell: UFOs, firearms, show dogs, groupie rock, movie gossip, soft-core pornography, and wrestling. And as if this sumptuous array of schlock isn't lifting me high enough, during a brief tour of the storage room, I discover that I now work for the publisher of *Bizarre, Shock Tales, Fright Tales, Legends from the Tomb, Voodoo Sagas*, and *Witches' Accounts*.

But the truly unspeakable ones, the rubbish that tops the bottom-of-the barrel, are Gassman's wildly successful "one-shots"—one issue magazines. The most lucrative of these arise when someone famous dies. It's rumored, for instance, that he made millions on his one-shot covering the death of President John F. Kennedy. And Gassman's theory for the success of these rags is stomach-turning in its cynicism:

"I believe it makes people feel good when someone dies," he has explained in interviews. "No matter what you thought of him, no matter how much you might have loved him, there's part of you that is going to feel good because you're superior to the dead guy now."

Unfortunately, in a very short period of time, I am going to learn way too much about Gassman's death-publishing cash cows. So, I decide to stop reading all press on Nationwide, and concentrate on doing my small part to push for quality. When I actually say this out loud to Al, he sneers, "You dragged my attention away from writing a really hot brothel story to tell me this?" Then, seeing my face fall, he recommends a "great new diet pill" his doctor gave him, and leaves me a handful of them as he hurries off.

Marvelous.

My never calm work area is also inhabited by a young man who always wears a suit and tie, corrects everyone's grammar errors, writes for all the magazines when called upon, and mostly makes a lot of phone calls to other men. After several weeks, Stephen takes me out to lunch and explains that this handsome well-dressed fellow is a big, big shot in the Mattachine Society of New York.

"Mat-uh-…?"

"Oh, Sweetheart, *really?*" Stephen says dramatically, "The Mattachine Society is renowned. It's a clandestine association from the 50s. You've never heard of it? Weird, well, it got started in L.A., to help gay men."

Something about this subject or the organization unnerves me, though I don't know why. I also don't want to be rude or insult Stephen in any way, so I push my fears aside and say as casually as possible, "Oh, and are you a member?"

"Oh God, no!" he spits back at me. "I'm not a fan of organizations. I don't do meetings. I'd rather bitch about unfairness by being a great writer or singer or…" he trails off dreamily for a second, then returns. "But they do good things, you know, try to help gay men who are isolated around the city. They also

3 Greenwich and My Lai: A Tale of Two Villages

help many of us who get targeted and beaten every day, and—well, that shit," he tosses his last words abruptly, shutting down more than he meant to bring up.

"I didn't know..." I say, reaching for my coffee quickly.

"What didn't you know?"

"That you...that gays...get beaten up."

"Not all gays, honey," he leans across the table and takes my hand. "More often it's little guys like me." He winks and grabs our bill. Stephen always pays my way. If we go to the movies, he buys my ticket as if I'm his date. If we grab a cab, he pays the driver before I can get my purse open. He walks on the traffic side of the sidewalk when we stroll. He opens doors for me. He is, in fact, the best non-boyfriend I've ever had.

And speaking of boyfriends, also seated in this jerry-rigged editor den, is Dan Wexler. I have no idea what Dan's original Nationwide job duties were, but this afternoon everything gets blown to Hades when Maurice Gassman himself strides brazenly into our little community wearing his usual attire of head-to-toe riding gear, tall black boots and a large whip. *(I am not kidding.)* I assume this wealthy publisher owns his own riding stables somewhere in upstate New York, but have heard much darker explanations for this nutsy Nazi outfit.

Gassman plants his formidable self in front of us all, and placing his whip-less hand on hip, barks out the following: "Who knows anything about astrology in here?"

After a stunned silence, during which I wonder if he wants his chart read, Dan (a smaller and more urban version of Robert Redford), lifts his hand halfway in the air and says:

"I once wrote an astrology article for..."

"Good!" Maurice howls at him; and pointing his whip like a rifle, says, "Then you're the editor! Go see Roy immediately. I want an astrology magazine on the stands as soon as possible.

Yesterday is even better. People are buying these prediction rags like lunatics and I want one of my own out there...now!" Dan picks up everything on his desk and flees into Roy's office. The rest of us sit stone still marveling at Gassman's level of audacity.

Early the next morning, one of the two artists responsible for the look of these tawdry publications saunters up to my desk and without so much as a "good morning," asks me if I would like to join him in "quitting his job today." He feels Gassman's behavior yesterday was borderline-criminal and people like himself and myself "exist on a level far above this kind of deportment."

"I am an artistic gay man," he continues forthrightly; and then—in a description that nearly takes my head off—adds, "and a gifted young *lesbian* like yourself..."

"What?!" I squawk. "What did you say?" I teeter between raging and laughing for a split second, then opt for a weird blend of both.

"I am not a lesbian. I'm not gay!" I huff while laughing unnaturally at him.

"Oh," he says," embarrassed, but clearly offended as well. "I wasn't insulting you, you know! To me it's a compliment!"

"Well, not to me!" I say, and turn my attention back to whatever hogwash I was writing. With my heart thundering in my ears, I check the room quickly to see who might have overheard, and believe I catch a glimpse of Dan—whom I really can't see anymore because he's stacked piles of astrology references high on his desk. Still, I'm pretty sure he's overheard everything.

Trying to feign nonchalance, I amble over to his desk; tossing my hair back, I sound off defensively: "Good God, did you hear that?" Although he shakes his head "no," I can't help but notice his face is flushed; Dan's blushing.

3 Greenwich and My Lai: A Tale of Two Villages

"That guy..." I say, pointing outside our editorial room, "...I don't even know his name, but he asked me to come along with him and quit my job today."

"You're kidding!" Dan gulps.

"Yeah, and then—he called me a lesbian!"

"Oh, wow," Dan says, with a new wave of blush sweeping his face.

"I know, I know. Can you believe it? That's crazy! I'm not a lesbian!"

"No, no..." Dan mutters numbly, still incredibly uncomfortable.

"*Sooo* embarrassing!" I conclude, rolling my eyes.

"Well...I heard that he—Neal, 'that guy'—just got the art director job at a new magazine called *After Dark*," Dan says, changing the subject with information and unexpected support for Neal. "It's supposed to be very upscale and arty, on glossy paper and all. But they're doing it on a shoe string for now, and no one's making any money to start."

"Oh, that's neat," I say, trying to sound less unhinged. Then, going out on a limb, I ask, "Are you leaving the office for lunch today?"

"What? Oh, I wasn't, but if you want to?"

"Me? Well, if you want to...yes, let's try that roast beef sandwich place around the corner!"

* * *

After the gunship Buck enlists delivers the terrorized but unharmed Vietnamese citizens to safety, the obvious next move is for OH-23 to return to their base and deal with what has happened. But Buck is too furious to face anyone. Just thinking about the men of Charlie Co. sitting in shock, eating their rations while dead bodies and body parts lay in chaos all around them, sends him into a renewed rage. Glenn suggests that they try to calm down by taking another pass over My Lai. So once again the three lift off from Landing Zone Dottie, fully fueled, with their eyes glued to the devastating sights below.

"I don't understand how all this happened so fast!" Buck yells into his headset.

Larry has his own questions: "Did they herd them into ditches before or after they shot them?"

Glenn can't listen. He feels himself starting to go into shock and tries to combat the feeling by staring as hard as he can at an irrigation ditch below. To his disgust, it's full of bodies, hundreds of bodies. Since Buck normally breaks left when he lifts OH-23, and Glenn sits on the left side, the now hyper-focused 23-year-old can't miss the sight below and suddenly begins screaming:

"Mr. Thompson, I think I see movement down there!" Indeed, the instant Buck brings the helicopter around, the men can see that several of the wounded must have tried to climb out of the ditch below. A few made it before they were shot in the back or head. If Glenn is right, if there are any survivors, they would have to be under two or three layers of bodies. *Oh, my God,* Buck thinks to himself, *who in his right mind is going to go in there and find anyone?*

"Okay, Glenn, Okay," Buck says into his mic. "I'm going down there to land."

Buck hardly has the OH-23 securely on the ground before Glenn bolts out and starts climbing down into the bloody pit. Larry jumps out too, but is secretly relieved it's Glenn and not him in the ditch.

Mired to his knees in what were once human beings, Glenn is forced to pull loose from some of the hands grabbing him during their last dying seconds. Summoning all his courage, the soldier focuses his awareness on the area he spotted

3 Greenwich and My Lai: A Tale of Two Villages

from above. There, completely buried but for his waving arm, a little boy catches his attention. Glenn reaches him somehow and tries to pull him loose, but the boy is still clinging to his dead mother. Eventually Glenn's able to lift him free, only to lose his own footing when he attempts to get himself and the boy out of the ditch.

Watching from the helicopter, Buck thinks, *This is what real heroism is about. Glenn Andreotta in this ditch doing what I could never do in a million years—this is a hero.* Larry also sees what's happening to Glenn, and—forcing aside his own terror—rushes to the edge of the ditch, leans over, and grabs the boy from Glenn by the kid's bloody shirt. All Larry can hope for, as he pulls with all his might, is: *I pray your buttons are sewn on well, little guy, because they're going to have to support your weight.*

Once the boy is out of the ditch, Larry helps Glenn get free. Mr. Thompson jumps out too and joins them as they lay the nine-year-old, obviously in deep shock, across their laps, and look for wounds. Since he is drenched in blood, they aren't sure if any of it is coming from him.

Larry tries to make him blink, but the boy only stares past him, totally limp, focused somewhere far off in the deep blue sky above. After a few minutes, they determine he has no bullet holes, no visible wounds, and no broken bones. It's safe to move him. Planning their next move, they look at each other, sharing a tiny moment of relief, while also noting that they are all totally soaked in the blood of My Lai.

Glenn holds the boy tightly as Buck lifts OH-23 away from this place of death and swings outward toward Quang Ngai where there's a hospital. Every hospital in Vietnam has an orphanage attached to it, so considering everything the child just went through, this seems the perfect place to bring him.

As Buck carries the limp kid in his arms up the hospital steps, he can't take his eyes off him. *My God,* he thinks, as tears leave filthy trails across his wind-burned face. *I have a boy at home his age. And he's just about the same size. This could be my son.*

A nun rushes out of the hospital to meet Buck, and he hands the boy over to her. They look at each other helplessly for a minute, then Buck says simply, "I don't know what you're going to do with him, but I don't think he has any family left."

OH-23 lifts off from Quang Ngai, leaving the child behind. Little do the men know that in two days, this young boy—whose name is Do Hoa—will leave the hospital on his own, and walk 10 miles through the humid jungle back to My Lai to make sure his parents are properly buried.

* * *

Two dozen hippies, draft dodgers, and troubadours attend my little concert at the Folklore Center. I don't know one person in the audience and purposely don't invite anyone in NYC that I do know. I want it that way. I know my songs are still tenuous, and not really ready for primetime, so I need a safe place to grow, and Izzy's store is it.

By the summer of '67, I join an organization set up by Izzy and others called "The Angry Arts: For Life and Against The War In Vietnam." It's made up of artists and musicians (some very famous; others like me), who volunteer to help various peace organizations bring in money on behalf of the movement by performing for free at their events. A Peace/Arts Center is set up as a central clearing house for the performing artists who are anxious to contribute and the organizations who need them. It's a breath of fresh air as it provides an opportunity for the peace movement to have the benefit of many performers' work, rather than the usual handful of familiar names—Joan Baez, Phil Ochs, etc. Naturally, I take

3 Greenwich and My Lai: A Tale of Two Villages

advantage of the opportunities being offered to lesser-known performers and score several gigs.

But the big, big event is taking place during a dramatic weeklong protest sponsored by The Angry Arts. All through Manhattan, the artists of New York are using their work to divorce themselves from the U.S. policy in Vietnam. I am so excited I could erupt. It's going to be the towering achievement of the 60s. I just know it.

My contribution is opening two folk-rock concerts that Izzy emcees at the Village Theater (soon to change its name to the Fillmore East). I sing three songs, two of which no one listens to because they're buzzing around looking for seats—inebriated on the event, grass, LSD, and whatever. But when I sing "What's the Big Blonde Boy of Freedom Doing Now, Ma?" (about callous American soldiers trouncing through countries and people they're indifferent to), I actually have listeners! So, in the spirit of overkill, and giddy on the continuing applause, I glance offstage at Izzy, thinking *maybe I can do an encore?* Alas, he's wearing an expression that would spook a wild beast. From where I'm standing on stage, he appears to be slicing across his neck back and forth with one hand. *What? He's going to cut off my head?*

I turn away from his negativity; take a bow, and exit the opposite side of the stage. There I collide with the Chad Mitchell Trio. I like their songs, especially a satirical one called "The John Birch Society." We chat a few minutes, and they introduce me to their new lead singer, John Denver—who's really cute and evidently a good songwriter. Izzy told me earlier that Peter, Paul, and Mary are holding some of his songs for future recordings, particularly one about a jet plane. Remembering Izzy, I decide to find out what I did so wrong that he wanted to chop off my head.

"No encores!" he hisses at me, barely looking up from the long, typed list of performers he is crossing out and adding to. "We barely have time for two songs per performer," he whispers sharply. "I've got to shorten everyone's set. Leonard Bernstein is bringing his protégé, Janis Ian, and she might play. Also, we may get Big Brother & The Holding Company to close the second show."

"Yikes!" I try not to shriek, "With...?"

"...*that* Janis!"

We're both quiet for a few minutes listening to the Mitchell Trio while Dave Van Ronk tunes nearby, getting ready to go on next. During the applause, I ask Izzy why he wanted to chop off my head, and he's flabbergasted. I imitate his gesture, then watch him collapse into hysterics.

"Stop," he barely manages to gasp after some time. "Where have you been? That's the universal sign for 'stop' or 'that's enough.'"

I too start to laugh, but a rock group called The Fugs knock us into each other before plowing down Van Ronk on their way to the roar now sweeping through the audience as it realizes who's taking the stage:

"Kill, kill, kill for peace/

Near or middle or very far east..."

"Wait!" Izzy shouts ineffectively at them. "You're *not* on now!"

* * *

Landing OH-23 after leaving the Vietnamese boy, Do Hoa, at the hospital, Buck can no longer hold onto anything resembling his "purpose." Half out of his mind knowing he'll never stop today's tragedy from haunting him, he is inconsolable.

At operations, he reports to his platoon leader, who immediately sends Buck to see the operations officer. Trying to find the right person to report his story to, Buck begins to

3 Greenwich and My Lai: A Tale of Two Villages

sense movement going on behind the scenes. In fact, though he has no proof yet, Part II of the My Lai massacre—The Cover Up—is in play. In truth, it began before OH-23 ever made it back to base.

With his operations officer at his side, Buck finally gets in to see his commander, and it's there that he falls apart completely, wailing and sobbing at the top of his lungs: "Take these wings right now," he points to his military decorations. "These wings are only sewn on! I can rip them off myself. If this damn stuff is what's happening here, I quit! You cannot make me do this. You cannot make me fly. I won't do this!"

With Buck's heated allegations of civilian killings now reaching Lieutenant Colonel Frank Barker, the operation's overall commander, something finally happens. Barker radios his executive officer on the ground, Captain Medina, to find out what is happening. Naturally Medina—who was observed by Buck, Glenn, and Larry shooting a wounded civilian—has a lot to hide. So, Medina feigns ignorance, but immediately gives the long-overdue "cease fire" order.

Instead of seeing himself as a hero, Buck begins beating himself up for not "catching on sooner and rescuing more civilians from insane soldiers on a rampage." In this despondent state, he cannot possibly understand that he—and his team of two—not only saved the dozen or so My Lai citizens that were airlifted to safety, but they stopped an operation that was supposed to go on for four more days! Charlie Co. was set to hit another village the same afternoon, two the next day, and two the day after that. Like ravenous wolves, their slaughtering could have gone on unchecked until as many as 20,000 were dead. But it did not. The very worst kind of human behavior came up against the very best:

An 18-year-old gunner and a 20-year-old crew chief covered for a courageous pilot, while he put them all in harm's way. Landing their small observation helicopter in the line of fire to save Vietnamese civilians, Buck confronted the primary leader of the massacre, and changed history. But dear God, will he pay for it!

* * *

Although I seriously consider throwing out the acetates Wayne made of my three original songs, another part of my brain refuses to do it. There's no question that I dishonored myself getting them, but I already did it. No one but me knows, so shouldn't I, at the very least, get some use out of them?

A righteous anger sets in when I pull the acetates out of my guitar case and begin adding lyric sheets to them. *Damn right I'm gonna get someone to hear these discs, you sleaze ball!* I make appointments with three big-name publishers who are the type that refuse to let artists play live for them in their offices. Instead they prefer face-to-face meetings, after which you leave demos of your songs for them to study at their leisure without pressure. Since no one hears your music during your first meeting, it's impossible to know if there will even be a second meeting when you leave. So, at this point, my favorite is the publisher whose office is directly across the street from Carnegie Hall. Luckily, he's the one who calls me back.

The owner of the publishing company, Ronald Holtauer, and I hit it off immediately. He's different from anyone I've met so far in the Manhattan music business. He's a real gentleman, around 50 years old, experienced, very professional in his approach to the industry, not only the owner of his own publishing companies, but the manager of several 1940s music companies. Although he's busy just licensing old songs, Holtauer tells me at our first meeting that he's looking for a contemporary, relevant singer-songwriter like "this new girl, Laura Nyro."

3 Greenwich and My Lai: A Tale of Two Villages

When he calls me back for a second meeting, Holtauer refuses to reveal anything on the phone. I am, in fact, peering out the window at Carnegie Hall's marquee when he tells me that he wishes to sign me and my songs to his publishing, management, and production company. His plan is to produce an album of my original songs in a studio and then shop the record to all the labels.

Suffused in the light of opportunity, suddenly I'm not sure I know what happiness feels like. I'm still very young, but I think this must be it. After calling my parents and everyone I've ever loved to tell them the phenomenal news, Holtauer and I map out a complicated rehearsal schedule around my equally full Nationwide time table. Working each other into a frenzy, we meet before, after, and sometimes during work hours, while my fellow editors puzzle over my sporadic attendance. Finally I confide in Dan, Stephen, and Roy, who all try their best to fence-straddle between feelings of jealousy and genuine encouragement.

"After all, we'd *all* rather take a shot at stardom than write about those who have it," Stephen huffs at me one evening after a movie. Later on that same night, when he lets me out of our cab at my apartment building and heads off for his own, neither of us notice the water dripping down from my window at 97 MacDougal Street and onto the awning over Monty's Restaurant right below my apartment. Oblivious, I walk upstairs to my front door and notice it ajar. Rather than take the chance of walking in on a thief, I run straight downstairs to the restaurant and ask for help from Monty who's at the bar.

"You caused a waterfall on my customers!" he screams at me. "First a fiery blanket floated down on them; then came the waterfall. I should throw you out on the street!"

Monty is an Italian-American life-force to be reckoned with. I've lived above his insanely popular restaurant for a year now and between its infectious, singing-at-the-top-of-your-lungs ambience, and bacchanalian hungry-man food, it's the kind of place you want on your side. So I burst into tears:

"I don't know what happened," I blubber truthfully.

"Ya don't know?" he leans in closer. "Girlie…"

"Judy…"

"Judy, you left a light bulb on in your closet. *That's* what happened!"

"What?" I snap out of it.

"I'm explaining what! You left a light bulb on and it got so hot it caught a blanket in the closet on fire!"

"What? You mean my apartment's on fire?"

"Was…was on fire. I called the fire department coz I saw smoke comin' outta your window.

"Oh, my God!" I shudder, and turn to go back upstairs. But Monty isn't through with me.

"So," he says, grabbing my peacoat tightly. "Here I am with a Saturday night restaurant full of customers, singing and eating my specials like always, and just when my second seating is lining up, out from your window floats down a blanket *on fire*—like a burning parachute, flaming down on them."

Honestly, the visual of this starts to make me laugh, but I know I'm finished if I do, so I quickly cover my mouth like I'm going to scream in horror.

"Yeah, right, right!" he agrees. "But then, it gets worse. The firemen are in your apartment doing God knows what, coz all at once comes a flood of water bursting out your middle window, splashing down on the same customers. So now they're drenched and scorched and screaming!"

Again, I cover my mouth to hide a burst of hysterics that I'm sure I can't stop. I rush past Monty and up my stairs. When I push open my apartment door, the perverse urge to laugh myself sick vanishes instantly. It looks like a war zone.

3 Greenwich and My Lai: A Tale of Two Villages

Everything in sight is charred and dripping wet. The FDNY hoses have blown every photograph and poster off my wall, unseated my television, ruined my record player, swept over my room divider, soaked my bed, and destroyed my desk and everything on it. I peek in the closet, half burnt up, with my clothes either drenched or roasted, and just stand there frozen.

Finally, I find the phone and call Stephen.

"I know you just dropped me off," I begin, and then tell him the rest.

"Honey, I'll be right over," he says firmly. "We'll put things in some temporary order, and after that you'll come and stay with me til things are right again." Then, he tops himself. Considering the undisguised envy he's felt all month, the nurturing side of his mercurial personality triumphs as he asks, "Judy, what about your guitar? Is it all right?"

I look around for it. Seeing it's been piled safely into a corner, I answer, "Yes, I see it. It's fine."

"Oh, thank goodness, then you'll be fine."

* * *

The day after the My Lai massacre, Buck, Glenn, and Larry are called to the command bunker at Landing Zone Dottie to give their statements in secret. There, Brigade Commander Col. Oran Henderson listens and takes notes, giving all three men the impression that the atrocities they witnessed, lived through, and are now risking their military careers to divulge, will be scrutinized and properly handled by the only "higher ups" who can do anything to make sure something this calamitous never occurs again.

Most of the men in Charlie Co. who didn't finish their tour of duty with the My Lai mission, are sent off to the most remote and savage parts of Vietnam's jungles, conceivably to die. Some are cut off from their officers for months with no direct orders, left in the grueling, moist heat. Their body parts literally rotting with illness, and half out of their minds from what they can't quite remember and can't quite forget doing in My Lai, some kill themselves, others wait and do it after they return and remember everything.

Instead of being decorated as heroes, Thompson, Andreotta and Colburn are sent back into combat—and assigned very dangerous missions. If the military higher-ups aren't trying to murder the snitches who are "telling tales on them," you could've fooled the crew of OH-23. Buck senses that the officers he debriefed in the chain of command have now begun a concerted effort to bury the truth. And if the truth is being entombed, then Buck and his story will soon become a titanic problem.

※ ※ ※

On April 3, in Memphis, Tenn., Martin Luther King hears that his plane received a bomb threat before landing. Although he's shaken up, King decides to give his speech as planned. About a thousand miles away, I sit listening to the radio in my recently redecorated apartment. After my "little fire mishap," I've taken the opportunity to buy some new things with my amazing $100-a-week Nationwide salary. As I've mentioned before, in my village pad, the radio is a better choice for entertainment than TV. I love watching MacDougal Street while using music or radio as a soundtrack, and tonight's no different. With the afternoon fading, I take a bowl of soup and sit at my street window, watching the foot traffic. The news comes on with an outtake of MLK's speech, and it just gets me how this man uses his church voice so passionately on words of peace. It's as if he's singing:

"I've been to the mountain top…and like anybody, I would like to live a long life. Longevity has its place. But I'm not concerned about that now…I've seen the promised Land, and I may not get there with you…" Obviously, the bomb scare has brought on major concerns about his own mortality.

The very next evening, Dan and I are working late in Roy's office at Nationwide, going over a story about Rock Hudson marrying his secretary. Roy and Dan are laughing at me because I don't know the whole thing is a farce and that Rock is gay. I ask why we don't just say that, and Roy responds that one of the things he likes about me is my "infectious humor."

Then, all at once, we hear something awful. Barreling down the hallway, Maurice Gassman is yelling and banging the walls. The three of us flinch.

"Martin Luther King was shot on a motel balcony in Memphis!" Gassman bellows triumphantly. And again, "Martin Luther King—shot in the head! Get ready! Nobody leaves!"

What? I don't know what to react to first. This is horrible. What does he mean: "nobody leaves?"

"Roy!" Gassman barks over my head. "Who else is here tonight?"

Roy summons a calm demeanor, and says serenely, "Easy, Maurice. Slow down. What's happening?"

"They shot him! They killed King!" he says, windmilling his arms and leaving no scenery unchomped.

"Okay, we heard that," Roy continues in a contrived, silken timber. "Is he dead? Maurice—," Roy actually snaps his fingers like Gassman is in a trance. "Do you know if he actually died yet?"

"What? Well, if he's not dead, he will be," Gassman fires back, refusing to be tamed. "Shot in the head!"

I start crying.

"Let's take a breath," Roy focuses his gaze straight at Gassman: "I want you to go back to your office and listen to the news." Then he shuffles some papers and casually waves a dismissive hand, pretending this buffoon can be managed.

Unbelievably, Gassman wheels around and leaves. Dan and I look at each other with bulging eyes. Then I continue crying.

"Aww," Dan says, at a complete loss. "It'll be okay…"

"Are you kidding?" I sob at him.

Roy walks over to his filing cabinet, opens a drawer and pulls out a Kleenex box. He reaches across his desk and hands me a tissue. "Oh, dear, dear, Judy!" he flutters about, showing me more feelings than I've ever seen from him before. I've already gone through my "big crush on Roy stage," which he mercifully handled by having me over for dinner with four of his best male friends who referred to him as "honey" the whole evening. *(Got it. Got it.)*

Static is all that squawks out of Roy's radio as he or Dan spin the dial, trying to find an update on MLK's shooting. Meanwhile, I continue racing down the dark side: "There's gonna be so much anger about this murder! If Maurice is right, there'll be riots, and looting. We better hope he lives."

"HE'S DEAD! MARTIN LUTHER KING IS DEAD!" Gassman screams from what sounds like an elevator shaft. Then, stomping through the hallways until he's back in Roy's office: "Now tell me, who's still in the office besides these two?"

"Oh God," Roy whispers to us. "I'm sooo sorry."

"This is fantastic!" Gassman bellows at us. "Let's get started. I want a *Martin Luther King Memorial Collectors Issue* on the stands tomorrow.

"What?" I blurt before I can stop myself.

Roy stands up quickly and walks over to Gassman, putting a hand on his shoulder. "Maurice, I'll take care of the

3 Greenwich and My Lai: A Tale of Two Villages

collector's issue on King. I always do. Please, you're overwhelming the staff..."

"Whatdaya mean?" Gassman snorts.

Roy sets his voice to a sing-song tone again. With his arm still draped around Gassman's shoulder, he begins steering him out of his office while talking:

"Let me get to work on the magazine's structure tonight. I'll get everything set to go for the morning. When the entire staff gets in tomorrow, I'll pull everyone off their magazines and put them to work on the King special." Slowly he leads Gassman away, assuring him Nationwide will have an *MLK Collector's Memorial Issue* ready to ship by tomorrow night.

"Here's what *you* should do..." we can barely hear him delegating a job to Gassman somewhere down the hallway. "You need to get with our printer in Atlanta. We're gonna need to send someone there with the boards tomorrow night..."

I realize my face is buried in my hands when Dan reaches over and lifts it up and out.

"You wanna go get a drink?" he asks.

* * *

After giving his report, Glenn Andreotta is immediately assigned to B Company of the 123rd Aviation Battalion, another assault helicopter not unlike the one he just served—except he no longer has his ace pilot, "Mr. Thompson," to make sure the crew is flown safely out of the endless death traps they get into. Thus, on April 8th—only a few days after My Lai—Viet Cong activity is reported near Quang Ngai City, and Glenn's little scout helicopter is sent in to ferret out the enemy. Accompanying two gunships to the location, Glenn hears VC gunfire coming from the ground. A single shot catches the young hero in the head, killing him. As Glenn dies, Do

Hoa—at momentary peace after finding and burying his family—looks up at the gathering storm clouds and remembers the face of the man who reached into the ditch and wrestled him away from the angel of death.

Buck and Larry are unaware of Glenn's death; they are too consumed with staying alive during their separate but menacing new missions. Buck continues flying observation assignments in OH-23 and is hit by enemy fire a total of eight times. Considering he loses his aircraft four of those times, he no longer understands what's keeping him alive at all. Finally, a couple of months after My Lai, Buck is all alone in his little copter when the VC spot him flying too low and open fire. The Plexiglas of the bubble bursts apart wounding Buck's legs and damaging the engine as well. The copter hits the ground hard, injuring Buck's back severely. Surrounded by VC on the ground and passing out at regular intervals from the pain, Buck has no idea how, but he holds off the enemy long enough to be rescued. His career as a soldier in Nam, however, is over.

Bedridden and immobilized in a hospital, Buck learns of Glenn's death. He has little time to grieve because at the same instant he is forced to confront something equally awful: Brigade Commander Col. Oran Henderson's report of the My Lai incident is as despicable as the massacre itself. Attributing his conclusion to the interviews he had with Capt. Ernest Medina, Oran's report states in part:

"…Twenty noncombatants were inadvertently killed when caught in the… crossfires of the U.S. and Viet Cong forces…" It is further concluded that no civilians were gathered together and shot by U.S. soldiers. "The allegation that U.S. Forces shot and killed 450 to 500 civilians is obviously a Viet Cong propaganda move to discredit the U.S. in the eyes of the Vietnamese people…"

3 Greenwich and My Lai: A Tale of Two Villages

* * *

All through March of '68, I record my album of original songs with Holtauer at the Bell Sound Studios on West 54th. We spend time getting my guitar parts down separately, then work on my vocals. Throughout the sessions, our mutual understanding is that these are only the basic tracks and we will add "sweetening" (strings, horns, etc.) afterwards. Lead sheets of all my songs are printed; discussions about orchestrations go on regularly, and our evenings working together are both heady and spirited. I feel very lucky. I insist on calling Holtauer "Mr. Holtauer," and he corrects me every time with a warm smile, "Please, Judy, call me 'Ron.' It would mean a lot to me." I try, but he's just "Mr. Holtauer" to me. That feels more respectful, and I'm so proud to have him hold this position in my life.

After we get the guitar and vocal tracks the way we both want them, Holtauer calls and says he'd like to do what Bobbie Gentry's producer did with her record, "Ode To Billie Joe." Apparently Bobbie Gentry only recorded guitars and vocals on her hit song before she got a record deal.

"After she got her deal," Holtauer explains, "they used the label's money to hire her arranger, Jimmie Haskell, and he added the strings and horns and rhythm section. So I'd like to shop your record the way it is, just guitar and vocals. Once we get a deal, then we'll go back in the studio, and put the sweetening on."

I'm a little disappointed, but also understand. I'm sure Holtauer would rather have the record company pay for arrangements and orchestral recordings than do it himself. Sensing I'm a little let down, he tells me that his first appointment is tomorrow, with RCA Records, a label he's had a lot of luck with in the past. We run through the list of other record labels he wants to approach, and he suggests we get together in a couple of weeks to discuss the outcome.

No sooner than two weeks have passed, right on schedule, Holtauer calls me sounding upbeat and secretive.

"I've made a reservation at The Russian Tea Room," he says, with something that sounds like excitement in his voice. He must have made a record deal. Why would he take me out to dinner to tell me bad news? I go through my usual shenanigans getting dressed in something I can stand and he might like, and meet Holtauer at the Russian Tea Room right by his office at the fashionable dinner hour of 8 pm. When I walk in, he catches my eye, waving enthusiastically from a table he's reserved tucked away from the Tea Room's more ostentatious crowd. When I take my seat across from him, he greets me with a kiss on the cheek and pulls me around the table to sit next to him. Then he hands me the wine menu.

"I want you to pick," he instructs, mysteriously.

"Why? I don't know a thing about wine," I say. "You're the expert, Mr. Holtauer, you pick!"

"Ron! Please, tonight especially, call me Ron," he pleads good-naturedly.

"Okay, Ron," I laugh. "But you pick the wine and tell me everything."

It takes some time, but eventually a bottle of something deliciously mellow and red arrives. Feeling safe and happy with him, I indulge in a full glass before Holtauer finally launches into the tale of my record.

"Well," he starts, "RCA passed."

My ears crackle with this bombshell. It's not that I didn't think this could happen. But what kind of lead-in is this?

"I know, I know," he continues, glancing sideways at my puzzled face. "I was totally shocked too. What bothered me the most," he leans against me, conspiratorially, "was that RCA kept referring to the tape as a 'demo.' Can you believe that?"

3 Greenwich and My Lai: A Tale of Two Villages

I try to open my mouth to express my feelings. *(Yes, of course, I believe that! Just me and a guitar, without any other instruments? That's a demo!)* But nothing comes out.

"I still have a few labels I intend to bring the tapes to," he continues, draining his glass, and refilling both of ours.

Finally, I find my vocal chords, "Wait! You've taken the tapes to other labels besides RCA? And they passed too?"

"Yes," he coughs self-consciously, and drinks. I take a drink too. "Columbia passed. So did Decca."

"But Mr. Holtauer..."

"Ron..."

"Ron, I don't understand. Why did you go on showing the tapes when you were told they sound like demos? We should go back into the studio and finish the songs the way you originally planned, so people understand what they're hearing."

"Well...Judy, you never know. Just when you think you've run out of options, some record label will surprise you, and love it. I just haven't connected with the right one yet."

"But, Mr. Holt—... Ron...I am afraid we'll get turn-downs from all the labels, and then we won't be able to bring the finished tapes to anyone."

"No, no. Let me handle this end of it. I know what I'm doing."

Our dinner comes, and I do my best to swallow my food and disappointment without seeming like a bad sport. He still seems so sure of himself and very motivated.

"I do have something good to tell you," he says, when dessert arrives.

"You do?" I perk up.

"Well, I've done a lot of thinking in the last months. You are a very special person, Judy. A very gifted artist, and a lady who knows what she wants."

"I guess..." I murmur, distracted.

"What I've come to realize is that I know what I want too. I see clearly now that I am deeply in love with you, and want to marry you."

Mother of fucks!

* * *

The powers leading all the way to the top of the American military chain of command are initially very successful in covering up My Lai. They work out a plan to give Buck, Larry, and Glenn (posthumously) the Bronze Star and Distinguished Flying Cross to keep them quiet. They say it's for their part in rescuing some children at My Lai. Unhappily, the citations totally fabricate what really happened. Buck's medal praises him for taking a Vietnamese child to the hospital who was "caught in intense crossfire between friendly and hostile forces engaged in a heavy firefight." Even worse, Buck's signature is falsified as a witness on Glenn and Larry's citations, which are also full of b.s.

Buck is so humiliated and miserable over being used that he throws his medal away, furious that everything they went through, everything they witnessed and reported has been turned into a lie—a deception that will be believed until the grisly and salacious truth of My Lai finally breaks through the iron grip of those holding it in place. And there are plenty of prestigious fingerprints on this cover up—leading all the way up to the brand-new president of the United States, Richard M. Nixon. In his mostly handwritten notes from meetings with his chief of staff, H.R. Robert Haldeman, Nixon directs Haldeman to get started on "dirty tricks and discredit the witnesses…in order to keep working on the problem."

"The problem" is that My Lai is a political threat to Nixon. Vietnam destroyed one president, and Nixon has no intention of being next. The witnesses he wants discredited are pilot Buck Thompson and gunner Larry Colburn. (Glenn Andreotta won't be a problem, of course, as he's already dead.) Nixon needs to get the other two to shut up about American soldiers slaughtering unarmed civilians in Vietnam. The war is unpopular enough and the American people are sick of it. So, while Buck and Larry puzzle over how the armed forces are getting away with the story that only 20 villagers were killed at My Lai, Nixon is working behind the scenes with two congressmen to successfully seal Buck and Larry's testimony for good; thus, damaging the cases against the real culprits of My Lai.

Unaware of what's happening, Buck can still sense the tide turning. After he finishes testifying against Lieutenant William Calley (who is scapegoated and court martialed by higher officers, who should be held accountable along with him), Buck walks into the Officers' Club for a drink. To his embarrassment, all the other officers get up and walk out. This scene is repeated over and over. The man, who should be receiving the highest honor obtainable for bravery, is being ostracized as if *he* is a traitor. And yet, to the military, Buck is breaking the brotherhood code. To them he's a snitch and a turncoat. If they don't reject Buck, then they have to believe him—and *that's* just too awful to think about.

Soon Buck begins calling himself by different names. If someone recognizes him in a bar—a place in which he's now spending far too much time—Buck says that they're wrong; he's not *that* guy. He was never in My Lai. He doesn't know anything about any of that.

And that's the way things stay until a soldier named Ron Ridenhour runs into several of the men in Charlie Co. who participated in the massacre. Finally back from their Vietnam jungle banishment, these men—to Ron's considerable alarm—can't stop telling the same story. It's a grotesque tale about being ordered to cordon off a village in Son My Village called My Lai, and then move through it, destroying the structures and killing the inhabitants. Overwhelmed by the facts he's collected, but committed to doing the right thing, on March 29, 1969, almost one year to the day of the massacre, Ron writes a letter with all this incredible information carefully documented, and sends it to every congressman in the United States. It takes a while, but a deep and significant crack in the deceit finally splits wide open. And in the new and safe space of this crack, someone remembers:

"Weren't there a couple of witnesses, some soldiers that kept trying to tell this exact same story? Where are they now? Can we find them?"

* * *

I don't throw my glass of wine at Holtauer. I don't sob. I am grateful he had me sit next to him and not across from him so he can't see me fighting nausea and tears. Still, I'm sure he knows. How could this have happened? I was so careful to pick a person and situation that presented none of the pitfalls I've ignored in the past. It must be me. My music isn't good enough to overcome the wolves.

"I'm sorry, Ron," I mutter weakly. "I had no idea." I can hear him clearing his throat next to me self-consciously. Defeated and feeling betrayed, I drop the truth on the table: "I'm very fond of you. But I just don't feel the same way..." *He's married and 30 years older than I am; where is this coming from?* "I was only thinking about our music project when we were together. That was the important relationship to me."

"Oh, for me too," Holtauer says in a swift mood swing. He's obviously pulling back; I feel him reaching for his wallet and signaling the waiter. "Don't worry about what I said.

3 Greenwich and My Lai: A Tale of Two Villages

Sometimes wine...I'll call you about the appointments I have this week. Let's see how things go."

I ask him what record companies he's seeing, but he either doesn't hear me as he finishes up the dinner paperwork, or doesn't want to talk anymore. He gives me a brisk hug at the Russian Tea Room door, flags a cab for me, and walks away without saying goodbye.

I tell the cab driver to take me to Dan's apartment. Ever since the night we spent writing the MLK Memorial Collector's one-shot, (Gassman had it on the newsstands in every major Southern town the day of King's funeral and made a fortune; we each made $100.), Dan and I have been "seeing each other." We're lovers and friends, and talk about most everything (at least I do), but I know something's missing. It takes several months before Danny finally tells me about a boy he's been in love with for years. Though he can't quite get this other relationship to work, it certainly explains the blush on his face when he overheard Neal calling me a lesbian. When I ask why he didn't tell me right away, he says he worried about my attitude, "You are a little homophobic."

"I am?" I ask, amazed. "I think I'm afraid of it," I add, a little surprised to be saying that.

"I wonder why?" Dan smiles, rubbing my back, and holding me while I bounce from subject to subject, including this latest defeat with Holtauer. Nothing ever surprises Dan. He's given to saying nihilistic things like, "Well, that's what you get for dealing with people." But, I have to admit these disappointments are getting harder and harder for me. I seem to have lost pieces of my highly polished fantasy life. My dreams feel exposed for all their fragility, and I'm tired. But I'm worried: won't the world feel smaller without them?

Mr. Holtauer does not call with any more reports. When I stop by his offices unannounced, he greets me warmly and introduces me to a new female artist he's signed. "She writes with a lyricist, but maybe you two could write together for her album too," he says, as if he and I never had a project. In no time Holtauer gets her a deal with Decca Records, and they both ask me to write her album liner notes, never giving any thought to how that might make me feel. Clearly, I am too busy stumbling around my own darkness, misreading everyone I encounter—especially myself—to grasp what's really going on, or to do anything useful about reeling in or letting go of my aspirations, no matter how stubbornly they elude me.

Then, just two months later in early June, my mother calls from California to tell me Bobby Kennedy was shot in the middle of the night at the Ambassador Hotel after winning the primary there. Everyone is hysterical, of course. Are all the good guys going down one by one? People with principles must go, is that it? Suddenly I start to feel a high degree of anxiety when I think about Robert Kennedy—but for a very different reason. As I ride the subway to work watching New Yorkers freak out over still another assassination, I dread what's waiting for me at the office. And I'm right:

At Nationwide, every single editor has piled into Roy's office. Maurice and his whip fill the doorway, but I can still hear Roy giving out assignments:

"Al, you're going to write about Bobby's actual assassination," Roy instructs. "Find out anything you can about what happened last night, and vamp, vamp, vamp."

"But what tense do I vamp in?" Al asks.

"What?"

"He's not actually dead yet. Kennedy's heart is still holding up. Are we supposed to write this as if he's dead or alive?"

There's a lot of murmuring. Then Maurice answers for Roy in his usual snarl, "Write like he's dead. He's gonna be dead any minute now."

3 Greenwich and My Lai: A Tale of Two Villages

Roy catches sight of me, and begins assigning me bits and pieces of Kennedy's life through the doorway: "Judy, write about Ethel; find out everything you can about Ethel, so you can write something believable about how she's gonna behave during this ordeal."

This is exactly the kamikaze mission I need to forever lose my mind. For Roy's sake only, I write diligently for a few hours about poor, dear Ethel. God knows how she's getting through this day; she's stronger than I am. So, at lunchtime, while everyone else opts for the slice of pizza Maurice so generously supplies each employee to keep them indoors and working on the one-shot, I find Dan and tell him I'm done.

"I'm leaving," I say simply, not really understanding what I'm doing. Somehow, Dan does, and asks to join me. We both exit Nationwide at the same time, although Dan comes back for a few months. Bobby Kennedy does, in fact, die in 26 hours. So, once again, Maurice is the very best at doing the very worst, and scores himself more millions.

Later that evening I call home, remembering the time John F. Kennedy was shot and my mother called me at U.C. Berkeley, saying: "Sweetheart, would you like to fly home to be with the family?" I definitely wanted to; and I want to go home now, as well. My parents think that's a terrific idea. We decide on a two-week visit; and at the end of the call, my mother changes the subject and asks me how the music project with Mr. Holtauer is going.

"Oh, not that well," I admit, sheepishly. "He seems to have lost interest in me."

"Really?!" she gasps. "Well, *that* surprises me. Did we ever tell you he came to visit us several months ago?"

I'm astounded. "In California?"

"Yes, he came to our home," Mother says. "Your father and I were somewhat taken aback by him, I must say," she adds.

"Why?" I ask, not sure I want to hear the answer.

"He seemed very naive and unhip for the 60s-record business; and yet, he seemed very taken with you. But like…like…"

"Yeah, I know." I say, softly.

"Oh? *Oh!* I'm sorry."

"Me too."

"Well, that's *that* business. Just awful! Come home."

[Defeated] "Yeah."

✳ ✳ ✳

4

On A Gender Bender

Shouldn't I be more excited? Packing my tape recorder, some cassettes, my list of questions, and a note pad into my catchall leather-fringe briefcase, I wonder, *what's wrong?* Ever since creating *Right On!*—America's first national black teen magazine—I've been trying to nail down this interview with Michael Jackson. I've been at the family's house so many times, talking to every other Jackson brother, that one of the magazine's columnists recently warned me, "There's a rumor floating around Motown that you're sleeping with 'Papa Joe' Jackson! Otherwise, they can't figure out how you're getting this much access to his boys!"

That's *so* wrong! What am I? Joan of Arc daring to speak directly to God without first clearing it with the Church of Motown? As editor of *Right On!*, which I started a year ago with art director William Cragun for Laufer Publications, it's true that I've had absolutely no trouble getting to know the Jackson family. I'm at their Encino home every week, charting their early years in Los Angeles after moving here from Gary, Indiana. But why go through Motown if their father, Joe, is calling *me*? He is, after all, the man who bench-pressed his five oldest sons into becoming the most successful pop-teen group ever. Thus, when Joe decides to use the "girl with the Jewish Afro" (Angela Davis freed my hair!) to write exactly what he wants said about his boys, he bows to no one, including the head of Motown publicity. So, I pretty much get to come and go at our mutual convenience.

Naturally, it helps smooth my way that we put the group on the cover of every *Right On!* issue. And, why wouldn't we? They are the reason the magazine exists. One afternoon Chuck Laufer, president of Laufer Publications, walked into my office and announced: *"Tiger Beat* [one of his hugely successful teen publications] is getting an awful lotta' letters about some black-teen group Motown signed. I think there might be something to it. I'd like to see if there are enough fans to support a magazine." Then, I swear, he gave me this zealous look and said, "I don't really understand that market, and I don't really understand you. So, let's give you a shot at being the editor."

At that time, 1971, I was the managing editor of a movie and gossip magazine called *Rona Barrett's Hollywood*. This was the first job I got in Los Angeles after returning from New York for what I thought was going to be a two-week vacation. Thank God for Bonnie and Marilyn, who packed up the pieces of my NYC life and put them in boxes headed for L.A. It will take me years to face how badly I feel about some of the queasy exploitation I head-longed into on the East Coast. I had every intention of returning when I left; unfortunately, the turmoil I experienced there upended my self-confidence. I didn't understand it yet, and felt sheltered 3,000 miles away under my parents' roof. And that's too bad really, because I also learned so much during that urban obstacle course, not the least of which was accidently getting a start in editorial work via Manhattan's pulp publishing world. Certainly, *Rona Barrett's Hollywood* is a direct descendent.

I was tapped almost immediately for the job when I got to L.A. because, apparently, finding someone on the West Coast with movie magazine experience was rare—especially before the 1974 birth of "legit" celebrity publications like *People*. So, when Rona Barrett resolved to use her television visibility on ABC news to launch a gossip publication with Chuck and Ira Laufer, it was one small step for TV-movie magazines, and one giant leap for star-muckraking.

Unfortunately, Rona's oozing-with-atmosphere presence on TV didn't make it to the pages of the magazine, primarily because she herself didn't make it into the office much. In fact, the first months of my *Rona Barrett's Hollywood* employment were perplexing. I was working with a very retrograde New York fan magazine editor who thought putting the Lennon Sisters on the cover was hip. When she was finally removed, Rona brought in a woman who had no editorial experience and spent ridiculous amounts of time telling me how different her sex life was now that she was married to "a real man," (as opposed to her first husband who might have been "...a fag because he didn't like to touch me!")

Full of prickly behavior, she enjoyed standing in my office, skulking over my shoulder, and making unpredictable demands like, "How about you write a cover story for the headline: 'John Wayne's Love Letter to America vs. Jane Fonda's Hate Letter.'"

When I said I didn't think Jane really hated America at all, she responded with the non sequitur: "Rona asked me to ask you if you were a lesbian."

Between this woman and the Laufer brothers, I had no real contact with Rona, so whatever "learning curve" existed in the gossip business was reduced to rumors about Miss Rona herself ("She's dating a married man," "She's bisexual," "She tried to kill herself," etc.). This was disheartening because there were plenty of skills to acquire, Rona was smart, and I was interested! Later, in the 90s, I'll get to know tattle titan, Liz Smith, when, as Editor-in-Chief of *The Advocate,* I conduct her coming-out interview. Liz is amazing, and her priceless interpretation of gossip as "the news running ahead of itself in a long red dress!" is more profound than most serious journalists will ever admit.

After a year toiling away on Miss Rona's magazine, and another year figuring out what black teenagers want from a magazine, by today, April 20, 1972, *Right On!* is a success. That's why I am driving straight from my Venice beach apartment to the Jackson's Encino home. But this time, it's finally Michael I'm talking to. The youngest star of the J-5 has already emerged as the biggest deal since Little Stevie Wonder. So again, I have to ask myself, *where is my excitement?* Perhaps it's just protection? Am I keeping myself in check as a journalist? After all, I have to return with a whole lotta material, enough to fill numerous articles for many months. That's how the teen publication business works:

You take one interview and chop it into a dozen tiny tales, add a few precious pictures from the one photo shoot you score, and with this you can do a year's worth of hot-selling teen issues. Sometimes when a teen magazine scores a new photo shoot of a teen star—like what happened last week with David Cassidy—some pretty Machiavellian shenanigans follow. One of our teen magazines had a cover story on Bobby Sherman all set to ship to the printers. The usual lame editorial inside birthed the cover line: "Bobby Cries: The Girl I Marry Must Have These 5 Things!" When the editors scored fresh photos of David Cassidy at the last minute, they only had enough time to re-do the photo layout. The story's type had been set some time back. So, they just changed headlines and star names, and ran with the exact same story. The cover now reads, "David Cries: The Girl I Marry Must Have These 5 Things!" Bonus New Photos!

I must say, I gasped when the layout artist pulled me aside

to show me the switch. "No one will be the wiser," she giggled. "The fans won't know. So why should we worry?"

Oh my God, why do I bother sweating everything?

Still, here I am flipping out over what I'll do if Michael Jackson won't reveal anything interesting to me! So far he has refused to say much in interviews. Maybe that's why I'm feeling so numb today! Am I just dreading the idea of trying to drag "goodies" out of a 14-year-old boy?

I push the talk box at the end of the Jackson's Hayvenhurst driveway. It's still relatively early in the spectacular rise of Michael and his brothers, so usually a family member answers the call or the door. This time it's "Mama" Katherine, the indomitable wife and mother of nine, also the 42-year-old daughter of Martha and Prince Michael Scruse. Everyone will think Michael names his first son ("Prince Michael") after himself in some grandiose way, when, in fact, he is named after his great-grandfather. Katherine, a child polio survivor who still manages a slight limp, is the rock of the family long before she emerges as a veritable boulder in the eyes of the world.

"That you, Judy?" she says in her Alabama-by-way-of-Indiana drawl. I confirm and the iron gates part. As I drive in, I can hear the Jackson's German Shepherds (Lobo, Heavy, and Black Girl), barking furiously somewhere out of sight. Parked in the driveway are Joe's Mercedes and Katherine's Audi—the subject of some staff snarking a few visits ago. ("He couldn't get his wife a Mercedes too? She only created and sewed the boys' costumes for years until they were finally signed by Motown!").

Fifteen-year-old Marlon Jackson answers the front door and leads me to the family room where I take my usual seat on the Jackson's vinyl, checkered couch. He runs off and I immediately begin unloading my tools and testing my tape recorder. Five-year-old Janet Jackson is sliding up and down on an overstuffed chair while she and a friend take turns trying to work out a new puzzle on the floor. I do my best to be subtle as I check my tape deck, but when I hit playback and "testing, testing" comes blaring back at me at full volume, Katherine appears with a loaf of bread in one hand and a surprised look on her face.

"You okay? Do you want a sandwich?" she asks. "Jermaine is in the kitchen eating now. Why don't you eat too?"

I mutter nervously about my interview with Michael but she makes a face. "Oh, he'll be here. Don't worry. He's in his room. Come eat something."

I join them in the kitchen where Marlon and his sister, Latoya, are doing homework, and Jermaine is hunched over his lunch plate. When I sit down, the frequently shirtless Jermaine looks up and smiles. (So gorgeous! Jackie and Jermaine—for my money—the two hot Jackson boys.) "You look great, Jermaine," I say, and he beams again.

"But his hair is too big!" Katherine proclaims. "Don't you think, Judy? Tell him his hair is too much. He's got to get a haircut."

Oh no! I think. She isn't going to drag me into this!

"Mom!" Jermaine objects, "My hair is fine."

"His Afro is out of control," she insists to me, but then drops it. Thank goodness. It's hard enough to get the boys not to feel guarded with me. It won't help if I'm seen as mom's assistant nag. The last time I was here, things went sideways when someone brought up that it was a little weird for a white girl to be the editor of the only black teen magazine in the world. I did my best with something no one can explain, when, in the middle of the wrangle, Marlon looked up at me aghast and said, "You ain't black?"—sending the conversation flying off its hinges!

We eat in silence for a few minutes. Then Jermaine reaches up into his enormous Afro and pulls out a buried comb which he looks stunned to have found. He's about to start primping when I give him the universal slash-across-the-throat "cease/stop" sign I learned from Izzy in New York. Jermaine understands, and shoves the comb back in his hair, glancing at Katherine who mercifully missed both our moves. Then to me, he says:

"We're gonna play basketball with the Osmond Brothers. We're gonna beat them so bad."

"Really?" I ask. Katherine turns from the sink and nods her head.

"Do you think the magazine could come too? You know, photograph the game and run the pictures?"

"Sure," Jermaine says.

"No," Katherine overrules. "This is a private family thing," she continues protectively. "The boys have been trying to put this game together for a long time. I don't want a press circus here. And I'm sure the Osmonds don't either. You understand, right?"

I say I do, and I do—as a "decent person." But as a journalist, well, there it is: the entire conflict built into the DNA of celebrity journalism. When they trust you, they show and tell you things that are ultimately of no use to you as a journalist. Sure, you have information other writers don't, and all the fans want; but you can't use any of it. If you reveal what you know publicly (which advances your career), you lose your contact (and friendship, if that exists) with the celebrity. And if you lose that, you lose your source of valuable information—which most of the time you can't use anyway. You're caught between semi-bland journalism featuring interviews that taste like under-cooked side dishes, and what people really want to know: the entree—often labeled "sensationalism" by more tasteful journalists who rarely score anything interesting.

"Hi," Michael says, appearing out of thin air like Peter Pan. "You ready for me?"

* * *

"Hej! [Hi!]" Steig Ekberg greets his friend Gunnar Skarsgård in the doorway of Gunnar's Stockholm apartment. *"Var så god!* [Here you go!]" he says, handing Gunnar a copy of *Dagens Nyheter,* Sweden's oldest and largest newspaper.

Both boys, just 18-years of age, huddle in the hallway, fiercely devouring an article headlined, "Sweden Passes The World's First Law Officially Recognizing Change of Gender." It's Friday, April 21, 1972, a temperate spring morning with no clouds in the wide Scandinavian sky. But for Steig and Gunnar, more than just the sky is unblocked; a world of possibilities has suddenly opened for them.

"What do we do first?" Gunnar asks in that sincere, breathy voice he's been cultivating so carefully, quite different from his deeper manner of speaking. Suddenly he doesn't care about being graceful or dignified. His eyes are wet with joy as he drops the newspaper on the floor and leaps on his friend, hugging him with crazy excitement. Steig lets himself be shaken about, but doesn't quite return the elation.

"Steig, Steig, you already read this article. I am too excited to read. Just tell me everything. Where do we go? How do we start?"

Steig retrieves the paper and reads aloud how there are many steps ahead of them. There must be psychiatric examinations, and many long applications filled out before they can go before the Health and Welfare Board's legal council for confirmation.

"That is fine," Gunnar says, still giddy. "We expect a big maze from them to discourage us. But nothing will, *ja* [yes]?" He looks hard at Steig, wondering why he isn't sharing in his elation. Suddenly worried, Gunnar asks, "Our parents don't need to be there, ja?"

"*Nej*, [no], because you must be at least 18, and we are. But, Gunnar, there is something else you don't know that we must talk..."

"Ja, I know. We cannot be married. Why do we care? We are not married. For us there is no need of a divorce." *[Gunnar pauses for a moment.]* "But I feel sorry for Dolph," he says, referring to a man they know who is married but says he still believes he is a woman. "Now Dolph must divorce his wife to have the operation?"

"This is a terrible thing!" Steig insists angrily. "Dolph's wife has been supporting him in this all along. It's cruel."

"Why would the health board care?" Gunnar asks.

"Maybe they don't want people to say that this surgery destroys marriages or families," Steig guesses, folding the paper and throwing himself down on the couch, looking sulky. "But Gunnar," he tries again, "listen, there's more. There's something I don't like at all. It is very wrong."

"*Vad?* [What?]"

"Gunnar, please, sit down here next to me..."

"Steig, just tell me! You are scaring me!"

Steig sweeps his wavy hair off his forehead and spits out the poisonous information: "We must be sterilized first, before we can have this operation!"

"Vad?!" Gunnar screams. "Why? What is the purpose of that?"

Steig turns and looks out the window. Their good news has come with a terrible twist. After all the years of waiting and wondering about himself, Steig feels that familiar distress building inside. Ever since he was seven and a teacher took his class to a nearby park, Steig has lived his life in a quagmire of anxiety. When the class was broken into two lines—the girls in one line and the boys in another—Steig knew he was supposed to join the boys. But he also knew where he belonged, so he got in line with the girls. His memories of the school trip up until that point are joyous: playing, singing, and laughing with the girls. Then he was discovered wearing one of the girl's hair ribbons. The teacher yanked him away gruffly, insisting, "This is where you belong! You are not a girl; you are a boy!" She browbeat him in front of the class, pulling his wrist hard. It was Steig's first experience with the world telling him who he was and what he could and could not do. The memory remains with him like a stringent smell he cannot wash away.

"What is the purpose of sterilizing us?" he hears Gunnar's voice pleading. It seems such unctuous politics to Steig, so obvious, really. After a while he turns his head in the direction of his childhood friend, the one with whom he shares more things than fate normally grants such a brotherhood—or perhaps soon a sisterhood. Taking a breath, Steig whispers, "I believe they fear us. We are a threat to gender roles. So they make us eunuchs. That way whatever madness is swimming in our genes stops with us. We have a present but no future."

When Steig finally turns completely away from the window to look at Gunnar, he's surprised not to see him. Looking down, Steig moves off the couch to the floor where Gunnar has collapsed with his head on his knees. He slides over and hugs him gently. He can feel Gunnar is crying. His sobs rock his rapidly changing body back and forth. Gunnar's physical transformation over the last year has been incredible yet subtle, so rich with anecdotal information: his smoother skin, long hair, his new small breasts, rounded hips, loss of muscle mass—all this from a little estrogen? Truthfully, there's been a massive rewrite of Gunnar Skarsgård going on right under Steig's nose.

Slowly Steig pulls Gunnar back up onto the couch with him, striving one more time to be the strong one. "Maybe," he whispers to Gunnar, "…maybe it will be worth it?"

Gunnar cries a little more, then they just stare at each other. For a moment Steig is speechless. The voice and features staring up at him are so different from that often intoxicated and emotionally numb teenager he grew up with. That chiseled, prematurely bestubbled-faced, that introverted mystery kid is really gone. Instead, this complex, gregarious, curvaceous, full-bodied character in his arms is…

"What is wrong?" Gunnar asks, sensing Steig's distraction.

"Nothing, nothing. I was only thinking how I still want to be a parent," he says, coming up with a different, but truthful subject. "I always assumed it would happen one day, so this is a terrible shock. I'm not so sure now."

"But Steig, at least we will be in the right bodies, ja? We must stay with our plan."

For the next hours Gunnar and Steig brainstorm ways to get around the dreadful sterilization requirement. Perhaps they can freeze some of their sperm before the final surgery?

* * *

"Should we do my photo shoot before the interview in case the sun goes down?" Michael asks, watching *Right On!*'s photographer pull into the Jackson family's driveway. In truth, Michael would rather do anything—eat mud, hold freezing ice cubes in his bare hands—anything but sit down and talk.

I tell him we have plenty of time for both the interview and photo shoot, and angle him onto the couch with me. He looks forsaken. What the world will come to know about his childhood in a few years, is sitting right in front of me today: a complex mass of undelivered communications. What's really going on inside his head, within his body? Only Michael knows—and I'm not even sure that's true. When all the voices outside and within are directing who you must be regardless of who you are, then self-knowledge has too many flaming hoops to jump through, even for someone as agile as Michael!

What's more, later revelations about Michael's relationship with his father are undisclosed at this time. Yet this is precisely when the alleged abuse would be going on. I, personally, cannot divulge fruits from any of the secret gardens I've walked through with him; I saw nothing. Family stuff is so complicated anyway; it can hide in plain sight. Relatives simply know too much about each other and have too wide a range of weaponry to choose from. What I do know for certain is that Joe is a disciplinarian; he's the ego and the enterprising engine driving his sons; his obsessive care and nurturing of each boy's particular needs is something I see played out every time I visit. But I guess there are boundless possibilities behind closed doors.

"I'm writing songs now," Michael says, giving me the one big smile I get all day. "We're gonna record this one song I wrote called, 'Got To Be With You.' It'll be on the new album. I really like writing stuff and I think we're gonna be doing more and more of it in the future," he adds. Then with no warning at all, he gets up, drops the copy of *Right On!* he was flipping through on the couch, and opens the door to his huge backyard. While I helplessly watch, Michael kicks off a series of hyperkinetic dance moves on the back patio, launching the dogs into a barking carnival.

"Wait!" I call after him. But I'm completely drowned out. Observing him, I wonder if he's aware of the operatic howling. Does he hear anything but his own soundtrack? Even as a mere cub, Michael roots out urban rhythms meant only for him. Avoiding all sappy-tappy dance moves, Michael stops, then kicks one leg in the air, twists, and leaps over it. I watch, open-mouthed until I realize he's forgotten me. Then I decide to use this unscheduled intermission to check on my tape recorder.

4 On A Gender Bender

I panic. In the dying afternoon light of the Jackson's family room, I can't see very well and decide that the tape hasn't been running at all. Flustered, I open my tape deck and pull out the cassette, mangling the thin spool in the process. Now I am sinking swiftly into a new state of incompetence, and my distraught energy has searched out and destroyed Michael's creative burst, for all at once he's back in the house.

"What's happenin'?" he asks, observing me in full-on panic.

I ignore him completely. My mind is moss thick; my editorial manners are gone. I'm sure that every word he's said thus far in our interview has been lost. Nothing has been taped, and I haven't been taking notes. I'll have to go back through the twisty territory of my memory with pruning shears to hack free anything worth writing. My big MJ interview—crashing along with my professional universe! I'm finished.

Being ignored must not happen to Michael very often. His entire demeanor changes. While I twist and pull the cassette tape into a scary cat's cradle, Michael shifts his graceful body onto one foot, lifts himself weightlessly over the arm of the couch and slips in close beside me. Gently he reaches over and takes the cassette player out of my hands and slides a pencil off my writing pad and into one of the two turning holes of the cassette. Then he begins rolling the tape backwards slowly.

At first I think he's trying to make me laugh by introducing a complicated way to further destroy the tape. After a few seconds, however, I grasp what he's doing: Using my pencil, he's slowly and steadily rewinding and straightening out my damaged tape. Immediately I pick up my smile where I left it in my mirror this morning while practicing for this interview, and try to salvage myself:

"Whoa, Michael, amazing! So, do you think maybe the tape was just stuck?" I say eagerly. He continues rewinding.

"Possibly we did record something?" He ignores me now. All concentration, he focuses only on the task. His perfectly cropped hair and still flawless young boy's skin encase the famous features he will one day cut out of his face forever. Adolescence is just around the corner, and with it will come the standard hormonal terrors we all suffer during puberty. But Michael will recoil from these signs of imperfection—acne and awkward face and hair changes—so vehemently, his misery and subsequent isolation become legendary. As his body becomes a man's, he will reject it, purportedly loathing any change that takes him away from the lithe, androgynous body of his boyhood.

"There," he says, in that effete voice that flies in the face of every muscular snarl and step he will make in a few years with "Beat it."

"Go on, try it."

I slip the rewound tape into my cassette deck and press play:

"Testing...testing...Well, Michael, so how are you doing these days with all this success?" I hear myself blurt insensitively at him. *God, no wonder he sat there appalled.*

"You fixed it! Thank you so much," I say as softly as I can after hearing my assault on tape. "You saved our interview."

"That's okay," he shrugs, and moves away from me again. Carefully he assembles himself at the far corner of the couch. Smoothing out his pinstriped pants and mock leather jacket meticulously, MJ once again prepares himself to do the thing that makes him so uncomfortable: talk. I check my list of questions for something easy but when I look up, I realize Michael has planted himself firmly on the outer limits of my tape recorder.

"Michael, I'm sorry," I begin, "but you're too far away." I indicate that my microphone cord is stretched as far towards him as I can extend it. "You've got to come closer to me."

4 On A Gender Bender

He looks over at me and winces.

"I won't touch you," I add, trying for humor.

He blanches and I can see a layer of moisture building on his face from here. Everything I'm doing is wrong. Our chemistry is crap. Not surprisingly, Michael pushes himself up and off the couch. *Oh Gawd, this is a disaster!* I think. *He hates me and I'm starting to feel the same way.* I watch him as he heads for the staircase that leads to his bedroom. Even in retreat mode, he moves elegantly, neither a boy nor a girl.

"Michael, pul-eeeze!" I call, "I'm sorry..."

"No, no, I'll be right back," he says sweetly, and he's gone again. The way he walks up the stairs, the way he tears up the patio, the music he talks of making in the future—I wonder will it someday create a safe space for him? A space to reimagine what dance looks like, what vocals sound like, and what gender can be? And if so, what on earth is he going to do with his macho, traditional father?

I sit on the couch with my own layer of anxiety heating up my clothes. I don't have one suitable thing for a teen magazine yet. "What's your favorite color? What's your favorite food? What kind of girl do you want to marry when you grow up?" If I start asking Michael questions like that, trying to crush his exhaustive creativity into teen pabulum, well, I'll get just what I deserve: more disappearing. Some teen stars just don't fit these magazines, but you can't tell the kids that. These poor teenage readers—with their hormones a'chugging and their pores a'clogging—actually believe that Michael is their perfect pre-boyfriend crush. After all, that's what teen magazines are about: a young girl's (or boy's?) first, safe, boyfriend tryout.

It's at least 10 minutes before MJ returns looking, well, brand new. As he descends the staircase, his jacket is now off and thrown casually over his left shoulder, in a move models execute. His hair and face have been noticeably attended to, and he is making the kind of entrance usually performed by a diva well-acquainted with the effect it will have on those in attendance. Like too many aspects of Michael's young life, this too has been well-rehearsed. For goodness sake, he's only 14, and I'm just a teen magazine editor. *Relax!*

When I get home to my dark apartment after a luminous day with the Jacksons (despite only fitful rays of info from the confounding MJ), I can see my answer machine flashing two messages at me. As I now live in the roar of my own heartbeats when it comes to my personal life, I'm not sure I'm up for playing either message. It could be her. It could be him.

As my mother said during our first conversation about my sexuality last year, "How *eclectic* of you!" Her voice was richly marinated in cynicism, as she didn't really believe that my affairs with men were much of a match for the "theatre of the tempestuous" being played out around my first woman. She was right, of course. Which is not the same thing as saying men aren't essential to my well-being. It starts with a father and brother I love, and spins out to some of my closest friends. As the patterns of my life indicate—from my early childhood years with the boys in the hood, to my future as the first female Editor-in-Chief of the male dominated *Advocate*, "Let's face it, Judy,"—to quote an editor friend, "it's Wendy and the lost boys, with you!"

I have no idea what makes me gay—a salacious confession from someone who will spend years assigning stories and asking interviewees questions on the subject—but it's true. Basically it all seems to come together in a bigger bang for me with a woman. That's my reason. Of course it also has a lot to do with the woman and the exact blend of male and female in that woman. Could I find that same mixture in a man? For me the 70s, and my own internalized homophobia, will give me the motivation and the opportunities to find out for myself.

"Hey, Judy, Judy, Judy, it's Chris!"

Deep baritone sounds kick off the answer-machine roll call. I can hear voices in the background, filling Chris Roberts' Hollywood Hills home. Actually, it's his father, actor Pernell Roberts's home, containing, no doubt, a small gathering of nice show biz people.

I met Chris at the Laufer Company. They hired him to assist the other editors and photographers. He's very handsome, a sturdy dark hunk of masculinity, just like his father. Right away he's in my office, interrupting my concentration, making suggestions, letting me know who his father is and how close to work they live.

"Why drive all the way home to Venice, tonight?" he reads my mind. "Come meet Dad and his wife and hang out with us." That's how it starts. He's irresistible, especially after a long, painful year of...

Ding! I press the second message:

"Hi-i-i-i-i. It's Kim. Where have you been? I've called you several times. What's been going on? I'd like to see you. What are you doing later? Call me, okay? Call me."

I walk through my tiny kitchen and open the glass and wood door leading to my back porch stairs. It's still warm outside and ocean breezes are billowing with odors from scattered sea shells and ripe seaweed; so I take a chair and seat myself on the cement landing, leaning back against the door—the same door Kim smashed through last fall during her breakdown.

* * *

Steig sits by himself in the waiting room of a busy Swedish hospital, biding time while Gunnar undergoes sex reassignment surgery [SRS] to become Astrid. No one else knows this is happening. Her family suspects nothing. Even friends who have watched her living as a woman for more than a year, have no idea that today her body is becoming one.

Although Steig still intends to have SRS as well, unlike Astrid, he is just beginning to fulfill some of the stipulations. The surgery itself is free of charge, but the steps getting to it are insanely stringent—and to Steig, one step in particular still remains unacceptable! He balks every time he faces the pre-op criteria of undergoing sterilization, or at least showing some proof that for other reasons he is incapable of reproducing.

Instead, Steig continues his copious ways of fighting it: He writes letters to newspapers and government officials. He sits in front of SRS hospitals waving signs that read, "Barbaric!" But no one cares, not really. He's already thought of as a freak. Just ask anyone. Everyday is a fight for him to drum up the white-hot rage he needs to keep the outside voices from damaging his psyche further.

Astrid, on the other hand, is amazing. When she was forced to declare she had "a mental health disorder" as part of this obligatory process, she did it without a trace of despair. Her clarity of purpose, outfitted with her usual wacky wit, is just plain inspiring: "Steig, my God, darling" she laughed, "When I was young, I told my sister that her doll got sick and died—so that I could play with it when she wasn't around. I knew I needed to hide playing with dolls, *but I never felt diseased*. I just felt a lot smarter than my sister who believed such a foolish lie."

Even after discovering that they would not be allowed to freeze their sperm in advance of sterilization, Astrid pushed on, fulfilling every requirement as fast as she could. She had a goal and she headed for it as if every roadblock—including sterilization—was just another dead planet on the way to a brighter star. Astrid always said self-expansion was in her nature. So changing her body is just one more way. When Steig freaked out over admitting to a mental illness, Astrid insisted, "Steig, before the possibility of SRS, *that's* when I felt I had 'a gender disorder.' Not today. What was I then? A pill-popping, rusted-out soul, whose life was sinking in front of her? So no thank you. I'd much rather tell them any lie they want to hear. I know my truth."

If only Steig—waiting here tonight under the flickering lights of the hospital corridors—had a thimble of Astrid's clarity. And *that's* the constant theme of Steig's interior monologue: Why isn't he as sure as Astrid about changing his body into a woman's?

* * *

Long before aerobic classes become the rage, Joe Jackson understands how to get his team into shape for victory. As far as he's concerned, it's simple: his sons are athletes as well as musicians. And as such they must work out everyday. What's more, being the first young black superstar teen idols, they have to work harder and longer than anyone else.

Although I'm not allowed to sit through a complete rehearsal, over time, I do get to peek in now and then. Watching Michael is the most exhausting because somewhere along the line you notice you're not breathing. He's bewitching. All that hunger, ambition, and anger, firing through his muscles like premium fuel. Everything is magically absorbed into whatever character he's creating in his head as he dances past race, sexuality, and gender.

In 10 years when MJ debuts his "Moonwalk" in front of millions of TV viewers on *Motown 25*, I will be among the lucky few who aren't astonished. For even now, I know he's soaking up other artists' dance routines and maneuvers. He told me recently that James Brown is giving him tips on the best way to throw a microphone in the air and catch it without missing a beat. In the case of the Moonwalk, Shalamar's Jeffrey Daniel teaches the step to Michael three years before he performs it live on television. But, oh, the practicing MJ does! Sometimes all night. And, of course, once MJ executes a step or gesture, it takes on stellar dimensions with his charismatic footprints all over it forever! Sporting a nasty scowl or a sweet smile, his non-conformist presence and androgynous moves are dancing him through new territory with no guides. He is literally that point in time and space when something new is born.

Today Michael and Jackie greet me like someone they're beginning to trust. Using a rehearsal break to talk with me, Jackie hugs me as usual; Michael does not—as usual. But he does smile. That's big. We pull up some folding chairs and sit together. Jackie starts off first, making sure the conversation swerves quickly into the brothers' upcoming solo albums.

I have felt a certain uneasiness of late from the other Jackson brothers over Michael doing a solo album, even though all the Jacksons are recording separate album projects. Could they be worried that MJ's LP will be a hit, and he will leave them? Dare I ask about that? I decide to go for it.

"Do these solo albums mean you won't be the J-5 anymore?"

"No, no, we're still gonna' be the Jackson 5," Michael pleads. I look up at him quizzically. *Why is he so defensive?* Remembering our recent conversation about his solo LP, and his unbound excitement, today's words seem tailored for Jackie's ears. I don't want to single him out in our conversation, but he played me two tracks, and it's obvious he is building something special. Michael is a musician working like an artist, painting new pictures on a blank canvas of silence. My question is what's going to happen to him and his brothers when that canvas gets exhibited, and the world sees it?

"Yeah, man, *we* are the main focus, the five of us, forever," Jackie jumps in, protectively. I watch his jaw muscles dance out a worried rhythm and try to think of some easy subjects that might release us from the tension I've caused. But when I glance at Jackie again, his normally radiant face has gone from worrying to glowering, like a shadow falling across the sun. Obviously, my question hit a bigger target than I was aiming for. In fact, it's gone straight into an open wound. Again, there you go, the double-edged "hard questions!" If I don't ask them, I have no chance at unearthing anything worth writing or reading. Fickle teenagers across America will want to know if Michael is leaving the J-5. They'll cry and complain, go off their rockers and write looney letters, but they'll buy the magazine and octopus onto every detail. So, I must poke into their beeswax!

On the other hand, I feel the interview losing air pressure, and have to revive it; I decide to obscure the tension with an abrupt subject change:

"I'm going to prison," I say casually.

"What!?" they both exclaim.

"Yeah, me and B.B. King are going to Chino Prison. Wanna come?"

"No way," Michael says, still unsure whether or not I'm kidding.

"Uh, no, no, me neither," Jackie laughs. Michael points toward the rehearsal room door, indicating he's gotta go; but doesn't. He is interested, and starts stretching instead.

"B.B. is doing a concert there and recording the whole thing for an album," I continue, relieved that they're both listening. "I might learn some interesting things about prisons. You might too."

"Oh, yeah?" Michael challenges, his voice cracking with hormones; but then softly, "Like what?"

"For one thing, nearly the entire Chino prison population is black," I say, repeating things I've been studying.

Jackie sits down next to me again. "Yeah, I heard that too," he agrees, looking aghast.

"So," I keep going, "I'm going to take some pictures for the magazine. Do you want to see them?"

"Yeah, I do. That would be cool." he says.

"B.B. King is cool," Michael echoes.

I continue pressuring them to join me on the trip. Michael tells me there's no way he can go. "They'd never let me," he says. I don't know who "they" are, but I stop while I'm ahead with him. Jackie is older and starting to flex his decision-making muscles, but he too signals that taking a road trip with a journalist would cause more trouble than he's willing to take on. I promise that our relationship during the trip won't be that of journalist/subject, and that no one but B.B.'s team has to know he's there. Then Jackie mumbles something about talking to Motown's public relations head about the idea, so I back off immediately. If Motown's PR still thinks I'm sleeping with Joe to get these interviews, then they're not active members of my journalism fan club.

So I drop it, and that seems to lift a curtain. We talk easily for another half hour about various unsolved predicaments before someone comes out of the rehearsal hall to get the guys. Then, I drive home thinking about my own unresolved dilemmas:

Like, what is the learnable lesson I can take away from falling in love with a girl I've known on and off since my late teens but barely noticed until, well, wham! It was the summer of '66 between my graduation from U.C. Berkeley and my cross-country journey to New York City to "begin my adult life." And there she was at my parent's front door: Striking, leggy tall, with thick ebony hair and sun-drenched-olive skin that didn't quite agree with her wintry blue eyes. She was artistic, bright, talented, and gregarious. Her family lived in the neighborhood, and she told me that as a kid she'd hidden more than once under our grand piano while I practiced or performed in recitals. The point of her visit that day was to let me know she'd heard that I was now writing my own songs and singing them with a guitar. And Kim felt confident she could bring something to this: "Why don't we jam together?" she suggested simply.

We did and our voices were meant for each other. Unfortunately, the rest of our molecules had problems. During the course of the summer we tried a few open-mike sessions at the Troubadour in West Hollywood and sang at parties for friends and family; but soon it was fall and I resumed my plans to move east. Two nights before my flight, I heard from her mother that Kim had tried to kill herself. She was in a psychiatric ward and had asked if I would visit her. Could I do that?

I said I could. Despite everything I needed to do before leaving town, all my plans seemed to fall away from me with that news. I had to know she was okay. I remember my hands trembling on the steering wheel of my folks' car as I drove into the night, leaving Mom and Dad puzzled at what would cause such a frantic pull on me at that hour. When I saw Kim in a community hospital room, she smiled one of her dazzling smiles, and assured me it was all a mistake: too many sleeping pills taken by accident. All she wanted to do was talk about New York and visiting me. I was confused and afraid, but I was also wildly captivated by her.

Before leaving, I easily agreed to a visit. That seemed to hold the separation crisis at bay for us both, certainly for me. And she did make at least one Manhattan trek, though I can't remember much about it. I don't think it went that well, however, as the outstanding image etched into my hard drive still alarms me: It's me coming home from my magazine work one night to my apartment on Bleeker and MacDougal where I found my friend Bonnie planted firmly in a chair, sharing her chaotic private life with Kim, who was sitting numbly in the center of my bed with a blanket over her head. Now, how could that have been good?

Frankly, my years in New York were so massive with people and work adventures, Kim was nowhere in sight; so time and a constant commotion kept her hidden from my heart. When I did return to Los Angeles, I arrived with my new magazine skill set. Although I was still running from pillar to post with my guitar and songs, now I was a professional magazine editor with a great new way to earn money while I pursued music. All I needed was a place to live.

"Live with me!" Kim said in early 1971, offering to share her one-bedroom apartment at Venice beach. The rent would be cheap. She'd take the living room and I would get her old bedroom all to myself. What a generous deal! I jumped at it without thinking; instantly setting fire to my life.

* * *

"Why don't you stay in my apartment for a while," Steig asks a pain-ridden Astrid [aka Gunnar Skarsgård] two weeks after her SRS. "I can care for you there. It is too hard on me running over here all the time."

"Ja, that would be wonderful," Astrid answers, trying not to grimace as she swallows another dose of pain meds. The all-inclusive procedure—especially in these early years—is substantial and traumatic, requiring a long, agonizing recovery period.

"But are you sure you want this silly girl in your home, in such sad, sad shape?" Astrid questions coquettishly. "Once I'm there, you may not be able to get me out."

"I can handle it—you, I mean." Steig smiles valiantly. Besides, it's a good way for me to get to know what's going to happen to my body soon enough, don't you agree?"

Astrid stares at her splendid friend, the one she needs and idolizes more than ever now. "I hope so, Steig," she says with an unexpected onslaught of emotion. These incendiary hormones she's been taking for a year make her wonder how "natural born" women can get through a day. A cacophony of swinging moods now rule her life.

"Steig, I just don't want to discourage your future plans with my childish handling of the recovery. You will do better. You are so much stronger than I am."

"Oh, no, Astrid. To me, you are the brave one. You are my hero."

"Heroine! Please."

"Ja, ja, heroine." Steig says, slapping his forehead and laughing at the glacial progress he's making with gender speak. They enjoy this light moment until, without much warning, Astrid begins sighing her way into a new disposition. Every flickering thought that zips through Astrid's brain, now appears on her face a second later.

"Yes? What?"

"Do you have a name yet?" Astrid asks, vexed. This is an ongoing point of contention between the two of them. Although Steig is seeing a doctor and has started taking a small amount of hormones, he seems unable to think about any female names. Everyday Astrid introduces two or three that Steig dismisses immediately. They have ridiculous disagreements that Steig tries to squelch by insisting he will know his name when he can see himself clearly in the mirror as a woman.

"But a name might help that happen," Astrid argues, ignoring his point.

Steig shakes his head at her. Astrid's new love of long flowing conversations is such a change from her past thread-bare, three-grunt, exchanges. Steig is often yanked out of their discussions completely just thinking about the difference.

"Astrid, I believe you have stepped into the high heels of a one-note nag with this name thing!" he laughs, amused with his pun. "You must stop or you will drive me away. Actually that's a good thought! I am going out for a walk."

"Oh? Running from me? Good, but first, tell me who do you see in the mirror these days, Steig?" Astrid calls after Steig, following him to the front door as he puts on his coat. "With your wavy blonde hair getting longer every day, you are getting to be quite a beautiful man in the mirror, ja?" Astrid laughs. Then wincing from another sharp groin pain, she adds: "And, I believe that no Romeo should be prettier than his Juliet! Oh, Steig—*Juliet!* What about 'Juliet' as a name?"

* * *

Waking up with Chris in his father's bed on a workday would be strange enough. Pernell is out of town, and although I set an alarm for myself, what awakens me are two odors: Coffee and pot.

"Hi!" Chris says, standing naked at the bedroom balcony door, with a joint in one hand and a big coffee mug in the other. It's 8 a.m.

"High, indeed," I say, trying to sound casual. "Isn't it a little early for that?"

"No, not at all. Don't you ever go to work stoned?" he asks innocently.

"Oh, geez, no. I can barely get things done stone sober."

"Maybe that's the problem," he smiles seductively, sliding into bed next to me with the joint and coffee. "Here, indulge."

"No, no, really, I can't," I say, sounding like somebody's stuffy old aunt. He seems so free and I feel so rigid. I hate that. Isn't that why I'm seeing him: to escape all the grown-up stuff I can't figure my way out of? I let out a sigh in spite of myself.

He senses my resolve disintegrating. "Judy, you work too hard on the magazines," he begins. "You're so diligent. Whenever I come into your office, you and Bill *[art director]* have so much going on. You need to step back a little."

"Chris, I know, but that *[indicating joint]* is what I do at the end of the day to unwind, like a drink; not before breakfast."

"Why?"

"Why? Well, because... Shit! I don't know why." (He had me at "Judy, you work too hard on the magazines.") So, I whip the joint away from him and take a new step with marijuana—alas, one that doesn't happen but once, because experiencing work ripped is way more than I can handle. At breakfast, where we finish up most everything in Pernell's kitchen, the pot affords me a more intimate glimpse into a side of Chris that is both tender and vulnerable. I hear hurtful things I don't understand at all that will one day lead him to a drug overdose, subsequent minor brain damage, and a way-too-early death in a motorcycle accident.

"Ya know," he begins, downing another bowl of granola, nuts, and fruit, "Lara was *my* girlfriend before she was Dad's."

"What?!" I erupt through a mouthful of toast.

"Yeah," he says, his rustic eyes moist at the memory. "I brought her home to meet dad, and after a little while, they just kinda fell in love."

"Oh, Chris! How lousy for you." I stop eating for a second and grab his bear-like self in a whopping hug.

"Wait!" I pull back suddenly, very stoned. "Is that true?" I start laughing inappropriately.

"Of course it is!" he shouts me to a halt, obviously hurt. "Do you think I would make something like *that* up?"

"No, no, no," I try to fix. "It's just...I hoped you were joking with me."

"No," his voice drops to a whisper, "She liked me but she wasn't in love with me—just like you."

I try to catch my breath. "Chrissss, come on!" I scramble defensively. "We only just started to date."

He turns my face towards his. *This is any stoned person's nightmare! Unmitigated confrontation while you're totally hammered.* "I just hope it doesn't happen again with you." he says pathetically.

"What?! Me? Chris...Listen..." I'm relieved. *This* truth I can handle: "Chris, there is no way in hell that I'm ever going to flirt with or date or marry your father. That happened to you once, and obviously it was traumatic. I know it must have shaken you to the core. But maybe...maybe, they fell in love because they were supposed to. You know what I mean? I'm saying people meet people in all kinds of ways."

An hour later, I am at the Laufer Company, listening to Bill Royce (whom I hired to replace myself as Managing Editor of *Rona Barrett's Hollywood* when I became Editor of *Right On!*). Bill is announcing himself, as always, by yodeling in the hallways. Bill will go on to be a cracker-jack editor for Rona's magazine, as well as a successful producer of Jay Leno's late night show for years. But right now, he's yodeling. On a regular day the sound is merely earth shattering. It's loud, piercing, meant for dogs, a great stress outlet for Bill, and good distraction for the rest of us. Unfortunately, today, with every sight and sound amped up way too high for me, I think Heidi is coming down from the Alps.

"Shit! What was that?" I run to my doorway covering my ears.

Kenny, the company photographer, pokes his head out of the darkroom with his typical response: "I hear nothing. I in darkroom."

Cragun looks at me confused. "What's the matter with you? It's Royce yodeling." He squints, and approaches me slowly. "You stoned?"

"Nooooooo..." I lie.

"You sure are!" he laughs. "Your eyes are red."

"Noooooo..." I sing out again, then, "They are?"

"Yeah, really. Here, let me give you some eye drops before Laufer sees you. Good for you, girl. Got any for me?"

"Noooooo...Bill, please. Shhh..."

Cragun's wife, Lynn, passes by my office and Bill runs out to join her and spread my sordid news. A minute later Lynn is back in my office with a cup of steaming black coffee and some eye drops. She smiles knowingly and leaves them on my desk.

By 6:30 p.m. I'm cold sober. Gathering up my stuff, I head for the lobby wondering why Chris never came by during the day to check on me. I'm not upset, just curious. I definitely don't want to see him every night. Tonight, for example, I want to get out of here and catch up on my Venice Beach life. But when I enter the lobby, I look up just in time to see Chris leaning over the receptionist's desk, whispering in her ear, flirting like his life depends on it. I'm so startled I just stand there staring. After a minute or so, he senses someone watching him, turns to see me, and jumps away from her like she bit him.

"Hey! Judy! Judy! Judy!" he blurts stupidly at me.

I'm so embarrassed. At the same time I feel like I want to burst into tears, like something ancient is hurting me all over again. I don't know what it is, but it's gotta be bigger than this ridiculous scenario. I walk with as much decorum as I can muster past Chris and the chagrined receptionist. She knows something's wrong, but can't figure out what. Calling out "goodnight" to me as usual, I find I can't respond. Suddenly she's way too pretty.

It seems to take hours to cross the lobby, but finally I walk out into the main hallway where I wait for the elevator. Damn. What an ass I am. Buying into all Chris' achingly intense looks and big emotions. Actually starting to feel guilty that I won't be able to match his passion, or that I might be the cause of more self-esteem issues for him after Lara. Truth is, I'm the one whose heart is breaking down my confidence. In the topsy-turvy sea of desire, I've fallen overboard. And neither my first woman nor my last man are reeling me in.

Riding down the office elevator to the garage where my little cocoa VW is parked, usually takes about a minute. But tonight, after the surprise "jealousy event" with Chris, it takes forever—or at least long enough to trigger a poop-load of memories that I've been pushing down for a year. Oh, the wonders of pot:

Living with Kim in Venice had gone from *ni*-ce to *ni*-ghtmare in the flip of a mind. The electricity between us was palatable. I felt a world of mixed messages flowing through my blood 24-hours a day. Our way-too-small place was a petri dish for shifting possibilities, always vanishing before any real physical engagement could prevail. Soon a chilly wind fell over the warm feelings I called love.

Neither one of us really wanted to cook meals or do much about straightening the apartment. I was probably worse than she, but our escalating ambivalence led to my disinterest in playing house in any fashion, particularly cleanup. At best we'd point to dirty dishes and announce whose turn it was, but that was about it.

Although I had the occasional male date, Kim was in an on-again off-again relationship with a guy who tended bar and would come over late at night. The walls were made of tissue, so their sexual encounters were impossible to escape. I felt trapped and constantly confronted with the part of her life I could not have.

Obviously, unable to make the apartment a home, our percolating anger over all the unexamined expectations we had of each other, led us to petty but hurtful arguments. After about six months, I found a place in Santa Monica that I hated but relished because I could escape my feelings, and moved out of Venice. This didn't last for long, however. Nothing lasted very long with Kim. Within a month she called with "great news." She'd found a magical, if small, one-bedroom apartment for me right across the alley from hers. I never hesitated. I couldn't wait to get back to Venice, and told myself the separate apartments would give us just the boundaries we needed.

They did not. From my perspective, we got more and more intense and passionate until one day, lying on the beach, attempting an intellectual discussion (my consummate downfall!) on Germaine Greer's lesbian riff in *The Female Eunuch*, something snapped. I don't remember exactly, but I think Greer's thoughts were something like, "go on, try it." To my rapture and amazement, Kim said, "Should we?"

That night, we did.

The elevator and I continue our leisurely journey downward to my car. The memory ends precipitately—just as the actual sexual event did. You see, the very next day, while I was still lying in bed inhaling fragile particles of new information about myself, Kim came over with three pieces of bad news:

1. The man she'd been sleeping with told her he had a venereal disease, so we would need to rush to the Venice Free Clinic and get a round of antibiotics.

2. During a standing appointment with her shrink earlier that morning, she talked about us sleeping together. Her shrink responded with, "Why did you do that?" which, naturally, threw Kim into a manic dilemma. And...

3. Her mother called to invite us both to dinner that night. The answer should have been, "no," but instead, there we sat at the dinner table in a swirl of messy moods, unable to eat. Her father, in particular, kept squinting at us suspiciously when we refused to partake in an expensive bottle of wine he'd bought for the evening. We decided against explaining that we couldn't drink alcohol because we were taking antibiotics, since he was a doctor and would understandably press on with some questions.

All of this was within just 24 hours of touching her. So, pardon me and any fantasies I had of an affair so intense it would wash away the rest of the world long enough to discover how I felt about these new yearnings. That wish went south fast.

Oh, shoot! I got off the elevator on the wrong floor. The vivid memory of Kim gradually losing her mind in the weeks after our sexual encounter, literally drives me out of the elevator too early. It's as if I believe the memories live in that tiny cabin on cables, and not in my head. Thus, I stand like a dolt in the lobby of a floor I've never seen before. And while waiting for the damn thing to come back up, I continue to reach into a part of my soul I never wanted to see again:

There I can hear my friend Marilyn's troubled voice clawing at my denial system after spending only 20 minutes with Kim one afternoon: "Judy, what are you doing about this? She's going crazy in front of you." But the mind won't accept what it won't accept. And mine got very creative at inventing reasons for Kim's more and more bizarre behavior. The fact that she was most certainly going bonkers—and I saw only stress—tells you more about me than her. Then one night she disappeared.

Going over to "the other side" is a very private journey. I speak of Kim's only because she so clearly took a part of me with her: Her mother called me frantic. Kim had "experienced a full psychotic break" that afternoon. After her doctor appointment, her psychiatrist and parents decided to install Kim in her parent's home while they came up with a hospital plan. Unfortunately, sometime earlier in evening, they weren't looking and Kim vanished. There was no trace of her anywhere. The police had been informed and were waiting the appropriate amount of time before investigating; but there was little doubt in the voice of the distraught matriarch calling me that her daughter was in physical and emotional danger.

"Wasn't anyone watching her?" I accused.

"Kim felt an enormous amount of pressure from *you*!" her mother blamed back. Her words—discharged out of fear—detonated my guilt. Her tone implied I'd squished a kitten with my perverted heart, and I believed her completely.

"It's all my fault?" I yelped, stunned, and began crying uncontrollably.

"I'll get back to you when we hear something," she sobbed as well, and hung up.

I couldn't stay still. *My feelings are lethal weapons.* I thought. I've killed the woman I love! So I grabbed a bag and ran to Bill and Lynn Cragun's apartment, a few blocks away. That entire, endless night, we sat together in their living room talking ourselves to death over what could possibly have gone wrong. Like me, the Craguns had spent time with Kim over the past weeks, watching her cling desperately to the lip of sanity, reaching around us for a foothold. They were more than up to speed. But by 6 a.m., I'd had enough. Words weren't helping. I knew I had to go back to my Venice place; I just didn't know why.

"Are you going up or down?" a man in a grey suit asks me, holding the elevator door open from inside. Since it's now going up, and I missed my ride to the garage again, I smile like a person who's all there, and say, "Going down." I rub my head vigorously, hoping the sudden circulation to my brain will derail this nightmare junket through my first gay love affair.

Instead, still waiting in this strange lobby, I continue remembering with distinct clarity what happened when I opened the front door to my apartment: Instantly I saw that someone had been storming about in a cape of madness, leaving bone-deep, indelible signs of suffering everywhere. Kim had broken in sometime during the night and, in her mania, gone through every inch of the place, upending possessions and leaving me cryptic messages I could not fathom. There were mysterious piles of odds and ends, meant to narrate something urgent; there were missing photographs off my wall from which I—in my own growing instability—tried to decipher clues of her whereabouts. For example, a large black & white photo that I took of footprints in the sand was gone. *Ah, ha,* I thought. *She's letting me know that's where she is: on the beach!* Of course, it was only my imagination coughing up encouraging scenarios to drive the gargoyles back to the unlit corners of my mind: *I was just loving her. I didn't know that meant pressure. Is this what happens when you love someone of the same sex? Did I unwittingly mess with her darkness, and now I've gotten it all over myself? I'm so sorry, Kim.*

"She was n-a-a-a-ked, naked," my next-door neighbor stuttered through my broken back window at me, later that day. Apparently, he had looked out his bedroom window at 5:30 AM. that morning because he heard breaking glass at my backdoor. There he watched "a beautiful dark-haired girl take off all her clothes, fold them neatly, put her hand through the broken window very cautiously, and turn the door knob. She just walked right in like that," he concluded, without his red face color ever returning to normal.

"I didn't really need to hear that," Kim's mother sighed heavily at me. But I was determined we both share any information we uncovered about Kim's whereabouts. "So I shouldn't have told you?" Another sigh. "Yes, of course."

As the days went by, chances of finding Kim alive passed with them. A close friend of her family's took up residence in my apartment and brought me great comfort by relating a more accurate history of Kim's past emotional strife. As a result, at least intellectually if not in my heart, I felt less responsible for the current situation. The new information also made me feel even more in awe of Kim for her courage and endurance in the shadow of this lurking Lucifer all these years.

"You know, Judy," the friend whispered hoarsely one morning over coffee, "we have to face the fact that Kim may die out there."

At last, the elevator finds me stranded on the wrong floor, and I step in. Only three more stops and I'll be in my car. But lucky me, standing in the middle of the group of people in the descending cab is Chuck Laufer himself. In my state, I'm just relieved I recognize him. Maybe he'll snub me.

"Judy, I was gonna call you in," he begins enthusiastically. "I want us to start signing and building our own teen stars!" his voice gusts past the other occupants to me with surprising chutzpah. Chuck isn't in the habit of making company plans in public places. So, when he continues in front of at least four strangers, telling me how he wants to find good-looking young guys, sign them to contracts, and put them in the magazines, (because we make these kids into big stars in our teen books, so, why shouldn't we be reaping the profits?), I'm quite surprised—and particularly love the "we" part, as if I'm going to share in this gigantic profit-making scheme. Although I never say one word to him, when we get into our cars on the garage level, Chuck yells to me how good it was to talk to me, and that I shouldn't forget to think about signing some black ones too!

What a boss. What a job. And, hey, I'm lucky to have it and him, really. It's the very job I'm doing, sitting at my desk, when I finally get the call from Kim's mother. She is crying and laughing at the same time, so I know my life can resume:

"They found her! They found Kim! She's alive, weak, but alive." After we both weep a long time, she tells me, "I'm so sorry, Judy. I love you. And I know how much you love Kim."

※ ※ ※

"My name is Tilda," Steig says to Astrid.

"Ohhh, wonderful! Finally! Tilda? Ja, that's so beautiful..."

"But wait—Astrid, stay sitting down. Listen to me: We must talk. I don't want to do it," Tilda says as gently as she can. "I don't need to do it."

Astrid stares blankly at Tilda.

"I am going to be fine this way, Astrid, in this body, just the way I am," she continues in the same practiced, calm tone.

Astrid's skin moves a little; she pushes her long locks away from her ears, as if the hair might be twisting Tilda's words into something she doesn't want to hear. "What do you mean you 'don't need to do it?' What are you talking about?"

"The operation, Astrid, I'm not going to have it."

"Vad!" Astrid cries out, although she can hear Tilda clearly and understands her meaning perfectly. The cry is one of panic and betrayal. All these years of dreaming and planning together about their sex change.

"How can you do this?" she yells. "How can you do this *to me*? How can you leave me here this way?" she begins to sob frantically.

"Astrid, please, please," Tilda tries to soothe, but Astrid has disappeared into her anguish. Her face is warped with despair. As she stumbles about aimlessly crying and accusing, Tilda sits stone-faced until she hears her friend finally leave the room with one last "Traitor!"

In the sudden, welcome silence, Tilda looks around the charming apartment that they've put together, as if she's never seen it before. Everything is the way Astrid wished it to be. While her health stabilized, the two of them spent weeks searching out the "perfect place for a new woman" to start fresh in Stockholm. It was Tilda who found the place and at just the right price, naturally. She even put down the security money—a gift, she told Astrid, for her tenacity about the life she always knew she wanted, in the body she now has. Yet all through it, Tilda remained taunted by her own puzzling circumstances—so similar to Astrid's, but craving a different solution.

Finally, last week, everything changed. First came the name: Tilda. After that, she started to feel different in small but vital ways. Certainly starting hormones has helped, but it was something else, something she read that finally released her from her marooned state. It was a tiny paragraph in a research journal article about transsexuals that she unearthed while haunting the local science libraries for scraps of information. This one she found enthralling. This one could have been written just for her. Tilda didn't have to know why. Her strong feelings told her that this information, and her reaction to it, held the key to her own private journey. The information helped Tilda see something with clarity:

She saw her own fog, yes, but for the first time, she saw the reason for it. Her numbness has been here to protect her from doing something that's not right *for her*. Her ambivalence has been a barrier, ja, but a barrier with a purpose. And now that she understands its purpose, well, aren't barriers meant to be knocked down? The tiny paragraph in the journal read:

> "Transsexuals have a 'deviation' that affects their brain development during infancy. The brains of men and women are different anatomically, and those who change sex have been shown to have the same brain anatomy as those born into the sex that the transsexuals change to."

Tilda read it over and over again. Although she did not think there was anything "deviant" about her brain, she realized that whether or not she had the operation to change her body, her brain was already a woman's. She'd been born Tilda all along. Damn, all those years ago, she was in the right line during that school outing, after all.

* * *

Frustrated with both Kim and Chris, I decide I am finally ready for a long-overdue visit to New York. It will be my first since fleeing my life there over a year ago. So I make arrangements to spend my Christmas vacation in the Big Apple, and let my Laufer coworkers know at the last minute. My parents are worried, concerned I'll get swept back into that "Manhattan madness" again; but I know better. It wasn't the city. If I belly-flopped there, I can belly-flop anywhere. It was me. I wasn't ready. I was looking outside myself to connect, instead of working harder to connect with my craft. So, unfortunately, I found what I was looking for: a slew of pretentious men unable to define themselves apart from seducing or sabotaging gullible young women, like me. Yes, it sounds like I'm toasting myself with a glass of sour grapes, but honestly, I'm the hardest on myself. Sometimes my skin feels so thin, its like a cobweb catching even the slightest whiff of negativity about me. All I know is it must stop. Nobody making a difference in this world can do it while giving a shit about all this.

It's an icy winter day when I step onto a stoop on East 72nd Street, where my friend Stephen is now living with a doctor whose claim to fame is that he used to be Maria Callas' physician. It must be so because there are posters and framed photos of the two of them in the apartment. But be that as it may, as far as I can tell, right now Dr. P. specializes in giving "Vitamin B" energy shots to half the Upper East Side. Although he and Stephen don't seem to be lovers, or at least not now, they are both incredibly generous hosts and put me up for weeks.

Naturally, now that I'm here, I realize how deeply I've missed the city. My sense of failure would not let me feel the towering love I've always had for this place that is, truly, nothing short of a masterpiece. And so, ignoring the occasional melancholy undertow from my last NYC life, I meet with Bonnie, dine with Marilyn, go to the theater with Roy, and spend several romantic nights with Dan. Because I tell Dan all about Kim, he is finally able to be fearlessly intimate with me and share feelings even he's surprised to have.

One snowy evening Dan gets a phone call from a friend of his, Joe, who knows a young folksinger living on a farm in Pennsylvania. Dan is very excited about this call because Joe has secured an invitation for the three of us to come for a weekend visit. Although I don't really want to leave the city, Dan is uncharacteristically intent on having me spend time with this up-and-coming singer-songwriter, so I agree. The following Friday we drive together, first to Camden, New Jersey to pick up Joe, and then all of us to Lyndell, Pennsylvania. On the trip, Dan sheds more light on his motives:

"I think you and Jim will really hit it off," he says, referring to the still unknown Jim Croce, that we're driving through this beautiful wintry countryside to visit. According to Dan, his friend Joe put Jim and his back-up guitarist, Maury Muehleisen, together several years ago. "The strange thing is, Jim used to be Maury's back-up guitarist when they toured," Dan explains, "but now they've traded places."

In fact, Jim is a dark and comic contradiction. He and his wife, Ingrid, welcome all kinds of musical characters into their cozy living room—which is tiny but bigger than a breadbox. I spend the first night sleeping on the kitchen floor, listening to Jim talk nonstop—the result of something he swallowed after dinner that no already-wired personality really needs. But, true to Dan's prediction, by the second evening, Jim and I are huddled in a corner swapping songs and trying out ideas. When he hears my tune about Dan ("Everytime"), he asks to put it on tape for a future album. The producing team of Terry Cashman and Tommy West, who've already produced an album for Maury, have just finished recording Jim's first album for ABC Records. Watching Jim try to cope with his mounting anxieties over the album's debut in two months, is like watching a man pretty much destroy all the peace that surrounds him. His 5-month old son, Adrian James—for whom Jim wrote "Time In A Bottle"—is an exciting new addition to the family. But the tug between his home life, that so obviously holds him together, and the essential, upcoming road life his new career requires, is causing a whole lotta stress.

Four months later, standing in line with Chris at a local Hollywood cafeteria on my lunch break, I recognize the singer and song coming over the radio. It's Jim singing one of his first singles, "Operator." Out of all the music he played me that night on the farm, this one is my favorite. It's so clever, beautiful, and heartbreaking. He told me he thought of the idea in the army when he watched solders call home. "A lot of the time, a guy would make a call to the girlfriend he left behind, and find out she wasn't waiting for him any longer." As usual, the material was incredibly sensitive, just like Jim.

We stay in touch and I see Jim backstage and in hotel rooms whenever he performs on the West Coast. Whereas he is always a captivating and funny performer, I have to say, off stage he never seems all that happy. He appears exhausted and moody, surrounded by back-slappers and fans he hardly knows. Especially standing next to Maury—who literally shines with sweetness and outgoing charm—Jim's dark side appears to be winning his war.

The last time I see him, Jim tells me he has made a rough tape of himself singing my song and that he'll send it to me when he gets back home. Unfortunately, before this happens, Dan hears from Ingrid that Jim needs a break from touring because he's homesick and wants to spend more time with her and Adrian. In an effort to speed things up between shows, Jim stops flying commercial airlines and uses small twin-engine aircrafts to get from gig to gig. One night, a little Beechcraft that he and Maury charter for one of his concerts, never makes it past the runway. It doesn't quite reach the altitude it needs, and crashes into a pecan tree killing all six people on board. Naturally it's shocking and devastating for his family and friends, but in that unpredictable way that the world can react to things, public interest in Jim's music goes bananas, sending many of his songs, including "I got A Name" and "I'll Have to Say I Love You in A Song," to the top of the charts and into several film scores. A small but kind compensation.

In the confines of my Venice apartment, I take out my guitar and play along with some Croce ballads on my tape deck. Although I don't yet know it, Ingrid will soon contact me about getting together to write with her and to take a look at Jim's catalogue, which she now manages in San Diego where she and Adrian James (A.J.) are currently living. Here in Venice, Jim's truck driver characters and macho highway men seem extremely far away—as does the distant yet familiar drumming on my front door. Only when I turn off the tape, do I realize it's Kim and we had a date...

"Tell me what happened with Michael Jackson," Kim says, laying back on one of two huge beanbag pillows Ann sewed for me when I first moved into my apartment. I look over at her, feeling the usual ache of excitement and disappointment simultaneously, the quintessential start-stop experience. It's not her fault. She's just being Kim. And I just want her to be different, "to want what I want," as the Sondheim song says.

Sitting across from her on the other pillow, sipping wine and jawing superficially about the Jackson brothers, I notice a familiar feeling. I'm starting to slip backwards in time, like I did in the elevator last week. When I see her, it's so obvious our relationship was never really cleared for a landing. It certainly wasn't cleared for a takeoff, either. So now, chafing against each other on a weekly basis, trying to sort things out and find equilibrium—especially when there are no scales to measure different needs—it's pretty hopeless.

"What the matter with you?" Kim abruptly asks.

"What do you mean?" I ask, casually. She bursts out laughing.

"No, wait," I try to laugh along with her. "I mean, I was thinking about something else, yeah, but..." My words dive hopelessly under her laughter like a baseline.

"You should have seen yourself. Where did you go? You looked so lost."

I feel a little panicked. What am I going to tell her? I have to think first.

"Is this about that guy you're seeing at work?" she pokes.

"Are you starting to like him?" Her face reddens a little. *Does she care? Is she jealous? relieved?*

"Who? Chris? No, I wasn't thinking about him; but yes, I do like him; 'though he doesn't know whom he likes." I stutter about, unorganized.

"What then?" she howls, untethering her laughter at me. "Are you loaded? I know you haven't dropped LSD since you tried to flush me out of your system. Remember that? I had to come pull you out of the ocean where you stood sobbing for hours and hours..."

"Jesus, Kim," I hiss at her, shocked to be tackled with that memory.

She lets her slightly manic mood run down a little, and we stare at each other like children.

"Okay, so what is happening?" she asks, warmly. "What were you thinking about?"

"I suppose I was remembering the morning after we became lovers," I betray myself pathetically. My words hang around the living room along with the gold light from the afternoon sun. I can see it fading now out my windows. Earlier in the day, the sky was convulsive with rain; but after Kim came over, it emerged into brilliant sunlight. Go figure.

"Ohhhh," she whispers, all amusement gone. "I remember that, of course. What about it are you remembering?"

"I think about it all the time," I say watching my hands twist the shit out of a rubber band. "I sometimes think it would be better not to see you..."

She eyes me carefully. "You know I love you. You are not alone. I understand why you feel like I betrayed you, like I left you stranded. But I do love..."

"Stop! Please! Not this discussion again. Let's not start our compulsive loop: 'I am gay. You're not gay. Blah, blah, blah...'"

"Aww, wait, it's not so black and white."

"Yeah, Kim, it's pretty elementary for me. This part is not something I want to continue chewing on with you because, honestly, your love doesn't help me," I writhe on.

"Judy, I'm just saying I see things more fluidly."

"Shut up! Dear God! *No one knows what that means.*" I let loose at her, flapping my arms like she's a plane heading for the wrong airport. But my histrionics only continue to entertain her until, finally, I too see myself as something absurd. The usual haranguing that's plagued our friendship ever since *that* night, can certainly use the trap door her light mood is providing this afternoon. The utter madness of one sexual experience discharging two people on such incompatible journeys is brain-crushing. Not getting whatever she needed from me after that night was at least one catalyst for her break last fall; while I spent the year in my own bat-shit-crazy state, believing—despite concrete evidence to the contrary—that I'd driven her mad with my unruly, arduous yearnings. *Shakespearean, really!*

Kim rolls sideways, holding her abdomen and sucking in her breath. "When are you going to get real furniture in here?" she says staring at a large stain her wine glass left on the pillow.

"What are you inferring?" I say. "I should stop camping out in my own home? Grow up? Figure out the shape of my life?" I ask.

"Well, yeah." she says, sitting up taller to receive what sounds like my earnest, uncrotchety, postmortem of what went wrong.

I act as if I'm going to impart something profound, but say instead, "Okay, here's the dirt on Michael Jackson," and jump up for a rag to clean the wine stain.

※ ※ ※

4 On A Gender Bender

Tilda's been sitting alone in Astrid's living room for so long, she's beginning to feel like she's been installed there along with the decor. Finally, after listening to the neighborhood children being called in for dinner from the cobblestone streets below, a loud sniffling in the room breaks her concentration. She turns quickly to see Astrid, dramatically, but bravely, pulling herself together in the doorway. With a dab at her swollen eyes, and a wipe of her running nose, Astrid lifts herself stiffly into good posture, and softly whimpers, "Why, Tilda? Why would you do this now?"

"I'm not leaving you, Astrid, honestly." Tilda answers. "Like you, I am trying to remain consistent. You still feel the way you do about yourself, inside and out. But I've been lost. Your solution, the operation, is a good one…for you. But it's not what I want for myself."

"I don't understand!" Astrid steps all the way into the room. "Are you saying that you want to live this way, in the body of man while you feel like a woman? Should I call you Steig again?"

With great care, Tilda explains about the study she read and how it has opened her mind to the right solution for herself. Astrid listens, but remains confused.

"But then you are not a match. Your body and your brain, they do not match. Your body says you are a man, and your brain says you are a woman. Tilda, darling, Tilda! How can you live that way? It's my fault, I know it."

"What are you talking about?" Tilda says, annoyed. "This is not about you. This is about me. I know we started together on this journey, but there are some differences we must..."

"I was such a baby about the operation..." Astrid interrupts, not really hearing Tilda.

"Oh, no, no..."

"Ja, I drove you away from doing what you should do for yourself. Tilda, you must think more about this."

Tilda takes a breath. "Yes, I know. And I will. And if I change my mind, I can do something about it—but Astrid, you must think too. We can be different and be alike. Your intolerance of my choices is the hardest part for me, you know?"

This hits Astrid hard. She's intolerant? Suddenly she looks tired and depleted from their talk. "It feels like a step back to me, that's all..." she sighs.

"I don't want to alter my body to be what I already am inside. I can be happy this way, living as a woman, but without the operation."

"But you will dress like a woman, ja?" Astrid asks, meekly.

"Ja," Tilda says. "Absolutely."

"But your body does not need to change?"

"No, Astrid. I do not mind my body this way."

"Ohhhh, my," Astrid sighs, then cries some more; but this time the despair is gone. She feels her situation with Tilda stretching past the claustrophobic premise of "abandonment," as she so dramatically labeled it earlier. She stares at Tilda, and has to admit that she looks happy, maybe for the first time. Sitting together in this new tranquility, Astrid realizes that her own melodramas have kept her from seeing how unhappy Tilda has been. Today she definitely looks different. They remain quiet and peaceful until the evening chill reaches into the open windows and demands a different activity.

"Dinner?" Tilda suggests. The frosty winds of change have ruffled Astrid's freshly washed locks. She fusses with them for a minute before responding.

Then turning her head to see Tilda's face better, she sighs, "Yes, what shall we make?" and smiles. Not waiting for an answer, she heads hastily for the kitchen, turning only to add, "And I *will* be happy for you, Tilda. You'll see. I can change, well, *obviously*. But I mean my *attitude*."

4 On A Gender Bender

* * *

I am sitting in an unused make-up room at Magic Mountain waiting for the Supremes to come offstage and finish up their *Right On!* interviews with me. These past months my life has gotten voluminous. I've met someone new, a woman. She says she doesn't know if she's gay, but there's a big difference. She obviously loves women and me. A shrink I'll go to in the near future will tell me: "You'll pick a woman who is solid about being gay, when you are." Right now, however, we're happy with each other even if we're still struggling with the grand narrative of being lesbians.

The Supremes are struggling too. It's not a breezy time for them or Motown. Diana Ross has split for a solo career, and it's a Herculean job getting audiences to feel that old love about the new line-up. Hauling journalists like me to distressing venues like this one, is a pretty good idea.

Across from me this evening is the Supremes assistant, Hazel, who—although devoted to the group—has gotten just as tired and bored as I have after so many hours of interviewing and then waiting to interview again. The Supremes have two shows a night, and during the breaks, I talk to each member. Hazel and I have done the required spurts of chit-chat with each other about absolutely nothing, just to establish that we're both nice people who love our jobs. But now I'm determined to accomplish something for myself before my last interview with Jean Terrell, Diana's replacement; so, I drag out my steno pad filled with handwritten lyrics, and begin working. Hazel watches me as I write and cross out words for about 10 minutes before announcing: "I *knew* there was something different about you!"

At this time in my life I am so hyper-sensitive, I wait for her to follow up with, "Lesbian!" But thank the Girl Upstairs, that's not the train she's on.

"You're a songwriter, aren't you?" she says, pleased as a pickle with herself.

"I am," I answer cautiously.

Then I hear the words that will forever change my professional songwriting life:

"Got anything for the ladies?" Hazel asks.

The ladies? I don't answer at first. *Songs for the Supremes? Me?* I write pop-ish folk songs. At this time in my music evolution, I play Beethoven on the piano and strive to write like Dylan and Joni on the guitar. Yet something tells me that's not the answer she's looking for. While I sit there vacuously, Hazel mistakes my silence for something intriguing, and takes out a pad of her own.

"This is what I'd like to do," she says hurriedly, as applause signals an imminent burst of activity and hoopla from "the ladies." "I'd like to get your telephone number," Hazel says quickly. "The Supremes are going to be recording a new album and I'd like to tell their producer, Frank Wilson, about you."

"Oh, wow," I say through a gaping mouth.

"Do you have a tape of some songs you've written?" she continues. "I'll give you my address. Send me a tape, and I'll pass it on to Frank. Who knows, right?"

"Right...who knows?" I echo, scribbling my name and phone number on her pad.

"I think it's my turn," a glamorous Jean Terrell says, opening the door. I know I should be making over her in a big way right now. That's my job. Instead it takes everything in me not to push her out into the hallway so I can keep after Hazel for her address. Jean senses something. "You are Judy, right?"

"Yes, yes, yes!" I gallop at her abruptly, from one extreme to the other.

"Oh, good. I wonder, since we're finished with the shows, could I just take another 10 minutes of your time to remove some of this sweat and make-up?"

"Of course, take your time!" I tell her with too much enthusiasm. Turning back to Hazel, I just grin. "This is terrific of you."

"Oh, no problem, honey. Listen, if they get a good song outta you, I'll be their hero—heroine, I mean, believe me. They need some hits. The ladies have something to prove."

"Yeah, I bet!" I say, my mind full of things I need to prove: Can I write a hit? Have I already written one that I can put on tape? Will Jean Terrell suspect anything if I ask her a few questions about the kind of music Frank Wilson is looking for?

Hazel hands me her address and says goodnight. Cindy Birdsong and Mary Wilson, two classic "ladies" who've fought hard to keep the Supremes going, join me for a few minutes then make their exits as well.

"Finally!" Jean says, materializing with a burst of newly located energy. "Let's do it," she says, and sits herself across from me looking radiantly refreshed; then to my secret delight, she demands: "Ask me anything!"

The following week at work I get a message: Michael is recording the title song from a dippy little film about a rat called "Ben." Joe Jackson wants me to be part of the listening party once MJ is finished recording. I know how much Michael wants to be in movies, so maybe this is his way of getting closer to his goal. I don't know. I'll try to hold off judgment til after hearing it—but a song about a rat? Who's going to listen to that?

My photos of B.B. King's Chino performance are coming out of the darkroom, so I stand at attention by my desk like a nervous soldier. I need to prove to myself that I saw what I saw: 700 inmates—poor, tough, and 99% black. If I hadn't been in the company of a really big black man, with an even bigger talent and a heart—a heart so embracing, the cold stone walls of Chino seemed to lean in toward him for warmth—I admit it, I'd have been scared witless.

Wailing through "The Thrill is Gone," "Whole Lotta Love," and "Lucille", B.B. King showed everyone how music transforms diverse people into one family. There I was, clapping hands and singing along with the same "alien, scary men" I was afraid of an hour earlier. I watched them sing and I watched them cheer. I watched B.B. distribute musical instruments to prisoners interested in playing along with him. And when he told the inmates that they could keep them to make music while behind bars, I watched the men weep through my own drenched eyes.

"I'm trying to give something more to the guys locked up inside," he told me when we left. "It's unnatural and if they learn something, I think they will be better for it when they get out."

I know I am. Riding the tour bus from Chino back to Los Angeles, I drop back in my seat and try to take stock of things:

Susan, my new girlfriend, mayn't become the ongoing love of my life, but her unwavering fire and encouragement of my music is categorically unequalled. Because of her, I have a giant upright piano stuffed into the bedroom of my Venice shack. "I've been hunting around pawn shops," Susan told me one evening, "and I found a piano for you. It's arriving Saturday!" The hulking pianoforte allows me to combine my entire childhood of classical training with my growing pop ear. Years after practicing every morning before I could go out and play, my fingers remember each note like it was yesterday. Susan's gift gives my songwriting a huge leap forward. She not only knew it was time to bring the piano back into my hands, it was Susan who figured out long before Hazel asked for that tape, "You gotta put some of your stuff down in a recording studio! What if someone in the biz wants to hear it?"

After my "making demos with demons" experience in New York, I was a little gun shy. But with Susan at the control board with the engineer, it was different. For months we recorded my new songs at a sweet little studio near Venice Pier called Spectrum Sound. Without that crucial experience, when Hazel asked, "Got anything for the ladies?"—well, you know the expression "Ready or not?" It woulda been *not!*

Susan is a child of psychotherapy. She has struggled all her life learning to deal with how traumatically different she is from her parents and brother. From her I learn to look at myself. It may be just the tiniest peek to begin with, but it's a start. In four years, after we break up, having flexed the self-examination muscle around Susan, I begin therapy for real—the most emotionally and creatively freeing activity I ever do for myself.

But in truth, I'm sure I wouldn't have been ready for Susan, if it hadn't been for Kim. Take your place on The Great Mandala, eh? I don't believe things burst out of nowhere. Kim showed me what I wanted; I just got stuck thinking it had to be her. We were like two blind girls feeling our way around an unfamiliar room. Unexpectedly, in the end, it turned out we were in different rooms. Maybe the fallout from it all just took too much out of us. I'm sorry an active friendship never flared from the ashes, but no one's dead yet.

A few weeks after sending Hazel a tape of songs, I get a call. It's Frank Wilson himself: "I like the songs. I like what you're doing," he tells me. "Can you play these songs live, just yourself?" I assure him I can.

The next day Frank and his wife, Bunny, arrive at my Lilliputian apartment with their two elephantine dogs. They all lay down on the beanbag pillows without once commenting on the absurdity of it. I climb over them and around the corner into my bedroom, where I have to walk on the bed to reach the piano bench, and sit down.

It goes like this: I sing a song, and after I do, Frank yells out, "Play another!" I have no idea what he is thinking. This goes on for two hours.

When I finish, I stand in the doorway between my bedroom and the living room (in which I could not fit because of all the space they are taking up). Frank and Bunny are chatting energetically with each other. Finally Frank looks up at me and says, "Here's what's going on. I am leaving Motown. I'm starting my own production company and signing writers who will work for me exclusively. I already have a lot of artists lined up to produce. I dig your stuff. I'd like you to be one of my writers, okay?"

Okay? This is the man who wrote for and produced Diana Ross, Marvin Gaye, Stevie Wonder, The Supremes, Four Tops, and Eddie Kendricks. *Okay?*

At that moment my own little mutt, Arnold, begins barking outside where I'd left him in my panic over "all these big visitors." I take the opportunity to step around everyone and savor this delicious moment, until I reach the front door. Frank's eyes are on me the whole time. He is absolutely gorgeous. So is Bunny. I try not to return their quizzical stares as I open the door and ask Arnold to "please shut up."

Then, turning to my guests I say, "Yes, I'd love to work with you." And with that, I see my future tumbling towards me faster than meteors falling on dinosaurs.

5

When Rhythm Gets The Blues

Record producer, Frank Wilson, did not call me for two years! Good thing I stopped sitting by the phone after a month. Seems it took him a little longer to break away from Motown than he originally thought. No, there wasn't a jam-up in the entertainment business gears. That's exactly how this perfectly calibrated machine works. Expect something, and one-two-three on you! If I sound bitter, I'm not. If I sound like I've learned a lot, I have: Everything's out of your control. You never know what, when, where, or how anything is going to happen. Take this for example:

"I should have called you sooner," Frank's gentle Texas accent cushions the absurdity of his opening sentence to me. It's a gorgeous summer morning under a brochure-blue sky in 1976. Briny ocean smells overwhelm me, so I know it's time to bolt out my front door down to the sand, where the breathless geometry of a vast Venice shoreline will help me chase the usual anxieties from my body. I will watch surfers form their line up on the looming swells to my right. Then, running until my mood burns off, I'll notice which surfer is in position to drop in, leaving the rest to miss out—or be wiped out—by the scruffy California surf. All life's lessons play out in the foamy tides nearby. One day I too will learn them from the sea.

Right now, I'm a freelance journalist and very rigid about my daytime schedule. I write for a set amount of time. I do my errands; I run; I eat; I take care of my dog, Arnold; I write some more; I sleep. With only me watching over my timetable, my anxieties intimidate me into believing that if I relax for one second, chaos will ensue. Below the surface of my inflexibility, I am sure bedlam lurks.

"It's Frank Wilson," the voice on the phone persists into my silence. "What are you doing right now?"

I stare at myself in the mirror dressed for a run, but answer, "Nothing."

"Great! I'm in the middle of a recording session with a group called the Mighty Clouds of Joy," he continues, "and I've got this track that needs…well, it needs to be made into a song."

"What?" I say, feeling a tidal wave of plans reversing themselves. "What did you say?"

"I'm at Crystal Sound in Hollywood; can you pick up a copy of this track we just laid down? It's a rhythm track, no melody or lyrics. I'll run off a cassette copy for you. That way you can start working on it immediately. *[Laughs, embarrassed]* We're very late. I shoulda' called you sooner."

I don't mention that at 32, I'm now two years older than the day he and Bunny came to my apartment and he asked me to be one of his writers. "Okay, but can you give me directions to get there?" I ask, hating to display one of my worst quirks right away. But without clear directions to the studio, I won't arrive until the album is finished and in stores. He shoots off some street names that I don't recognize, and the address.

After we hang up, I race to the trunk of my VW and begin searching for my *Thomas Guide.* Obviously, Google Maps, MapQuest, and Waze programmers will have photos of me driving in circles for inspiration when they create their amazing software in years to come. *But really, why now?* I wonder to myself. Susan and I broke up less than two weeks ago, so I can't exactly phone her with the double-barreled newsflash: "He called me to write, at last! I'm going to a Hollywood studio to work on my first song that's going straight onto an album!" Along with: "Please drive me, or this golden opportunity will croak!"

No, I have to manage both these terrorizing feats myself. And, honestly, finding my way there freaks me the most. I rush back into my apartment with the *Thomas Guide* and start drawing a map on a big piece of cardboard with Venice Beach at the bottom and Crystal Sound (1014 North Vine Street), at the top. I remember how to get to the Laufer Company. Hey, how far can it be from there?

Crystal Sound is nowhere near the Laufer Company; so, after seeing half of Hollywood, I finally arrive. I've been in many small recording studios before, making demos or helping others do the same, but Crystal Sound is the real deal, what every songwriter and artist dreams about. These are the days before digital and sequencing or other magical means to correct everything you do. Here, if you don't like something you've recorded on expensive two-inch tape, you do it again! And Crystal has what it takes to make that work: several well-stocked studios with impressive consoles, microphones, effects, preamps, and compressors.

Gold and platinum albums of the superstars who've recorded here fill all the vertical surfaces; from Leon Russell to Jackson Browne, from Carole King to Marvin Gaye. My eyes spin from wall to wall until, instead of asking to see Frank, I suddenly blurt, "Where's your bathroom?" because I'm sure I'm about to pee my pants from sheer excitement.

Without looking up, the hulky receptionist points to a wooden paneled hallway. I take off but wind up in the studio kitchen with some back-up singers who are snacking on sandwiches and gossiping. I turn and push open the very next door. The good news is it is a bathroom. The bad news is it's the men's room. Worse yet, I've opened the wrong lavatory door wide enough to have a clear view of Stevie Wonder brushing his teeth. It's absolutely surreal. While he spits out rinse, unaware anyone is gawking at him, one of his handlers reaches across the sink and slams the door in my face.

"Oh, sorry, sorry," I babble to no one.

"And you're here to see who?" the receptionist shouts at me authoritatively. Lifting his bouncer body out of his chair, he addresses me the way he now realizes he should have when I asked to use the bathroom. "What's your name?" he huffs.

"Frank Wilson," I say, answering his first question. "I'm Judy Wieder. I'm supposed to get a tape from Frank Wilson, but I really need to use the lady's room; I made a mistake with the men's room, so I'm going to..."

"No, no you are not. You take a seat right there," he points to a couch near the entrance. "I'll check with Mr. Wilson before you go any further. Really, who knows who you are?" His big voice slams into me with all its might. Now I have everyone's attention. I sit humiliated, like some demented fan who has crossed the etiquette line, trying not to exacerbate my first impression by urinating on their chichi couch.

It takes a minute, but my reprieve is well worth it. Apparently, Frank's "I should've called you sooner" distress was transmitted to Mr. Muscles with some oomph. Suddenly bouncer boy is standing in front of me blinking and professing, "I'm very, very sorry. Yes, Mr. Wilson will see you right away. Please, he's in Studio B—but, wait; you need the lady's room, I believe? It's down the hall. Um, further than the men's," he adds, slipping in some humor I wouldn't have guessed he had in him.

Studio B is cavernous, a giant cosmos. I feel like a tiny speck falling upwards into a bowl of stars (literally and figuratively),

5 When Rhythm Gets The Blues

all wrestling for space and attention. At the center of this tantalizing universe, doling out his attention, is Frank, seated at the console and surrounded by engineer, Kevin Beamish, (later to produce REO Speedwagon and give me the nickname "Wudy Jeeders"), plus various members of the gospel group, Mighty Clouds of Joy.

"Judy! Oh, girl, I'm so glad to see you!" Frank calls out to me in what has to be one of the warmest welcomes a person could ask for. "Hi, Frank!" I wave back, feigning casualness. There are several highly pedigreed male musicians also sitting in chairs around Frank; one is guitarist Ray Parker, Jr. ("Ghostbusters"), another is Nathan Watts, bassist for Stevie Wonder's band, drummer Alvin Taylor, and keyboardist Jerry Peters. *These people are famous.* So, having absolutely no idea what's expected of me, I stand at the door, grinning inanely.

"Come in. Come in. I want you to hear this. Come over here and sit down near me," Frank's voice reaches across the vast room. Everyone in the studio is now ogling me, trying to figure out why their kingpin is giving me the time of day. As I walk further into the studio I'm knocked down by a skull-cracking blast from the overhead speakers. My instinct is to scream and run out of the building; but a quick glance at Frank's smiling face cues me to freeze and do the same. *Why is this so loud?* I think to myself in a panic. *Who listens to music at this volume and lives to hear another thing, ever?*

"Isn't it great?" Frank screams at me, even though I'm now standing right next to him. Bass, drums, and rhythm guitars are all bouncing along in a pleasant enough groove.

I scream too: "Yeah, yeah. I like it. What is it?" A worried look shoots across his face, like maybe he should have gone slower for the Venice Beach nutjob. Then he laughs so loud I can actually hear him.

"It's *your* song!" he shouts at me, delighted.

I'm sure I didn't hear him right. "*My* song?"

"Okay, Okay, *our* song. This is the rhythm track. I'm running you off a cassette copy right now."

"Oh, I understand, uh-huh," I say, shaking my head up and down vigorously to let the celebrity spectators know I'm no goofus. I'm cool and I'm gonna be onto this funky stuff real fast. Everyone's scanning me hard now, without a single smile. They all know each other from their Motown days, from years of studio and songwriting work, and from the Baptist church they attend regularly. I, on the other hand, am not black; I'm not a born-again Christian; I'm not a guy; and I'm not straight. I will get used to this. But in the end, will they?

* * *

In 1976, 19-year-old Ella Mae is in the throes of a tumultuous love/hate relationship with her church. She joined the Temple six years ago, when she was only 13.

It all happened way too fast: After her mother's divorce, Ella Mae's older brother started using drugs. Suddenly their home was in an uproar. The battles between her mother and brother only made him act out more. Finally, having tried everything else, Ella Mae's mother heard about a radical substance rehabilitation program run by a church in northern CA. The program was said to have a very high success rate.

So, with nowhere else to turn, Ella Mae's mother made the trip north. After that, it didn't take long before the whole family began traveling regularly to Redwood Valley to hear a charismatic minister preach his own special gospel to the country's first fully integrated congregation. And that, Ella Mae had to admit, was something to behold.

The first time Ella Mae heard the temple's choir and watched the beguiling preacher pull off one of his Pentecostal healings, the gullible, but adorable teenager thought her Afro curls would fly off her head. Of course, being an exceptionally bright child, it didn't take long before Ella caught on to some of the tricks Father used to pull off these elaborate deceptions. In fact, Ella Mae began to feel downright embarrassed for the new church members who believed their pastor was a prophet because he "mysteriously knew" private things about their personal lives. In truth, 3x5 cards—full of information about each new Congregationalist—were assembled by guards who then fed the information into Father's headphones while he pretended to be in a spell, magically experiencing a member's deepest secret. The only miracle that took place was how well it always worked.

And yet, other church activities really are miraculous in Ella Mae's eyes. She believes many of the programs Father has put in place for the elderly as well as the neighborhood foster children, are truly heaven sent. The church's work in local communities is stellar, a model for other organizations in the future. And the things this man says! In the early years, Ella Mae loved every word that came out of Father's mouth. He spoke the truth boldly: "The Bible is a tool to oppress women and non-whites...Christianity is a fly-away religion... A Sky God is no God at all. Nobody's gonna come out of the sky... You're gonna help yourself, or you'll get no help... There's no heaven up there. We'll have to make the heaven down here."

If only the Church's move to San Francisco hadn't touched off a wave of paranoia in Father. The once loving and trusting atmosphere of Ella Mae's youth has been replaced with discipline, extensive observation of the members, and intense, restrictive rules everyone must obey day and night. Although she's allowed to attend school, Ella Mae can't talk to anyone who isn't in the church. In fact, she can't talk to anyone in her own congregation about anything church related. Why? What does Father think will happen? She wonders if anyone else has these questions, but the rules won't allow her to ask.

* * *

Somehow, I navigate my way back home from the studio without getting lost. The cassette of Frank's track must have played a dozen times along the route. I like it. Very poppy, very upbeat, but I've never done anything like this before. I've never collaborated with professional songwriters. What's more, the Mighty Clouds of Joy are a gospel group—contemporary and popular—but still gospel. What do I have to offer their sound or church message?

"This is your chance to be Carole King!" Frank said to me when he walked me out of the studio. "I want you to really say something in this tune. I want you to write a...a 'You've Got A Friend' kind of thing for the Clouds. You can do this."

I should stop right now and say that one of the most discouraging things I learn when I become a "recorded songwriter," is why so many good, unknown songwriters never get their songs recorded. It's one thing to have a producer ask you to write a song with the same "feel" as a song that's already been published, as Frank did when he talked about "You've Got A Friend." But in time, I will sit by the side of many lionized record producers as they open song submissions from unknown songwriters for artists they're currently producing. I will watch as these producers listen to the demos, get excited over a song on the tape, then turn to one of their own signed songwriters, and say, "Write me a song exactly like this for the project." No wonder so many of our song submissions get shuffled back to us with those dreaded kiss-off form letters.

Regardless, for now, I'm grateful to be one of the chosen ones at the higher end of the food chain. Once I'm back from

5 When Rhythm Gets The Blues

the studio and in my apartment, I begin arranging my crowded desk so that all my magazine freelance work is shoved off to the side, opening a space for my cassette recorder and several pads of lined paper to sit prominently in front of me. Then I begin sharpening pencils until even I'm bored.

Start, just start. Put down anything, my mind begs. Sing something to the track. Use dummy lyrics. Make it pretty. What would the Mighty Clouds sing? What would Carole King do?

I pummel my brain like this for a few more hours before finally falling asleep around 10 PM. In the morning, I begin what quickly becomes my modus operandi for the course of my early songwriting career: wake up at 6 AM, drink a cup of coffee, run five miles, shower; feed myself and my dog, write until 4 PM, take a 10-mile bike ride, collapse. Of course, all of this topples if I have to go into the studio to attend a recording session for one of the songs.

By the middle of the second day I think I might have something worth showing to Frank, so I decide to call him at the studio. He takes my call immediately. (I am fooled into thinking this will always happen.) I tell him I have a verse I'd like to present to him, and suggest driving in to sing it.

"No, no, just sing it over the phone," he says. I can hear loud instruments playing in the background on those titanic speakers, and resist: "Frank, how can you hear me sing a new song on the telephone with all that going on? It's okay, I can drive in."

"I can hear you fine, don't worry. Let me hear whatcha got," he bids.

Very worried, I turn on the cassette and stare at my notes. When the verse part of the rhythm track comes 'round, I shut my eyes to block out what I imagine is happening on Frank's end, and sing what I've written so far.

— 233 —

"That's it," I say, snapping off the machine. Nothing. I only hear studio din on the line. "Frank?"

"Yeah...yeah," he says slowly. "Sing that again."

I knew it! I knew he couldn't hear me. I sing it again anyway. When I finish, I hear more hoo-ha on his end. "Listen, Frank, this isn't working..."

"Judy," he cuts me off, "I like it a lot. That's good stuff. But I want you to take it apart and make it the chorus."

"What?" I ask, starting to worry that I can't keep up with all his moving parts.

"You know the segment of your verse where you're singing: 'That's what friends are made of/ talking 'bout a true love/ coming to the aid of/ your body and soul/' —those lines of your verse?" he persists.

"Yeah?" I'm astonished he can quote the words back to me so accurately amidst his mayhem.

"Make that into the chorus...some way," he continues.

"Ah," I say.

"Ah!" he echoes. "Okay?" It's obvious he's got to get back to his own pandemonium, and is finished with me; so, I attempt one last question.

"So, Frank, um, I just sing these lyrics—using a different melody—over the chorus chords? Maybe tinker with the chords, and add other lines too? 'Cause, you know, the chorus is structured differently than the verses," I add doltishly.

"What? Yeah, do that. Do that. But you *can't* change the chord structure. The rhythm track is cut. Just make a new melody line to work with those lyrics and chords in the chorus."

"I...I...?"

"Yeah! *You! [He's now yelling so loud he's stripping the paint off my walls.]* Look, Judy, I really like this. I knew you could do it!"

"Do what?" I say, clasping my forehead to contain a coiling migraine.

5 When Rhythm Gets The Blues

"Come up with something so perfect: 'That's What Friends Are Made Of.' That's the chorus and that's the name of the song. Good girl. Finish it"

* * *

Loretta is 50 years old in 1976, the year she gets word from "Father" that he wants her to be the official writer for the church. She can hardly believe it. All around her, the mixed-race choir is singing; those joyous voices in blue robes, filling the congregation with the sounds of hope. And now *this* honor: to tell the story of idealism in action, of America's greatest freedom fighters.

It's true, there are church members who don't trust Father. After all, a preacher who admits he's an atheist? A reverend who doesn't believe in God? A man who uses religious theatrics to mobilize people for social change? The world is always threatened by imaginative leadership. Just look at history. And Loretta knows her history: from Jesus to Siddhartha, from Gandhi to the Dalai Lama. She understands and believes Father is a genius. Loretta has seen his greatest vision come to life: blacks and whites together, functioning as a community day and night, in and out of church, building a better, more equal world for each other. When has that ever happened before?

And what about all Father's new fans? Harvey Milk, Angela Davis, George Moscone, Jerry Brown, Willie Brown—every one of them has visited the temple and spoken many times. Whenever right-wing crazies attack the church or Father himself, renegades like Angela and Harvey step up to send letters or broadcast speeches defending the great work of the temple and its innovative leader. Father is all about change; and his church is a political organization fighting the noblest war of all against a dying government system that's proven over and over it simply has no idea how to equalize the wealth of the people it governs.

It's true there are a few who whisper of defecting, but in her new role as historian, Loretta will be sure to write about the majority of temple members who feel the way she does: grateful to have their lives made whole again by a leader whose goal is to bring the world together before it self-destructs. Loretta never feels any doubt because all she ever has to do is remember her own journey here. An injured adult with a heart full of anger and helplessness, she could barely hear her name called the day Father invited her up to the podium with him. With tears pouring down his face, he spoke to her like a prophet who already seemed to know all her deepest secrets. Hearing his voice in the packed church, talking about things only she knew, Loretta realized she could finally follow someone again. The experience that day remains utterly divine in her memory. He is divine. She vows she will follow Father forever, like an eternal flame.

※　※　※

"That's What Friends Are Made Of" (not to be confused with "That's What Friends Are For," written six years later by Burt Bacharach and Carole Bayer Sager to help fight the stigma of AIDS), rounds out a mix of traditional and contemporary gospel songs for the Mighty Clouds of Joy. The fact that the album, *Truth is The Power*, goes on to earn a Grammy nomination for Best Soul Gospel Performance, knocks the breath right out of my little Jewish lungs! I might have been even more astounded if I'd had one free second to celebrate. But the same fever flapping around Frank's schedule like a demented bat, is now yammering at the edges of mine: "More, more, more."

5 When Rhythm Gets The Blues

The minute I finish with the Clouds, Frank has me over to his home to begin working on a song he's started for Stevie Wonder. He and Stevie are old friends, so showing Stevie songs is no problem for Frank. Can you imagine? In what universe do people play Stevie Wonder their new songs? And how many toads must you kiss first?

I'm so nervous, I practice driving out to Frank's house a day before our scheduled meeting. (I still do this today for important appointments that appear to me to be located on the far side of the moon—which most do.) When I arrive the next day, Frank sits down at his grand piano, and gives me a taste of what will become "Look Up With Your Mind." He already has the title and, of course, he wants to make those words start off the chorus. I get it. Stevie cannot see with his eyes. So, the whole song should be about "looking" with your soul, your mind, your entire being. Suddenly, Frank stares past me, out over the piano, and very softly says:

"Supposing, for example, you saw two girls holding hands, walking down the street?"

My eyes pop open. I notice his living room ceiling has lowered about three feet.

"What?" I say, carefully. Could his creativity be turning rogue, becoming a nasty force headed straight for me?

"Well," he chuckles self-consciously, "what I'm saying is: seeing these two girls holding hands could mean different things."

Why is he saying this to me? I sob silently behind my carefully composed face. All at once I see my fragile foot-in-the-record-biz door being crushed between slamming bibles. After all, it's only been a few years since Frank left Motown and his run-amok days, by throwing himself into the mandates and directives of Jesus Christ—as interpreted by the Mt. Zion Baptist Church—which lavishes no praise on "two girls holding hands."

"If you look only with your eyes," he continues, jarring my thoughts, "you might get the wrong idea."

"Right, right..." I mimic his detached tone. At this point I am so freaked out, I have started counting my dead relatives. Although I am not in a romantic relationship at the moment, and have begun experimenting with dating men again, I have no intention of sharing the arc of my sexuality with this man for any number of very good reasons. First and foremost, he's about to become a minister, and I'd rather not appear in his first sermon. All I know is I don't want to lose what little professional progress my hard work has finally brought me, so I decide to take control:

"Well, we certainly can't use *that* as an example in the song. It's way too complicated for listeners to follow. But I see where you're going with it." Then I point to his tape deck for the cassette he's made me, and to my wrist watch: "Oh, no. So late? The traffic will be a nightmare. But if you give me the tape, I can listen to what we've done so far on my ride home."

With that, I start grabbing things up with my agitated energy and throwing them in my briefcase. Frank reels around on the piano bench and watches me with fascination. I feel him measuring my semi-coherent body language down to the marrow. Then, abruptly, he's on his feet, responding in bright splashes of kindness. Despite this one unfortunate, yet cavernous, fissure destabilizing our relationship at all times, the communication and collaboration we share is mighty. Frank's hypersensitivity, warmth, and mentoring—including the vast knowledge of R&B and gospel music he embodies as one of Motown's early disciples—are always there for me. But it's too early in the world for us to build any stable bridges over my sexuality, so we're left with trying to ignore the elephant in his church.

"Hey, okay, okay, let me get the cassette for you," he says, darting around the piano, snapping the tape out of the deck and handing it to me. He takes my purse from me and carries it until he realizes that's wrong. We talk over each other nervously as we walk to the front door. I can't look at him so I have no idea if he's looking at me.

When I'm seated in my car, he leans his head into the driver's window and notices (he notices everything!) that I've velcro'd the face of an old Timex wrist watch to my dashboard. "What is this?" he questions.

"It keeps time and the VW has no clock," I answer, hurriedly starting the engine. He laughs elaborately: "Girl, I swear, you are the Renaissance woman. It's a wonder you know what to do first!" Even though I realize he has just said something wonderful to me, the atmosphere between us is so layered with unnerving subtext, I can only laugh inanely, push him back out of my car window, and flee. "I'll call you with some verses," I say with false cheeriness, and nearly run him down pulling away from the curb. I keep up the performance 'til I'm off his street; then exhale the entire ride home.

What in Hades was that? "Two girls walking hand in hand?" Why did he say that to me? An accident? A probe? A Test? When I finally get home, I can't remember the drive at all. Seriously, how did I get here? Arnold greets me, happy and hungry, but I can barely shove through my exhaustion to feed and walk him. What's more, I fear this isn't the kind of fatigue that a good night's sleep is going to fix. This is going to be hard—not the songwriting—the hiding.

※ ※ ※

That special community spirit that Ella Mae once drew such comfort from, is being replaced by people telling her what to wear, what to eat, when to sleep, and when to rise. It's as if there's a growing psychosis coming down from the top—which makes no sense because so many things in the church are expanding and going well. Why isn't this a time for great celebration?

Instead, Father has been preaching negativity and warning about nuclear wars and the need to stockpile supplies to survive all the inevitable disasters heading the temple's way. If you listen to his sermons these days, it's clear Father believes someone or something is out to get them—first and foremost, our own government: "We must move our church out of the United States as soon as possible," is the recent, relentless theme of his sermons.

Ella Mae is starting to feel like she's suffocating every time she walks into the building. If only she hadn't married another Temple member. If only she didn't have a three-year-old son she adores. Still, is it time for a break? After all, she's been working for "the cause" since she was a kid.

Then one day, despite all her obligations, Ella Mae surprises herself and takes a job at a hotel. First, she makes sure that her work hours conflict with all the church meetings she doesn't want to attend anymore. Then she tells everyone something vague, and leaves. As soon as she does, a new world opens to her.

✳   ✳   ✳

Frank and I follow each other's creative bursts throughout the writing of "Look Up With Your Mind." Letting my ideas come at him right and left, he basically steers the song where he wants it to go. It's his world when it comes to expertise in R&B music, and there are many times my "pop soul" is called out for not being "soulful enough." I secretly long for our work to be given a little "popping up," but at this point, I'm just grateful he never again mentions the "two girls walking hand in hand." And he doesn't. It's as if it never happened. But the creepy incident worked perfectly. Though his motives remain obscure, I'm still receiving dark messages in the murkiest part of my unconscious: *He's on to you. Be careful. Don't do or say anything gay or the fires of hell will swallow up your music career.*

Well, that's the closet for you. As most of us eventually learn—no matter why you're in that hurt locker—get out as soon as you can! It has no moral bottom. Eventually, you will freefall.

At this point things are moving at turbo speed. Despite feeling like I've made a tentative debut as a "talented oddball" in the eyes of Frank's born-again teammates, I have apparently gotten through the appraisal process. Frank never officially signs me to his publishing company, and therefore he never pays me a regular weekly salary. Still, I am treated like a permanent member of his core writing team, and he uses me frequently. At the onset, this team consists of Frank (rarely), John (a terrific melody writer), Terri (an ace lyricist I'm very fond of), and now me.

When Frank takes on an artist to produce, part of his payoff—in addition to his producing fee—is getting a certain amount of songs from his publishing company onto the album he's producing. This translates into his writers writing songs at the speed of sound. Additionally, as part of his deal on certain projects, Frank is expected to write a song or two himself. Being a proven writer with such past hits as "Love Child" and "You Made Me So Very Happy," some of the artists he produces bank on getting a hit song from the master himself. However, since Frank's gotten so busy producing, he has less and less time for songwriting. This results in his need to add his name to at least one song his team has written for each album. John and I have been surprised a few times—after Frank added an inspired production element to one of our songs—to find that he then added his name to the song's writing credits as well. Was what he did writing or producing? Since Frank already takes the publishing side of the songwriting royalties, adding another name to a song's writing credit (a widely practiced custom by producers), subtracts from the writer's visibility, and money.

Having experienced this behavior several times makes it all the more amazing in 10 years when hit makers Peter Bunetta and Rick Chudacoff listen to a song I co-wrote, "I've Never Been The Same," and have Darlene Love record it. Darlene is one of the most recognizable voices in American music (finally acknowledged in the film *20 Feet From Stardom*). Her manager, Kenny Laguna, along with Bunetta and Chudacoff, are all hit songwriters. Yet none of them jump in and rewrite "I've Never Been the Same" just so they can take writing royalties away from me; none of them insist on taking publishing royalties as payback for having Darlene record the song; and none of them tell Ken George, my song runner at the time, to just leave the tape with them so they can "study it"—i.e. tell their own signed writers to "write a song like this." Honestly, I don't know what's more surprising: the common unscrupulousness or the uncommon ethics?

Getting back to the saga of "Look Up With Your Mind," I will never learn the real story behind why Stevie Wonder doesn't record it. I do know that long before Stevie has another recording project, ABC Records comes to Frank with Lenny Williams, the lead singer of Tower of Power, a well-known Oakland, CA band. Lenny is about to make his first solo album, and his record label is looking for the perfect R&B producer to make him a star. The next thing I know, Frank is selling me on how much Lenny loves "Look Up With Your Mind," and, "Guess what? We're gonna be cutting the song with Lenny at Crystal Sound next week."

5 When Rhythm Gets The Blues

"What about Stevie? Did he get to hear it yet?" I ask, meekly.

"Oh, this is gonna be even better!" Frank snows me. "Lenny is a rising star who's had hit records with all the groups he's led. This is a big opportunity. And—I've got more good news for you: John and I need lyrics for another track we're putting together for Lenny. We want to get you on it right away."

"Another song for Lenny?" I ask, trying hard to get swept into his enthusiasm. "Great, great..."

The first time John and I hook up to write a song together, we meet on the second floor of Los Angeles City College, in a tiny music room with a piano. We work on a ballad for the former lead singers of the Fifth Dimension, Billy Davis, Jr. and Marilyn McCoo. It's December of 1976, and the duo, also on ABC Records, is topping the charts with their first solo LP and television show. And after only four months of working together, Frank's team is in the running to do their second album.

When I get to the school rehearsal room (the Thomas Guide and I pull over several times with a flash light!), John is waiting. He's striking looking, with a large Afro, polite, eager to write, sweet, and very grateful I'm there. He already has the title that he wants for the song: "My Reason To Be Is You."

Right away I don't like it. But my reaction isn't an artistic one. After the break-up of my last relationship, I'm experiencing, maybe for the first time, what it's like to depend on myself in life. It's rough, for sure, but very growthful and long overdue. So, writing a whole song that says the reason for living one's life is solely because of someone else ("My Reason To Be Is *You*"), is about as far away from my current truth as I can possibly get. The very thought of it makes me itch.

Sitting beside John at the piano, I feel like there's an unhealthy sheen building on my face as we sing a melody for his lovely chord changes. I suggest, "not getting married to the title," for a few days, until I build a chorus, but there's definitely no negotiating. He's clearly in love with his title, and I don't want to get on his bad side long before I even know he has one. Also "My Reason To Be Is You" is one of those phrases that sings beautifully, which is the unfathomable thing about words: some are just naturally lyrics. And, for reasons no one understands, some words sound very profound—even if they aren't.

"I hate the song title of this new tune," I whine at my therapist.

"But, Judy," she says astutely, "You *know* what those feelings feel like!" With her impeccable way of illuminating the emotional debris of my past, she does her "leaning in thing" and tells me, "Even if this is a more solo time in your life, you can still write a song about those mad, passionate, crazy in-love times. It'll feel good for you to do that."

"No, no, it won't!" I blurt, my outburst surprising me so much I start crying.

"What's this?" she asks softly, covering her mouth with her hand so I won't see signs of a smile playing with the corners of her lips. She looks sideways for her Kleenex box but knows better than to make a move for it.

"I miss those times," I whimper pathetically. "And I don't want to start longing for them. Not now. Everything will fall apart."

"Nothing will fall apart," she contradicts, knowing how tightly I hold onto structure, trying to push down my dread of chaos. "There's room for all of it. Just because this isn't your time to experience that kind of love, doesn't mean you don't know what it feels like, or that you won't feel it again one day."

"I will?" blubber, blubber. I try not to smile back at her, but take the damn Kleenex.

5 When Rhythm Gets The Blues

* * *

Being older and hailing from the segregated South when she first joined the church, Loretta has experienced enough prejudice and marginalization to know what a gift it is to find a leader filled with compassion and tenderness for people like herself. A white man able to understand the needs of the nation's outcasts because he himself feels like one? That's a wonder to behold. Building sturdy, rent-free homes for church members to live in, setting up free clinics for the elderly, providing healthcare for all, preparing free feasts nightly, making sure armed guards are everywhere to protect temple members, these are but a few of Father's many gifts to his congregation.

Even on the hard days, when a few church members misunderstand the intent of Father's disciplinary measures, oral condemnations, or daylong sermons, Loretta's devotion never wavers. *Let others desert, if they must.* Though why some bad-mouth the greatness of the temple's work, bewilders her. And to attack him personally? Where on earth are they ever going to find another dedicated fighter with the desire and power to go into jails and free members of his flock who are locked up for crimes that they had no choice but to commit? You steal what you gotta steal to live. Loretta knows this from her own life experiences. Angela Davis knows this! The Black Panthers know this!

Equally important, Father's wise enough to go one step further and create cutting-edge programs that can redirect a freed convict's talents into a career that will be of real service to the church in the future. *This is how the world is changed for the better.* Bold actions from a benevolent thinker.

And yet, Father is still a humble man at heart. There was a time he confided in Loretta that he never really wanted the thankless job of leading this rapidly growing cross-section of America's underdogs. But who else was going to do it? Everyone else had been gunned down or quit. Somebody had to pick up the torch. Somebody had to roll up his sleeves and lead the people to the Promised Land.

※　※　※

By the beginning of 1977 my world order completely detonates. Everything is an adventure and a stretch. Nothing feels like old territory or autopilot. Often Frank's team pulls all-nighters in the studio and still has to get up and write new songs the next day in order to entice potential recording stars.

I wind up with two songs on Lenny Williams' album, *Choosing You*, ("Look Up With Your Mind" and "Riding The High Wire"). Because of his pivotal work as lead singer in the bands Graham Central Station and Tower of Power, Lenny's first solo outing is successful, prompting ABC Records to ask Frank to produce his next two albums.

On the other hand, Billy and Marilyn's second solo album, *The Two Of Us,* is an upset—to use an unfortunately perfect word. Their first single doesn't get enough airplay, so by the time they release their second, "My Reason To Be," it's too late. Listeners have the attention span of fish. You only have a teeny window to sell them new product, and then the fish move on. This never changes.

One day, when I'm deep in the writing of at least three different projects, Frank calls to say he's decided to produce Renee Geyer's fifth solo album. Renee is a bluesy Australian soul singer who has her own band, but is looking for "that Motown sound," and has tracked down Frank to add some rhythm to her blues.

"I need you to write two songs at once. Can you come hear the tracks today and meet Renee?" Frank doesn't wait for my answer. "Hurry over to the studio," he gasps before hanging up. By now I can get to Crystal Sound on a pogo stick. I've become fearless on the freeway; not minding the traffic at all, as it usually offers me another 30 minutes to bang my head on the dashboard over something I'm writing.

When I get to Crystal I stand amazed and delighted to meet another "white chick." Ironically, Renee—with her restless blond hair and intense green eyes—sounds more rock-soulful than any of the black singers I've written for so far. I dwell on this for a reason: When Renee's LP is ready for release down the road, her record company, Polydor, fights a losing battle to get her to forego putting an image of herself on the packaging. Before the final album is ready, the label sends out a few finished song mixes to several hundred R&B radio stations across the USA, trying to create a buzz over their Australian star. The results are terrific, with a wide range of stations jumping on the cuts and playing them in high rotation. It's clear that people who haven't seen her, assume Renee is black. Naturally record execs want to capitalize on black radio's expanding excitement. They believe including a photo of Renee on the record jacket will confuse and drive away buyers.

Renee, however, who calls herself "a difficult woman," won't have it, and insists on a full-blown album cover shot of her "big pink face." They hassle, and she wins. Sadly, the Polydor execs are right. As soon as listeners become aware of the color of the artist making the soulful sounds on their R&B radio—Renee's airplay and record sales stop mid-air.

Reverse racism? Certainly, a racism I'm unprepared for. I've experienced creepy things like eating dinner at Crystal Sound when drunks poke their heads in hollering: "Niggers, niggers, all of you!" Then one sees me and adds, "Nigger lover!" *Well, yes.* But *this* I hadn't heard of. Isn't "crossing over" all about launching a record in one category and expanding to others? Maybe it's too early and rare for a white woman to launch herself from black radio. I'll go through a similar thing with an R&B song I co-write called "I'll Love You Through It all" for a Hawaiian group (Society of Seven). Although the record goes to Number One in Hawai'i, on the mainland we hear, "they're not black enough!"

"Judy," Frank says late one night after a long day at the studio, "You 'n' Renee gotta come up with something great, really amazing." With this kind of expectation, I'd always rather wait until morning when I'm fresh. But the studio is booked for Renee to put down her vocals on this song tomorrow morning, so we have no choice. We have to finish the tune tonight.

So I drag out the 'ol *Thomas Guide,* and start charting how I'm going to get from Crystal Sound to where Renee's lodging at the Beverly-Comstock Hotel on Wilshire Blvd. The place turns out to be so small and well hidden, I'm reduced to yelling at people on street corners, glancing at the stars, and pretty much feeling like Columbus looking for America.

Unfortunately, after tonight, the hotel will be a far more conspicuous landmark.

* * *

Life outside the church in San Francisco is one tumultuous adventure after another for Ella Mae. She finds herself indulging in all the things the church forbids: sex with strangers, drugs, alcohol, dancing all night in night clubs. It's as if she's finally having her adolescence. And what's wrong with stepping away from years of nonstop commitment to one person? The only thing that haunts Ella Mae is her son. Left in the care of others—who will surely tell him bad stories about his "weak, deserter mother"—Ella Mae knows her little boy must think she has abandoned him.

But whenever these thoughts rise up, Ella Mae finds new ways to escape them. Dating a heavy-duty drug dealer, she tastes "happy powder" for the first time and narrowly misses getting sucked into his exceedingly dark and illegal world. She is, however, sucked into cocaine; and that changes her life significantly. Suddenly, without the "happy powder," Ella Mae doesn't have much energy for anything, even her job. But with it, she can do anything; especially blot out the church, her family, friends, husband—even her son.

Then one night someone at a club gives Ella Mae what she thinks is marijuana. But when things begin to get blurry and grotesque, Ella Mae knows something's wrong. Soon she can't even stand up or walk. The weed turns out to be PCP, a chemical used as a tranquilizer in veterinary medicine. By the time she is loaded into someone's car, Ella Mae can't move a muscle in her body. She decides it is a sign from God: she must return to her temple family and repent.

And so, she does; at least she tries. Attending non-stop meetings and participating in work projects, Ella Mae can't seem to make things gel any more. She isn't allowed to visit her son very often because Father always prefers to break up families like they do on communes. By breaking down family bonds, members are more likely to bond with Father.

Then *New West* Magazine publishes an investigative piece on Father and the temple, and the sky falls. The article, which church members tried in numerous ways to derail, is immensely critical of the organization and its leader. Based primarily on interviews with ex-members, the piece exposes life inside the temple as a mixture of regimentation, bullying, and humiliation. It reports that members must attend services four nights a week, and reveals that services can last until daybreak.

There is no way to read the magazine probe without believing the church and its pastor are fakes, frauds, and worse: they are thieves, since joining means signing over all your personal valuables—from your income to your home to your social security checks. Yet despite her relief over the temple's public unmasking, Ella Mae knows there is a darker side waiting: *What will Father do about this exposure?* she wonders.

* * *

It's really late by the time Renee and I push aside our take-out dinner, spread ourselves out on the carpet of her suite in the Beverly-Comstock Hotel, and take aim at the song. It's long after midnight. I worry about playing my cassette of the track at this hour; it's so quiet my wristwatch is the only audible sound, scattering the early morning minutes around the room with weary precision.

The song, "Moving Along," seems to let the lyric hold a lot of meaning despite its funk 'n blues melody; so, I push Renee to let me say some things I've been learning in life lately. Displaying an astonishing lack of stage-hoggyness, she's up for letting me do it. We hit a great stride quickly, but seeing as the track is a six-minute opus, we're still writing in the middle of the night. That's when it happens.

"What's that?" Renee gasps, jumping straight up.

"What?" I'm concentrating so hard on words, melody, and not falling asleep, I don't hear a thing. I shut off the tape recorder and listen. Renee doesn't need to say it twice. Somewhere outside in the hallway, not far from her room, we hear a heart-halting scream. When I look at my watch, it's nearly 3AM.

"Jesus!" I say.

"Oh, God," Renee echoes. She is on her toes, sneaking towards the door.

"*Wait!*" I hiss at her.

"Oh, right," she turns toward me. "I shouldn't open it, should I?"

"What if there are, I don't know, guns?" I whisper, channeling my cautious father. It's quiet again, so we stand there sucking all the air out of the room. "Okay, open it," I say, bravely pushing her toward the door.

Renee peeks out. "No one's there," she says. "Well, so, then what was that?"

"And other people haven't come out of their rooms?" I ask, trying to peer over her shoulder. The hallway is empty and silent.

Is it possible two sleepy people under a lot of stress can have cognitive breakdowns at the same time? Is it possible the scream came from the street, maybe from a passing car, and perhaps we were too focused on the music to place the sound correctly?

Just as Renee and I fold ourselves back onto the floor, there's a sudden charge of footsteps down the hallway, and it definitely sounds like more than one person. This time I urge Renee to the door immediately, and when she opens it, we're both shocked at the sight: Men dressed in white ambulance gear are carrying a stretcher and storming full throttle past Renee's room.

"We *did* hear something!" she gasps at me, her relief at getting it right trumping her horror at whatever might be going on. Between the long studio day and interminable writing night, we're just not up for adventures that pivot on the unexpected.

By now I'm putting my jacket on. Watching me, Renee has a small panic moment: "Judy, are you going to finish the lyrics and meet me at the studio in the morning before Frank gets there?"

"Absolutely, absolutely," I lie, thinking only about sleep.

She opens the door again for me, but once more there's drama. Now the stretcher has someone on it. After about five minutes, we try again. They're gone, but now other hotel guests have finally roused themselves over the commotion. I walk down the hallway to the elevator shaking my head and repeating the mantra, "I have no idea," to the inquiring sleep walkers popping out at me.

The next morning—which comes in a couple of hours—I oversleep, so by the time I get the lyric finished and myself to the studio, it's noon, and Frank's already there: "Renee's looking for you!" he says, when I hand him the lyric. Then, glancing at the typewritten page, he adds: "Give me a few minutes to see what you've done, and then come in and sing it for me. I think Renee's out front waiting to flag you down. She seems very agitated. She needs to talk to you."

I wonder if Renee got any sleep at all with the hotel in such a tizzy. I see her coming in the main Crystal entrance and when she sees me she yells:

"Judy! Did you listen to the radio coming in?"

"No, I was singing the lyric to..."

"That commotion last night at the hotel? You know what that was?"

I have absolutely no guesses.

"Freddie Prinze shot himself in the room down the hall," she answers.

"Who?"

"*Chico and the Man?*"

"No way! Down that hallway? On *that* stretcher?"

My words are now bolting ahead of me. "Last night? Wait, while we were writing this song...!"

"Yes! Yes! He's in critical condition at UCLA hospital. And they say he's not gonna make it." We stand facing each other, breathless.

5 When Rhythm Gets The Blues

Frank bursts out of the studio and into the lobby where we're standing. He holds up the lyrics in one hand, completely oblivious to the three-alarm fire in our eyes.

"Ladies, I love this lyric. Whatever happened last night with the two of you, it was magic." With that he turns and heads back into the studio, calling for Renee to get ready to sing.

We continue to stare at each other, helplessly. "Oh, Wow," Renee eventually whispers. "I can't sing. I feel sick."

"You can do it, Renee." I say, as she follows Frank in.

I stand in the lobby for a few minutes trying to absorb this weirdness: It's always such a shock when someone famous does something fatal. Isn't fame supposed to shield you against your bad feelings? I guess there are no shields big enough for that. How isolated, frightened, and hopeless Freddie must have felt to take his own life.

"Can you come in here?" Frank sticks his head out the studio door and motions to me. "I don't know what's bothering Renee, but she says she wants to *see* you when she sings today." He laughs self-consciously. "Come in and sit with me."

* * *

Loretta is proud of Father. What courage and grace under fire. If only she could take on some of his pain and disappointment. She would do anything to unburden him. How grossly unfair this so-called "investigative news" piece is! Such fake reporting. Naturally, the people interviewed for the article said heinous things about Father and the church. Those people defected! There will always be church members who refuse to accept constructive criticism; and Father knows they must be punished or they'll bring harm to the greater community.

Loretta can only watch helplessly as the man she worships paces the temple hallways at all hours. His stone-faced mask, only half visible now behind aviator glasses, doesn't fool her. Neither do his fierce mood swings. After weeks of watching him obsess over the damage inflicted by the *New West* article, no one is shocked by his solution: the People's Temple will move to a raw piece of land that Father purchased in 1974.

The accelerated move will mean that all those currently working with him to complete housing construction in the South American jungles—will not have the time they need to finish the infrastructure. Fortunately, Loretta is prepared. She knows this is what happens when jealous people spread resentful lies about all your progressive accomplishments. You must go far away and start fresh in a remote country that understands socialism, appreciates the battles you've won, and will allow you to live free.

Loretta also knows that soon she will hear Father give the command for every single one of them to leave the United States. And she, for one, is ready.

* * *

It turns out that climbing the record charts is as precarious and essential to the life of a songwriter as ascending summits is to a mountain climber. You're simply not in the game if you're not on the peaks or the charts. Thus, *poof!* goes another Judy illusion, one that harkens back to my days of believing that the only important thing was to write a beautiful and relevant song that people wanted to hear. After that, the record-buying public would move in and take care of the rest. People would begin to notice your name on songs they liked; a connection would be made; and, presto, you'd begin to make a steady living, right? *Wrong!*

And so, in the Spring of 1977, the first time I optimistically ask Frank when I might receive some songwriting royalties for my recorded songs, he not only takes the opportunity to laugh himself sick at me, he entices a studio full of royalty-poor writers (who prefer laughing to crying) into joining him.

"Girl, you're funny!" he finally manages to snicker. "You gotta have a hit before you start seeing money worth counting."

"You mean we don't get any money unless we have a hit?"

More hooting and howling at the dunce. Nothing new. For the first year, laughing at Judy seems to unleash some unspoken feelings the group harbors about me, feelings that probably run the gamut from affection to resentment. Usually the laughter pivots on the wide variety of ways that the media and record companies misspell my last name on record labels and in trade magazines. No doubt I set myself up for this kind of ridicule by showing how much I care about getting the name spelled right. With a famous work-out equipment company spelling its name "Weider," and the pronunciation of my last name sounding like it should be spelled that way, naturally it's everyone's first guess. And it doesn't seem to matter how carefully I submit the correct "i before e" spelling on every song sheet; they always get it wrong, and naturally it gets picked up from there.

"Oh, Judy, look! They did it right—'i before e'—just like they should," John calls out to me about the listing of one of our songs as a "pick hit of the week" in *Cashbox*. But when I rush over to see what he's talking about, I see that they listed my songwriting credit as, "Judy Nieder." When I turn to John confused, he's sliding off his chair in hysterics.

At first I try joining in on the laughter, but that makes me feel like I know why they're laughing, and I actually don't. So soon I get into waiting them out any way I can—even if it means counting their teeth while their mouths are wide open.

Since it's often Frank who kicks off the "joking," at some point he catches himself bearing witness to something he can't bear to witness any longer—my humiliation—and pulls back to kinder, "more godly" behavior. Skipping over any apologies or explanations, he addresses whatever's been accidentally set off at my expense:

"Okay, okay, Judy, yeah, you'll get some money, but we're only talking pennies. Honestly, you get a couple of pennies for each record sold. So, you gotta wait. That's what the 'big-hit mentality' is about," he explains. "If you have a song that starts getting national airplay, all kinds of things happen."

Now everyone in the studio has stopped working and is listening: "First, people hear your song from some early radio play or a live performance and start goin' into record stores to buy the single. That's one sale for the song. Then when the album comes out, they buy the album. That's another sale for the song. The longer twelve-inch mix of your song is another sale. Then the cassette, another sale, and so on. Record sales drive radio to play your song in higher rotation, and that gets you more record sales which drives more radio play. All this action gets added up and reported to *Billboard* and *Cashbox*. Their weekly song charts track your song's rise—or fall."

No one can teach or preach like Frank Wilson, so even though there are some famous songwriters in the studio, the room is dead silent while his words shimmer through the clouds of myth that usually surround him. Picking up the two trade magazines he's just mentioned, Frank lands on the dance charts pages.

"These two publications are the bibles," he continues, using a word I often hear coming out of his mouth. "They report the record charts every week. And if your tune gets to the top of these charts—stand back!" He slaps one of the chart pages for emphasis. "That money's gonna come pourin' through your windows and doors and bury you!" He punctuates the last sentence with a deep, rolling laugh.

This time his laughter is so inclusive, when it stops I say, "Thank you for explaining how all this works, Frank,"—and instantly regret it. To my utter horror, he says:

"Oh, that's all right, Judy. I expected you'd be asking about your money. That's the Hebrew in you."

What? My ears start ringing in a register so high-pitched my dog back in Venice must hear it. Did he just make an anti-Semitic remark about Jews and money right to my face without the slightest realization of how offensive that is, or how absurd it sounds coming right behind his soliloquy about moola "flowing in the doors and windows?"

For a second I'm not sure something like this has ever happened to me before. Has anyone ever said anything so obtuse about Jews to me before? Then—probably because my whole life is whizzing before me—I remember a time I got lost on the lower East side of New York. When I saw an older woman with a kind face walking towards me, I felt a surge of relief and asked her where I was. She answered without hesitation: "You're in Jew Town, honey!"

"Jew Town?" The "Hebrew in me?" Wow! It's true that we are what we're taught; and Frank has been carefully taught. The man—who has my royalties locked up in his publishing company's bank earning interest *for him*—was indoctrinated into believing that I'm the overly focused money person because I enquired about payment and I'm Jewish.

John, who's not Jewish, but who, in a few years, insists on making larger royalty percentages *[money]* than his co-writers by claiming he sometimes comes up with a title or word (that we co-writers are rarely knocked out by), is never chastised by Frank. In fact, when John and I have conflicts over this royalty policy of his, and go to Frank for help, Frank "rules" in favor of John.

The royalty arithmetic takes another misshapen turn when John and Frank collaborate on all the music for a song and ask me to write the entire lyric. Instead of giving me 50% for the lyrics—which would leave them to share the music royalties 25/25%—they divide the song evenly into thirds. Okay, I get it: three people working on a song, sure, that makes it nicer for everyone. However, when I co-write the lyrics with another lyricist, and John writes all the music, those freakish royalty mathematics return. Instead of dividing the song into thirds, the pie chart mysteriously reverts to 50/50%, with the two lyricists splitting the lyric royalty 25/25% and John taking the other 50%. So, it's okay to be greedy if you're not Hebrew?

Although this obviously frustrates me, I continue to see Frank as a complicated man straddling a multitude of roles all tangled around these changing times and cultures. Despite the rebellious past he talks about, he's a man of tradition. Family and the support of a large church community are everything to him. What's easily lost on many people, including me, is how very close to the insurgent 60s, these 70s really are. While it's true, he isn't chanting, "Black is Beautiful," it's also true that *that* mindset is only a few stormy years ago. Yet here he is, sharing his rarified studio situation—in which nearly everything I write is recorded—with a little white (Jewish) girl, when he could be saving every grace note of it for his own community.

On a practical note, however, diminished percentage points and long waits for royalty checks mean that in addition to the unfinished songwriting all over my desk, I must now start up my magazine freelancing business again. Fortunately, I just got a review assignment for a wildly anticipated film called *Star Wars*. So, I RSVP for the screening and feel grateful to have a plan B. Because, honestly, I don't know what the non-Hebrews do, but without song royalties, this songwriter still needs to eat.

5 When Rhythm Gets The Blues

* * *

When Ella Mae hears that Father plans to move everyone to some godforsaken jungle located on the northeast bulge of South America, all she can think is, *How stupid! Their sudden evacuation will make the public think every accusation in the* New West *article is true.* Instead Ella Mae wants to stay and show the world the good sides of Peoples Temple, if there are any left to show.

But by now the man who insists his congregation call him "Father," has turned into a full-blown megalomaniac, bragging about his sexual prowess day and night on the PA system, "I'm the only real heterosexual here!" She used to live in fear that he'd come onto her too until one day she noticed he never slept with black women. *What a hypocrite!*

* * *

In a secluded hotel room in North Hollywood, I'm sitting on an overstuffed chair more than ready for this meeting to get started. Across from me is Lenny Williams, whose lanky body is lying along the entire length of a single bed. He is staring distractedly at the lead sheet to "Think What We Have." It's a song I wrote in which I stealthily released my disappointment over John dive-bombing our co-writing partnership over a few royalty percentage points. It has broken our trust and sent me on a new journey writing with different cowriters. Even Frank, who now regrets his culpability in mishandling this royalty squabble, tells me, "This kind of stuff happens in writing relationships all the time. But usually it occurs further down the road when the team has achieved real stardom, like Bernie Taupin and Elton John."

Regardless, now that Frank is producing Lenny's next album, the team is beginning to show Lenny the songs we've been working on. Naturally, Lenny loves "Think What We Have," sensing some authentic passion stewing around in it. I like Lenny a lot. He's a big flirt, but smart and immensely dedicated to his career. Although I personally savor a lower, huskier voice, Lenny's trademark alto—oscillating in the frequency of woe—accentuated with his distinctive "ah-ah-ah" calls, has made him a truly recognizable voice in contemporary R&B music. And that's hard to do.

"So, who is this song about?" Lenny suddenly questions, with a little grin.

"Oh, no one..." I try to close the query down.

"It's so moving, and the sentiment about thinking over what you're about to walk away from, is so real. It's great subject matter. I just figured, it had to be about a guy you really love or loved, yeah?"

Help! There's no way I'm going to get into this with one of Frank's recording artists. I need to end this conversation quickly. But when I open my mouth to speak...

"You know, Judy," Lenny interrupts. "I'm very attracted to you."

"What?" I blurt, laughing wildly.

"I'm serious," he sits up on the bed, offended. Although he's been married for many years and has several children by his current—and a former—wife, he's Lenny "Lady-killer" Williams, and when he flirts with you, you don't laugh in his face! It is just that I didn't see this coming at all. I'm still so thrown by this new attention. Throughout my teen and young adult years, I always looked different from my other—more popular—female friends. My hair isn't straight or long. My face features are bolder, darker, and definitely not as delicate and yielding as the 50s and early 60s required of its young ladies. In short, boys did not choose me. Especially not the boys I liked.

Now, years later, surrounded by handsome black men my

age—everything's changed! They like my looks. Forgive such a narcissistic annotation, but this has never happened before. Whether it's with fellow songwriters, or recording artists like Lenny or Ben Vereen, these flirtatious experiences are both exhilarating and confusing. Naturally, this bewildering new adolescence has me asking: Am I gay because I genuinely like women better, or because I've given up on men liking me? It should surprise no one that my therapy sessions have hit the motherload!

"I'm sorry, Lenny," I try to recover from my reflex rejection. "I was just shocked. I'm very flattered, of course."

"Don't be flattered," he says, smiling. "Just say 'yes.'"

"To what?"

With that, he gets off the bed, pulls me out of my chair, and kisses me.

"Whoa," I manage. When I pull away, I hold him at arm's length, and we look at each other for a long moment, then:

"Wasn't that a wonderful kiss?" he asks with such guileless delight, I need to fight off laughing at him again.

"Lenny, you are a married man!"

"That's okay."

"Not with me!"

"Judy, we're separated," he half lies.

"I realize she's in Oakland with your kids, and you are here in Los Angeles working on an album, but, Lenny, that's not what I call 'separated.'"

"It's a long ways away…"

"Yes, and you're lonely, but we have a professional relationship; and I feel very protective of that right now."

"No one has to know," he offers."

"*I* know."

Another long look, then, "Judy, we should have a baby together."

"*Lenny, shut up!*"

* * *

Loretta is packing. She holds an old shoebox in her hands tentatively. In it she has tucked loose notes and notebooks, journals and letters, her thoughts and dreams, all of it carefully hidden away for the book Father wants her to write about Peoples Temple. Someone has to put down the truth, not these unhappy lies that a few others—who couldn't fit in—are spreading. Really, if everybody felt like these disappointed few, would nearly a thousand Congregationalists be leaving their creature comforts, cozy beds, cars—everything that is familiar—to move to the middle of a rainforest?

Contrary to what some are saying, so many church members are like Loretta: people who felt like misfits in their own lives, like they were born into the wrong world. The first time any kind of society made sense to most of them, was when they became part of Father's church. *Do people really think we are all brainwashed, mindless robots?*

Personally, Loretta is excited to be going to Guyana, far from the creeping fascism currently taking over America. She's done some studying and discovered it's a former British Colony—where people speak English. Today it's a Socialist Cooperative Republic, and the government is happy to have them. The land is plentiful; and all they have to do is be strong enough and willing enough to work it. It literally makes Loretta swoon to contemplate what Father has done: he's found a black country where the black members of Peoples Temple can finally feel at peace and at home. Her skin color means more to him than his own! Father also promises to make this their final move.

* * *

5 When Rhythm Gets The Blues

I sit dead center in the orchestra section of the Los Angeles Motion Picture Academy's largest screening room, waiting for *Star Wars* to begin. I am trying to relax, let go, and make conversation with Bill, the tall, sandy-haired man I've been dating for several months. It's part of my ongoing "keep the door open to all experiences" M.O. Bill and I met in Venice during the winter when he called out his window to me after watching me jog past his oceanfront apartment every morning. We chatted, shared stories, then dinner, more conversations, and now dates. Still, I can't quite put my heart on it, but something's not right. Is it me? Him? Us together or...?

There's a disturbance and I look up to see two girls edging into the center section of the row in front of us. One stops for a second and waits for the other to catch up. There's something about them. They seat themselves directly in front of us. I can't stop staring. I hear Bill still talking to me on my right and force myself to turn and watch him. I breathe in his cologne. He's very dear; but, suddenly he smells like the past.

I switch my gaze back to the girls. Their heads are tilted together and I'm glued to every tiny move they make, looking for signs. They're cautious, so I'm not sure, but there's something electric between them, something I can almost taste sitting this close, something that's totally absent from the air around Bill and myself.

The *Star Wars* theme blasts from the Academy's huge speakers and the curtains part. As the lights dim, I can see the girls reaching for each other. Then, a second before the auditorium goes completely dark, one girl tosses her coat over their clasped hands.

My God! Maybe these are the "two girls holding hands" sent from Frank's imagination to test me? Suddenly I feel like crying and laughing at the same time. Really? All this therapy and careful exploration of "my feelings towards men," all this dating, seeking, and looking again at why I haven't been able to make a go of it with a guy—*kaput!*

Bill takes my hand and I hold his. Just because I like men and can sleep with the ones I'm attracted to doesn't mean that's where I belong. I don't have to be in a galaxy far, far away to recall the moonlight and meteors that have torn through even my least satisfying relationship with a woman. It's called passion. And that fire is so verifiable and strong that the mere fact of it makes me feel insecure, like I'm in the wrong clothes.

So! An epiphany during the opening sequence of the noisiest movie I've ever seen? Too bad this revelation turns out to be the most exciting part of the entire screening for me. The girls in front whisper into each other's ears under the reverberant soundtrack, giggle, and then snuggle over their popcorn. Well, well—may the force be with them! And maybe me too someday?

* * *

Ella Mae gets a call from a church official telling her if she ever wants to see her son again, she better be in the next group of Peoples Temple members leaving for South America. Something tells her this will be the most important decision of her life. She is told to join a group that is taking a bus from S.F. to Miami. *Miami?* Ella Mae puzzles. Then she realizes that Father doesn't want to raise any suspicion over sneaking a thousand people out of the country, so he's purposely chosen an East coast city as a departure point rather than San Francisco. But regardless of where they start, the pilgrimage will be a long and grueling one.

After days of humid, sweaty travel, they finally land in Georgetown, a 24-hour boat ride from their destination. The waterway takes them to Port Kaituma—where only small planes can land. A broken down cart is sent to get them, and in the twilight of evening, Ella Mae looks up just in time to see a crude sign in the near-dark jungle. It reads "Peoples Temple Agricultural Project." Off in the distance music and voices can be heard. "Welcome to Jonestown," the driver yells back at them.

Well, of course, Father named the Promised Land after himself.

* * *

I finally get an "advance" on my royalties from Screen Gems-EMI Music, Frank's publishing company partner. The check is for $200, and I nearly run people down on my bike trying to get it to my bank.

"That's it?" my mother comments predictably when I share my good news. "Two-hundred dollars? Oh, honey, I'm sorry."

I'm elated. To me this means it's finally real. I'm a paid songwriter, at last. It's not just in my mind. I've taken my dream out of my bedroom where I used to spend hours writing songs on my guitar and piano, and I made it real. Little did I know it would be rhythm and blues and not folk, acoustic, pop or Broadway; but it's a door, and I'm walking through it with my head high—and I'm not talking about drugs:

While every club in the U.S. is incorporating pharmaceuticals into its dance steps and moving an edgy new social scene to the forefront of America's consciousness, those of us writing for Frank and responsible for a portion of this trendy soundtrack, are as clean as unused water pipes. We're an oxymoron. No alcohol, no cigarettes, no weed, no coke, no nothing! Just work.

Furthermore, I seem to be totally out of touch with crucial parts of the music world itself:

Mary Wilson, of the Supremes, once told me a story about a time "the ladies" were on the road working so hard at the beginning of their career, they had no idea they had a hit record being played all over the country. I recall thinking that was very sad and kinda hard to believe—until this morning. Standing in my Venice kitchen, with the back door open, I heard a song of mine coming out of a radio next door. I ran out onto my back stairs stoop, and found two workmen painting my next-door neighbor's front porch while their little radio blared "Look Up with Your Mind" on KDAY, a Top-40 AM station.

"That's my song! That's *my* song!" I screamed at the top of my lungs, pointing at the radio. One of the workers—who didn't understand English—grabbed the radio in his arms, and ran into my neighbor's house calling back, "No, no! This *our* radio!"

Funny? Yes, but pathetic too, like discovering something really important to you by way of jungle drums. I have a song on the radio and I'm too busy writing one song after another to know or relish an achievement I used to dream about—way back when I had time to dream.

One day, Frank, John, Kevin—the engineer—and I are mixing a tune of mine and John's, (we're writing together again), "Love Magnet," for Freda Payne's album. These are the days when mixing takes at least three or four sets of hands. Programming hasn't happened yet, so everything is done live, in real time. Although you can make edits—by literally cutting the tape with a razor blade—you generally don't risk it. If you hear something in the final mix that you don't like, you have to start all over again from the top with every single instrument turned back up in its track. And Frank is a producer who likes his arrangers to fill all the spaces in a song with music. So, during the mix, we all sit around at the same console, pulling the volume up and down for each track. Meanwhile another tape recorder is copying the results of our live mixing onto a 2" tape. That tape becomes "the master" mix from which the different products are made.

For example, if I'm the one who pulls the keyboard volume down during the verses in the mix, and brings it back up for the choruses, and after doing this correctly in the first two verses, I forget to do it in the third verse, we have to start all over mixing everything from the top. This is true no matter how many other tricky maneuvers everybody else got right while they were mixing their tracks at the same time. Tedious? *OMG, the screaming.*

During this particular mixing session, a representative from Freda's label enters the studio while we're working on her single and sits down next to Frank.

"You've gotta start to make the songs longer," he says matter-of-factly.

Frank, Kevin, John, and I stop what we're doing and look at him. *What does that mean?*

"Stuff is going on out there," he continues, nodding towards one of the studio walls. I take him to mean "the world."

"Add breakdowns to the songs, and make the breakdowns that you've already got in the mix much longer," he instructs, playing with a gold pen he's removed from his suit jacket. "There's a record that the Bee Gee's kid brother just cut called 'I Just Want To Be Your Everything,' and it's gonna be massive."

"Andy Gibb?" Kevin, who knows about everything, asks.

"Right, him, check it out. Anyhow, all these songs gotta be longer. There's gotta be *lonnnng* breaks for people to dance through, longer than you've been cutting. So, don't be afraid to copy measures and add them back in later. Triple what you've got for this single. I need 12" mixes of "Love Magnet"—yesterday! Hurry. DJs are trying insane things with these discs in clubs. Prep me two different versions by tonight."

And with that he returns the gold pen to his suit jacket and walks out.

"Who was that?" I ask. "What's his agenda?"

"Dancing! It's about dancing," Frank answers, matter-of-factly.

None of us are clairvoyant or we'd realize that was the "Paul Revere of Pop" announcing, "Disco is coming! Disco is coming!

* * *

Despite the dripping heat of Guyana, Loretta feels like she's in paradise. Spending long days recording the words of her master teacher, she doesn't mind sitting side by side with other devotees for up to 10 hours at a time at the Jonestown pavilion. This is her job, her duty, her promise. How else will the teachings of Jim Jones stay pure and untarnished throughout history?

Father's voice often serenades them all: "If you only knew how much I love you." Jonestown is real, a living community, where residents subordinate their personal desires for the greatest desire of all: the equality and happiness of everyone. This is not about Father's ego. "If anything happens to me, forget me as a personality because all that gives life meaning is principle…I don't want you to worship me. I want you to become what I am."

If only Loretta could take away his heartbreak whenever someone leaves. The tears that roll down his face are agony to her. "I will never leave you," she whispers up to him. But he doesn't hear. No matter how many stay, the desertion of one person from Jonestown is so devastating to Father, he has started to spend periods of time away from his followers, locked up in his private cabin, alone with a few chosen women and a pharmaceutical doctor.

And now this appalling custody suit has surfaced to distract him even further. Two Jonestown members have not only deserted the utopia they once helped to build, but now they're demanding the return of their son—who wishes to remain with his biological father: Jim Jones. He had relations with the child's mother and has never denied that or that the boy is his son. Father can't help it if these two weak adults left Jonestown. Their betrayal set their own destiny in motion, not anything he did. Father merely responded by never letting them see the child again.

* * *

"Now you're gonna' see your record tear up the charts," Frank says to me early one evening at the end of 1977. We're sitting in our usual seats in front of the sprawling console, lead sheets spread out, working on a ballad for a new group he's about to produce called Alton McClain & Destiny. Frank's been looking to sign an all-girl group like the Pointer Sisters, Bananarama, Sister Sledge—any successful girl group, really—just as long as they're his. He's made hit records for all the ladies, from Tina Turner and Brenda Holloway to Diana Ross. And now he wants to make more of the money; and that means signing them to his production company and publishing as many songs from his publishing company as possible on the group. Thus, the recruiting of a fresh-faced 22-year-old killer vocalist from Baltimore, Alton McClain, and two accomplished back-up singers: D'Marie Warren (later to die in a car accident) and Robyrda Stiger.

As we sit together working on a demo for the new all-girl trio, Frank continues talking to me about a phone call he got earlier in the day from Lenny Williams' manager: "With a record promoter on your tune," he says, able to do two things at once as usual, "everything's gonna be different."

I thought the labels always had record promoters working our records. "No, no, this guy isn't from the label. He's being hired by Lenny's management just to push this one record. And it costs a fortune, so, there's only a limited amount of time to use him. You better start praying, girl."

"Payola?" I ask.

"Praying!" he snaps back.

"No, I heard that part," I say, trying not to laugh. "Does it include payola?"

"No, it's promotion! The radio stations get dozens of new records a day. You can't just leave these guys alone to pick what they wanna play. Somebody's gotta snow them, ya know? Push 'em. But, no, not payola." Then turning to face me so I get his meaning eyeball to eyeball: "But for you, it's about praying. That's your job, praying," he says again.

Telling me to pray is Frank's lead off into a mini-sermon about a better way of living: his way, or his idea of Christ's way, or some combo. I know I should just relax, let the words flow over me. But I feel my body stiffen and my attention flee the minute he starts.

Although my family's Jewish, my brother and I were not raised in a religious tradition. Over time, Jonathan and his wife do make temple a place of comfort and guidance, but I never do. I guess if pushed to say something cogent, I'd say I agree with my mother who used to tell me, "The only way to explain my Jewishness is to say that I would never stand up and deny it." So, for me, it's more like race or nationality, something that's a part of my culture and history.

I've definitely glimpsed appealing ideas that I embrace from many different religions; but I see them more as philosophies than divine truths. I love believers, and join them in feeling there's way more to everything than our little lives. But the stuff too many zealots do in the name of their faiths, *oy!*

5 When Rhythm Gets The Blues

The trail of destruction surrounding their actions reaches up through the ages into today and beyond.

"So, what do you think?" I hear Frank ask, cracking my thoughts to bits. Shoot. I meandered away from his sermonizing so successfully, I have no idea what he's talking about. I smile, hoping he'll repeat some tiny shred of it to help me jump in.

"It'll be fun!" he says, offering no help at all.

"What will?" I finally say.

"Coming to my church the Sunday after New Year's," he huffs, bewildered.

"What?!" I gasp.

"You seemed interested, willing to try it."

"When?" I struggle.

"Just now, when I brought it up. Weren't you listening at all?

I quickly regroup. "Of course, yes." Okay, maybe if I do this, maybe if I actually go to Frank's Mt. Zion Baptist Church where other members of his writing team attend services regularly, maybe it'll matter. Maybe it's something I need to do so they'll realize that even if it isn't my way, I care about all of them enough to take the time to observe an activity that brings them so much fulfillment. Who knows, maybe that'll make them respect my journey too?

"Okay." I say simply.

"Really?" Frank jumps back in his chair with joy. "That's great. That's just great. I'll even draw you a map," he adds with affection.

* * *

The first time Ella Mae experiences "White Nights," she knows something in Father's mind has snapped. The isolation and alienation now permeating much of his daily life, has taken its toll. He is ill, mentally and physically. There are whispers he's been medicating himself with drugs, even shooting something new called Meth. The select few that surround him won't talk. In fact, no one speaks of his escalating, erratic behavior.

The first White Nights begins with distant gunshots. Then a siren is sounded and Father's voice blasts across the PA system yelling, "White Nights! White Nights! Everyone to the pavilion immediately! Hurry, hurry!"

Hundreds of men, women, and children run from every corner of Jonestown to gather round Father, to encircle and protect him, to listen and learn from him. Ella Mae runs too—although she is not afraid of the guns in the jungle. She doesn't believe there is an enemy out there at all. She knows it's Father's inner circle shooting pistols and pretending to be a threat to him and to Jonestown. But why?

"They are trying to kill and destroy us," Father repeats over and over. "We are under attack. You hear them out there? They tried to shoot me. We are being threatened. Everything we have built here is endangered. They will never let us live in peace."

White Nights is also the first time Ella Mae hears Father talk about something called "Revolutionary Suicide." This, in Father's paranoid thinking, is a far better thing to do than allow all these evil, determined, outsiders to take over their beautiful life at Jonestown. The exhausted temple members watch blurry-eyed as several paper cups are filled with "poison and fruit juice," and put before Father.

"Ella Mae," Father says. When she looks up, he is holding out a cup for her to drink. Without skipping a beat, Ella Mae bluffs, swearing she'll most assuredly drink poison for him, if that's what he desires. Her words of loyalty seem to be enough. He moves on, giving the cups to other willing followers who

5 When Rhythm Gets The Blues

drink the mix and wait to die. When nothing happens, Father claps his hands joyously, laughs and bellows into the PA: "Not this time. This was just a dress rehearsal."

That's it! Ella Mae has heard and seen enough. Something very bad is happening; others may not see it or agree, but allowing a person to dictate the course of your life is one kind of mistake. Allowing a crazy person to do it is a tragedy. She knows she must find some way to sneak her son and herself out of Jonestown immediately. But how will she do this? If she tries to walk out, she could get shot, or more likely, wind up lost in the jungles of Guyana forever.

* * *

Wendy and I rustle through my tiny closet looking for the right thing for me to wear to Frank's church tonight. Jeans, no. Sweats, no. Shorts, no...

"My blue, pin-striped pants suit!" I cry out triumphantly. I purchased the tailored suit at Aardvark's, a Venice thrift store full of used-clothing treasures that dominate my wardrobe.

"Perfect," Wendy—who's as naive as I am—agrees. "And you can drape this scarf of mine around the top of it, to sort of femme it up a bit, you know, church and all," she adds, pulling off a bright blue scarf from around her neck and lying it across the suit.

"Great, great. But what about earrings and stuff?" I panic.

"I have tons of things you can use. I have earrings and bracelets and necklaces. Why don't you stop over at my place on your way to his church. But you better get going, look!" She points to a clock on my piano.

"Oh help! Wendy! This is freaking me out."

"It'll be fine. You'll be fine. And you'll look beautiful. Frank will be so happy to see you there," she encourages, knowing that taking on this church visit for me is like growing a new personality.

"I don't do this," I bark at Wendy, as if she doesn't know and is the one forcing me into this.

* * *

Loretta ignores the dull ache in her tooth. But the next morning one of Father's children finds her with a message saying it is time for her to take that long-awaited boat trip to Georgetown for her overdue dental appointment. Although she's very touched that with everything else on Father's troubled mind these days, he should think about her, Loretta resists. She tells the child to let Father know it's okay. She will be fine with the tooth pain a bit longer. She doesn't want to leave him just now. In her heart, Loretta feels she should remain close by. Although she doesn't know why, she senses he may need her.

But the care-taking flows both ways: Jim Jones's daughter returns with a personal message from her father: "No, my dear, you've had that toothache long enough; enough is enough." He also apologizes for not acting on Loretta's dental request sooner. And so, as Father wishes, Loretta prepares herself for the daylong boat trip down a watery 125 miles to visit a dentist in Georgetown.

* * *

The pictures, diagrams, and notes I'm juggling in the car in order to avoid getting lost on my drive to the Mt. Zion Missionary Baptist Church in Watts, are absolutely humiliating, even for me. I forgot to factor in fear. Not that I personally am afraid to go into Watts—where riots have occurred on more than one recent occasion—but because like an ass, I told my hyper-fretful father I was going there.

"No, no you are not. You can't go to Watts!" he bellowed at me. Dad only "goes off" when he's afraid.

"Oh, Daddy," I cooed unsuccessfully. "I'm just going there this once to show Frank and the rest of them that their church, their community..."

"Show them somewhere else!" he roared back.

"Dad, that's ludicrous. That's where the church is."

"Then find another activity to show your respect, but stay out of Watts! Anything could happen there. It's not safe! They're black. You're white. And a white girl—the only white girl!"

"Dad, believe me I know I'm the white one." Finally, I realized that standing up for myself and insisting I'm 30 and don't need his permission, would only leave him spinning and phoning me all night with grim statistics on muggings, murders and other Watts tragedies. So, I did the only honest thing I could; I fibbed:

"Okay. You're right. I'll change the plan." I figured if he follows up and asks what I wound up doing, then I'll tell him the truth. After the fact, he'll be able to see that I'm still alive and take the Watts outing better. Maybe.

✳ ✳ ✳

Father has many, many spies everywhere; after all, the act of turning in friends and family is one that's well rewarded by him. But Ella Mae has moved past her own fears, so there's no going back. She needs to find someone else who wants to leave, and she senses her new friend at the health clinic is as good as it's going to get. Mercifully, she's right. Not only is the woman deeply disturbed by the exploitation and madness escalating in Jonestown, she and a few others already have a plan in place. They intend to sneak off on the very day that United States Congressman, Leo Ryan, is due to visit their settlement. They are banking on a lot of excitement and confusion due to Father's obsessive preparations, which have been going on for days.

Ella Mae knows how hard Father has fought to stop this "visit" from the Congressman. The legal battles literally went on for months. By now everyone recognizes Ryan's sojourn to Peoples Temple for what it really is: a government investigation kicked-off by the concerned friends and relatives of several temple members who've reported feeling abused and trapped in Jonestown. Thus, on the evening of November 17, 1978, Ryan—along with a number of professional news journalists and some troubled family members—are treated to a massive extravaganza of faux Jonestown happiness, rehearsed and staged by Jim Jones himself.

※ ※ ※

After driving twenty miles away from the sea, I pull into the parking lot of Frank's church. There I nervously give myself the once-over in my rear-view mirror: straightening Wendy's scarf, untangling one long dangling earring from the strap of my purse, combing my eyelashes with a toothbrush, pinching my cheeks, and putting on another layer of lipstick.

All right, honky, Hebrew, homo girl: in you go! I think, taking a breath and pushing open my driver's door.

Naturally, as usual, I'm several minutes late, so no one's in the parking lot to help guide me into church. But as I come around the side of the building, I see a man standing outside by himself in a dark suit. He turns my way and I know instantly it's Frank. I wave and pick up speed—as much as possible, clomping along in these heels I have little experience wearing. Frank grins and waves back when he sees it's me. I'm honored that he's actually waiting outside for my arrival.

However, when I'm about two yards in front of him, he literally puts one hand up to his mouth and gasps: "Oh no!"

"What?" I ask, feeling my heart die.

"You can't wear pants in church," he bleats, eyes huge.

"What? No one told me. I mean, I didn't know."

"No woman wears pants in there," he continues, with zero awareness of how much work went into the outfit before him.

"Okay, then," I say, trying to recover, "I'll come back another time."

"No, no," he counters firmly. "Come with me."

"But I thought..."

He steers me abruptly to a side door, away from the main entrance. The door leads to a small, dark room in the church, where he leaves me in the company of two other "unclean things" who haven't attired appropriately enough to worship with the dress-code flock. In this dank, wooden room, we can hear but not see Pastor E.V. Hill's Sunday sermon—which for us disparaged outcasts, seems to go on til kingdom come.

It's pitch dark when I clunk irritably back to my car. None of my cowriters even know I came. How would they? What a stupid waste of time. No good deed...

"Judy! Judy!" I hear Frank calling across the parking lot where he's standing with his family. "Next Sunday you'll come again and wear a dress and sit with Bunny and me and the kids, right?" He's grinning one of his half-sheepish half-confident beams. Very seductive and very manipulative, but not very effective tonight.

"Sure, sure!" I flash back one of my brightest smiles, then slide in behind the wheel, very happy to be wearing pants in this damp weather. When I turn on the engine, I immediately get the giggles as I think, *Oh gee, next Sunday? I forgot. I'm already booked, running with my doggie along Venice Beach and worshipping in the Cathedral of the Great Outdoors, where you can wear a Hefty bag and still receive the blessings of the sun, sand, and sea.*

* * *

In the pandemonium and turmoil of Congressman Ryan's brief stay at Jonestown, a small group of Peoples Temple members—including Ella Mae—tell nervous Jonestown guards that they're going on a quick picnic, and vanish into the jungle. After walking for more miles than they thought they ever could, the group hitches a ride on a train headed for Matthew's Ridge. There, Ella Mae hopes to find a phone and call the American Embassy. However, before that can happen, police officers question the group about their escape from Jonestown. They want to know if any of them know anything about the shootings at Port Kaituma. Apparently, a congressman and several others were killed at the tiny airport a few hours earlier.

The following day, Loretta and Ella Mae—two women with entirely different perspectives on life at Peoples Temple—pass each other in Georgetown like bewildered vagabonds. The surreal news about yesterday's mass suicide-murder of all their friends and family members at Jonestown—918 people including Father himself—has them too traumatized to think. They're in deep shock and will remain that way for years.

Although neither woman knew anything about Father's plans for yesterday, Loretta will spend the rest of her life trying to forgive herself for not dying by his side. He needed her and she wasn't there. Ella Mae too will grapple with massive guilt over leaving behind her mother, brother, and sisters to die in

Jonestown. *What did they think while they were dying—that she knew of Father's grotesque plan and didn't take them with her?*

Years of suffering will hound the few survivors; for unlike other catastrophes, where a sudden and immense loss of life causes the world to offer sympathy, aid, and understanding to the victims, Jonestown survivors will only experience condemnation and rejection. Most will hide or change their identities in order to exist. If they attempt to live openly, no one will befriend, hire, sell, or rent to them.

For years Loretta and Ella Mae feel like pariahs and outcasts, when all they ever meant to do was improve things. As a result of this pervasive survivor shame, most of the world doesn't completely grasp that anyone lived through Jonestown. And yet they did and they're scattered all over America. What's more, most of them do not characterize what happened in Guyana as mass suicide, but as mass murder. And the tapes made during the horrific event support their reality unequivocally.

* * *

"What are you two working on?" Cheryl Lynn, a young back-up singer asks John and me. Cheryl is in the studio rehearsing her part for one of Lenny's songs. We are off to the side of the studio, huddled around a piano, fussing over the final touches of a new song. Outside the pouring rain is holding up the delivery of our take-out lunch.

"I won the *Gong Show* last week," Cheryl continues, "so now I'm going to be taking the lead myself."

"What does that mean?" I ask, looking up from the piano. John and I have been seated so long my back aches. *Gawd, I'm hungry.*

"I'll be singing lead vocals! I just got a record deal," she pauses dramatically and waits for us to do exactly what we—and all sane songwriters—do when we hear someone's gotten a deal: Turn and pay them a lot of attention! It's amazing how the mere thought of getting one of your songs recorded trumps everything else in your psyche: hunger, pain, bad weather—anything!

Cheryl and John continue the courtship while I ruminate over one lyric still bothering me. We've been working steadily on this particular song, "Star Love," for a week. I love the melody and the lyrics flowed out of me like smooth wine thanks to my love affair with the cosmos.

"*Star Wars* is so huge," John told me over the phone. "We should write a song that capitalizes on all the attention it's getting."

"I hated that movie," I replied foolishly, knowing he was right because *Star Wars*' box office was atomic. And in one of those lucky instances of synchronicity, we both said, "How about 'Star *Love*?'"

Yeah, make star love not star war! I thought, remembering the epiphany I had during the screening of *Star Wars*. Wow! That's the feeling I'll try to get into this song.

Abruptly, Cheryl decides to drag me into the conversation: "David Paich—from the band Toto—is producing my album along with his uncle, who's an arranger, Marty Paich," she says happily. "And CBS signed me. So, I'm looking for songs, and like I said, what are you two working on?"

John and I give each other a look. "Star Love" is being prepared for Diana Ross. Frank's known her for years, so getting Diana the demo we're cutting tomorrow is easy. But Cheryl is right here, leaning over our shoulders, dancing around the piano, and asking to hear it.

"Play it for me, please, go on!" Cheryl insists in a

commanding style we'll come to appreciate. Picking up on each other's thoughts, John and I pause a moment: *Why not? It's a good chance to get an outside opinion from a terrific singer.*

John begins playing the provocative intro chords. Still hearing Diana Ross's breathless voice in my head, I begin singing, "Come with me tonight/ All across the universe/ we'll sail for the sky..." When I open my eyes to sneak a look at Cheryl, she's swaying to the verse groove and smiling broadly as the song begins to take off.

I don't know why, but right there and then, *snap!* I get the memo: It's her song. It will take me months to be happy about it. As with "Look Up With Your Mind," a tune intended for Stevie Wonder, here again is a song written specifically for a certain singer who never gets to hear it. That Cheryl Lynn does a killer, number-one hit job of it isn't the point. It's that you just never know the destiny of anything, even a song.

Because I meet Cheryl at one of Frank's recording sessions, I do not object when he takes all my publishing royalties for "Star Love." I certainly don't have to give them to him. He didn't produce the song, and I am not signed to him. It will take a while before I realize I did it because I was afraid he would stop using me as a writer if I didn't. And that's not a good reason. It shows me I am starting to lose confidence in what I bring to Frank's productions. Coincidently, over the next year, people stop bringing artists to Frank to produce. The entire disco explosion disappears as quickly as it materialized. Dance music for blacks and gays is stomped into the ground by AIDS and good old boy rock 'n' roll.

Frank enters a theological seminary to become a full-time minister. Not surprisingly he begins serving as a personal pastor to many entertainers. He is extremely popular, well loved, and respected. I continue writing and getting records with different R&B cowriters, until all at once R&B artists don't want melodies. They want to rap their lyrics. I love melodies and take rap to be a fad that will soon pass. So I wait. It's a long wait.

* * *

6

A Mother of A Meltdown

Oh, Gawd, how am I going to deal with her letter?

It's another painful time for Mother and me. She would call it "devastating," as in me destroying her. To make sure I deal with it, she's sent a single-spaced, typewritten letter, letting me know how wrong I am and how badly I treat her. She didn't even sign or date the letter. There are x'd out words everywhere and little rips and tears all along the sides of the creased paper. Are those water or tear stains? The condition of the stationery tells me more about her distress than her words. She writes:

"I have tried very hard not to intrude on your personal life, but I might have hoped that time spent with me was not a total drag," her hurt feelings leapfrog over any facts I am aware of. "I have suggested many times that it would be nice to take a walk together. Do I need to remind you that it's been years since anything of the kind has happened with us?"

After the x'd out words, the letter just ends. Or maybe she didn't mail the second page. I don't know. I can't guess. Our perspectives are so far apart. Even though I'm working on music all the time now, I could swear Mom and I see each other once a week. Maybe not walking on the beach, but, come on. Does she just want more attention from me like she says? I could do that. But is that really true? If so, why, when we get together, do I feel she's so unsatisfied when I leave? Something's always wrong. I didn't put some dish in the right place; I didn't take something with me that I should have. I didn't ask about someone I should have; I couldn't fix something I should have; I never walk out her front door thinking, *There, that went well, didn't it?*

Honestly? The bottom line is I'm just not the daughter she wants. So, I'm surprised she isn't saying, "Whew! *That* visit's over with. Don't come back." But, there you go: She wants the daughter I'm not. And I want her to love me for being the daughter I am. *Brain-vaporizing, isn't it?*

All right, she hasn't been feeling well. It's the late 1970s, and Mom has entered a time in her life when her body keeps bringing up a subject she hates. It's the same subject that the woman—who once walked the runways of New York City, modeling fall and spring fashions for name designers of the 1940s—has been rejecting for years: aging. I remember when her friend, Eva Landecker-Menkin, wrote a book on how to deal with getting older called, *Aging Is A Lifelong Affair*; Eva gave me a copy of the book because I took the author photo. When I showed it to Mom, she spotted the title before I had time to explain why I had the book, and threw it across my apartment.

Right now, it's mom's feet. She tells me, "they've collapsed." More precisely, "I have foot collapse!" She had surgery three weeks ago, "and you only came by once to fix us a meal!" I remember more visits, but it doesn't matter. That's how she sees it. So now she's in pain and learning how to wear ugly shoes that offend her sense of style. And I don't blame her for feeling anger and disappointment about any of this. If only she wouldn't take aim at me? I am not responsible for what's happening to her anatomy, and it's very hard to feel compassion for someone who's spitting mad at *you* for the pain she's in. It's easier to run. It's actually essential.

6 A Mother of A Meltdown

I'll tell you one thing, I'm sorry I didn't get to see those now painful feet walking in snakeskin high-heels on wooden stages while department store merchants chewed their pencils and made hard choices in the dark. No doubt the years she spent pushing her feet into new shoes that didn't quite fit, with experimental designs and unorthodox materials, didn't help to slow down this hoof collapse she now suffers. But at least she has that exciting time to look back on. She had her "glory days." Wouldn't it help her now to recollect them with pride, and feel some sort of trade off? You know: "I may be hobbling around now, kids, but you shoulda' seen me knock 'em dead in my black suede, open-toe, sling-back, 4-inch heels!" It's that wonderful balance that great memories can offer us. But, I'm sorry to say that everything I've heard about Mom's years as a Manhattan model, I've heard from her, and it isn't glorious:

"It was no fun dragging on and off those heavy fall wool suits after the July 4th weekend; I promise you that!" She often told me. "We were all horribly sun burned and very uncomfortable after vacationing on the beaches of Far Rockaway—which were teeming with people." Mom's always had a way of setting fire to words. "We absolutely never got away, so when we actually had a holiday, of course we overdid it. And there were no suntan lotions then. There were no air conditioners. It was *insufferable*. It was the middle of the summer and we were schlepping on the heaviest materials imaginable for the fall fashion shows. It was murder!"

I honestly don't know what makes my mother happy. As I say, it's not me. There are those who have said she told them otherwise, but isn't that the kind of thing you develop a sense for—whether someone likes you or not? And why didn't she think it was important to mention it to me? I once asked her how come she never complimented me about anything, and she said *(I swear!):* "I never wanted to make the mistake Willy Loman made in Arthur Miller's *Death of A Salesman*. He puffed up his kids so much with compliments that they didn't know who they were or what to do with their lives."

My God, Mother! From one extreme to another? So, her strategy was to rarely let on that she was pleased with me? There are sad plays about that too.

I've checked through every postcard and letter she's ever written me. Never once is there anything more demonstrative than "love, Mother." No "you make me proud" or "you make me happy." There was one nice letter she wrote when she was in France for the first time in 1962. After asking, "How is your piano practicing and weight loss coming along?" she wrote, "How is your cold? I know I must get home soon because you need me now, especially with so many events coming up and big decisions to make." The events and decisions were all about my leaving for college. And although I don't think there was anything left to decide, I clutch at straws thinking that her wanting to be a part of those crucial decisions, indicated her love for me.

I don't look like my mother. I actually have quite a few memories of her telling me exactly that: "You don't look like me at all." *Really, what is a child supposed to say to such information?* Although early photographs of the two of us together show me dressed exactly like her, as I got older and did my own dressing, that image evaporated quickly. A Hopalong Cassidy outfit (without the black hat and white horse, unfortunately) was my wardrobe's pièce de résistance, and I'm sure that was "very last century" for Mom. Every parent wants her kid to reflect her in some way; boy, did I muddy that mirror. As I've gotten older, I can look back and see how she might have felt rejected by me as well. But, hey, *she* was the mother. I had no idea what I was doing.

6 A Mother of A Meltdown

My pre-teen best friend, Wendy, once told me she dropped by our house unexpectedly and found, "Paula screaming at you. You were at the piano, crying your eyes out. Paula kept yelling, 'You will never become anything if you don't practice more. You will never make anything of yourself!'" Wendy said she was so traumatized, she ran out of the house. It took her years to even tell me about it. "My goodness, you were only 10, Judy. How could you 'never make anything of yourself?'" Wendy asked me, without humor. "She scared me so bad, I was amazed that you could practice at all."

Thankfully, I don't remember the incident. But I do remember lots and lots of practicing. Throughout my childhood, from nine years old on, I wasn't allowed out of the house to play with other kids until I practiced. It was just the way I thought things had to be. It made my parents happy. And it made me feel special, like I'd accomplished something. I learned discipline at such an early age that to this day I need to get the hard stuff over with before I'm comfortable having any fun.

By my early teenage years, I had added the cello to my hours of practice because I wanted to play in the school orchestra and pianists were useless there. Luckily, I caught the ear of renowned cellist, Caesar Pascarella, of the Roth Quartet. He occasionally worked with the Los Angeles Conservatory of Music and Arts, and was interested in assembling young musicians and coaching them to play fine chamber music. Although he became my cello teacher, he also decided to put together a classical trio with me on piano and two amazingly talented, if quirky, boys: One was Peter Snyder, who later became the first cellist of the L.A. Philharmonic, and a real-life character in the book *The Soloist*. The other was Michael Schnitzler, the violinist prodigy grandson of Viennese playwright, Arthur Schnitzler. Michael's mother told us some scary stories about what it was like for her and Michael to flee the Nazis during WWII, leaving behind her husband—a famous theater director—and older son.

The Malco Junior Trio (as we became known) toured the Los Angeles area on weekends, getting great reviews and building all sorts of self-confidence for me. I was so swept up in the intensity of our schedule, I didn't immediately notice the psychological toll my heady cultural life was exacting on my adolescence. I was so awash in ignorance about the "important pop figures" of the day, I asked one cliquey classmate, "Who's that?" when I caught her sighing over a picture of Elvis Presley glued to her notebook. As if I wasn't weird enough dragging a cello around school—remarks like that finished me with the "in" crowd.

I do remember one time, being in a classroom full of students who had long ago crossed me off their "people to know" list, when our teacher announced that we were going to compete against another classroom in a talent contest. Unsurprisingly, no one in our group had any talent. Unfortunately for me, our teacher knew I played in orchestra. So, to my horror, in front of this band of assassins, she asked me to play the cello. Well, there was no way in hell I was dragging out a 19th century instrument that you played between your legs in front of this too-hip-to-breathe set. So, at my own desperate suggestion, we all went next door to a music room that I knew had a piano. Kissing my ailing social life goodbye forever, I played a Schubert Etude. At first I heard giggling. My heart stopped, but my fingers kept going. Then it got very, very quiet. When I finished, they all jumped up and cheered. After a juggler from the other classroom dropped all the pins on his head, our class was declared the winner. I'd won one for the team; and suddenly people who wouldn't even look at me before, were slapping me on the back gregariously. It was a truly stellar moment, though mind-boggling in its complexity: *"And she doesn't even know who Elvis is!"* —whisper, whisper.

Music also rescued me in the family. Despite what Wendy remembers and I've repressed, the piano gave me a role and made me feel unique. I had something. Whether it was a ruby or a rock that I rubbed until it looked like an actual jewel, I don't know. It made Mom happy. Dad too—partly because she was happy, and partly because he loved to walk around the house humming off key to the great melodies of Beethoven, Haydn, and Mozart while I practiced.

One very intense summer evening in 1957, during an important concert with the trio at Schoenberg Hall, I remember mother smiling at me. We knew beforehand that the *Los Angeles Times* was sending its critic to review the performance and everyone was pretty uptight. Mom was whiteface terrified. Dad told me years later that the only time she relaxed was when I unexpectedly looked up over the grand piano, caught her eye, and smiled at her. "I felt her whole body relax," he told me. "She was so worried about you. But then you smiled like that in the middle of all those notes!" he recalled. "Your mother whispered to me, 'Well, if she's okay, then I'm going to enjoy the music like everyone else.' And she just smiled and smiled the rest of the time."

I have the *Times* review in a scrapbook, and although it's flattering, it's not what I remember about the night. It's my mother smiling at me. I felt her pride and maybe even her love.

My mother, Paula, was born on October 24, 1914. She was by her own narration, an "accident." Her parents were in their forties, and had grown sons and another daughter with careers and families of their own. Paula's father, a Polish immigrant named Koppel Rosenberg, died suddenly of an aneurysm when she was just four. Her only memories of his death are of her mother, Anna Rubinstein, "going crazy" racing around

New York trying to collect unpaid bills still owed them from his tailor business. When the dust cleared, so did Anna's understanding of their situation: he'd left them destitute.

As my mom told us many times, "My mother was an old lady that I had to take care of." In fact, Mom was forced to quit high school to do this. According to my father, the District Superintendent of Mom's school actually went to her home and urged her immigrant mother to find a way to keep her young daughter in school. The school requested that other family members be present during the meeting, hoping that more ears would help to hear how wrong it was to take this exceptionally bright child out of high school. Although Mom had several brothers, only her brother Ben came.

"She has a real chance to succeed," the Superintendent pleaded with Anna and Ben. But it was out of the question. Not only was there no family money for schooling, but for her elderly mother who struggled to communicate in Yiddish and Polish, Paula was her best defense against starving. And so, the 17-year-old threw herself at the job market, vowing to finish high school at night someday in the future.

What no one could have expected was the surprising work Paula landed. Indeed, it was a major revelation for the family that had treated Anna and her daughter as "the black sheep, always looking for a handout." All at once the undignified atmosphere permeating their lives and the meager apartment they shared in midtown Manhattan, lifted. Mom began to score one modeling job after another in the Garment District for $40 a week—an amazing amount of money during the onslaught of the depression years. To be frank, I'd have trouble believing all this myself if I didn't have a photograph of Mom walking down the runway in Madison Square Garden during a plush fashion show that featured Cab Callaway—a break-through in itself—leading the band.

6 A Mother of A Meltdown

Because she lost her father so early in life, Mom clung to her brother, who doted on her, my Uncle Ben. He was a pharmacist during the prohibition, which was rumored to mean he was also involved with booze, and therefore had money. Unhappily, their relationship, so precious to my mother, took an ugly turn when Ben married. His new bride was determined that her husband cut down on his contributions to the support of his mother and sister. She not only refused to let Ben give them money so that Mom could continue high school, she literally pulled a very young Paula off Ben's lap when he was talking and singing to her as he often did. Grabbing mom by the arm and yanking her away, she said, "Enough! He's got his own baby to take care of now!"

I'm sure Ben *did* have a new world of responsibilities with his young marriage, so I certainly don't blame him, but the number of times I heard my mother repeat her sister-in-law's devastating words, surely indicates how frightening and damaging the incident was for her. Even today, my heart breaks thinking about her as that vulnerable child. It's so true what they say about giving what you get. My mother did not get a nourishing, nurturing, childhood. And what was given to her as a child is what she had to give back as a mother. Mercifully, I bloomed in the dawning of Aquarius—a time of change. Absolutely every song, piece of art, or political event shrieked at us to look at ourselves—and evolve.

But for Mom and her peers, they didn't think about their wounded psyches. Traumas, emotional injuries and the rest just happened and they moved on. They told themselves, "We toughed it out alone, and got over it." But, we the children know better. For sure, long-term neurosis is the engine driving so many people of that generation. Freud, Jung, and the genesis of any tools for "how do I stop some of this pain?" didn't come in time for them. And when it did come, Mom's generation considered it a weakness to indulge. Real adults don't examine themselves. They splatter all their confusion and unrealized dreams onto their young. Then their kids go to therapy.

My far more privileged father, living with his family on Riverside Drive on the Upper East Side in New York, met my mother while she was modeling. Though some said she was marrying "above her economic class," others (including my father), saw it as the cool college grad gets the successful model. When Mom finally brought him home to meet "Mama Rosenberg," Dad says, "To us snobbish middle class guys, Anna belonged more with the recently arrived immigrants, like my grandfather. But I liked her and she liked me. I took her to the Broadway Theater with Paula, and she couldn't stop grinning the whole time." And when Anna didn't think anyone was around, Dad caught her calling her son Ben and bragging, "My Paula, she's dating a college boy who took me to the theater—and a grand dinner!"

My brother, Jonathan, and I were out of the house when Mom eventually decided to finish high school and go to college. She simply wanted to complete what had been taken from her. The thing I remember the most about that time, is how proud my father was. He read and re-read her papers, pointing out to us the high grades and good comments she got from teachers. A poet and literature aficionado himself, who had abandoned his English major to do the more practical thing and become an engineer, Dad took on the role of Mom's old District Superintendent checking back in on her: "I told you she had it in her—a very bright kid!"

I think that made Mother happy for a while. Maybe she was "making something of herself," I don't know. She never used her degree for anything specific. Instead she went into real estate and made a real bundle now and then. She showed her independence, her earning power, her ability to provide for herself and others—even though underneath, she always worried. She stuffed food and leftovers into the freezer. Just in case. Poverty? Another Depression? You never know. Nearby there's always darkness, cheaters, traitors, double-crossers—even daughters who don't really care about you...

Which reminds me—what do I do about this letter of hers?

There's no way that writing back to her is going to make things better. If it's true that she's mad at me for not paying enough attention to her, and I can convince myself she's right, then I should make a date with her and try again. But taking a walk on the Venice Boardwalk, which she says she would like, isn't a good idea if her feet are recovering. So, I'll take her to the movies. Even though I'm writing songs for a living full time now, I still get screenings to upcoming films thanks to my journalism career. In fact, I just got one for a hot new film opening in March called, *The China Syndrome,* starring activist actress Jane Fonda.

I pick up the phone and dial. "Hello, mother?"

[Icy] "Who is this?" She says, knowing perfectly well it's me.

"It's me, your daughter," I answer with a neutral tone.

"OH? I have a daughter?"

[Taking a minute to stop myself from hanging up on her] "Yes, your first born."

"Really? No, I'm not sure I recall that. How would I?"

[Not taking the bait.] "I was wondering if you'd like to go to the movies with me?"

"Me? Are you sure you want to take me? I'm sure you'd rather take someone more exciting than..."

"Mom, please, stop. I'm inviting you to..."

"Did you get my letter?"

"Yes, it was delightful, thank you."

"I wasn't kidding! I've been very, very hurt." she begins to launch herself into a live version of the letter.

"I know, Mom, I know," I say, throwing myself in the path of a mounting fit. "I'm sorry that I've hurt your feelings, *again*. I never mean to do that. It seems that's what happens no matter what I do; but it isn't what I ever wish to do. I love you."

[Silence] "No you don't."

[Deep breath] "Okay, Mom," I manage to spit out between clenched teeth. "Would you like to go see an advance screening of *The China Syndrome*?"

[Voice lifts] "Really? Oh, I've read about that somewhere... *Time* maybe or *Newsweek*? Uh, when?"

[Feeling hopeful] "This Thursday night at 8. But I doubt that you've read about it. No one has seen it yet."

"Oooo, excluuusive?" she teases. "Are you sure you wouldn't rather be bringing someone... special?"

"That would be you, Mom. You are the only person—dead or alive—that I want to take!"

[Sighing, but pleased] "Well, okay, if you're sure. Will you pick me up?"

"Naturally."

* * *

It's March 1979, and Randall Thompson is shuffling through some old notes he wrote criticizing the safety conditions of a nuclear plant where he once worked. He can tell from the tone of his writing that even back then, he was skeptical that anyone would read what he had to say, or care. How stupid. In Randall's view, cutting safety corners to make higher profits should not be an option in any business. In the energy business, it's just crazy; and in the nuclear energy business, it's potentially disastrous, and should be a crime.

6 A Mother of A Meltdown

That's why, after being a Navy nuclear program veteran for years, after spending much of his life in a field he loves, Randall is finally quitting. Somehow, he's just going to walk away from his past at Peach Bottom nuclear plant in York County Pennsylvania, just south of the larger PA nuclear plant, Three Mile Island *[TMI]*. Rather than continuing to batter their heads against the entire nuclear industry over the issue of safety reform—something so many others have tried and failed at—Randy and his wife, Joy, are getting out of the nuke business altogether. Sometimes it's better to admit defeat, and hope someone else can do what you can't.

Instead the Thompsons have decided to try their hand at something they've always been interested in—something quite different. They're going to publish a skateboard magazine! That ought to create a less stressful lifestyle. It's about as far away from something you can't alter as a frustrated person can get. Like they say in that serenity prayer: sometimes you just have to recognize the things you can't change, and let go.

* * *

"Holy God that was scary," I say to Mom who is sitting stone faced next to me in my '67 VW. She definitely looks uncomfortable, like she wishes she had driven instead in her new Volvo. We are still parked in the Columbia Pictures parking lot, just a short walk from several plush screening rooms. Certainly, one of the best things about viewing a movie at a screening, is the comfy seats and cozy rooms we get to share with other film critics. But sometimes that atmosphere can lull you into a sense of well-being that leaves you utterly unprepared for a shock-punch like *The China Syndrome.* The picture, a film about a nuclear power plant accident and a reporter's determination to publicize it despite an ominous conspiracy to hide it, is terrifying.

"That was nerve-wracking," Mom says, a little irritated. "I don't think they had to take it that far, making it so cloak and dagger, I mean."

"What are you talking about?" I react, as usual.

"Don't get excited," she dismisses. "It's a movie. Why don't you start the car?"

I start the car. We drive through the lot alongside many other cars filled with nervous, unstrung *China Syndrome* passengers. She glances over at me.

"Well, I understand what it was saying," she begins, wanting me to know that the point of the film wasn't lost on her. She rummages through her purse and pulls out a stick of gum, slips it in her mouth, and begins rolling the wrapper around in her fingers nervously. "But they always take these things over the top, and sensationalize them."

"How can you say that?" I keep my eyes on the other cars but really want to pull over and shake her.

"Because it's true. Even the title. Why call it that?" she asks.

"They said why. It's when the reactor core melts, and all the radioactive poison burns straight into the ground," I say. She looks at me like I'm making it up. "Mom, you just saw the movie too. Then the core seeps down past the center of the earth to the other side, to China!"

"Oh, come on!"

"Mom, when I was a kid playing in the sandbox, didn't you ever tell me, 'Here's a shovel; go dig to China?'"

"No, I did not. That wasn't me."

"Gawd!!" I growl, frustrated.

"So, then..." she begins, "if there's a nuclear meltdown in China, it would be called 'The America Syndrome?'" *[She smiles at her remark.]*

"Oh, my God, Mom. Did this movie not frighten you at all?"

"Yes, of course. I'm just teasing you. But you get so excited all the time. You were always that way, right away as a baby. Jonathan was different. My mellow baby. *[Pauses]* Do you still do things with Jane Fonda?"

"What? Oh, that was years ago..."

"I can't remember what you were doing..."

"...when she was dating Donald Sutherland. Bill Cragen and I used to meet with their group, E.I.P.J."

"E.I...?"

"Entertainment Industry For Peace and Justice. We were trying to put on a big show at the Hollywood Bowl against the war in Vietnam. It was called *Acting in Concert*. But stuff went wrong and it fell apart."

"She's very excitable too," she murmurs to herself."

"Who is? *Jane?* Mother, does everything I say just irritate you...?"

"Jane irritates her father a lot! And Henry is a good, liberal, man—but you and Jane...your whole generation is on a tear!"

"Mom, that's ridiculous. Please! Are you sitting there pretending you didn't give a damn when you were younger..."

"I still do!" she finally responds. "I don't fancy nuclear reactors! I'm not keen on having them built all over California. There's that one in San Onofre that they had to shut down. Ask your father. He's more versed in these matters. But I just think this movie took it to a fare-thee-well." *[She waves her hand above her head to make sure I understand it went over the top.]*

I try to speak without emotion: "I think they laid it out for us pretty straight, Mom. I think these things could happen—if they haven't already."

"Going by this movie of yours, if they've happened, we would know."

"Movie of *mine*?"

* * *

Randall is sound asleep when his phone rings. It's one of those groggy, jumbled times, when dreams and reality are still pressed cheek to cheek like the lovers they really are. The voice on the phone only adds to his confusion. It's familiar, but why? He pushes at his temples with his free hand, as if to goose his brain awake.

Joy rolls over squinting at the clock, then looks up at him concerned. "Who is it?" she asks, letting her head fall back on the pillow.

Randall shrugs and tries to listen. Suddenly he recognizes the voice and sits up straight. It belongs to an old acquaintance who now works for a private company, Rad Services, that measures radioactive material. Pushing the phone tight to his ear, Randall concentrates as the Rad Services contractor sputters and stops, trying to explain why he's calling. Usually a pretty quick study, Randall's concentration balks at the distraught voice going absolutely rogue on the phone.

"Randall, they, that is to say Metropolitan Edison, just hired Rad Services because there's been an…uh, an…accident at Three-Mile Island."

Joy wakes up again hearing her husband gasp loudly. She turns to see him mouthing, "Oh my God."

"A problem at TMI's' Unit 2 reactor has sparked a series of "mishaps" which—right this very minute—are leading to the meltdown of almost half the uranium fuel inside." Randall bolts out of bed dragging the side table phone with him. He searches the small bedroom for a pad and pencil to write all this down for Joy to read:

"There has been an uncontrolled release of radiation into both the air and surrounding Susquehanna River," Randall scribbles. Joy runs out of the room looking for her glasses because she simply doesn't believe what she's reading without them.

I knew it, Randall thinks to himself. This is exactly what he's been carping about for years. Hardly a peacenik or anti-nuclear doomsayer, Randy has always considered himself the voice of reason. "Do the little things along the way to head off big trouble," has been his motto and advice. Unfortunately, that's not the way nuclear plants work. They don't want to spend a dollar to be proactive when they can roll the dice and bet against something bad ever happening—even if that "something bad" could be a disaster big enough to threaten the very existence of the planet itself!

Joy lays her head against the back of the receiver as Randall tips it so she can hear too: "...Metropolitan Edison has their own in-house health staff," the voice is saying, "but that staff observed what was going on in the first hours of the crisis, and split..." When Joy hears this, she gasps, "It was *that* bad right away?"

The contractor, undisturbed by hearing another listener on the line, answers, "That's right. They saw the dials, read the printouts, talked with other scientists, and decided that spending another minute inside TMI was suicide. That's why the responsibility for monitoring the radioactive emissions has gone to a private contractor—us. But now we're calling you, Randall, to step in and pick up the sword," he concludes, hopefully.

Randall looks at Joy to be sure she heard all this as well. His eyes are huge with excitement. After years of wielding his voice and pen at the higher ups who all refused to reward his instincts with so much as a reply, *the bastards finally need him.* It's happened! All that catastrophic violence stewing right beneath their feet, is loose. And look at them run...

"Yes!" he yells into the phone. "Yes! I want to be a part of the investigation. Get me cleared for TMI immediately."

* * *

It's March 22, my 35th birthday (and Dad's 62nd). The family has gathered at a friend's Venice beach house, where my girlfriend for the next decade, Carol, and I are house-sitting. The beautiful yellow two-story house is a landmark halfway between Muscle Beach and the Washington Pier. It has a large grand piano that I play all the time, and a telescope we brought over ourselves to find the moon on clear nights, and gasp.

I'm trying very, very hard not to go into my usual depression that these family birthday congregations bring on. *Just don't expect anything,* I tell myself over and over. For years, I accepted my mother's decree that I was "so lucky to have your birthday on the same day as your father's!" It certainly seemed true. I adore him, so it should make the day feel all the more special, right? Then I went into therapy. *Never do that unless you're ready to learn the bloody truth about things!*

"Haven't you ever wanted to have your very *own* birthday?" my therapist, Ruth Steiner, leaned in and asked me thoughtfully one day. I'd been talking about my propensity for getting depressed around my birthday. *Hmmm, my very own birthday?* A day where I didn't run around shopping for someone else? A day when I didn't sit there half the time watching cards being read for someone else, or presents being opened by someone else? When Ruth brought this up, I couldn't even go there. "Don't be silly!" I shrugged. "That's selfish. How many people get to share a birthday with someone they love?"

"That's not what I asked you," she pushed on, in that deadly but dead-on way the good ones have. "I'm not questioning your affection for your father. I'm talking about *your* birthday. Everybody wants to feel special on their birthday. Even your father got to have his own birthday for many years before you came along. Right?"

I still wasn't ready. "Well, my friend Michael was born on his mother's birthday and..."

"We're not talking about Michael. We're talking about you. Think about it." Session over. *Ick, I hate when they do that. Leave you to spin in your own thoughts.*

So here I am, on a profoundly beautiful 1979 Spring afternoon, in a sprawling beach house, right outside the soothing Pacific Ocean, with my girlfriend, my brother and his wife, Marie, my mother and father...and my birthday. And it's not just any birthday; I now have this extra knowledge stewing around inside me called: "my hidden birthday feelings." So, I'm both melancholy and agitated.

As usual I've hand-made a card for Dad, using my photographs of the family and quotes from his favorite Shakespeare characters—typically someone like Polonius in *Hamlet,* known for spewing the nonsense of his day to the annoyance of all the other characters. While some men might be insulted by the comparison, Dad gets a perverse kick out of it. He takes pride in being a pain-in-the-ass, worrywart nag. Go figure. Somehow my folks have completely forgotten to get me a card. Somehow, I'm not surprised. Brother Jonathan hasn't gotten me a card or a present. This is his own special tradition with me. On the other end of the spectrum, Carol walks into the living room carrying presents and a generous tray of cut fruit, cheese, and fresh shrimp that she's spent the morning assembling.

Carol, originally from a small town in Montana, learned early and well the indispensable skills of community and giving. I can honestly say my first visits to Alberton, MT with her, were life-changing. The state's huge, flabbergasting, unfastened skies, wood-paneled everything, home-spun steel women, estranged, monosyllabic men—all western remnants living in the past and present at the same time—are now a part of me.

Alberton mornings produced a miracle of camera angles on Carol—dressed in her father's checkered, worn-to-soft flannel shirt, sitting under the trees with the breezes stirring her hair. Mother Lois would join us, twisting her daughter's yellow locks into French-braids—Montana dreadlocks—while relaying the latest town gossip: "A giant pine cone fell from a tree and killed Little Jimmy dead; right in the next town over!" Americana life in the margins, while all around us the ghosts of Lewis and Clark gathered to fill up the endless sky...

Sadly, today I must watch this same bountiful girl from Alberton look up just in time to see my mother pull out a loosely wrapped birthday package from her purse—and pitch it at me across the coffee table. I'm so startled, I duck.

"Pau-la, really!" Carol scolds.

"What?" Mother says with feigned innocence. "It's not going to break."

"Well, that's not the point," Carol laughs, putting the tray close to Mom, Jon, and Marie, who dive in. "It's just not very 'giving like' to throw it at her."

"Oh, don't be silly," Mom says, dismissing her. "Judy understands."

Carol and I look at each other wide-eyed.

Jonathan takes off his handsome brown leather jacket, a birthday present from my parents this past January, and explains that he was going to get me something for my birthday but he ran out of time and wasn't sure what I wanted anyway. Mom looks up and chimes in:

"It's true. It's so hard to buy for you, Judy," she says between bites.

"Why?" I ask, knowing better, but unable to stop myself.

"I don't have any trouble buying for Judy," Carol says, passing around napkins. "She has a million interests, and besides all you have to do is ask her."

Dad senses trouble brewing. "Well, I'm going to open my gift from you girls," he says, nodding to Carol and me, and tearing open his present quickly. Having spent the Christmas holidays in New York, we are stocked with great gifts this year. Carol is a stupendous shopper. While I would lean over her shoulder in "Bloomies" mumbling, "But really, who will we give *that* to?" Carol judiciously snagged every blue-ribbon sales item in Manhattan, and sent them all back to L.A. So, I breathe easily anticipating the big grin Dad is about to unleash as he pulls out of his meticulously wrapped birthday package: a hunter green, cashmere, crew-neck sweater.

"Ahhhhhhhh," he sings predictably. Mother reaches over to the sweater and feels it, reluctantly impressed.

"That's quite beautiful, girls. Try it on, Jack," she instructs, and he disappears up the stairs to the bedrooms.

"I don't know where you girls get the money for these things," she says, looking for trouble.

"Carol is a good shopper, Mom. She finds great sales and..."

"It's not about the sales," Carol stops me, annoyed that I'm making excuses. "People are just worth nice presents. That's all."

Dad returns looking marvelous in the green sweater. It was made for him.

"Oh, Dad, that's great," I say. Marie, herself a good shopper, stands up and straightens the sweater on him. Everyone fusses for a while. Then Mom gets up and retrieves the present she threw at me from across the room.

"Open it," she says, handing me a rapidly decomposing sheet of tissue paper with silk material hanging from it. "I hope you like it. I didn't know what to get you."

This is a disaster; I can tell, even before I fully unveil the long silk scarf I have no interest in. At this time in my life, I don't think I've ever worn a scarf anywhere, not once. "Oh," I say, trying to think of something, anything, to follow up with. The room is quiet. I know this is the part where I say, "It's wonderful. Thank you. Just what I wanted because I use scarves all the time—as you all well know—and I've worn my others to shreds." But instead I just sit there staring glumly at the scarf.

"*You hate it!*" Mother's voice slices through the silence.

I look past her to Carol. Her face is in her hands. I feel my eyes suddenly well up with tears. *What's the matter with me? Why am I falling apart? Why don't I just push on the way I always do on this day? Damn therapy!*

"Yes, I hate it." I hear myself saying before my censor can kick in. *Crap, that shook the sugar off my birthday cake!* My words hang like unsightly laundry around us.

"Well! That's nice!" Mother yowls, threateningly. "What's the point, really? I don't know why I even try!"

"You don't try, Paula!" Carol foolishly jumps in.

"How would you know anything about my efforts...?"

"Mother, whose scarf is this?" I ask, bringing the bickering to an abrupt halt.

She looks at me confused, then a little worried. "What do you mean?"

"Is this your scarf?" I sniff it, smelling a faint whiff of perfume. "Did you get this for yourself and decide you didn't want it? Or did someone give it to you?"

"*That's it!* We're going, Jack!" she screams, as if outrage will shut down my suspicions.

"Now, Paula, Paula, please..." Dad tries, but knows it's over.

"Oh, God," Jonathan sighs, signaling something to Marie who is busy looking for her wrap.

"Take this with you," I say, starting to lose my mind, and catapulting the scarf back to her over ducking heads. "If you had the slightest idea who I was, you wouldn't give me something that has nothing to do with who I am!"

Everyone freezes trying to fathom that statement. Something's wrong with the grammar, but Dad doesn't dare point it out under the circumstances. So, I nosedive on hopelessly: "I'm tired of these birthday disappointments. Don't give me anything ever again..."

"Oh, don't worry, I won't..." Mom shouts at me from the foyer, stuffing the scarf back in her purse.

"...unless it's really for me! It's MY birthday too today."

"Well, of course it is, honey," Dad stalls, helplessly walking towards me while watching his distraught wife stomp out the front door.

"And I know it's your birthday too," I say a little softer; but taking him in wearing his elegant new garment, I'm cornered by my anger all over again: "Just look at your sweater, Dad. It's all about you. This scarf isn't about me. Crap, at least don't give it to me on my birthday."

"I...I understand, Judy," he exhales. "But honestly, sweetie, why make such a big deal? Mom and I get you things you want during the year. Why is this birthday bit so important?"

"I don't know, Dad. It just suddenly is. Okay? It just is," I whimper.

"Are you coming? *I'm waiting out here!*" Mom hollers from the beach walkway in front of the house. Foot traffic heading toward the pier disperses around her nervously. Dad hugs me with a few extra pats thrown in, and leaves.

"Well...happy birthday, Judy," Jonathan chuckles nervously, trying to get out alive. "I didn't say we weren't getting you anything. I just said we didn't get it *yet*. I'm working on it," he stretches awkwardly.

"That's great, Jonny." Carol says, ushering them all out with one last sweep.

When the front door closes, I walk past Carol, outside to a large wicker chair on the side porch that faces the beach. I sit down and cry as hard as I can.

* * *

Eight days after "the incident," Jean Trimmer walks outside her farm in Lisburn, PA, about 10 miles from TMI. Standing on her front porch, she starts looking around for her cat. Jean hears him howling somewhere close by but can't see him. Leaning over the porch rail, she calls, "Here kitty, kitty." Just then, a blast of scalding hot air knocks her hard against the railing. Jean, who's wearing a scarf over her hair and a short sleeve dress with an open neckline, covers her eyes and stumbles around for a few frantic seconds. But before she can cry out, the scorching wind passes, and she's drenched in a mysterious rain that starts falling out of nowhere.

"What was that?" she yells to neighbors who are too far away to hear her. Finding her cat crouched low under the floorboards of the porch, Jean grabs him and runs inside. She immediately locates a towel and begins drying off both herself and her cat. After a few hours, she notices something strange: her skin has taken on a bright red color, as if she'd been sitting in the sun too long and gotten a bad sunburn. It even itches. Trying to remain calm, Jean walks into her bathroom and stares at herself in the mirror. The sight shocks her. She wonders if any other residents in the area are seeing this.

Jean Trimmer turns away from her mirror, picks up the phone in her kitchen, and starts calling around.

* * *

My phone rings. Before I even pick it up I know it's her. I swear my mother has the power to change the timbre of my apartment phone's bell.

"I thought we should talk," Mom says a week after the birthday debacle.

"Okay. But are you going to reprimand me about 'going over the top' about a simple scarf, a nice gift that you went to great lengths to buy for me?" I ask, surprised she's calling at all, but still too upset with everything—including my part in it—to be gracious.

"How are you?" she says, perplexing me further.

"I...I don't know what to say to that, Mom. Fine, thank you."

"Good. I am not."

"Me either," I grumble.

"Judy, what do you want for your birthday?" *Okay, I'm now stupefied.* "Do you even know?"

"Mom..."

"I'm not kidding!" *[Surely her favorite expression]*

"Okay, *[I decide to take her at her word]* I actually need a small, portable tape recorder for the studio when I'm working with Frank," I answer, going to the top of my "need list."

"Fine," she says. "But I don't know where to get that. You'll have to get it and bring me the receipt."

"R-really?"

"Yes. Just do it. That's how we're going to handle these things from now on. Buy it, and we'll pay you back. Naturally, within reason," she adds, gruffly.

"I...I don't know what to say. Um, thank you. *[Pause]* When I bring you the receipt, do you want to have lunch so I can show the tape recorder to you?"

[Startled] "Oh? Okay, yes, that would be fine. When?"

"Well, I'll try to get one tomorrow, Saturday, so maybe on Monday?" I say.

"Good. I'd like that."

After she hangs up I stare at the phone. *What the hell just happened?*

* * *

Jean decides to attend Sunday church despite her strange appearance. Still operating in semi-denial, she hopes her itchy red skin and burning scalp doesn't draw undo attention from the congregation. In fact, she decides it will be a great reality check. And it is. Every single friend she has at the chapel takes one look at her and asks some variation of: "Why didn't you mention that you were going on vacation?" or "Too much sun, eh, Jean?"

Later, after several more days pass, the exposed areas of Jean's skin turn from red to blotchy, and develop little hard white bumps in place of the sunburn. And that's not all: Jean's natural brown moles, scattered about her face and back, turn flesh colored. Finally, she can no longer pretend that nothing is happening to her body. The time has come to investigate. So, after getting a few referrals, Jean holds her breath and begins making doctor appointments.

* * *

Mom and I are sitting across from each other in a small bakery on Wilshire Blvd., where she enjoys lunching. I have already shown her the portable Sony tape recorder that I purchased over the weekend as my replacement birthday present. She is meticulously writing out a check for the $57.98 it costs.

"Here," she says, stopping herself from tossing the check at me across the table.

I take my time examining the check, making a big deal

out of the gesture. "I really appreciate this, Mom. I need it, and it's gonna be a big, big help.

"Good, I'm happy to hear it," she says, "though I'm not sure why."

"Oh!" I begin explaining, hoping she really cares. "Each time we record a new track to add to the song, Frank plays back a rough mix of the entire song up until that point. I want to copy the song in progress, even if it's not finished, so that I can study it overnight, and make suggestions the next day. To do that, I turn on my tape recorder while he's playing the song back..."

"He doesn't mind?" she interrupts.

"What? No, no. It helps him too," I continue, unsure of her real interest. "With this new tape deck you got me, the recording quality will be perfect for what I'm trying to do. The song'll sound a little muffled..."

"And that's good?"

"Yes, by the time these songs are played on AM radio, or on some kid's little transistor, the quality of the sound is pretty dim, like how it sounds being played back on a small tape recorder like this. So, it's like a preview for all of us to work with. Otherwise, those huge studio speakers can hype you into believing..."

"I see." She abruptly cuts off my explanation. "Well, you have the gift you want."

"Yes," *[Feeling guilty]* "thank you again. Listen, Mom...I wanted to ask you something."

"What?" *[Suspicious of my tone.]*

"What do you think about this Three Mile Island mess?" I ask as nonchalantly as possible.

"Oh, that," she shakes her head. "Thank God they've got a handle on it."

"You believe that?" I ask.

"Well, I certainly hope so," she answers authoritatively, as if that will make it so.

"I have trouble believing it," I say. "Doesn't it make you think about the film?"

"What film? Oh, *The China Syndrome*? Yes, of course, I thought about it. It's almost like a publicity stunt!"

"What? Three Mile Island is a publicity stunt for the film?"

"Oh, no, I...don't know," she looks agitated. "Let's not get into all that again. It's been a nice lunch."

"It has," I agree. "I just couldn't help wondering if you had any second thoughts about the film now that a real accident has occurred?" I press on.

"Well...yes and no," she says. "I'm not a fan of those reactors. I told you that. They worry me. But I think they can be useful, if the people in charge don't risk our safety for foolishness.

"Foolishness?"

"To save money! But, Judy, really, what can one person do about it? These outfits are big and powerful. It's like poverty..."

"What is?"

"Trying to change things like corruption or poverty. The numbers are against you. There are too many poor people starving and not having what they need to live useful lives. And the nuclear business? There's too much money in nuclear energy. How can you or I make a dent in any of this?" She concludes, satisfied, and looking over the lunch bill.

I sigh, trying to digest her words. Then, "If everyone thought like that, Mom, we'd be so screwed. One person *must* do something; that's where it starts.

"Well, I've been around a little longer..."

"Oh, please! That's preposterous. Let me never get to a place in my life where I say the things that are wrong in the world are too hard to change. What's more, I think it's farcical coming from you."

"Why?" *[Pained]* "My beliefs are my beliefs; they are not cockamamie!"

"Mom, no, that's not what I meant," I say. Then leaning across the booth until I force her hazel eyes to meet mine, I say as firmly as possible, "Because you aren't really that way. You do care. You've known real poverty, and you feel for those who know it now. You're the woman who loves to go to Mexico and visit small villages where you can speak Spanish and stay with poor families so you can learn about…"

[She abruptly breaks our eye contact, and sits straight up in our booth.] "Judy, there are too many of them in this world. Trust me."

"So, do nothing? Let crap situations bungle along everywhere?" I lean back too, suddenly tired. "Please, let me pay for lunch. I asked you."

"I'm happy to pay. Just…just…don't ask for my support."

"For what?"

"You and Jane Fonda can fight the idiots at Three Mile Island. Just don't ask for my support."

"Me 'n Jane Fonda, again? *[sigh]* Okay, Mom, thank you for the tape recorder; and lunch. Thank Dad too. The gift is perfect! It means a lot that you wanted to get me something I want."

"I always try to get you something you want! I just never know. You're an enigma to me."

I know how she feels.

※ ※ ※

Three weeks after the sunburn enigma, Jean Trimmer is rapidly becoming the star of several doctor symposiums at Hershey Medical Center in PA. To begin with, her hair is turning white and falling out. And the small hair growth that's coming back is salt and pepper, not her normal black hair. Add to this, the mysterious case of her left kidney. "It just dried up and disappeared," her doctors tell her after several examinations. Hershey Medical Center offers only one conclusion: all Jean's symptoms are consistent with high doses of radiation exposure. But where would this exposure have come from?

Farmers in Jean's area are reporting that many of their cattle and goats have died. On top of that, some of the livestock are suffering miscarriages or giving birth to deformed young. And the mysterious plague is not just attacking the animal population: Trees are losing their leaves out of season. There are unsightly tumors on the stems of plants, and huge dandelions—at least 31" long—have popped up sporadically throughout the areas closest to TMI.

Every single day, human, plant, and animal mutations are added to the daily reports that make up a very grotesque picture. And yet, TMI refuses to accept responsibility for any of it. Although the nuclear plant willingly reviews evidence brought to them by local residents claiming instances of non-Hodgkin's lymphoma, lung cancer, leukemia, and skin cancers, researchers for TMI insist there simply is no "convincing evidence" that radiation released from their nuclear plant as a result of the accident should be linked to any of these health problems. They stubbornly and publicly continue to refer to the "low estimates of radiation exposure" documented in their original report.

* * *

I am reading a clipping from the Wall Street Journal that my friend Marilyn sent me from New York. It is so inflammatory, it's sending me into an incoherent fury. I'm jumping out of my skin—an expression that always made me very nervous, but finally feels perfect for what's happening to me. My outer layer simply cannot contain me. I really wish Marilyn were here in L.A. so we could scream and laugh and eviscerate this article into the sleek piece of weasel crap it really is! But alas, she's not, so I re-read the words of this idiot clown, and wonder what my mother might think.

The article, dated July 31, 1979, is headlined: "I Was The Only Victim of Three-Mile Island." The piece is written by Edward Teller, the German nuclear physicist known as the "Father of the Hydrogen Bomb." While it's true Professor Teller taught at my alma mater, U.C. Berkeley, and originally helped to keep the Atom Bomb out of Hitler's hands, he's also the dunderhead who believed the scientists at Los Alamos working with J. Robert Oppenheimer were "too ambivalent about developing nuclear weapons," and not gung-ho enough about dropping the big one. So, he successfully lobbied Congress to establish his own atomic lab in Northern California, and got it. While there are nuclear scientists who have come to regret the potentially devastating genie they've let out of the bottle, Dr. Teller clearly isn't one of them. Anxious, I phone Mother:

"Mom?"

"Oh! I've been meaning to call you," she cuts me off immediately. "I need you to come by and give your father a haircut."

"What? Oh, okay, but it'll have to wait for the weekend. Listen, I want to run something by you..."

"Judy, please. *Your father is desperate for a haircut!*" she hits me with high drama.

"Mom, that sounds so silly."

"I'm not kidding! He looks awful. Can't you come by sooner? We never ask you for things."

"Why do you say stuff like that, Mom? Yes, okay, I'll come by very soon," I fudge, not wanting to have this conversation at all.

"Please, dear, he can't go out of the house looking like this."

"Mom, I just saw Dad Sunday," I squawk, suddenly realizing how loony this is. "He doesn't look bad at all."

"It's grown...!"

"Sure it has!" I capitulate, annoyed. "I'll cut his hair tomorrow,"

[Sweetly] "Thank you. Why did you call?"

"Mom, you know who Edward Teller is, right?"

"Of course."

"He's taken out a two-page spread in the Wall Street Journal blaming Jane Fonda for the heart attack he had three months ago," I announce.

"He had a heart attack with Jane Fonda there?"

"No, no, Jane wasn't there…

"That was hard to picture..."

"This is about *The China Syndrome* and the Three Mile Island accident."

"What is?" she says confused.

"Okay," I start again, "Teller is a big supporter of nuclear, nuclear…anything. Right now, he's trying to resuscitate nuclear energy. When the Three Mile Island accident happened, Jane and a bunch of anti-Nuke people were everywhere protesting the incident."

"I'm sure they were," she says, drolly.

"Mom…! Please. Listen to what Teller wrote:

[I quote Teller from the Washington Post] 'On May 7, a few weeks after the accident at Three-Mile Island, I was in Washington to refute some of that propaganda that Ralph Nader, Jane Fonda and their kind are spewing to the news media in their attempt to frighten people away from nuclear power. I am 71 years old, and I was working

20 hours a day. The strain was too much. The next day, I suffered a heart attack. You might say that I was the only one whose health was affected by that reactor near Harrisburg. No, that would be wrong. It was not the reactor. *It was Jane Fonda.* Reactors are not dangerous.'"

"What a worm!" Mom says.

"Thank you!!" I say, feeling something alien: Mother's support.

"Okay...so your father's hair tomorrow?"

* * *

After witnessing first hand that the radiation leaks inside TMI were easily hundreds if not thousands of times higher than what the plant was willing to acknowledge, the Thompsons and a few other bold scientists who documented all the acute health side-effects and animal deaths, made their findings public. Not surprisingly, their reports were rejected out of hand by the nuclear industry.

Still the Thompsons try to hang in. They continue to meet with others in the TMI area to discuss and chronicle the experiences they had after the accident. But soon things get creepy. They hear rumors about threats and bullying, even some disappearances. While there are those who consider this meaningless gossip, Randall and Joy worry. They know that the nuclear energy industry has too much at stake. So, when a stranger comes up to Randall in a parking lot outside a local market, and tells him that his life is at risk, that's enough for the Thompsons. The family decides to flee the state as soon as possible.

Joy's brother, Charles—another Navy nuclear vet and former nuclear plant worker in Georgia—now lives in New Mexico. Randy and Joy decide to stay with him for a while.

However, leaving the area doesn't mean Randall is really giving up on exposing the truth about TMI, at least not yet. He and Joy decide to work on a book that will detail their experiences at the plant right after they were brought in to analyze the radiation damage. Joy's brother agrees to help them write it. God knows, considering all the shady stuff he's seen, Charles will be a real asset.

*   *   *

Mom and I are sitting in my VW again. This time we're parked in the driveway of my parents' beautiful Rustic Canyon home, just outside the Pacific Palisades. We are arguing. I know you're surprised.

"This is the last money you will ever get while I'm alive," she says unpleasantly.

"Oh, that's nice. Please take it back, Mom," I huff, pushing the check back to her.

"No, your father and I are giving Jon and Marie the same amount, so you should have it too," she says, pushing the envelope into my hands and trying to open the passenger door.

"But…wait, why give me anything if you can't stand to do it?" I say, exasperated with the same argument over and over. "You ask to get together, and then in the end tell me you and Dad are giving me money—which should be such a lovely event. But you dynamite it by saying something obnoxious."

"Giving you money is obnoxious? *Ungrateful!*" Her face is on fire and she's too close to me in this little car for a confrontation, so I open the driver's door and get out.

"You know that's not what I meant," I say standing just outside the car. "The money is fantastic. Of course, it is. What I don't appreciate is: 'This is the last money you will ever get while I'm alive.' Mom! What is that about? You're not dying!"

[She looks a little sheepish.] "I just don't know if we have money to give you in the future, that's all."

"I didn't ask you for money. And, Mom, even if that was true, why say it like that? Why say something bad when you're giving me something wonderful? Are you that ambivalent? It's like when you serve a great dinner; and just as I'm about to take a bite, you announce, 'Have you any idea how much this meal costs?' It kills my appetite!"

"Oh, don't be ridiculous. I'm just kidding," she dismisses.

"No, you're not. You're dead serious when you say these things. You play hide-and-go-seek with giving…"

"Now you're being dramatic," she concludes, gathering her things out of the car.

"I'm being dramatic? *[Imitating her:]* 'This is the last money you'll ever get while I'm alive'" I needle.

"Well…maybe I was kidding about the check…"

"Mom, *that's* not kidding. Kidding is when you say something funny and everyone laughs. What you do is take a dump on nice things."

"Judy! That's disgusting."

I just look at her, perplexed. I guess this is how it will always be. Not exactly enemies. Not really friends. But, yes, family. Well, they say I came out of her, so it would seem so. What's more, she's obviously as dumbfounded with me as I am with her.

* * *

On a warm New Mexico night, Randall and Charles decide to leave Joy at home, and do some shopping for the week. In the trunk of Charles' car is a rough draft of the book the three of them have been working on for months. After marketing at two local stores, the men begin the drive back to Charles' place; soon they become aware of another car coming up on them very, very fast. In one explosive moment, they are run off the road. Losing control of their vehicle, they turn over wildly, finally crashing the car hard. Randall is alive but injured. Charles is dead at the scene. Later, when the car is searched, the manuscript detailing the Thompson's evidence of what happened at TMI—is missing.

* * *

As I drive through the canyon down to the sea along Highway One—a route I use year after year to return to my Venice home after visiting my folks—the check I left on the passenger seat next to me floats with the ocean breeze down to the floor. I start to reach for it but stop myself, preferring to leave it there until I get home. Maybe it'll float right out the window next? I don't know. Mom's ambivalence about giving it, gives way to mine about receiving it. How gross. *Think of all the suffering in the world, Judy!* I tell myself. All the need, all the people who wouldn't die today if they only had a check like the one lying on my dirty car floor.

I'd like to write here that I sent the money to UNICEF or Greenpeace, but that's what ambivalence does. It's a curse. You feel so many different ways, you start to feel nothing at all. So, I did nothing with the money. I put it in the bank, which is like putting it in the freezer, a la Paula. Keep it on ice for... for...what? In fact, the freezer's a pretty good metaphor for the place my feelings about my mother dwelled for a very long time. Of course, I had no idea I was doing this. Our visits and conversations went on unchanged.

And my emotions didn't really open to me 10 years later, when she suddenly died within two weeks of her diagnosis of an inoperable, malignant, brain tumor; or the years before that, when she struggled despairingly with Parkinson's disease. Although I was there for all of it, I felt like I was of little solace to her. What can you really say about two people who loved each other but couldn't really find each other? "Wake up! Life isn't forever."

Now, after decades of meeting her in my dreams, and finally feeling fragments of the love I missed while she was alive, I'd give anything for that long walk on the beach with her. And these days, I'd be the one wearing a long scarf. I like scarves now.

My father lived for 22 years after Mom died. That, of course, is a huge story in itself; the way he emerged, grew and changed, becoming both parents to Jon and me, and a committed grandfather to Jon's children. When he died at 95, I was able to not only grieve for him, but to really, finally grieve for my mother. I better understood her because without her around, I had come to really know my father, who'd preferred her shadow during her lifetime. From him, I learned that although he'd been the source of so much good in her life, he'd also caused her pain. Simply put: I knew so much more about my mother by knowing my father, who couldn't be known while she was alive. Really, what an opus grieving is, with its winding corridors of unexpected information. No one returns unchanged.

"So, Mother, my only Mother, wherever you are, put your sarcasm aside, and listen: I do really love you. *And I'm not kidding!*"

* * *

7

Between Rock And A Hard Place

"Run! *Run now!*" Bret Michaels, lead singer for the glam metal band, Poison, shrieks full fire into my face.

I stare into the beer that's taken a half hour to reach me in this rowdy New Orleans club. I don't want it, but after the chronicle of horrors I've witnessed for 72 hours, being sloshed could be helpful. It's March 1989 and I've been on the road with my favorite flock of cuckoos for several days and nights, moving ever so slowly through the South in their dolled-up tour bus, where even I rate my own bunk. But the drama that lurches out from every corner of their world has finally taken its toll on me.

How did I go from writing songs for R&B stars to writing magazine articles about heavy metal bands and traveling the world to do it? Easy. In the music business, you don't make a living; you make a killing. Every blue moon a song you've written is a major or minor hit, and you make money. When that isn't happening, you create a different life. So now I'm a songwriter without a current hit who's parlayed her music background and writing passion into rock and glam-metal magazine reporting. Nobody I know believes I'm doing this, and I know exactly how they feel.

"I'm serious, Judy! Get up and *run!*" Bret yanks my arm, pulling me out of my seat and sending the heavy beer

7 Between Rock And A Hard Place

glass flying over my shoulder, somewhere. I'm afraid to look. Tethering my purse to my body, I let Bret pull me up and into a running position like a water skier leaving the dock. With my leather jacket now sealed tightly in the grasp of his fist, he flings us both through the bar door, mowing down unsuspecting drunks right and left. I am horrified, but I'm running.

"What the hell, Bret?" I manage to gag at him as he continues dragging me down Bourbon Street.

"Just run!" he hisses. "I'll tell you when we get to the bus."

"*The bus?* The bus is nowhere near here." I say, vaguely recalling tour manager, Scotty Ross, walking me around for an hour before we got to Bourbon Street.

"Please, stop!" I whine.

Bret glances at me, and realizes I'm serious. In another whiplash motion, he heaves us both into a different bar—there's a bar, a club, or a strip joint in every building along the French Quarter and Upper Bourbon Street. No matter where we are, it's clear the main attraction is chugging alcoholic beverages in the middle of the street and falling over.

"We'll lay low in here," he whispers breathing hard.

"Oh, my God, what happened? Why are we run…"

"We beat up a fag!" he blurts.

"*What???*" I shriek loudly enough to cause a couple, swilling something called "hurricane cocktails," to choke on them and turn our way.

"Shhhh! Shhhh!" Bret warns. "Me and Bobby *[Dall, Poison's bassist]* beat up this guy who hit on Bobby in the men's room."

"Oh, you did not!" I say hopefully. Bret stares at me. "Shit, Bret, no…!" I plead.

"He was homosexual!" Bret scoffs, like that's an answer.

Suddenly my worlds are colliding in the worst way possible, and my mind is too sour and tired to deal with any of it. Being in the closet usually works fine with these guys. I wouldn't dream of telling them anything real about myself, and they wouldn't dream of asking. It's all about them, anyway. Since I'm a decade older than most, I trade on the big sister vibe and usually do fine. But lately, I can feel little cracks in my pretense spreading wider. It's actually how I got on this Louisiana meltdown to begin with. During a phone interview with Bret several months ago, he asked me what was wrong:

"You okay?" he halted our interview. "I mean, you sound so sad. You're always laughing and knocking me around with personal questions."

"I'm in the middle of a break-up!" I announced, as if it was his business.

"Oh, baby! That's such heartbreak," Bret soothed, with surprising sincerity.

I was stunned, and quickly tried to suck back my outburst: "Oh, no, it's nothing. Really I…"

"Break ups are never nothing, Judy. Take it from Mr. Break-up," he boasted with self-deprecating laughter. "But I know exactly what you should do."

"What?" I worried.

"You are going to pack a bag and come out on the road with us," he said, pounding something on his end for emphasis.

"What? No, I don't have the money…"

"Poison will pay," he cut me off. "Or Capitol *[Records]*. But not you. I know you'll be worth it. Being on the road will make you forget your pain. I'll make sure you have a blast, and we'll get lots of good press out of you! Do it!"

"How?" I asked, warming to the idea, but not quite believing it.

"I'm going to have our tour manager fax you our schedule. Just pick any dates or places where you wanna join us. I'll call him right now."

7 Between Rock And A Hard Place

"Really?"

"Yep" Bret concluded, delighted to be somebody's hero. And so I did. I picked Baton Rouge, Louisiana, because I'd never been that far South. But somehow, after a very successful gig there at Centroplex Arena, Bret talked me into getting on the back of his motorcycle for a ride; and that one little lapse in Judy judgment pitched me onto this thoroughly hammered road trip to New Orleans in the middle of the night, a couple of nights ago—I think.

The truth is, people who don't drink, shouldn't drink. It's pointless. And I'm *so* not a drinker, that I can actually remember the only other time in my life, in college, when I tried to keep up with classmates and got so pickled, I fell into a bush outside my Berkeley dormitory and wasn't found until early the next morning. My boyfriend at the time—yes, I only had boyfriends in college—spent the entire night driving around the campus looking for me because, apparently, I found a way to call him from somewhere or other (before I lay out in the shrubbery), and beg him to, "Come get me quick! I'm not feeling well." Then I hung up.

But honestly, I'd rather be back in that bush than hiding out in this New Orleans bar with Bret because he and Bobby gay-bashed someone. This just can't be happening.

"Did you hurt him?" I manage to ask.

"Well, he was flat out on the floor…" Bret brags.

"Oh, my God! We have to go back!" I snap and stand up.

Bret pulls my purse strap so hard I become a human yo-yo landing in his lap. "No! The guy called the cops. *That's* why we're all running!" he explains.

"I need a bathroom," I whimper.

Bret stares at me worried. Am I going to go back to the scene of the crime? Can he trust me? We've been good pals for three years, since the day I interviewed the band at their

Woodrow Wilson, Hollywood flophouse in '86. It was the first real interview Poison ever had.

"Su-ure, of course, you can go to the bathroom!" he says magnanimously, never taking his eyes off me. As I turn to leave, a blur of spiky blonde hair circulates in front of us, and even in my freaked-out state, I know its C.C. DeVille, Poison's guitarist.

"Wait! C.C.!" Bret yells. But C.C. is so out of it, he doesn't recognize either of us. He's holding a monster size plastic cup filled with something called "Huge Ass Beers," and despite Bret's bellowing at him, C.C. can only manage a spacey "Hello, Kitty," and wobble totally trashed into another bar. Later, Bret's younger sister, Michelle, insists she saw C.C. jamming to "Wild Thing" with a bunch of black musicians somewhere, but no one else hears from him again for three days.

In the bathroom—which I don't want to talk about—I run into Penny, Poison's lighting and pyro tech. After working 25 feet in the air, and then trying to keep up with the band and crew's crapulous behavior afterward, unsurprisingly, she isn't feeling her best. So together we try to figure out where the bus might be parked. When I walk back into the club, I'm very grateful Penny is with me because Bret is nowhere in sight. Bravely the two of us walk Bourbon Street, which, after 2 AM, looks more like a thoroughfare of brothels engulfed in a spectacular blues 'n jazz soundtrack. We watch an unwieldy parade of boozers eat, drink, gamble, and have sexual encounters right in front of us until, finally, we run straight into Scotty and Bret, who are—surprise!—drinking, eating, and ogling in the middle of the street. Well, at least Bret's eating.

"What is that?" I ask Bret, famished.

"It's called 'Lucky Dogs,'" he says, pushing another piece of something putrid into his mouth.

"I don't want *that*," I say, as if he actually offered it to me.

"You really don't!" Scotty confides, pointing to a filthy street stand where Bret bought it.

"Why?" Bret asks, suddenly alarmed.

Scotty goes in for the kill: "Bret, an old friend of mine who lives here just told me that 31 people were killed in 31 days—here, on Bourbon Street!"

Bret stops eating. "That's *dark!* What's that got to do with…?" He looks at his Lucky Dog, worried.

"Well, you know what they did with the 31 bodies?" Scotty whispers.

"Made them into Lucky Dogs?!" Bret freaks; then re-thinks it, "Oh, Shut up!"

Scotty's face remains a mask of concern. "No, no, really, Bret, I didn't want to say anything while you were eating that, but, remember *Sweeney Todd*?"

"You're not funny! I am already sorry I ate it," Bret says, agitated. He wipes the remaining mustard off his face, and stares at his napkin as if it holds the gospel about Lucky Dogs. Scotty can't stand it any longer, and breaks out laughing.

"Very funny!" Bret laughs, despite himself, and hurls his napkin, which sticks onto my jacket.

One close look at the oozing green and red napkin tips me into woozy. I beg to be taken back to the bus, where I know I've stowed a few cups of fresh yogurt and some crackers. But before I can get anyone to move, a loopy discussion ensues about who is accountable for C. C.'s whereabouts if we leave Bourbon Street. After 10 minutes, no one can follow the conversation, so we default to wishing him the best of luck and leave. Bobby has apparently made it all the way back to the bus, running non-stop the whole time; and drummer, Rikki Rockett, turns out to be the genius of the group. Side-stepping this nightmare-before-rehab, Rikki flew home to his girlfriend in Florida after the gig. Whenever that was.

Once aboard the bus, I head for the bathroom, determined to wash away everything I just saw before attempting to eat anything.

"Oh, no! Don't use *that* bathroom!" Bret yells at me.

I stand in front of the loo frozen. "Why not?"

"It's clogged," he says.

"Clogged?" I choke on the word.

"Yeah. I just looked, unfortunately."

Suddenly I get an appalling visual. The thought of a clogged toilet on this bus with all the foul things that probably clogged it, makes the room start to spin. I think I must have begun to sway because out of nowhere a *very* young groupie grabs hold of me and pushes in close.

"Aw, honey, you can *probably* use the toilet." she sing-songs into my ear with an overplayed Southern drawl.

"Don't use it!" Bret bellows again, snapping me out of my slide to the floor. In a flourish of lead-singer sovereignty, he whirls away from us and disappears.

I unfasten myself from the groupie and hobble off to lie down. Regrettably, I can still smell and hear everything.

"Where did Bret go?" Ms. Groupie asks someone outside my bunk.

"How old are you, honey?" Penny answers with a question. I hear in Penny's tone a lot of worry over the anticipated answer.

"Bret asked *me* to come here," Groupie grumbles, defensively.

"How old are..?"

"Fifteen!"

"Fifteen!" Penny hollers. "Help us! Fifteen? Bret doesn't know you are 15, does he?"

"You all are making me feel like a whore," teeny-bop whimpers.

"Where do your parents think you are?" Penny tries the maternal approach.

"With friends. *[Pause] Bretttttt!*" she yells, and darts off toward the band's end of the bus.

Penny sticks her head into my bunk. "Judy, I swear to God. I don't even remember fifteen. Do you?"

"I'm kind of nauseated right now, Penny," I implore.

"Really, what is going on in this world? Fifteen? Can you *believe* her?" she continues, as if I'd said, "tell me more." To add to this queasy carnival, as Penny bemoans the state of morality aboard a rock tour bus, I can see the window behind her opening, and two pairs of legs—long beautiful legs—drop into the bus, followed by the busty top halves of what is obviously double-trouble, Southern style. I feel my mouth fall open, but no words come out.

Penny stops rambling, stares at me, and asks, "Uh, oh! Judy, you gonna puke?"

The best I can do is point toward a blur of butts and boobs dropping their bras and panties behind them as they streak down the hall. Penny turns to catch the last seconds of the show. She blinks a few times.

"You saw that, right?" she checks back with me. Even shaking my head at this point makes me sick, but somehow I communicate, and Penny chases after them.

Relieved, I lie very, very still, chanting quietly to myself not to throw up. After twenty minutes of my tiny berth whirling 'round like a ferris wheel, things finally start to slow down. I wonder if it's safe to close my eyes and sleep for the first time in I-have-no-idea. Apparently not: Bret sticks his head through my curtain and whispers sheepishly:

"Judy, can you do me a favor? Would you go to the kitchen and get me a condom? I'm out of them at my bunk; but we have a stash in the kitchen."

"Me? Oh, Bret, please, I'm not feeling well. Couldn't you...?"

"*I'm naked,*" he hisses urgently.

* * *

It's been nearly eight years since Joel Weisman became one of the first physicians in the U.S. to identify the bizarre illness patterns in several of his patients as being the onset of the AIDS epidemic. Should he have known that the two seriously ill men who visited him at his Sherman Oaks practice in Los Angeles in 1981, were suffering from the same thing? Displaying an ominous constellation of unrelated symptoms—fevers, swollen lymph nodes, rashes, thrush, low white blood cell counts, shingles, drastic weight loss—the men also shared something else: both of them were gay.

Weisman found all this more than a little unnerving since he himself had left his marriage and hometown of New Jersey in 1975, to cross the country and start a new life in Los Angeles as an openly gay man. Why was this—whatever it was—coming to his door? Was this phenomenon happening to this population anywhere else?

The first thing Weisman had to rule out was Lymphoma, the usual culprit when an immune system falls apart. And *that* was the one thing Weisman was sure of: all these men were dealing with malfunctioning immune systems. After all, a normal immune system would have knocked out any one of these unusual maladies.

Realizing he needed help, Weisman sent two of his patients to a young doctor at UCLA named Michael Gottlieb, whom he'd heard had a patient with the same mysterious symptoms. Ironically, Gottlieb and Weisman, soon to be the West Coast pioneers of this plague, had a lot in common long before they began pooling their patients: they were roughly

7 Between Rock And A Hard Place

the same age, both Jewish, and both from New Jersey. They were both practicing medicine on the West side of the country when the worst health scourge in modern history caught the attention of the white medical and science community. Unlike Weisman, Gottlieb was not gay. But like every trailblazer in the AIDS battle, he too would soon suffer personal setbacks for daring to be on the right side of history.

Weisman remembers the first meeting he and Gottlieb had, and what it felt like to grasp that together they knew three patients with the same symptoms. After all, *three* is the magic number that takes coincidence out of the equation. "My sense was that these people were sick," he recalls, "and we had a lot of people that were potentially lining up right behind them."

Over the next months, all Weisman and Gottlieb's patients were diagnosed with Cytomegalovirus (CMV). CMV, a member of the herpes virus family, typically causes little or no problems in healthy immune systems. But these men—joined now by at least 20 more with similar manifestations—displayed drastically impaired immune systems. Several went on to develop Kaposi's sarcoma, a rare skin cancer usually found in older men or immune-suppressed kidney transplant recipients.

Then one of Gottlieb's first patients reentered the hospital with pneumonia in both lungs. Since he wasn't coughing up phlegm, an astute intern took an unusual step and requested a bronchoscopy. A tube was put down his windpipe, and something no one was looking for was found: Pneumocystis carinii.

People with Hansen's Disease came down with Pneumocystis carinii! What could this mean—aside from the fact that if doctors hadn't been so terrified of Hansen's Disease (Leprosy) patients, maybe more progress with immune deficiency diseases would have ensued by now? If AIDS information was mishandled as well, fear and ignorance would stir up the same hysteria that led to Hansen's Disease patients being quarantined in leper colonies on Moloka'i, Hawai'i. In fact, the Surgeon General, C. Everett Koop, visited Moloka'i and reported that many of the great missionary hospitals founded a century ago for leprosy invalids, could soon be filled with AIDS cases.

Clearly a human catastrophe of ginormous proportions was coming at the medical community; and not knowing every single thing about the disease was no longer an excuse to keep it a secret. So, Gottlieb and Weisman sounded an alarm. In June of 1981, they shot off the first warning flare, using the CDC's *Morbidity and Mortality Weekly Report* as the messenger; a more elaborate report followed six months later in the *New England Journal of Medicine*. The latter was headlined: "Pneumocystis carinii pneumonia and mucosal candidiasis in previously healthy homosexual men: evidence of a new acquired cellular immunodeficiency." At the time, most people didn't know what the hell they were talking about.

Today Weisman stares at the historic clippings before pushing them aside and resting his head on his palms. Whenever he gets discouraged, Weisman tries to look at all the facts he knows now that he didn't know the day he and Gottlieb rang that tolling bell a decade ago. Like so many others, he originally believed that a killer strain of CMV was the culprit. But today he knows nothing that simple can be held accountable for the 100,000-and-counting cases of this insatiable disease. And with half of those afflicted—nearly 50,000—dead, the search for a cure has turned into mass hysteria. Add to this the escalating rage over the length of time it takes the FDA to approve experimental HIV drugs—drugs that could possibly slow the nefarious thing down—and you get a brutal portrait of AIDS and the U.S. medical community in the 80s.

At least doctors and scientists are no longer wasting time arguing over how AIDS is transmitted. All those doctors who maintained AIDS was caused by inhaling amyl nitrate poppers? To Weisman, that theory was an attempt to blame the epidemic on gay men, rather than a virus. And *that* disease has another name: bigotry.

Today the medical establishment understands that unless tainted blood transfusions or shared needles are involved, the condition called **A**cquired **I**mmune **D**eficiency **S**yndrome (AIDS) is sexually transmitted. And that fact alone is the main reason Weisman has become the first chairman of AIDS Project Los Angeles (APLA), as well as the founder of AmFAR (an AIDS research organization): he needs a platform, a way to be more than just another hoarse voice screaming in the wind, pleading with his patients and friends to, "use safer sex practices." Things have to change in the gay community—in the habits of any sexual person, really. Isn't it obvious? How many must die? All of us? Even his lover of nearly a decade, Timothy Bogue?

* * *

Aboard Poison's darkened bus, I finally get enough sleep to find myself wide-awake in the middle of the night. There's something comforting about being rocked gently in the confined solitude of a sleeper bunk. Maybe I'm rediscovering some ancient cradle? I don't know. But in this peaceful and vulnerable state, I find myself able to lift the veil on some recent events I could only walk through—not really face or feel—while they were actually happening. Pushing through the cosmos tonight, they've found me, with all their vivid and emotional precision:

Minna—Ralph and David's mom—is standing very still in her kitchen doorway. I have walked over to the Mitchell's Rustic Canyon home, around the corner from my parent's house. The night before I got a phone call from Ralph and it scared me. He's been sick for a month, causing a joint dinner our parents set up during that time to be cancelled more than once. When I heard his voice on the phone, I can't explain it, but I thought I heard a once indestructible bond to my old neighborhood, shredding. I had hoped he was calling to reschedule the family dinner, but instead he said, "Can you come over and visit tomorrow? Dave and I have something important to talk to you about." I didn't like the sound of that. I was already avoiding a nagging terror that was ringing my shit-detector bell.

Two years earlier, the Mitchell twins came to visit me when I was house-sitting for my parents; and during a casual conversation we were having while making dinner, I decided it was time to tell them I was in a relationship with a woman. While I was mid-sentence with this exposé, I noticed that David's face was turning red. I stopped talking immediately.

"Are you telling us you're gay?" he asked through his blush. Ralph turned around from the kitchen sink where he was washing lettuce; his grin was ripe to the point of rupture.

I confirmed his conclusion, but didn't understand their growing elation. They stared at each other for another second before signaling mutual approval to proceed:

"*Us too!*" David announced, springing across the room and hugging me.

"*Really?*" I whooped inside his embrace. "Ralph and David? The two smartest boys in L.A. are gay? Oh, that's so great! *That's* going to help mom and dad with, you know, [accepting] me."

"Same here," Ralph said, throwing his arms around both of us. Really, we were suddenly back in kindergarten, bouncing around the playroom.

"Our folks are going to be so relieved to know that you—Jack and Paula's daughter—are gay!" David relishes. "They respect your parents so much. Wait til they get together. I'd like to be a fly on the wall of wherever *that* conversation takes place!"

"How did your parents take your being gay?" I asked.

"Mom knew," Ralph said. "Nothing gets by her."

"But Dad didn't; and he wasn't happy," David added, with some sadness. "They were worried about us. They didn't know what 'the gay life' was like."

"So, we took them to Studio One to show them the scene," Ralph explained, as if *that* was the next logical step.

"OMG," I laughed at them. This was *so* Mitchell boys. Their guileless response to parental alarm: invite them into the epicenter of the raunchiest party.

"How did that go?" I teased.

"Not that well," David chuckled.

"Well, at least I hope they were playing 'Star Love?'" I joked.

"I don't remember, but we usually hear it there," Ralph said, working the salad again. "We were a little distracted *that* night."

I told them of my own calamitous visit to Studio One, after Carol and I heard the disco was playing "Star Love" at 2 AM every night. We decided to go and check it out because we were informed the guys were making up special dances to the song, and I didn't want to miss *that*. Unfortunately, when we arrived, they wouldn't let us in because we were women. Of course, the bouncers couldn't actually say that, so they told us we were wearing the wrong shoes: "open-toe shoes." After returning the next night in closed-toe shoes, only to be turned away again for some other bogus reason, I decided we'd try one last time and bring my gold Cheryl Lynn album. Lugging the big thing to Studio One's entrance, we pointed to "Star Love," and my writing credit. Finally, after showing them my driver's license with the same name, we were granted an audience with the breath-catching erotofest inside. The experience broke audacious new pathways in my brain lobes.

"Did *you* know they don't want girls in Studio One," Ralph asked his brother.

"Ralph!" I stopped Dave from replying. "You are kidding, right? How many girls have you ever seen there? I mean, unless it's Liza Minnelli or Cher. And they're not girls; they're divas."

"Oh, no, I've never seen *them* there," he said, referring to Liza and Cher with such earnestness, I laughed 'til I couldn't breathe. We were now shouting this subject matter at the top of our lungs near the open windows of my parents' home—much the way we used to squeal for joy when we were 10 years old and riding rubber rafts in the ocean. I, for one, was ecstatic. Discovering this unexpected camaraderie, after a childhood thick with admiration for their nonstop, high IQ achievements, was the closest I'd gotten to pure euphoria over being a lesbian since owning it…

But this joyous memory is eclipsed by the more recent one of me standing in the Mitchell's living room, looking at Minna's broken face. I turn away from her, and try to take in a nervous and pale Ralph, sitting on his parents' couch. Across from him, David is seated in a large chair. He takes a deep breath and speaks:

"You better sit down."

"Really?" I ask, already choked up; and take a seat across from them both.

"Yeah, Judy, I've got 'the Big A,'" Ralph says, trying to lighten the news somehow.

"Oh, Ralph. I…" my voice dies on me. I turn and look at David. I don't even have to ask.

"I'm HIV+," he confirms.

Looking up a few inches, I see Minna moving further into the living room. Her eyes are full, and she raises her shoulders and both palms toward the ceiling, as if to say, "What does all this mean; and what are we going to do?"

We talk in muted tones for a while; me asking how long they've known, and discovering—as I'd dreaded—that Ralph's "bad cold" had been Pneumocystis carinii, and the cancelled dinners were due to his hospitalization. He tells me he has a lot of faith in his doctor, someone in Sherman Oaks named Joel Weisman. Their father, Bob, is sequestered in the bedroom, heartbroken and completely unable to join us. I try not to break down sobbing in front of everyone.

"Are they going to come to our home and paint a large X on our door in blood?" Minna suddenly vents.

"*What?*" I say, appalled.

"Mom!" David flares, at the same time.

"Mom, stop it," Ralph says sweetly, reaching out a hand to her, and indicating she should sit next to him. She does.

"Minna, you can't be serious," I begin.

"I *am* serious. They are throwing people with AIDS out of their homes, out of their schools. Kids are being taken out of clubs and organizations. I read everything. This is a plague, and people are frightened. *I* am frightened," she weeps.

We all comfort her. I've never seen Minna come apart. All my life, since I was a small child, Minna was *the* consummate mother, so proud of that role. While other mothers in the neighborhood went back to school and started new careers and jobs, Minna remained devoted to her number one occupation: being the mother of Ralph and David. And now this menacing calamity has loomed up out of nowhere, threatening to deep six not only her sons, but her whole reason to be. If she can't protect them, why is she here?

"Judy," Ralph says, looking over his mother's shoulder at me. "Do you think you can reach Michael Deming and tell him about me?"

"Michael? Why?"

"He's a doctor at the CDC, right?" he says, a little piqued that I'm not immediately following his thought process.

"Oh, yeah, of course."

"Maybe he can help me find new drugs? I can't wait around. *This is an emergency!*" he shouts, a reservoir of desperation bursting through his last sentence.

"I'll call him, Ralph, I promise. I'll call him as soon as I get home."

* * *

Continuing his clinical research at UCLA, Michael Gottlieb is able to publish more than 50 papers on HIV infection and possible AIDS therapies. Amazingly, he also manages to obtain one of the first AIDS research grants from the National Institutes of Health, [NIH]. But in terms of getting the general public's attention about the disease, everything pales in comparison to what happens when Gottlieb becomes the doctor of the most famous AIDS patient in the world: Rock Hudson.

Most people agree that the history of HIV can be divided into pre- and post-Rock Hudson. When Rock was forced to come out because he needed to get the best medical help, Gottlieb says, "People finally got it that something bad was happening, and that it was something that they ought to have an interest in."

Instead of pigeonholing the handsome actor with the growing population of sick gay men, Rock, a movie star, was seen as a familiar personality. He was someone the public had grown up with, like a relative or an old friend. People couldn't dismiss him as "the other"—a costly mistake made by "straight people" because it allowed them to believe AIDS was someone else's problem. Of course, the karma of all this wasted research time and money during the crucial early AIDS years will come back to bite the mainstream's butt when the delay in treatment breakthroughs cause many of them to join the dying later on.

※ ※ ※

"It's a fag disease!" Bobby barks at me with bogus authority at 6 am the morning following my night of reminiscing about the Mitchell twins. His blood shot eyes look like someone's scaring the living brown out of them. I believe it might be me. He doesn't like our discussion; so, he flips more ice into a bourbon glass, and watches me take notes. Or at least try to take notes as our shaking vehicle pulls out of New Orleans.

"That's just not true," I sigh for the umpteenth time. But no one wants to hear what I say. I ride these tour busses all the time with bands like Poison, Def Leppard, Ratt, Tesla, Metallica, Skid Row, Warrant, Bullet Boys, Motley Crue, Cinderella, and Slaughter; and most of the time, I just try to get my magazine story, learn more about one or two band members, and get the hell home in one piece. If I pay too much attention to what's going on around me, I will turn into a party pooper of towering proportions. Like what just happened after Bobby plopped down next to me with *this* fabulous news:

"Tommy Lee [Motley Crue's drummer], sent Rikki a note about a real sexy groupie he had recently. He even sent along her measurements. *So...*she'll be waiting backstage for Rikki at the next gig. Cool?"

No. Not cool. But Bobby—joined now by Bret—is irritated.

"It's a fag thing," Bret agrees amiably, trying to side with Bobby. "That's why they're the ones dying."

"Bret, Bobby, look... *[They turn my way obediently.]* AIDS is a virus. AIDS doesn't know or care about the gender of your sex partner. Doctors now get that the virus is passed from person to person through the fluids you share in sex."

"*Ewww, come on, Judy!*" everyone wails at me.

I probably should stop. All these years listening to machismo rock star babble, and suddenly I'm going to throw up a bunch of rickety scaffolding to build a case for safe sex practices? Why? Am I losing my mind over losing Ralph and David? I don't know, but I can't quite shut myself down the way I used to. In truth, I like the guys in Poison; they're sweet beneath the posturing. Yes, their ignorance about this is baffling, but in time I believe they will be among the first to get it—if they live. Besides, aren't they the kind of people I should be talking to? The ones who need to hear it? So, I hold my breath and jump in again.

Bret, both sensitive and smart, sees me take that breath, and stops me: "I'm not saying heterosexuals *can't* get AIDS; it's just we're not the target, and, besides, we're careful." Then he adds, boasting, "Hey, I asked you to get me the condom!"

I don't know what to say first. "Gay guys are not 'the target' either." Ignoring his reference to my part in his sex life, I dig in, "There are no actual *targets* that the virus is aiming at. Do you know that it's only in America where HIV hit the gay male population first? In Africa…" Then, noticing the rapidly clearing room, I snap, "Hey, wait! Can I just say one more thing?"

"Sure," Bobby surprises me. He comes back and leans against the kitchen counter. Bret and Scotty take a few reluctant steps back into the room as well.

"I'm just saying, I wish you wouldn't share groupies," I finish up.

Bobby groans and drops his head back like a child barely tolerating an annoying adult.

"Wait a minute!" Scotty interrupts, holding a fax up and sliding closer to Bret. "I just got a message that says the first message was a mistake. The groupie isn't for Rikki. She's for you, Bret."

Bret snickers and flexes his muscles.

"Oh, my God!" I bellow at Bret. "These girls are sleeping with every rock star that passes through," then I flop back on the long sofa bench, defeated.

"That's the *cool* part!" Scotty needles me. I turn my stiff neck to look at him, unsure of whether he's serious or commenting on how stupid the whole groupie-go-round is to begin with. But he's gone back to studying his notes for the next gig and his face is a blank. So, I swivel back to Bret and Bobby and finally drop the big one:

"This will mean that *you* are sleeping with Tommy Lee and everyone Tommy Lee is sleeping with."

Their mouths drop open.

"Well?" I shrug, as if it's not perfectly obvious. "If one person in this petri dish of cool rockers and groupies is HIV+…?" I let them do the math.

"My hand fucking hurts," Bret blurts, crashing his way out of the subject matter.

I stare at him, annoyed that he's taken to riffling through anything that crosses his mind to terminate our conversation. "I'm sorry? Your hand, Bret…?"

"From popping that guy in the head in the bathroom," he says, proudly.

"Oh, Crikey, Bret! That's the other thing…" I flounder.

Bobby lights up at the new subject: "Yeah, well, you gotta hear the whole story…"

"No, no I don't." I put my hands on my ears.

"I go into the bathroom…," he persists. *Will they never run out of gas?* I feel so weird even listening to this story, I fight the urge to stick my fingers in my ears and make droning noises. Instead I drop my face in my lap and think about the last time I saw the ocean.

Bobby takes a swig of something and walks up next to me

to be sure I don't miss a word: "So this dude says to me, 'Are you guys a bunch of faggots like me?'"

"Wait, what? Who says that?" I sit up ready to listen.

"The guy in the bathroom!" Bret leaps in. "He kept going on and on like that. Talking about our band like *we* were the faggots, wearing make-up and…"

"But, you *do* wear make-up," I insist.

"So what? So what? A lot of cool bands wear make-up, like, like KISS, Alice Cooper, Bowie, Ozzy, the Crue and…"

"I understand," I say, switching to my more accommodating voice to calm him down, "but the guy in the bathroom didn't get it. He made a mistake. He thought the band was gay. Big deal."

Now Bobby and Bret both start screaming at me at the same time, they're so adrenalized:

"We're glamorous!" "It's what we do! That's our band's image." "We tease our hair; we wear heavy make-up and flashy clothes." "We strut around on stage." *[Bret demonstrates strutting through the bus kitchen.]*

"He hit on *me!*" Bobby screeches through the commotion. "He put his hand on my butt!"

"Oh, great horrors!" I mock, trying to drag the conversation to a finish.

"No, no!" Bret admonishes me. "He was serious. Very serious. He kept going on about our band. He was homosexual and asking us, 'What's the band doing tonight?' I mean, what the fuck? So, finally I just popped him right in the back of the head and he went straight down. That was it."

"*Ohhhhh, in the back…?*" I say, disappointed.

"Judy, don't cry for him. He got right up after, and went out the door and started hitting on C.C.….!"

"…who wouldn't have noticed anyway, he was so blasted," I inject.

7 Between Rock And A Hard Place

"...So, Bobby goes 'boom, boom' *[indicates slugging]* and the guy went out!"

I look at Bobby, who, oddly enough, looks like he might be revisiting the testosterone-fueled evening using different optics. He is standing perfectly still and staring into his empty glass, now clutched tightly in his swollen fist. He too hurt his hand punching this unfortunate guy. Bret gets upset.

"Wait, why are you defending him?" Bret asks me, with genuine chagrin.

"Who?" I ask.

"The guy in the bathroom!"

"This 'guy in the bathroom' doesn't sound like he was in very good shape, Bret. He obviously misunderstood the make-up thing. Maybe he was attracted to the band? It's a compliment. Just walk away."

"It takes a real man to wear make-up!" Bret says rejecting the idea that Poison's make-up could be confusing. His blue eyes look pleading now; it's time to support him.

"I like that," I say, escaping into my journalist role; I jot down his quote. "'It takes a real man to wear make-up!' That's cool."

"Yeah, you don't have to be a faggot…"

"Oh, please, stop with the faggot stuff!" I hear someone— oh, no, it's *me!*—yell! I am definitely off the rails now, and I need this job. Bret arranged this trip out of the generosity of his heart. And here I am quarreling with everyone and embarrassing him. They're used to spending their interview time inhaling the intoxicating perfume of their own rock yarns, while exhaling hilarious explanations about all the dumb-ass things they do. That's the rock playbook. I should let my negativity go. I need to find a way back to pandering. But I must have pulled a tendon groveling because I can't seem do it. I don't know why they haven't thrown me off the bus!

— 341 —

"Really, I just had this conversation with some of the guys in Ratt as well as Motley Crue," I say. "All of you rant on and on about 'faggots.' You bait each other, even call each other 'faggot,' like 'hey, faggot, did you take my beer?' So, I've gotta ask, *What faggots?* Where are the faggots here? Do you just like using the word?"

A mighty silence follows, unsettling the few of us left in the kitchen. After a while we just give into it.

I look away, and say, "I'm going to ask Lonn Friend *[editor in chief of RIP Magazine, Larry Flint's rock publication]* if I can do a story about rock stars, groupies, and AIDS. And if that doesn't work out, I'll write it for *Creem Metal [of which I am Editor in Chief]*."

"Cool," Bret says. I look at him expecting a smirk, but see he's serious.

"Cool," I smile back.

Bobby finally stops staring into his glass, glances over at us, and winks at me. "So…you *really think* this AIDS thing is waiting out there for guys like us?" he says.

"I'm afraid 'this AIDS thing' is waiting out there for everyone," I respond. Then annoyed, "Do you think I get off making up sadistic fire-and-brimstone mumbo-jumbo to freak you…?"

"Oka-a-a-y!" he and Bret bray at me like a loud horn.

I can barely believe it, but that makes us all laugh. Soon we're belly-laughing. I'm not sure why Bret and Bobby are doubled up, but for me, it's the first full-on laugh I've had since the twins died. So, I just let myself get deep into the wonder of it. Maybe someday our worlds can merge for real; but for today, I'm laughing out the relief of sharing this little bit of intimacy with people who need it as much as I do.

✳   ✳   ✳

7 Between Rock And A Hard Place

And now Rock Hudson's familiar face is on the cover of *People* and *Newsweek* along with the word AIDS, offering the disease that has been a matter of indifference, a face—and a handsome face at that. Finally, America believes it "knows" someone with AIDS, and the effect is staggering. And when Rock dies, the huge space he leaves behind is filled by his longtime friend, Elizabeth Taylor. The two had been close since 1956 when they co-starred in *Giant*; so, when Elizabeth witnesses her old friend's painful AIDS death first hand, she takes up his cause with unexpected energy and courage. For this is not a popular disease to risk your career on in the late 80s. The mere subject of AIDS is treated like a plague itself. "Let his death not be in vain," Elizabeth begs the world, and never leaves the cause until the day she dies. Gottlieb, who often travels with Elizabeth to lobby senators in Washington and speak out against the epidemic, says it is Elizabeth, and only Elizabeth, who finally gets President Ronald Reagan to say the word "AIDS," a *mere* seven years into his white house stretch.

※ ※ ※

The afternoon weather on the day I bring Michael Deming to the Mitchell's is sunny and welcoming. Rustic Canyon, with its majestic Redwoods and deep forest brooks, is always the perfect place to be when the sun is shining. Somehow the trees, so tall and dignified, filter the sunlight into a soft green afterglow that's now rubbing against the sliding glass doors of the Mitchell's living room. For at least a half hour we talk about nothing while the winter light above us stays trapped in an unstable sky.

Then it begins. I hang onto the tiny details, bone deep and indelible; but it's the unspeakable uselessness most of us are feeling that I can't bear. Ralph sits, then stands and paces, wearing his customary geeky corduroy pants and buttoned-up, short-sleeve, polyester shirt. His head twists to find each of us at one point or another, as he reviews and explains, asks and insists, gestures and points, until his lovely hands give up and fold into fists that rest against his slim hips. I want so badly to say something encouraging, but when I see despair collecting on his body like a second skin, I can't think of a thing. He hardly needs another voice scratching and clawing against his laws of diminishing returns.

"*I can't wait for that!*" he yells at Michael, who suggests contacting someone at the NIH, because he himself knows of no one at the CDC who can get ahold of new HIV drugs.

"Michael, I am going to die if I don't find something to slow this down," Ralph says more slowly, trying to bring his panic down a level. "I thought for sure you would know someone at the CDC who's working with AIDS."

"I'm sorry, Ralph, but I'm not working on HIV/AIDS myself; and it's not part of the work of my office," Michael says, his face a crucible of pain. "But I will do something. I will try to locate someone, some contact at the NIH who is working on AIDS."

"Didn't you do AIDS work in Africa?" David asks, also disappointed but more sympathetic to Michael's distress in this ordeal.

"Yes, but not drug research," Michael mutters. "Are you taking AZT?"

"I don't know!" Ralph shoots back.

"What do you mean?" Michael asks.

Ralph explains the all-too-common scenario torturing HIV and AIDS patients who are trying to get Zidovudine (AZT), a drug first used as a cancer treatment but now showing signs of being able to slow down HIV:

"Dr. Weisman got me into a clinical trial, but its divided into patients who are receiving AZT and patients who are receiving a placebo. I don't know which one I'm getting, but I can guess," he says, unsteady, and sitting back down next to David.

"The placebo?" I ask.

"Right you are!" he snaps. "I don't really feel any better, and I just found another Kaposi's lesion. I think that AZT would at least stop anything new from developing."

"Oh, Ralph, I am so sorry," Michael says with such heartbreak we all turn to look at him. He feels the attention, blushes slightly, and tries to dig up something reassuring.

"I really believe the FDA will approve AZT soon. I mean it. I hear things. I realize it seems crazy to you that they're holding back approval at all…"

"It's insane! We are dying anyway, so most of us are willing to take chances on these drugs. It's an opportunity not only for us but for the FDA and drug companies," Ralph rails at all of us. David puts a hand on his arm to calm him.

"I know, I know," Michael says, "but it *will* happen soon, I know it."

"*Soon* isn't going to work for me, Michael," Ralph says, giving up. "Maybe for David, but not for me."

There's a soft knock at the Mitchell's front door. Michael and I had left his mother and father at my parents' house around the corner when we walked to the Mitchell's. When Minna opens the front door, we hear Michael's mom, Margaret, greeting her. Then she turns and sees all of us.

"Oh, dear, hi," Maggie says cheerfully. We sit stone-faced in the living room, lost in a deluge of human-frailty we can't fix.

"*Oooh…*" Margaret sucks in air, instantly reading the psychic weather around her. She takes another breath and does her best: "I, um, we…Paula and I were wondering if all of you—or, if you prefer, just the boys, the twins—would like to walk over to the Wieder's later and have a light supper with us?"

We all stare at her as if she just suggested skydiving.

"I can't, Maggie," Ralph finally says quietly. "I'm not feeling well enough."

"Not tonight," Minna explains. "Both boys are…under the weather…" her voice breaks.

"It's just not a good idea for me to go outside," Ralph steps back into the conversation to cover for his mother. "I can get sick easily."

Maggie nods and finds Michael's eyes; examining her son carefully with that special affinity some mothers and sons have, she quickly grasps what must have come before the information void now engulfing her.

"That's fine, just fine. We'll do it another time," she recovers. "Michael, I have your violin." She points to a case sitting by the front door. "Why don't you and Judy play something?"

"What?" I shudder. *How can any of us even think about playing music in the midst of this tragedy?* "No, no, I'm sorry. I just can't."

"I can," Ralph surprises us. "Let's play some Mozart, Michael," he continues, pushing away from the wretchedness of the afternoon. I'm astounded, but so relieved I don't mind skipping across this major mood swing at all. No one does. Minna wipes the tears from her face, and stands to help Ralph move to the piano. Michael throws open his violin case and begins tightening his bow and tuning to the piano. As he and Ralph tune and look for sheet music, they begin reminiscing about old classmates and their years together in school. David walks over and joins them, filling in details from the exhaustive material that makes up their memories.

The phone rings. It's Randy Schrader, Ralph's good friend from an AIDS group he attends when he's well enough to go. Minna holds up the phone in the dining room, and Ralph excuses himself for several minutes. I can see him talking from where I'm sitting; he's huddled over the receiver with another distressed look laying claim to his face. When he returns, he explains briefly: "Rand isn't feeling well. So, neither of us made it to today's meeting," he pauses, and then adds, "He told me someone in our group died last night."

Another silence sweeps through the gathering as we all race through every comforting thing we've ever heard, but in the end, choose silence. Somehow Ralph looks different, lighter in some way.

"He's amazing!" he exhales.

"Who is, Ralph?" Minna asks, clinging tight to her son's rising spirits.

"Rand. Whenever we talk, even for a few minutes, he always says something that starts me thinking," he looks directly at David.

"Like what?" Dave asks.

"He was talking about letting go of things, and how hard it is to do that; but, you know, what's really important in the end, anyway?"

"Oh," David says simply, understanding completely.

I think my heart must have stopped and started again. Is that what happens when a heart breaks? Ralph walks back to the piano. David sets up a music stand for Michael. Whatever transpired between Ralph and Rand—not the words or the information, just their end-of-life bond—liberated him to be alive here and now.

Minna brings in slices of fruit and crackers along with tea and fresh coffee. The music agenda restarts as she hovers around everyone, making sure we're comfortable, even coaxing her elusive husband into the living room. Maggie and I huddle together on the couch, and when she puts her arm around me and lets me rest against her, I'm reminded how she, like Minna, has the supreme gift of mothering—that great, joyous force that may not prevent dying, but sure as hell improves living.

Finally, the busyness in the room quiets down, and Ralph looks over the piano at Michael. He smiles with genuine pleasure. "Are you ready?"

"I am," Michael says, so happy to have something to give after all.

* * *

By the mid-80s, despite all the sickness and dying, the AIDS epidemic is still being framed as a freak (gay) accident on the side of life's main road—something to rubberneck at, then forget about. Weisman and his professional partner, Dr. Eugene Rogolsky open a new practice dedicated to acutely ill members of the gay community. Soon, the doctors are completely overwhelmed by all the sick men flocking to them, and must move their practice yet again. This time they open two AIDS Units—one at Sherman Oaks Hospital in the Valley and one at Midway Hospital in downtown Los Angeles.

It's common knowledge within the pandemic that gay people are dying hourly every single day in these hospitals, and that their deaths are devastating their lovers, families, and friends. But, the toll on the doctors, nurses, and caregivers experiencing these same daily tragedies, can never be underestimated. Like soldiers in some ghastly war, the post-traumatic stress is immeasurable; the wounds too deep. Too many losses can blacken even the most generous heart with the permanent grime of sorrow. No one knows how to care for the caregivers. For Weisman, everything is magnified by the helplessness he feels watching his lover lose his AIDS battle. Despite all the drugs he's tried on him, Timothy dies anyway, becoming another statistic on the endless list of casualties. And although Weisman pushes on for

7 Between Rock And A Hard Place

several years, something creative switches off inside, refusing to turn back on for at least five years.

* * *

I have now moved on from torturing Poison about AIDS, needles, and safe sex, to scheduling interviews with every single hard rock band I can trick into talking to me about the disease. I think the word is out that I'm on the warpath, but fortunately so is a lot of hefty fear and reality about HIV. Now plenty of bands want to talk to me. True there are those who still insist they're immune to AIDS because they're "not queer," but I pretty much crap all over that until they shut up. And if they don't, I'm pleased to see other members of the band kick them under the table and say things like, "No, A-hole! It's *not* the Russians and their germ warfare trying to get rid of the really decadent people in our society!"

The hair-brained ignorance—of which there is beaucoup—that spews into so many of my interviews, exhausts me. What are parents teaching their male children? True the current government and its trickle-down stupidity isn't helping, but still it's depressing to hear the gifted musicians you admire belch out this remorseless bigotry. The heavy rock community is made up of young men who come from everywhere in the world. A band can have a number one hit in America and not speak a word of English. But whether they hail from the smallest town in Holland or the largest city in Kansas, by and large, their ideas of manhood are asinine. And now they're totally spooked. The once confident battle cry, "Sex, Drugs, & Rock 'n Roll!"—yes, that's it, the entire post-bebop creed in six words—is crashing down all around them.

First came the bad news about drugs, when "use" morphed into "abuse," and the intoxicating thrill of having a few

— 349 —

of your nuts and bolts temporarily loosened became an utter nightmare when you found you could no longer tighten them. White rubber rooms at the Betty Ford Center were helpful but costly; and when you left, the whole cycle began again. And now another fright show is sinking its teeth into the battle cry and ripping away "sex?" So not only can drugs kill, but *sex kills?*

Naturally, there are a few exceptions to these wincingly dim rock star interviews: Both Gene Simmons and Paul Stanley of Kiss show their maturity by admitting that although they'd rather not be monogamous, "we must be careful, like if you have a cold," Gene philosophizes. "You stay indoors until they find a cure in a couple of years. Then we'll be able to be as crazy as we want again and hang from the chandeliers. And I don't accept the oft heard remark from the 'moral majority'—which is neither moral nor the majority," Gene insists, "—that AIDS is God's way of ridding the earth of undesirables, and that the family structure is the only place in which you should express your sexual desires."

Paul wonders aloud if Kiss should have given out condoms with each copy of their latest *Kiss Exposed* videos, and bemoans the fact that "somebody who is suntanned with a great body and blonde hair, now leaves me wondering what I'm going to do about it!"

A couple of the most sought after members in Metallica are forced to "come out" to me as having steady girlfriends they are monogamous with and thus are not worried about groupies and diseases. This works counter to the usual game plan of widening your appeal to young girls by appearing to be available.

"I'm very lucky," echoes drummer Lars Ulrich. "I have a lovely girlfriend, so I have nothing to worry about. Actually, everyone in Metallica has a steady girlfriend! We're all washed up at 23!"

7 Between Rock And A Hard Place

On the other hand, there's Sebastian Bach, lead singer for Skid Row. One day Sebastian gets photographed wearing a t-shirt that says, "AIDS Kills Fags Dead!" Naturally, getting to him or the band for an interview after this stunt is practically impossible. But I finally lure him onto the phone.

First he tries to lie: "That wasn't me!"

I just laugh at him; then I ask what the hell he was thinking.

"It was a mistake!" he squawks.

"It certainly was!" I respond.

"No, what I mean is I came offstage and I was a sweaty mess. The guys from L.A. Guns were backstage with all of us too. Gerri Miller—do you know Gerri Miller?" he tries to sidetrack me.

"Editor of *Metal Edge*, yes, so what?" I shove him on.

"So, so, she wanted to take a picture of us, of all the bands. I was a mess, so I just grabbed that hideous fuckin' shirt. Some fan had thrown it up on stage, and I put it on."

"Oh, come on. Blame it on a fan? You didn't look at the shirt?"

"No. Well, yeah, sure, all of us saw it and we all knew it was the most awful shirt of all time. But I wasn't on a crusade."

"I wonder what you think a crusade is? People were dying of AIDS while you were posing in that shirt."

"*You* know I'm badly behaved, Judy!" he sighs, hoping for some weird mothering, "and I do think it's important that you know I didn't wear that shirt onstage. I also did not wear it at a press conference like people are saying. I was backstage really drunk and shit and…and I stuck on that hideous shirt."

And finally, there's my head-on collision with the self-aggrandizing Christian metal band, Stryper. Lead singer Michael Sweet, whose howling clerical outrages I've usually managed to evade, pushes one too many of my buttons during this interview, and we never talk again:

"Personally, I feel AIDS is a judgment of God," he proselytizes, not expecting anything but cheers from an interviewer. "The majority of AIDS is passed on from homosexuals; and homosexuality is a sin. That's what the Bible says."

"Michael, here's the thing," I say, pissed, "if God is punishing homosexuals, then why are homosexual women the very *lowest* statistic in this disease—even below heterosexuality?"

He literally gasps. *"Really?* Oh…Look, I don't have all the answers…" *[You think?]*

Weeks on, when I talk again to the members of Ratt and Poison *[I know, that sounds like a joke]*, I discover some real remodeling going on in their thinking. It's not exactly enlightenment, but, it's barely the 90s and, truthfully, most rock stars say the main reason that they got into the music business is because they want to have lots and lots of sex! So, having to go out there, play rock 'n roll, and call it a night, is a big adjustment. Thus, even in the midst of their "we'll-try-condoms-now-and-sort-out-the-damage-later" solutions, I do my best to cheer the guys on with an impressively *straight* face. 'Cause given how they're struggling with this subject, I doubt that they're ready for my *gay* one.

* * *

All the disappointments and failed trials in the AIDS war finally give way to the advent of medications known as Protease Inhibitors and Nucleoside Reverse Transcriptase Inhibitors. The jaw-dropping outcome of these name-twisters is that very sick people begin to get well. Medical researchers discover that if you drive people's viral load down to levels that cannot be detected in their blood, their immune systems will come back. Even young men, literally at death's door, upon receiving these cocktails, recover, get healthy, and leave the hospital. It is an amazing and celebratory time for the thousands and thousands who can finally get well, and their loved ones.

Yet for the families, lovers, and friends of those unlucky patients who got infected too soon in the epidemic, it is a bittersweet breakthrough. What if a supportive president and government, medical community and mainstream society had risen to the challenge a decade ago? Things could have ended so differently for all these missing souls. Instead, the dead are now playwright, Tony Kushner's, *Angels in America*, circling all of us every day. We can't call them back, but each time we stand up to intolerance, or educate against bigotry, we pay tribute to the brave fight fought and lost by these beautiful spirits no longer with us.

※ ※ ※

Two days before Minna dies of a broken heart, she tells me an astonishing story that epitomizes her late sons. She's sitting in her bed, not particularly unhappy, maybe even a little relieved. Months earlier—less than five years after David followed Ralph out the hereafter door—her doctor found cancer in one of her breasts. Although she allowed them to remove the tumor, she refused to fight the disease.

"I'm done," she said, without any signs of regret or sorrow when she called and told me. "This is all right with me. Once the boys left, I had no reason to stay. What for? Every day I look in the newspaper to see if there's been a breakthrough in fighting AIDS. And it's terrible to say, but I'm ambivalent. I'm afraid to read there's still nothing hopeful. And I'm afraid to read there's a cure. Honestly, Judy, I don't think I could stand it. And *that's* just selfish! So, really? The cancer is fine."

Of course, I understood her words perfectly; in fact, I had been expecting something like this to happen for some time.

But now that it had, I wept at the unbearable reality that AIDS had literally killed her entire family.

So now, trying not to cry again in Minna's darkened bedroom on a rainy canyon day, I gaze at her, lying back on her puffy old bed, and remember all the times Carol and I came into these rooms to visit first Ralph, then David, bedridden like Minna, until they could no longer find comfort here and had to make that final trip to Sherman Oaks Hospital in the valley. And though we often promised Minna that we'd sew together a panel for Ralph and Dave, to be added to the AIDS Memorial Quilt *[The Names Project]*, the truth is, Carol and I were coming un-quilted ourselves when they died, and we simply lost the threads to a lot of things.

"I want you to listen to me, Judy," Minna interrupts my reflections with a half-whisper and a strange smile on her lips. "I have something interesting to tell you, and I think that you, of all people, will enjoy it. This is such a sweet story: Years ago, when the boys were in grad school at Harvard, David called to tell us that Pan American World Airways was selling tickets to a future trip the airline would make to the moon."

I feel my face begin to tear apart the way it sometimes does when I'm about to deliver my full-throated aria, *"WHAT?"*

"No, no, listen, I mean it; this is true, and I don't have much strength," she continues. "Pan Am really did sell tickets to one or two moon flights. It's true."

"O-o-o-kay," I say, remembering the cancer is now in her brain.

"Well, I always thought it was so sweet and just like the twins that David bought *four* tickets. See, they wanted to be sure Bob and I could go too."

Oh, my God. Of course, they bought tickets for their parents too. And now, even though they're not going to the moon, they—Bob with his weak heart, and Minna with her cancer

7 Between Rock And A Hard Place

that she won't fight—are all leaving anyway. I try my best to laugh in support of her strange happiness, but all I can manage is weeping again.

"No, don't cry, Judy," she says, reaching a hand out to me. "You see, I want *you* to have the tickets. And I know the boys would too." With that, Minna pushes a white envelope with the Pan American World Airways logo towards me.

"Oh!" I say, truly stunned. "Really? Me? Yes, yes, of course I'll go. I'll go to the moon."

"Wonderful!" she says, with breathy relief. "Then it's all taken care of."

I put the four tickets to the moon in my purse; hug this faithful mother one last time, and say goodbye. Forty-eight hours later, when Minna dies, I walk outside my new Venice home, and look up at the night sky quite sure they've all made it past the moon by now.

8

"Judy Wieder—*Lesbian!*"

Suzanne found the want ad in the *Los Angeles Times*.

It's the end of 1991 and my music magazine writing outlets are vanishing. Classic rock publications like *Creem* and *Music Express* are closing up shop and taking with them the editorial and writing positions I've held for years. I'm trying not to have a cow, though I do get a kitten, my beloved "Piano."

Every day I nag myself to think positively. After all, when disco died a decade earlier, I was able to use my songwriting connections to write reviews and interviews for all these now collapsing magazines. Maybe something will levitate out of their ashes too. But, really, what? What am I qualified to do with my unconventional music background and my college education in theater and psychology?

"Listen to this," Suzanne calls out to me from where she is seated at the sunny kitchen table of the Venice home we've been sharing for exactly one year. "It says, 'Gay *Esquire* looking for editor.'"

"What does *that* mean?" I answer glumly, barely looking up from my desk in our dining room, where I'm throwing old *Creem, Metal,* and *RIP* magazines into a wastebasket.

"Who knows, but it actually gives a phone number," she continues undeterred.

"You're joking!"

"No, look."

Suzanne comes in, unfolding the *Time*s on my desk, as if laying a map of the future over the dying echoes of heavy metal, and circles the ad. "What does it hurt? Call it," she says, before returning to the kitchen.

I dial the number. After a few rings a *very* gay sounding man's voice comes on saying: "If you have called about the editorial position, please write up a table of contents with a list of story ideas for a gay men's magazine; then submit your table of contents to the following address…"

"*What?*" I scream, drawing Suzanne back into the room. I tell her what I think I heard.

"No way."

We dial the number again and listen together on speakerphone. While Suzanne has a good laugh, I find myself jotting down the address.

"Are you going to do it?" she asks, surprised but tickled.

These kinds of things always tempt me. Is it the challenge? I don't know. The maverick in me feels provoked, I guess. And what a clever racket for a publisher to devise to steal good ideas for his magazine! Of course, the fact that this exact scam is done regularly in the future on the Internet under the guise of being "interactive," means nothing to me now.

But what do I know about the things gay men want to read? Well, I know gay men; I can start there. And recently I lost my childhood friends, Ralph and David to AIDS. *That's* got to be a familiar subject to any gay man. So, before an army of censors takes up residence in my imagination, I stick a piece of blank paper into my word processor and bash out a table of contents in twenty minutes. Suzanne reads it for spelling errors, and off it goes to the Venice Post Office.

A week later the phone rings. I recognize the male voice immediately as the one I heard on the answer machine.

"Is this Judy W*iiii*der?" he begins, mispronouncing my name as usual.

"Yes," I say, quickly, while waving an arm around wildly to catch Suzanne's eye. *It's him!*" I hiss with my hand over the receiver.

"Well, Judy, I am the publisher of *Genre* magazine and you are our number one candidate for editor," he announces.

"Really!?" I gulp, naively.

"Well, there are a few other candidates, but you are number one, yes," he reiterates. "We would like you to come into our offices for an interview. Could you do that?"

I tell him I can and I'm about to ask for directions when he says, "I do have one important question for you, Judy."

"Okay," I say warily.

"Why would you, a woman, want to be the editor of a gay men's magazine?"

Before I can think it through I hear myself declaring, "Because I'm gay!"

"Oh, wonderful!" he responds. Then he gives me what turns out to be his home address, which is where his "offices" are located, and we hang up.

"*Oh, my God!*" I yell at Suzanne. "I just told a stranger that I'm gay! Who is he? He could be anyone! He could publish it somewhere. He could..."

"It'll be okay," Suzanne says in her sweetest don't-wig-out voice. Even more importantly, she crosses the room and holds me while I continue chanting, "Oh, my God! I told a stranger that I'm gay," as if repetition can make something go away.

The next day I arrive at the publisher's "offices," and wait in his living room while he finishes interviewing a candidate in another room. As I'm sitting there, I chance to glance over at a large pile of resumes he's left sitting right in front of me on his coffee table. To my horror my resume is on top—with the handwritten word "lesbian" scrolled across it.

Internalized homophobia is a treacherous thing. The precise moment you think you are happy and past the many pitfalls you've bruised yourself on since the day you found a name for what people will call you *("lesbian!")*, kapow! Something like this rears its ugly handwriting just when you're trying to look and feel confident.

I can't swear that my heart is still beating, but I sense I've stopped breathing. I force air into my lungs hastily, and the sudden sensation clears my thoughts like steam leaving a mirror: *Wait, I can't edit Genre. My name, my life, my resume, with "lesbian" flaming across it in red ink? I must be insane. I gotta get out of here.*

"Judy! Judy! Judy!" There's that voice again, calling out before the door even opens, and uttering the most hackneyed greeting anyone with the name "Judy" can hear. My favorite part being that most "Judy! Judy! Judy!" greeters follow it up by asking if anyone has ever said that before. ("No, only you.")

After depositing his last candidate in the hallway, *Genre*'s publisher grabs my resume off the top of the stack and—before I can bolt away—ushers me into his office. I'm afraid to explore the terrain but I think it's his bedroom with a makeshift desk, which he promptly sits behind. The interview takes about a half hour and I don't remember one word of it. All I can say for sure is that he seems positively buoyant after we talk, so I must have said the right things—whatever they might be.

"I'll call you very soon," he threatens. I rush to my car and sit for a minute, resisting the urge to bang my head rhythmically on the steering wheel. Once that passes, I drive home from West Hollywood determined never to go to that place again. When I get to Venice, I collapse on our bed and relay the story of seeing "lesbian" scrawled across my life's work.

"It doesn't matter, honey," Suzanne implores. "No one is going to see that copy of your resume but him."

"*And* his partner, whom he faxed it to in New York, and therefore who knows who else!"

"And who cares, really? It's a gay magazine. You *had* to tell him you are gay…"

The phone rings and it's him. "You got the job," he chirps brightly.

Now here's the thing about competition and winning. It must be a basic animal need, like food or water, to hear "you've been chosen." It can momentarily make you forget you don't want the prize at all. Suddenly I'm one of Pavlov's dogs responding to a bell. Woof! Woof! All puffed up and exhilarated, wondering what marvelous quality I possess that aced out all the others.

Before I can recover, I find myself agreeing to hang up the phone—since we only have one line—and hook up an old fax machine that may or may not work, so he can fax over "the managing editor's editorial duties." Suzanne's puzzled face slides further and further into the features of an acutely concerned person when she hears me say, "Cool, can't wait to read them. I'm sure this will be great fun."

For several unpleasant minutes, a long list of job descriptions makes its way over the fax line to my disbelieving eyes. It reads: story assignment, story writing, story editing, proof reading, monitoring the traffic flow of all stories, providing payment to writers, problem solving, and being accessible "at all times" to the publisher. So, at least four editorial jobs rolled into one. Then comes the kicker, the payment is $1000.

"For what?" Suzanne and I say in unison.

"For each story? I venture. "For a week's work? A month? $1000 for what?"

When I call the publisher for an answer, he does what I will come to learn he always does: utters the most preposterous statement in a tone of voice usually reserved for the most levelheaded remarks. "$1000 for each issue of *Genre*," he says calmly.

"You're kidding me? I earn $1000 for one cover story. What are you talking about? *[Pause]* How many issues of Genre are there each year?"

Again, he slides into his answer as if it's a good one: "Four, there are four issues."

"So you want one person to basically perform all the editorial duties for the magazine all year long for $4000?" I say loudly so Suzanne can enjoy this psychosis with me.

"Why don't you come into the office where we can talk about all this, Judy?" he croons. I hesitate, but figure that by now he might realize how foolish all this sounds? Maybe he'll even call his partner and they'll offer up an entirely different deal. Incredibly, I determine this is bound to be the outcome and agree to drive back there the next day.

And so on the 1st of January, 1992, I am hired as Managing Editor—despite being told I'm really the Editor—for pretty much $1000 per issue. Since being a woman won't sit well with *Genre*'s gay male readership, the publisher decides to call himself Editor in Chief and be "the face of the magazine." This part is fine with me. Better his face than mine.

I should mention here that I reference only *Genre*'s beginning years, for that's what I know. With its two publishers, one in New York and one in Los Angeles, *Genre*'s the first national gay men's magazine on glossy paper to have a go at publishing *without* sex ads. In time, the magazine's success will push the quarter-of-a-century-old *Advocate* onto glossy paper and make way for the entrance of the initially groundbreaking, co-gender *Out* magazine on the East Coast.

Sadly, *Genre*'s two owner-publishers agree on nothing and fight constantly. The one I work for yells things at me like, "Pay him $50 bucks!" when I secure world-famous fashion photographer, Francesco Scavullo, to shoot Charles Busch and Lypsinka for a fashion spread in the magazine. He's accustomed to having gay men do everything for free in *Genre* and is puzzled by people (me, professionals, women, etc.) who want to be paid. The situation is surreal. But two wonderful things come to me out of the experience: the magazine's Associate Publisher, Joe Landry, and *The Advocate*. For this I owe *Genre*, so I will say no more about the inner workings of this gonzo factory.

One afternoon in 1992, I accompany the publisher to a brunch where we are seated across from *The Advocate*'s Editor in Chief. He is drop-dead gorgeous with his model looks and regal carriage (something I truly believe the magazine needs at this time in a world besieged with images of sick and dying gay men). When *Genre*'s publisher sees him, he starts to spin out. I have no idea what's happening, but all at once he begins elbowing me and shoving a note into my hand as if it isn't obvious to everyone around us that he's doing this. From the corner of my eye, I see The Advocate's EIC watching, and looking away quickly as if he isn't interested. I pretend not to care either; instead I open the crumpled note in my hand:

"Judy-
Don't look now. It's him! *The Advocate*'s
Editor in Chief. HE IS LOOKING AT YOU."

So? Certainly, *Genre*'s publisher doesn't fantasize that we are in competition with *The Advocate*? When I turn to ask him, I'm surprised to see his face has grown pale. Before I can say anything, he says, "I need you to drive me home right now; I'm very tired and I don't feel well."

I stand up so quickly to help him, I actually catch *The Advocate*'s head editor staring at me before he can look away.

It's probably a lousy thing to do in the middle of assisting someone, but I take advantage of the moment, stick out my hand, and say, "I'm Judy Wieder…"

"I know who you are," he says.

What does that mean? I have no time to find out. The publisher's grip on my arm has turned claw-like after that exchange. "I feel faint," he hisses into my ear. Later, in the car, he sulks until we are parked outside his apartment.

"You introduced yourself to him," he sighs, opening the car door.

"He was looking right at me, so I thought…"

"Yes. *That's* what I wrote in the note," he huffs, and slams the door with surprising strength. The next day, knowing the publisher still isn't feeling well, I decide to do something I rarely do. I come into the "office" to work instead of working out of my home as usual. While I am editing a story, one of the guys who answers *Genre*'s phones for free, comes to me with his eyes popping.

"It's J.V!" he gasps, as if Paul Newman is on hold.

"I have no idea who that is," I mumble, without looking up.

"He's *The Advocate*'s EIC's assistant!"

"Oh…" I try to sound casual. When they transfer J.V., I hear someone—whom I'd never have guessed was in a t-shirt and flip-flops—say officiously: "This is J.V. The Editor In Chief would like you to join him for lunch this week. Would this coming Thursday at 1 pm be convenient?"

I look around the room. Seeing that I am alone, I say simply, "Where?"

I meet the EIC for lunch in West Hollywood and we hit it off immediately. It turns out he and *The Advocate*'s Editor have been tracking me since I landed Madonna on the cover of *Genre*. He wants to know how on earth that happened, and when I explain that my music career still fuels my Rolodex with formidable contacts, he is intrigued. After he learns I wrote the disco hit, "Star Love," he offers me the job of Arts & Entertainment Editor on the spot.

I race home ablaze with excitement. *The Advocate* is the most prestigious magazine in gay journalism. It just added the word "lesbian" to its subtitle so it couldn't be better timing for me.

When I meet with *Genre*'s publisher a week later to let him know I am leaving, I assume he won't be shocked because of his behavior at the brunch. Despite that, he reacts like I have staged a surprise attack on his business, his livelihood, and the rest of his life. After screaming "How can you do this to me?" until he's hoarse, he takes another tack. He calls his partner in New York and they offer me more money and the chance to edit "*Genre*'s sister magazine," soon to be entitled *Curve* (a name thought up by a friend of mine after a late-night brainstorming session, and no relation to the future lesbian magazine called *Curve*). I will be given a "terrific budget" and "...be able to make all the creative decisions...Just don't leave us."

I'm a total wreck. The decision is coming at a very vulnerable time in my psyche. Only a few years prior, my girlfriend of 10 years left me for another woman. The experience cracked me wide open, severing a main cord and leaving dozens of little wires inside zapping and shorting-out in the wind as they flapped around attached to nothing. I oscillated between the extremes of outrage over being left, and self-pity over believing I was completely unlovable. When I told my friend, Janis Ian, she gave me a look of instant comprehension and said, "I know that syndrome; it's the old: 'How dare you leave me?' followed by, 'Of course, you left me; who wouldn't leave me?'"

The apartment we shared in Venice became a place we took turns staying in as we fought and grieved. I would pack up a small sack with a few personal items and stay with close friends who took me in and listened to me cry and laugh and blather my side of the story, while my love for them grew deeper than I thought possible with "mere" friends. This profound discovery about friendships changed me more than anything else that can happen to a person who's been raised to believe that blood family is your only defense against an indifferent universe.

Amidst this swirl of activity, orchestrated to keep my pain at a tolerable frequency, I let myself take occasional comfort in the company of a young musician who sang in a friend's band, The Riveters. I'd met Suzanne before my relationship broke-up. One evening, a mutual friend asked us each to play a song, and Suzanne played something so unexpectedly intense and exquisite, I was left speechless. Where did all that come from?

I occasionally asked Suzanne to accompany me to the screening of a new film for my magazine work. But because I was feeling like such a failure, it took me some time to tell her anything about my "broken home life." When I finally did, she was reserved, careful about what she said, but supportive and kind without once trashing anyone. I liked her.

One day I was driving somewhere with my close friend Linda, and telling her that I was seeing Suzanne again that evening. Linda literally hit the brakes. "Wait a minute!" She said, ignoring the honking cars behind us. "You mean you are seeing her every week?"

I was thoroughly startled by what she was making me confront. I'm never that consistent about visiting friends. "No…well, yeah."

"What's going on!" Linda concluded, making her question sound like a statement. Then she hit the gas and left me to freak out.

OMG! I was attracted to Suzanne, a gorgeous, smart,

talented, woman—*sixteen* years younger than I was. My poor injured ego was blinding me. *Stop! I don't need any more rejection.* This was an unconditionally stupid thing to be entertaining. Suzanne would be horrified; her trust in our friendship would be completely betrayed.

"Put your observer on," I recalled my therapist cautioning me during times of confusion. "Take a step back and study your behavior."

And I did. When Suzanne came over that night I observed myself nearly black out after a minor miscommunication between us led her to say, "I'm not sure what to do. You see I am very attracted to you."

When she left, I called Linda frantic. "Suzanne said she's attracted to me!" I screamed at her.

"Oh dear," Linda gulped, knowing a crazy-ass train was about to leave the station. "How do you feel about that?"

"I…I am really, really surprised, Linda."

"Why? I'm not," she said confidently.

"You're not? But she's never, ever done or said anything to me that would make me think…"

"But you guys hang out a lot!"

"But I also see you and Helen a lot…"

"Oh, come on! That's very different."

"There's been no flirting, none. [Pause] *Linda! Did I tell you she said she's attracted to me?*"

"Yes!" Linda managed to say through an eruption of laughter.

Unsurprisingly, things took off rather fast after that. I'm not sure there is anything in this world more intoxicating and passionate than a sexual connection that is wrapped up in a fierce, creative relationship. We wrote songs constantly, together and apart; each one mapping our expanding affections; we discovered startling similarities in our parents' work and personalities—despite hers having died when she was just a teenager; we lay on the beach at night and gasped at the vision of shooting stars blessing us overhead; we marveled at the catalysts we so obviously were for each other's much needed changes. The spark glowed til it burst and we were like crazy, erotic fire.

Then my former girlfriend returned, and decided she wanted to try again. And this is where the decision to stay or leave *Genre* is influenced by what happened in my amorous, emotional life. When you've been with someone for 10 years and she's the first woman you ever lived with, and she knows your whole family, and now your mother's dying and there's no time for your mother to even meet your new girlfriend, and there's all this history you share, and she's mad as hell 'cause you've moved on despite the fact that she split first, and you could kill her for this entire clusterfuck even though you still love her and always will—*it torpedoes your mind into stupid useless chunks.*

I felt so guilty, heartbroken and confused. I knew I still loved her deeply. And I also knew I didn't want to give up Suzanne. My head was telling me she had been a wonderful dalliance to help heal my rejection; she was a brilliant, sexy girl who was way too young for me; in time, we'd be out of sync and thus a limited lifetime match. *That's how things look on paper*, my exhausted brain lectured. But my heart...

Sooner or later, we learn our hearts have minds of their own. Hawaiians call it "mana," that intuitive spirit we all possess that can lead us, rock-steady, if we let it. And when the promise of true love is whispered, just watch us become relentless seekers, turning over marriages, families, relationships, friendships, attachments, dresser drawers, old habits, bank accounts, anything and everything that might reveal the road. Even me. Old Faithful, loyal by nature, needed to leave for this treasure.

Somehow, twist by turn, I trudged away from my comfort zone: my rigid opinions about aging, ancient anxieties about losing loved ones, and one particular Evil-Witch that taunted, *"She'll leave you one day and you'll be a very OLD fool."* My intellect remained in conflict for nearly two years, a distance that felt as interminable as the expanse between the Earth and Pluto to Suzanne; and yet she—the so-called "younger one"— soldiered on, faithful and constant, always letting me know, "You are the one."

Yes, I was lucky, blessed obviously, for one day, in the space between heartbeats, I grasped the truth: I had not tumbled out of paradise with Eve for some terrible betrayal. I was still there and everything and everyone I thought I'd lose was right there with me. I could finally exhale the fear of impending consequences for breaking the rules, and inhale the rewards of letting Suzanne, and my own nerve, shepherd me home to the most ardent and perfect partnership anyone could have wished for.

That's why, while *Genre*'s publishers are begging me not to abandon their road, I find myself in *The Advocate*'s EIC office saying, "I can't do it. I can't come over to *The Advocate*. I can't ditch *Genre*."

At first, he just stares at me speechless. It's the last thing either one of us thought I'd be saying. "I don't understand," he says, at last. "Why?"

"Because I just went through this in my personal life. I turned away from the relationship I was in and chose a new road. I'm happy with that decision, but I feel like my work life is offering me a chance to make a different choice, to choose the road not chosen in my personal life."

"Really?" he asks. When I go into further detail, he listens to every word, and when I'm finished, I swear, he comes around his desk and hugs me. Then we both cry.

8 "Judy Wieder—Lesbian!"

"If you change your mind," he whispers, "call me right away."

* * *

Angela Wright feels the day's newspaper slip out of her hands as she sits transfixed staring at Anita Hill giving testimony against Supreme Court nominee, Clarence Thomas. *Is this really happening to Clarence?* She thinks, fumbling for the remote to turn up the TV volume, but not finding it. Frustrated, she dashes across the room to the controls on her television and jacks up the sound. *OMG*, she shivers to herself. *Somebody is actually nailing him for this stuff.*

On the same October 11, 1991 night, an old acquaintance of Clarence's from the 80s, Kay Savage, is holding her breath in front of the televised hearings. Kaye, who knows Anita as well, feels herself swoon as her memory coughs up old clips of Clarence's first bachelor pad, decorated with naked centerfold pinups torn from his *Playboy* magazine collection. *Maybe pictures of naked women with huge breasts on his walls doesn't prove Clarence was hitting on Anita, but still...*Kay rubs her head, trying to remember. *Wasn't that exactly when Anita was working for Clarence?*

Lillian McEwen isn't the slightest bit surprised at the words coming from Anita's mouth. *That's the Clarence Thomas she knew, loved, and even encouraged* after being romantically involved with him for over six years in the '80s. Like Angela and Kay, Lillian suspects Anita Hill is telling the truth. During her relationship with Clarence, Lillian shared his interest in pornography, sex clubs, threesomes, and a lot of drinking. In fact, if you asked Lillian, Clarence changed when he stopped drinking. He had no idea how to relax after that. He was irritable, mean, and distant. Worse yet, he became a full-time tool for the Far Right, with his eyes fixed firmly on their prize: a seat on the Supreme Court. She even remembers how President Reagan could never remember Clarence's name, but how his Vice President, George H. Bush, always could.

Watching Anita Hill testify today, Lillian finally understands what was motivating Clarence when he insisted she come with him to the office of his Equal Employment Opportunity Commission [EEOC]. He told her that he needed her there to show one particularly difficult woman who was working for him—Anita Hill—that he had a girlfriend and wasn't interested in her. Although she'd taken him at his word, now Lillian wonders, *maybe he was worried he had pushed Anita too far?*

* * *

The West Coast publisher of *Genre* had one spectacular gift, and he had it right from the beginning: audacity. He started his publication with that and a couple of credit cards. Few people have such gall. I certainly don't. Despite some of the leaps I've taken in my life, I'd stroke out just stewing over all the things that could go wrong launching a magazine. But if you have 100-proof moxie, along with a solid denial system to bolster you on the down days, you can do anything!

You can, for example, tell an employee with another job offer not to leave you because you'll give her something better, something you know she's been dying to do, like edit a great lifestyle magazine for lesbians. You can tell her you'll match her salary offer, and get her a full-time assistant (one she doesn't have to pay for out of her own salary like she's been doing thus far); you can promise her a reasonable budget, even encourage her to hire women for the magazine's positions if that's what she believes it will take to win over lesbian readers.

You can actually tell her whatever she wants to hear as long as she throws that big *Advocate* job offer right back in the face of the magazine's EIC! You can even cement the deal by leaking a gossip item boasting: "*The Advocate* loses Wieder to *Genre*..." in a local rag just to embarrass everyone and presumably seal off her return route.

You can, and he did. He told me things he had no ability to deliver on, and I made an important decision based on his words. Lies are so unfair. Their corrosive nature not only ruins the situation they're dumped into, lies rust through to other occasions, injecting suspicion into circumstances that don't deserve it. There's only one thing you can do when someone lies: tell the truth. So, I call *The Advocate*'s EIC and request another meeting.

Over lunch in West Hollywood, I explain that after walking in on *Genre*'s publisher's brother designing a prototype cover for *Curve* without my knowledge; after being told the lesbian I've hired to do the first cover shoot can't be used because she wants to be paid; and after hearing there won't be any budget for the first issue because "men can write the stories for free and who will know?"— I wonder if that arts & entertainment *Advocate* position is still open?

I can see *The Advocate* EIC struggling to keep his normally inscrutable composure intact after my update; he recovers after a few minutes and says: "Good, I've actually been waiting for this to happen." He adds that he's been holding an important assignment for me—when I return.

"Return from what?" I ask. That's when he tells me to take two weeks off and rest up, because, "You're going to need it."

When *Genre*'s publisher hears I'm really leaving, he decides to make a peace offering for reneging on everything. He comes up with a free stay in a Maui hotel. Although Suzanne and I get awful colds the minute we arrive there, the

Hawai'i trip launches a long and soulful affair with the islands that will one day result in a second home. From the moment a Polynesian beauty in a long silk muumuu drifts up to me and my swollen sinuses, offering, "Guava juice?"—I understand that an alternative to everything I've ever used to soothe myself, exists. True graciousness awaits, floating between the mainland of the United States and the Eastern coastlines of Japan and China. But for now, it must remain an aroma, a hurried taste, a dream.

When I get back to Venice, a week of sweet Maui trade winds are promptly blown out of my head by the earthquake shaking under the EIC's voice: "Judy! You must know a way to get to Marky Mark!" he insists into the phone, as if we've been working together for years.

"Marky Mark? The rapper? No, I don't think so…"

"You've got to find and interview him for our Year In Review cover!"

"*Marky Mark?* Is he gay?" I nearly shriek.

"No, but there's a big scandal going on with him and the gay community and Madonna, so we've got to get him to talk to us."

With that, he explains that Marky (yet to become the gifted actor/producer Mark Wahlberg), has allegedly been involved in some "gay-bashing incident," followed by a big screaming fight with Madonna—considered the patron saint of all good gay deeds. And because of this, gay men from coast to coast, are in a turbo-charged outrage, tearing down Marky's Herb Ritts posters in their bedrooms, even throwing red paint on Marky's 40-foot-tall Sunset Boulevard Calvin Klein underwear ad.

"Wow!" I exclaim, thinking how far away Hawai'i really is.

"So, it would be a huge selling issue for *The Advocate* if we could get his side of the story," he concludes, correctly.

I begin making calls. I know my entrance and immediate positioning at *The Advocate* is going to depend on my ability—or lack of it—to "get" a 22-year-old Boston street kid to talk to me about something he'd probably rather puke on than discuss. Because Marky is a rapper, I start by tearing through my R&B songwriting contacts until I land on someone who knows someone who knows Marky's tour manager. After a day or two, I get the kind of call back that I soon learn is a blueprint for many handlers when *The Advocate* calls: "What publication? *The Advocate*? Oh, no, no. Marky is unavailable, holed up in Fort Jackson, South Carolina, where he is doing his first film, *Renaissance Man*, with Penny Marshall. Goodbye."

The glory days of *The Advocate* magazine are made up of many magnificent and exasperating things. In 1993, if a celebrity is gay and ready to "come out," the mainstream press won't touch it. It will take an avalanche of national interest in Ellen DeGeneres and the skill of her press agent, Pat Kingsley, to change this in 1997 with *Time* magazine's "Yep, I'm Gay" one-page Q&A cover story. In the early 90s, even the *New York Times* is cautious about covering gay subjects. This makes *The Advocate* the only place to go for gay-centric news, or as a popular ad we run for the publication says: "When the famous speak, they speak to us!"

While this is certainly a powerful force to have behind you, I quickly discover the down side. If I tell people I'm calling from *The Advocate,* all they hear is *"G-A-Y,"* and all I hear is a "click." It's sad, not to mention rude, but I guess that's why they call it homo*phobia*.

With the early 90s still breathing in fumes from the AIDS dragon, the fear factor is astronomical—on all sides. Many activists have had it with the closets that countless gays won't budge from even in this all-out emergency. Gabriel Rotello's publication *OutWeek* was born of this disgust in the late 80s, and exposed many of these closets, claiming a new era with new rules. Michelangelo Signorile's "Gossip Watch" column in

OutWeek stripped public figures as diverse as Malcolm Forbes, Liz Smith, and Chastity Bono of their privacy for what was judged their collusion in a deadly silence forsaking gay activism against AIDS. (Two of these public figures tell me a very different side to this narrative in future *Advocate* interviews).

OutWeek's defense of "outing," rests on the argument "strength in numbers": if you only knew all the people who are gay, things would be different; as well as "fair play": the media should treat the homosexuality of a public figure the way it treats any other aspect of his or her private life—report it. "Is it fair to write that Julia Roberts is dating Lyle Lovett but not to report who Rosie O'Donnell is dating?" Signorile asks me during an argument over why *The Advocate* should *not* have rules about outing (revealing a person's sexuality without their permission.)

It's a question with no right answers. Playing God and punishing "bad closeted gays" for doing something or not doing something by outing them may be tempting, but it's no longer possible at *The Advocate*. National advertisers are finally coming into the magazine and outing is not something they'll tolerate. Most advertisers are straight in every sense of the word, and it's a big enough deal that they're displaying their wares in a gay magazine. To do that in one that's involved in controversial politics such as outing—something its own readers don't all agree on—*is harebrained*. In truth, I still see my own resume with "lesbian" scribbled across it. You must be ready. It's like the cliché about throwing a dog in a swimming pool to get him to swim. Oh, he'll swim all right—right out of the pool and never get back in. You can't grow a movement, a community, or a cause that way. If it *is* about strength in numbers, then you need everybody in the pool.

This collision between the right to privacy and the need to show the homophobic world how many people are gay, is the emotional centerpiece of a struggle that takes many forms throughout my career. My job, in fact, sits in the hub of this cradle of thorns. Almost immediately I am handed a list of closeted film, TV, and music stars who "...could save a lot of young lives and inspire many people if we can just get them to come out!" Additionally, I am told, "Being the A& E Editor, this is *your* territory. How well the magazine does, depends on how well you do your job!" But it isn't just a "hit list" to me. I believe in our "truth will set you free" mission.

As for Marky Mark, he mayn't be gay, but he too has a truth to tell that is stuck in his sense of well-being. And seeing that it's all about gay issues, the only useful place he can tell it is *The Advocate*. Once I grasp this, I am "a dog with a bone," as the magazine's president calls me. What's more, these are the days when getting straight stars to talk to a gay readership is important. To everything a season, and this is the season for strong, supportive hetero voices to counter the destructive ones howling, "AIDS is God's punishment" and "fags brought this on themselves." Thus, I push on.

I call Penny Marshall's office and get more names to call. From them, I get still more names and phone numbers. Finally, someone helps. I am told exactly where the filming is taking place at Fort Jackson; and with that tiny piece of information, I go into *The Advocate* offices for my first full day of work.

* * *

Like Anita, Angela Wright also worked in Clarence's office, but if she ever saw Anita there, she doesn't remember. What she does remember quite clearly is the behavior of the man described in Hill's testimony this week, and it's pure Clarence Thomas through and through. Still, what is *she* supposed to do?

Currently a North Carolina assistant city newspaper editor, Angela decides to write a column detailing her own experiences with the Supreme Court nominee. Although the column won't be for publication, she feels it will be a relief to put down some specifics and then perhaps even show the piece to her publisher as an example of how fast she can turn around a topical item if given the chance. So, she does.

In her commentary, Angela writes of Clarence's inappropriate behavior towards her and other women, including all the times he asked her out after she told him she wasn't interested. But even more than his inappropriate sexual conduct at work, Angela's convinced Clarence simply doesn't possess the temperament to have a seat on the Supreme Court. His social skills are immature and he's given to making course and cruel remarks about people's age, intelligence, and looks.

Leaving the first draft of her column on her desk to percolate overnight, Angela fully intends to reread it the next day and do a rewrite. But to her dismay, someone from the paper gets to the article first, and without her permission or a word of warning, slips it to the investigators on the Judiciary Committee. They, in turn, contact Angela for a telephone interview right away. Suddenly things take off much faster than Angela expected. Does she actually want to join this media circus? She wants to report the news, not make it. Writing about something and being a part of it are two very different things!

Deciding to seek the advice of her paper's publisher, Angela feels a sense of relief during their conversation. His council is simple, moral, and direct: Can she live with herself if she *doesn't* tell the committee what she knows? After all, she knows a lot. For most of the world it's 'he says, she says.' But Angela is sure this frightened but determined Oklahoma law professor is telling the truth. She's sure because that's exactly the kind of thing Clarence would do.

Furthermore, watching her old boss hold forth about the hearings being "a high-tech lynching for uppity blacks," and daring to insist he doesn't remember arguing against Roe vs. Wade—is just too hard. He's lying to America.

✳   ✳   ✳

My first full day of work at *The Advocate* quickly turns into me getting back in my car and going home to pack. When I brief the EIC, he agrees that I need to fly to South Carolina, hole up in a motel room, and wait. Wait and nag. This, you see, is what I do from now on; first as the Arts & Entertainment Editor, then the Senior Editor, then the Executive Editor, and finally as the Editor in Chief. I hound and bother, badger and coerce the handlers and celebrities—be they entertainers, scientists, or politicians—to talk to the magazine, to tell their stories exclusively, passionately, and truthfully to *The Advocate*. Some dislike me for my persistent, take no "no" for an answer approach. But it's a lot better than "outing"—something I'm against long before *The Advocate* declares its own "no outing" policy when I become EIC in 1996.

I begin by asking, inviting, and suggesting ways to get together and discover what might make someone feel more comfortable before doing his or her *Advocate* interview. During these meetings we discuss timelines, family members who might be affected, children or parents who aren't ready. Chastity Bono and I will meet over lunch for nearly a year before she's ready to come out as a lesbian in 1994. Jann Wenner and I get together in his *Rolling Stone* offices almost every time I go to New York, batting around when he might be ready for his *Advocate* close-up. George Michael does his first tell-all interview with me in *The Advocate* because I stay close to him for five years, even flying to London on my own dime to demonstrate my sincerity.

But if someone isn't ready, my tenacity can be very unsettling. Rosie O'Donnell screams at me out of sheer terror for making calls to her publicist in 1994, but gives me one of the most gracious, forthcoming, and educational interviews ever in 2003. At a dinner when she's reminded of her initial outburst, Rosie's so horrified, when I return to my hotel room, I find a huge bouquet of flowers in a Tiffany bowl with the card, "Sorry I yelled at you." And the awesome Ellen DeGeneres? Ellen and I will go through one stormy mix-up after another until we finally sit down to chase her "Yep, I'm Gay" 1-page *Time* cover with *The Advocate*'s 11-page interview in 2000.

Sometimes it's as harrowing for me as it is for the interviewee: Lily Tomlin agrees to "officially" come out in *The Advocate* as part of our cover story with filmmakers Rob Epstein and Jeffrey Friedman in 1996. Presumably Rob and Jeff originally asked Lily to narrate their documentary, *The Celluloid Closet,* because Lily said she'd "come out" by the film's premiere date. The late Vito Russo, who wrote the book on which the documentary is based, was a good friend of Lily and her partner, Jane. How could the narrator of a movie about the history of LGBT film be in the closet?

And yet, after a fun cover shoot (featuring Lily spoofing "tough" by wearing my leather jacket, smoking a cigar, and holding a beer bottle by her thumb—all at her own direction!), Lily decides she's *already* out, and doesn't need to talk about it—even though she's *never* spoken candidly about her personal life in the media. In other words, she reneges on her promise.

When *Tales of the City* author, Armistead Maupin (who wrote Lily's narration for *The Celluloid Closet*), gets wind of this, he has a fit during a radio interview, and outs Lily for narrating the film from the closet. Armistead's outing of Lily gets picked up and printed in all the local rags, which sends Lily over the moon. However, not wanting to take on someone like Armistead, Lily goes after me instead. She's upset that I refused to cut one sentence (something she said) from her *Advocate* interview: "Vito was a close friend of mine, and I'm proud to say that he wrote part of *The Celluloid Closet* when he stayed at the house Jane Wagner and I have lived in together for many years." It is literally the only thing she says in our article that can be vaguely construed as "coming out." The sentence goes to press with the rest of the cover story, and I'm left with very unfriendly messages from Lily on my home answering machine.

What's unfortunate about all this for me personally, is how well she and I got along during our pre-*Advocate* dinner at Kate Mantilini. Alone, just the two of us, Lily told me her whole life story, with details I still remember. It was a great evening with lots of laughs and exchanges about all kinds of subjects. If I had wanted to betray or hurt her, I had plenty of "private information" to do it with.

As the critical "coming-out years" lurch through my early work at *The Advocate*, one dependable guideline emerges: People, who really *don't* want to come out, don't! Rock Hudson would have gone to his grave without saying he was gay. AIDS outed him, period. Jodie Foster doesn't "accidentally" show up at lesbian bars or get caught on camera making out with her latest flame until she's ready to tell her truth. But Ellen does! And Melissa Etheridge does! When George Michael propositions an undercover cop in a Beverly Hills men's room, he's definitely throwing caution—and his "secret"—down the nearest toilet!

Sure, to some extent it's a generational thing; older celebrities like Rock, Richard Chamberlain, Liz Smith, Tab Hunter, and Lily—still feel the bad old days lurking nearby, when the word "queer" was a club to bash you with, not something hip to call yourself. During my early A&E editor years, I have unavoidable run-ins with many closeted stars that tease at coming out but feel terrified if something truly defining breaks through in their interviews. Doors open when they open, but it's my job to knock on them regularly.

Marky Mark is very important for many reasons. He represents the first time that my phoning and imploring brings someone out of the dark to discuss gay issues with me. Though it takes time to get Marky to the other side of the door in my small South Carolina motel room, it finally begins when I hear, "Judy, it's me, Marky. Let me in. I'm psyched!" When I let him in, we're both so nervous, we just pace the room, circling each other like kids. I know it's up to me to take control, but, in fact, it's Marky who finally grabs a desk chair and says in thick Boston street, "Judy, you should sit down." *Thank God.*

The interview is amazing in the only way that an interview can be—the things he says! You can read every word of it in Advocate Books *Celebrity*, but nothing there will illuminate what happens to me when this tough kid slides over to trusting me—opening like an oyster, raw and vulnerable, his words rushing straight into my notes and recorder. At the end of our multi-hour session, I reach into my briefcase to pull out the *Advocate* t-shirt the EIC wants me to give him. Although by now I assume that Marky will be gracious and take the T with him, I'm unprepared for him to pull off his own shirt on the spot, put on *The Advocate* shirt, and rush out of the motel room to find someone who will take pictures of us together. Marky is so happy and relieved he can't stop grinning. And I can't tell you how many times interviews end like this when everybody involved does the work it takes to get there.

✳ ✳ ✳

8 "Judy Wieder—Lesbian!"

Kaye Savage is trying to work things out in her head. Why hadn't Anita brought any of this Clarence stuff up when it was happening? Was it all too embarrassing? Listening to her testimony, she can understand why it might have been.

A divorced, single mother today, Kaye originally met Clarence when she was a civil servant assigned to the Reagan White House. Clarence too was going through a divorce and so they bonded. Soon, their relationship included jogging dates, and one day, Kay agreed to pick Clarence up. That's when she learned more about her friend.

Clarence's bachelor pad was a junior efficiency apartment in D.C. It was completely unfurnished except for a mattress on the floor, a stereo, and a compulsively organized stack of *Playboy* magazines—five years' worth, all carefully lined up on the floor. But it didn't end there: When Kaye looked around the main room of Clarence's small apartment, she saw she was surrounded by a gallery of *Playboy* centerfolds. Even his tiny kitchen and bathroom door had been wallpapered with "large-breasted nude women." Nothing could have prepared her for this sight. Certainly the Clarence she knew casually in and around Washington never showed signs of having such risqué interests. He was an avid churchgoer and hyper-disciplined about everything else in his life. He'd even shared his Supreme Court dreams with Kaye. How did any of *this* fit with such lofty plans? She felt she had to say something, but knew better than to sound critical.

"Why," she wondered, "Do you keep such sexually explicit material around?" Clarence's response was unexpected. He said the magazine collection was the only thing he thought worth keeping from his broken marriage. That only created more questions. So one day Kaye was at lunch with Anita Hill and told her about Clarence's vast *Playboy* collection. At the time, Kaye hadn't understood Anita's response. After telling her friend what she saw all over Clarence's walls, Anita had said simply:

"Yeah," as if there was nothing unusual about it, "*that's* Clarence."

* * *

The "Year-In-Review" issue of *The Advocate* with Mark Wahlberg on the cover performs just as the EIC predicted, rapidly becoming one of the magazine's biggest sellers for years to come. While the EIC and company president seem pleased, there is a decided whiff of jealousy coming from the other, more established male editors. Fortunately, around this time, Joe Landry breaks out of *Genre* and joins *The Advocate* as Associate Publisher. He helps immeasurably by sending up flares of enthusiasm for my work when he sees the Wahlberg story. I definitely need all the support I can get because I still haven't won over the magazine's editor who doesn't think a rock journalist and Grammy-winning songwriter make for a good copyeditor. He's right, of course, but I wasn't hired as a copyeditor. I have faith I will get better at copyediting *if I work at it*. Unlike everyone else employed here who appears to be in their late 20s or early 30s, I am about to turn 50; so, I know my strengths by now. What I know is that if I study hard, I can and will learn anything. It usually takes me a while, especially if the atmosphere is more jeering than cheering, but I get there.

The brass ring I insist on reaching for in this job, is to help people reveal their individual, unique journeys. I'm sure that hidden in the details of every idiosyncratic tale, is a universal coming-out story, and I believe that people reading these stories will discover they are not alone. Even if it's not about coming out, there are always very intimate revelations in a good *Advocate* interview. *The Advocate* Q&A Interview is an award-winning standard-bearer during this time. Whether the interviewee is gay, straight or somewhere in between, the subject of sexuality is in the interview. Once you've got someone talking about something as private as his or her sexuality, they've entered into a level of trust and intimacy with the readers that disarms other discretions. I've had people suddenly tell me about their facelifts and depression, family rifts and past jail terms. It's just amazing how confessional and cathartic these interviews can become.

So, for now I study the long list of names I've been given to court and interview. Although I am much better at this in person, I lift my office phone and start dialing Kenny Laguna, Joan Jett's manager. I know Kenny because he also manages Darlene Love, who recently recorded one of my songs. I will start by "schmoozing" Kenny, knowing the Holy Grail here is Joan Jett—who refuses to discuss her sexuality.

Amazingly my call hits pay dirt. A few short weeks later, the three of us wind up downstairs in my office building, eating lunch at the Hamburger Hamlet. Although I will never get Joan to do a "coming out" interview with *The Advocate* during these crucial years when I believe her words would matter so much to all the riot grrls of the world, my favorite exchange during this lunch comes while I am giving Joan an idea of how an *Advocate* interview might go:

"So, Joan, have you ever been romantically involved with a woman?" I ask her. Joan jerks her head up from her burger, then realizes this is an example question. She turns her chestnut eyes first on me and then her longtime friend and manager, and says, "Hey, Kenny, I could answer that! *Yeah, I have.*" One beat later, Kenny blurts, "No, no, no! You could *not* answer that." The exchange is so breakneck and unexpected, all three of us crack up, literally spitting food across the table. It's not the result I was hoping for, but it initiates a bond that remains unbroken. Joan comes to the office more than once, even destroying my "thinking yo-yo" while attempting "around the world" as I take cover. She insists Suzanne and I join her for a small dinner with *Interview* magazine's editor-in-chief, the late Ingrid Sischy, after attending the *Rocky Horror Show;* and she and Kenny even buy their own tickets to hear my speech at the Kodak (now Dolby) Theater when GLAAD honors *The Advocate* in 2002.

I don't think Kenny Laguna keeps Joan out of *The Advocate.* Even if he holds the reins tight whenever she's tempted to confirm her lesbianism, Kenny works for Joan. If she didn't like it, she'd fire him. This is their deal, their plan of action. I just couldn't bust through it.

※ ※ ※

What amazes Lillian is not Anita Hill coming forward with these accusations, but Clarence getting away with separating his robust sexual appetite from his saintly Religious Right image all this time. For her, it's like the other shoe finally dropping. When the two of them used to go to Plato's Retreat, a sex palace in D.C., he didn't even bother giving a phony name. He was the head of the EEOC, and he used his real name! It was just a big candy store to him. Like all the pornography they rented together, Clarence wasn't particularly worried about any of it. Truth be told, it was Lillian who always worried that someone would get a hold of a piece of film with her in it from Plato's Retreat. Why no one ever mentioned their attendance there or Clarence's frequent rental of erotic films from local D.C. video shops, she'll never know.

Not that Lillian thinks either of them should feel shame about their sex lives. What she understands, probably better than most who've known Clarence, is the miserably dysfunctional family life he endured as a child. She understands because she lived the same nightmare. Their abusive childhoods were as big a bond for the two of them as sex. Lillian even facilitated a trip to Clarence's boyhood home in Georgia. To give him support, she went along, viewing for herself this nightmare place called Pinpoint, Georgia. But Lillian was dumbfounded by what she saw. Southern beauty that stretched as far as the eye could see. Not understanding what was so awful about the place, Lillian thought, *It must have been the people.*

But when she finally met the great villain of the piece, Clarence's grandfather, Myers Anderson, on whom Clarence so often harped, she only saw a feeble old man. He may have made Clarence despondent, bullying him physically and emotionally as a kid, but here he was at the end of his life. The only power he had over his grandson was the power he always had: Clarence's deep-seated desire to please him.

Lillian realized that that the man she cared for had become the man he hated. She recognized Clarence in Myers Anderson, a man who despised the poor black families around him. Myers called them "no good niggers who'd never amount to anything, always looking for a handout from white people." All Clarence's young life Myers had drilled this into his head, along with the decree that white folks are your heroes; they should be respected, feared, and imitated.

How often did Lillian overhear Clarence mumbling his grandfather's favorite ditty? "Niggers and flies, I do despise. The more I see Niggers, the more I like flies."

* * *

Anne Stockwell, my new associate arts & entertainment editor, literally bursts into my office: "Oh, good God," she says, like there are unidentified life forms in the hallway. "Did you see the cover photo of Martina (Navratilova) that they're using?"

I had not. The "boards" or pages of each *Advocate* issue in production are hung on the wall outside my office. While the current issue is being worked on, editors and artists refer to the boards often to see how their stories are progressing. I step around the corner to observe what has ruptured Anne's veneer, and find myself face to face with Martina's distorted face. The tennis ace is twisting to make a backhand, resulting in a very unattractive cover shot. I wince.

"Oh, no, no…" I half-mumble to myself, positive I can do something about it. "*That*'s not pretty." I immediately head into the EIC's office: "Hi! I'm really pleased to see a lesbian on the cover."

He looks up a little wary. "It happens."

"Did you see the picture the art department is using as a cover photo for the Martina interview?" I continue.

He gets up and walks into the hallway to double-check. "Yeah, yeah, it's great," he calls back to me.

I feel a wave of nausea. "No, it's not. It's ghastly." I say quickly, joining him in the hallway.

He looks annoyed. "It's an *action* shot, Judy" he says, his tone indicating he's talking to someone who's up past her bedtime. I try to pull my tone back.

"Listen…" I purr carefully, aware that we've never butted heads before. "I know it's an action shot. But it makes her face look contorted…"

"Aww, Judy, it's fine. Her fans will love it!" And with that, he pushes by me, and heads back to his desk. I stand in the hallway staring at Martina's buckled face. *He's the editor-in-chief. It's his call,* I tell myself; but I also believe there are things he hired me to help him with, like, for example, "what do lesbians like?"

I return to my own desk and compose myself. I know I can't just argue with him; in fact, if I bring up the cover picture again, I've got to approach it in a completely different way. Fortunately, something perfect falls into my lap as a communication tool:

The Advocate's art director, who picked this particular Martina photo, flies by my office door very excited about a photo shoot that's just come in for a cover story on "Mr. Universe" Bob Paris, and his model/husband, Rod Jackson. He is racing for the EIC's office like a human pinball, bouncing off other employees caught in the hallway. Without being asked, I follow him in. The two of them are literally swooning over the sumptuous, homoerotic photos. They're so gone, neither of them sense my presence. I can feel my heart beating in my throat. In the depths of my left brain, I overhear a familiar argument going on: *Say something! /Shut up! / Say something! /Shut up!* Eventually, I open my mouth, and despite the lack of saliva, push out the words:

"Why don't you use an action shot of Bob Paris struggling to lift heavy weights and grunting?"

The art director spins around like I just drove a tractor into the room.

"What?" the EIC gasps.

"Why would we do that?" the art director snorts. "These guys are hot! Look at this stuff."

"I know." I walk up to the desk they're huddled around as if they've invited me. They're both in such a state, they stand back to make room for me. I point at the photographs and begin:

"You are using these great photos of Bob and Rod because it's going to turn-on our male readers and spark a buying frenzy. Right?

They gawk at me.

"It's a simple, basic law of sexy cover physics, yes?"

"What's your point?" the EIC snaps, suddenly annoyed.

"Who asked you...?" the art director picks up on the EIC's permission to be rude.

"My point is, you are absolutely right—and *that's* exactly what you need to be doing for the Martina cover, and for the same reason!" They stare at me for a second, letting my words sink in, then the EIC straightens up and with a loud exhale, says: "Enough about Martina!"

"Martina?" the art director groans, baffled.

"I am not trying to be difficult..." I attempt to go on.

"But you are," he insists. "Martina's cover is done."

"But women feel the same way men do," I plow on desperately. "We need to be turned on. That picture of Martina is *no*t a turn on."

"It's fantastic!" the art director huffs, suddenly grasping what could be going on. "*I* love that picture."

"Show it to any lesbian working here *[not many, at this point]*, and you'll find out how attractive that picture is."

"I don't need to show it to lesbians!" the art director howls at me.

"Yes, you do! I wouldn't know how to pick the best Bob Paris cover photo. I'm not a gay man. It takes time to learn what turns on..."

"You better learn what turns on gay men," the art director threatens, pointing a finger at me.

"I agree. But you should learn what turns lesbians on before you waste this rare lesbian cover opportunity."

"Okay, okay, Judy, that's enough," The EIC steps between us, assuming control. "You did your job. You informed me." With that, he gives me a final, dismissive wave.

I leave defeated. I thought a spark of understanding would ignite when they got the connection between the two cover images, and some reasonable, productive outcome would follow. But nothing. Maybe the EIC couldn't deal with it in front of the art director. I guess the confrontation was too blunt. I blew it.

It's so perplexing, this gay men/ gay women bind. We have the umbrella of our civil-rights struggle that should be holding us together no matter what. But all the communication difficulties straight men and straight women have, we have—without the flirting and sexual attraction to get us through the hard parts.

Up until the AIDS epidemic, when lesbians became the first line of defense against the intolerant external world, our lesbian and gay movements were pretty separate. Our interests are decidedly different, which is not easy when you're organizing a movement; and it's a colossal conundrum for a co-gender LGBT magazine. Even though *The Advocate* is now being called the "LGBT National Newsmagazine of Record," the news doesn't seem to be the great common ground we'd hoped for. Men turn past articles with women, and lesbians skim all the "boy pages" hoping to find a feature on lesbians. When I first came to the magazine, the percentage of lesbian readers was very small, only 3%. The best way to grow that percentage is to do editorial that interests lesbians, obviously. But all too often, the concern I hear is, "We must be careful not to turn off our male readership. They're our core buyer."

When I walk through the hallway where Anne's cubicle sits, she pulls me in. "What did the EIC say?"

"He likes the cover," I sigh. "I think he and the art director honestly believe *that*'s a good photo of Martina."

Nothing changes about the Martina cover. The issue does well enough; after all, besides Martina, lesbians only have a few recently out stars like k.d. lang and Amanda Bearse to read about. How would the issue have sold with a "hot" picture of Martina on the cover? My money is on "a whole lot better." But my days of being able to influence how the magazine uses and treats women are not here yet. Even though I couldn't get through to my boss today, in just a few short years, he will fight by my side like a warrior to get photographer Greg Gorman to sell us something eye-poppingly sexy of Martina for her next *Advocate* cover. But first I must get through a lot of days like this one.

✳ ✳ ✳

During her days with Clarence, Lillian remained focused on her career. She has been a prosecutor, a criminal defense attorney, and a federal judge. Ironically, and incredibly, today she's working for Senator Joe Biden, the man heading up this ridiculous and inept Committee dealing with Clarence and Anita. Lillian really wishes she could be of some use, but how? She doesn't know what she thinks of Anita or Clarence, so she can't really align with either of them. But she had enough of Clarence's anti-black, anti-reform attitudes a long time ago. What a nightmare for civil rights if he *does* get on the Supreme Court.

And he certainly might if he can get past this Anita Hill mess. His desire to become the perfect Supreme Court Justice for the Right will make him their tool for the rest of his life. All these conservatives defending Clarence, propping up his lies on TV, attacking Anita's character instead of considering his, means he will be beholden to them. He will never be able to mellow or change his reactionary opinions as other Judges have done over time. The deal is being sealed in front of America, right now, as we watch.

After a lot of thought, Lillian decides to write a note to Joe Biden. She reminds Biden of the many years she spent with the nominee, noting that because she knows Clarence well, she might be a very useful person for the committee to interview. Unsurprisingly, nothing ever comes of it.

8 "Judy Wieder—Lesbian!"

✳   ✳   ✳

Anne and I are locked up in my office trying to piece together the right editorial mix for the back of the magazine. It's a free-floating session of ideas, and like any creative process, it works best when trust is firmly in place:

"Oh, this is awful," Anne says, reading from her reporter's notebook, "… 'Isabelle Miller has cancer…'"

"Aw, really? Wait, who is…?"

"Author of *Patience and Sarah*," the classic novel. "I guess we should see what happens," Anne continues.

"I loved that book so much. What about asking the girl who wrote and starred in *Go Fish* to interview her?" I scheme.

"Oh, yeah, Guinevere Turner!"

"Wow! Good for you!" I scribble down the name. "I'll call what's-her-head, *Go Fish*'s producer, to get her number…"

"Christine Vachon," Anne easily remembers. "Judy, did you ever hear that Laurel and Hardy slept in the same bed?"

[Laughing] "*Stop!*"

We take a few minutes to sort through our notes, both landing on Robert Altman's new fashion film, *Pret-a-Porter*. I look up at Anne and confess, "Oh, gawd, this is so embarrassing! I called Lois Smith, who handles Altman and the film. I was nervous because she's such a major-league publicist. Lois asked me to tell her what writer I was sending to do the *Pret-a-Porter* interviews. And instead of saying 'Charles Isherwood,' I got flustered and said *[the late]*, 'Christopher Isherwood.'"

Anne roars.

"Yeah, well, there was a pause, and Lois said, 'No, please, don't send the dead guy. Can't you get anyone who's alive?'" Now I start laughing, remembering how deadpan-funny Lois was. "Thank goodness! She has a sense of humor. Did you know that Lois once represented Marilyn Monroe?"

"Really? Ask her if Marilyn was bisexual."

"*What?* No! *[Belly laughing]* No one will ever take my calls over there again."

"What about some of these iconic women whom we know are lesbians, like, like…"

"Angela Davis?" I offer.

"*Ye-ahh!* Is that door locked?"

I flip through my pad until I find a number written next to Angela's name. I stare at it for a while trying to remember exactly what happened. I see notes in different pen colors and in pencil. Obviously, I've visited this subject a few times. Somehow, I'd gotten Angela's direct line where she's teaching at U.C. Santa Cruz—which I particularly love because the University of California drove her out in the 60s, saying she'd never teach there again. But today, she has an appointment there in African American and Feminist Studies."

"Holy God!" Anne says, looking over my shoulder at my notes. "What did she say?"

"Oh, she wouldn't talk to me when she heard it was *The Advocate* calling," I sigh.

Anne looks positively wounded. "They just said 'no' point blank to you?"

"No, no, they first told me she'd call back, so I was all hopeful, as usual. Then some assistant…*[squinting at my notes]*… Stephen?…no…Stephanie? called back the next day and said Angela had already given her heart and soul away as a feminist and as a person of color, so, sorry, she wasn't about to make 'gay issues' another battle field."

"Really? *Really?*"

"She didn't use those words, but, yeah, really." Honestly, I thought to myself, *I get it! This woman has gone to prison; she's seen people she loved murdered in prison. I mean, even I'd say, 'Someone else can take this one; I'll sit it out, thanks.'* [Note from the future: Angela Davis allows herself to be interviewed by *Out* magazine in 1997 and indicates, hesitantly, she is a lesbian.]

"What about the first woman astronaut, Sally Ride?" Anne brightens, examining her list.

"I actually talked to her, but she said no."

"She did?" She whispers.

I can see Anne's face color slowly fading as the afternoon's disappointments pile up. Then, after a few minutes, she throws her shoulders back and straightens in her seat: "Why not, damn it? She's not going up there anymore," she snaps, flinging her arm straight up in the air and letting it circle her head to create the image of space travel.

I laugh, treasuring her tenacity, and feel great comfort knowing this smart woman is going to swim through many celebrity riptides with me in the future without drowning. "True," I answer, "but apparently, she has another career: she goes around the world—*on the ground*—and lectures, including in schools, about her astronaut experiences. And she says she can't do that as a lesbian astronaut, at least not as an out lesbian. We didn't talk long. She was sweet and honest and very clear she wasn't going to risk a decent living by coming out. [Note from the future: Sally came out posthumously; her partner of 27 years, Tam O'Shaughnessy, wrote her obit.]

After a few minutes, Anne regards me seriously and asks if it's true that the EIC really told me Melissa Etheridge could *only* have an *Advocate* cover if she posed with Don Henley from the Eagles? My head starts to throb. Yes, he definitely said exactly that. When Melissa's manager called to tell me that she was now on tour with the Eagles, I figured that would be it: the EIC loves the Eagles, and Melissa is getting mainstream exposure opening for them; so, I thought it would be perfect timing for Melissa's *Advocate* cover. And he agreed, but only if she shared it with Don Henley.

"What do *you* think? Can she sell *Advocate* magazines alone?" Anne asks.

"I hope so because that's what I'm aiming for. She's never been photographed very well," I venture. "At least that's my opinion. So, I think if we can pull off a sensual shoot with her, using just the right photographer…"

"Oh, noooo," Anne wails. "Don't get *that* hopeless hope up again," she says, referring to the Martina cover.

"I know, but this is different. It has to start with the interview. I think if I can get a sexy story out of Melissa, then I can talk the EIC into a sexy photo shoot…"

"That's a lot of 'ifs,'" Anne warns. "Can I ask what Melissa's people said when you told them she had to share a cover with Don Henley?"

"Oh, Anne! There's no way in hell I told her people that. That'd be the end of getting Melissa on *The Advocate* cover."

"But they're demanding a cover, right?"

"Oh, sure, yeah, of course," I answer, like everything is fine. I look up to see that Anne is now rubbing her temples.

"So," Anne begins carefully, "you want to convince our EIC to do a solo cover of Melissa by bringing in a killer interview, which you can't get without promising Melissa a cover, which we can't do without Melissa agreeing to pose with Don Henley, which you won't even bring up to Melissa's people because you're sure the whole thing will die then and there, correct?"

I walk myself through her statement. "Yes, that sums it up. I'd only add that even if Melissa would do the cover with Don Henley, what makes anyone think Don Henley would pose on an *Advocate* cover with an out lesbian?"

"Oh, *that's* an irritating detail, isn't it?" Anne reflects.

"Look, I know this is the right thing. She's the right gay woman to be on the cover of *The Advocate*—right now. I can feel it. Besides," I say more softly, "her management just bought my plane fare to Amsterdam to interview her there. So, this *has* to work out."

Anne looks at me, aghast, then grins and says, "You have the job from heaven…and hell."

✳   ✳   ✳

Angela Wright is mad as hell pacing around her lawyer's D.C. office. The Commission subpoenaed her to appear at the Thomas hearings and tell the Committee the same story she told them. And yet, for three days she's literally been sitting around Washington waiting.

Although word has gotten out that there is "another woman" ready and willing to testify to Clarence's sexually inappropriate behavior in the workplace, the Committee has yet to call her. What could be going on? She's explained several times to Senate staffers about the time Clarence asked her what size her breasts were; she's given them other examples of inappropriate comments he's made in front of her; they've questioned her thoroughly about the night Clarence came to her apartment unannounced, and how upsetting that was to her. So, why isn't she saying all of this in front of the entire senate committee? Why are they wasting time rehashing the same things with Anita Hill instead of looking for a pattern in Clarence's behavior? She is living proof there's a pattern!

In the end, Angela Wright isn't called. Instead, stories circulate that "the second woman" got cold feet after watching the Committee tear Anita apart. Infuriated, Angela's lawyer refuses to let Joe Biden run with this offensive lie as their official explanation for Angela's no show. If they won't call her to bear witness to things Anita is saying, then Angela's lawyer insists they must have his client's testimony written into the official record. The committee agrees, but this too gets murky when Angela's carefully formulated words are buried so deep in the report, no one from the press reads far enough to find them or report her story.

Now the bipartisan Committee is in a panic: Republicans don't want Angela's testimony for obvious reasons. But Democrats are worried too. When Clarence learns that Angela's in D.C. ready to testify against him, he tells the committee that he fired Angela because she called someone a "faggot." Flabbergasted, Angela responds that she never in her whole life called anybody a faggot. "All I can say is the whole incident was plucked out of the clear, blue sky." Angela's North Carolina newspaper is so distressed by this accusation, it hires a lawyer who uncovers information that the "Bush administration was calling up people looking for dirt on Angela Wright." In fact, one Republican Senator admits: "If Angela wants to expose herself to the committee with damaging information about Clarence Thomas, I am fully ready to damage her character in the process…"

Thus, it is determined that the catastrophic hearing must be halted. "The country simply can't take another ugly 'he said/she said' farce," the good senators of D.C. decide. In an after-hours vote that some congressmen don't even know about, it is settled: The other woman's voice will not be heard; Angela Wright will not testify.

※   ※   ※

Chasing down a bi-weekly column from Lance Loud has become the task that ate my job—even with a new assistant to help me. And yet, the edgy, often hilarious rock 'n roller, who initially found fame coming out in the 1973 PBS documentary, *An American Family*, is undeniably a terrific catch for the magazine. He's eager to tackle anything and anyone, and his fascination with contemporary pop culture keeps the magazine hip and fun for readers. Unfortunately, his word count generally comes together at the last second, and not without massive nagging and mayday calls to his mother, Pat. Although I'm crazy about him, I must find an alternative to hounding Lance.

Fortunately, the answer fits in nicely with my push to entice more women's voices into *The Advocate*. Why not let Lance rotate with another arts & entertainment columnist? Maybe a lesbian! To my surprise, everyone agrees. But who? What well-known lesbian is out, opinionated, entertaining, and can write? The EIC calls his favorite, Sandra Bernhard, who says no.

I'm not disappointed because I already know who would be perfect. Last week I interviewed Janis Ian for her first new album in 12 years, *Breaking Silence*. The record is fantastic, and to celebrate finally telling the truth about several forbidden subjects on the album, Janis comes out publicly as a lesbian. She has a new girlfriend of four years; and she lives and writes in Nashville, where she's also quite boldly out. It would be impressive, indeed, to land her, her devoted fans, and some new Southern readers, all in one net.

I call Janis's manager, Simon, with my column pitch, and get a "no" a few days later. "Janis doesn't write prose," I'm told. "She's a songwriter. Thanks anyway."

I go into battle mode: "Janis is *so* talented, her songs are *so* deep, smart, insightful, and funny, learning to write words *without* music will be simple. I did it. I'm a songwriter too." There's a long pause on the phone which I immediately fill with silent assaults on myself for mentioning that I write songs. Other songwriters never want to know this. And their managers really don't.

"I...I...only mentioned that because writing anything

professionally means you're not starting from zero, so for Janis..." I stumble around.

"Did you ever get your stuff recorded," Simon asks, unexpectedly.

"What stuff? Oh, my songs, I did, but I didn't mean to bring that up; it's not my point."

"I get your point. I'll ask Janis again."

And he hangs up on me.

A few days later, Simon calls to tell me that Janis said no again, but that she and her girlfriend, Pat, will be in L.A. for a gig, and want to know if I can have lunch. This is what I call the "go away closer" response to *The Advocate*. I am elated, of course, and slightly hopeful that an in-person meeting might lead to more trust and a new columnist.

We meet at a Hollywood restaurant and talk nonstop over bowls of soup and glasses of ice tea, all of which eventually send Janis rushing for the ladies room. When she's gone, Pat—who's just started law school—tilts herself into the table closer to me, gives me an exacting look, and says in a divine Southern drawl, "So what would she really have to do for this column thing?"

In the time it takes Janis to use the restroom, I lay out everything for Pat: I will hold her hand, talk to her day or night, let her write about anything that makes sense, and make sure failure is not an option. We actually shake hands on it, just as Janis joins us.

"So, what have you guys been talking about?" she asks, suspiciously.

"I'm gonna let Pat fill you in," I say, dashing away from the table before anything can go wrong.

I know that Janis is being honored this evening at a nearby venue, so I've already hatched a plan to set up a photo shoot with her after the gig. But I need to get the art department in on this. After all, Janis is going to need a fabulous picture to go with her new *Advocate* column, "Breaking Silence."

When I hand the valet my ticket, I also slip him a few dollars and whisper, "Hurry!" Just as the restaurant door is swinging closed behind me, I'm sure I hear Janis's voice choking out: *"What?"*

* * *

As for Faye Savage's supportive voice detailing the reading material in Clarence's apartment, Joe Biden decides that no behavior outside the nominee's workplace can be brought into the hearings. In this case, it's clear Faye is talking about Clarence's apartment from his younger years. Why dig all that up now?

Fortunately for history, Faye's memories of Thomas during the times he was harassing Anita do not die with the Committee's rush to "shut this thing down." She crosses paths with two *Wall Street Journal* reporters, Jill Abramson and Jane Mayer, who, in 1992, set out to follow up on all the "leads left dangling by the Senate Judiciary Committee." For these two journalists, the premise is simple: Clarence and Anita couldn't both be telling the truth. After a few years of hard work using extensive interviewing and investigative reporting, they pry open new leads, witnesses, and much of the pathetically ignored information that the committee ran from—the majority of which is explosive and damaging to Justice Thomas. While writing and reporting what will become their prize-winning book, *Strange Justice*, Abramson and Mayer publicly relate Faye Savage and Angela Wright's distressing experiences with Clarence.

D.C. conservatives demand *Strange Justice* be discredited and fast. Right-Wing journalist for the *Spectator*, David Brock, picks up this torch and uses every dirty trick he's mastered.

Tracking Faye down, Brock divulges personal information about her sealed divorce proceedings, and threatens that he will go public with it. How did he get this secret information? Faye is so alarmed she caves.

The final twist of fate is karma incarnate: David Brock (pressured by the lionhearted journalist, Frank Rich), has a change of heart and politics. In his own book, *Blinded by the Right*, he reveals that the secret, sealed "negative information" he used to discredit Faye, was passed along to him from Supreme Court Justice Clarence Thomas himself.

Although Anita Hill will suffer personally for years after the hearings, the crushing blow dealt her and those silenced while waiting in the wings does not go unnoticed by millions of women who sat glued to their televisions. History will show that in the years immediately following the Hill-Thomas hearings, more women run for public office than ever before in history—and win.

* * *

I'm sitting in my favorite European city, Amsterdam, with Melissa Etheridge and her girlfriend. Last night we rode her tour bus back from Rotterdam where Melissa blew away an arena full of near-hysterical, bra-throwing women and equally enthusiastic men. Although the morning after has been a little fuzzy, the three of us are now drinking strong English tea and getting more and more jazzed.

"It was so easy to start answering questions truthfully," Melissa explains about why she came out when she did. "I had been talking about my lesbian following as if I wasn't a lesbian myself, and I'd feel sick after those interviews. Then when k.d. [lang] came out and did well—I just started thinking, why not me?"

We drink more tea and continue down this road of good feelings for at least another half hour before I feel it's time to introduce my agenda. "I wanted to talk to you, Melissa, well, both of you, really, about an idea I have for the, uh, main thrust of your cover story."

The dining room in Amsterdam's famed American Hotel gets very quiet suddenly. Or maybe it's just that our table is no longer the center of overlapping chatter that it's been. Both women look at me sharply. I panic.

"Oh, no, no, it's nothing to worry about," I lie. *I hate myself.* "Here's the thing; as you know because you both read it, *The Advocate* has primarily been a gay men's magazine for most of its history. We are trying to make it co-gender, and obviously, doing a cover story on you, Melissa, is going to be part of that effort."

Melissa smiles warmly, but remains quiet. Her girlfriend leans forward, resting her elbows on the table and placing her head on her palms. She stares at me in such a no-nonsense way I want to pee out all the tea we've been drinking. Instead I do my best to chant down my fears while reminding myself that I am trying to do a good thing—for Melissa, for the magazine, for lesbians, for me. I take a breath and continue, deciding to look only at Melissa.

"I believe that *The Advocate* staff knows how to package gay male celebrities and make them look sexy," I push on trying to sound focused and professional. But this…*lesbians* are still new territory for them. The challenge is putting lesbians out there in a sexy way. There have been some close calls, but in my opinion, we haven't done a great, sensuous photo shoot of a lesbian."

"What are you saying?" Melissa's girlfriend breaks in.

"I get it," Melissa says calmly.

"Oh, thank God! It's new for gay men to think of lesbians

as sexy women. They think a lot of straight women are sexy—divas and movie stars—but not lesbians. Lesbians are dependable, great nurses in AIDS wards…"

"What about this new 'lipstick lesbian' thing?" Melissa asks.

"That's a pretty new concept and there aren't a lot of them in our offices. But what I am thinking about—and I really need your cooperation in the interview—is doing a sort of *'Dangerous Lesbians'* theme with the two of you, and getting you to talk about sex…*a lot.*"

To my great relief they both break out laughing.

"Sure," Melissa giggles. "I'm not sure we can tell you everything…"

"*Definitely not…!*" her girlfriend punctuates, though she clearly looks game.

"Really? Oh, that's just great! Thank you. This is really going to help. I want to bring back an interview that calls for the kind of photo shoot the magazine has never organized around a gay woman before. But I can't force it to happen. Only our editor in chief can okay it. But we can give him something he can't resist."

"*Oooooo! Dangerous Lesbians*" they both make fun of me.

"Okay, let's order more of this nasty tea and go for it, ladies. Or, do you think we need something stronger?"

* * *

9

Matthew and Nicole

It's November 22, 1997, and I am standing at the podium of the Los Angeles Ballroom at the Century Plaza Hotel. *The Advocate* is receiving the "Special Board of Directors Award" from the Los Angeles Gay & Lesbian Center, and as Editor in Chief, I am giving the acceptance speech. I've been EIC for a little more than a year, and the enormous banquet of events leading up to my appointment and beyond have been too rich for me to digest. So, even though my concentration is fierce, I can feel the year bubbling up under my speech.

I hold up an *Advocate* issue with a woman's breast on the cover. The sight of me at 53, the first woman EIC in the publication's 30-year history, together with an issue of the primarily male-driven magazine featuring a woman's body part on the cover, causes a hush to fall over the sold-out dinner. It's a watershed moment. I show the cover to the audience, slowly turning until everyone has had an opportunity to see *The Advocate*'s Breast Cancer issue. Then I speak:

"The men looked at this cover and said, '*That* doesn't look like a penis! What *is* it?' *[Laughter]* And the women? Ahhh, the women! They called me to complain. Instead of being thrilled that *The Advocate* was finally covering an important lesbian health issue, they bitched at me: 'The breast is too perky.' 'Why didn't you use an older breast?!' 'Why not a black breast?'

'What about a Hispanic breast?'...A politically correct breast?' *[Explosive laughter and applause]* Ladies, you are scary!"

I am a study in opposing forces up here, fighting to tell a humorous story about the magazine cover, while thinking about the exquisitely difficult road that led to it ever happening. As my remarks continue their own journey, my mind gives up and falls backwards a year...

When I became EIC after the former EIC's departure in the summer of '96, it wasn't a big surprise to anyone behind the scenes. The former EIC had positioned me to take over his job. Despite our early struggles, in the end he was a solid ally in advancing the magazine in a co-gender direction. I was aware of his flirtations with other editors for my future position, including my friend, the editor of *Out*, Sarah Pettit, but in the end, he picked me to follow him into his job. And in doing so, for better or for worse, we made our own kind of history.

It's the "woman component"—meaning for one brief, luminous moment in LGBT history, two women are helming the two biggest and best LGBT publications in the world—that initially sends folks swooning en masse. The mere fact of it both energizes and aggravates the community. On more than one occasion Sarah and I get to hear how we wouldn't have our jobs if AIDS hadn't knocked out so many talented men. We don't agree.

The stress of the first year was hard-core. Everyday fiery sinkholes opened up in front of me at work as my appointment provided the company an opportunity to redesign and restructure the magazine. Although I was definitely relieved and excited to push the publication in a more "newsy" direction, with fewer straight celebrities on the cover (a past ploy no longer interesting to readers), by this point in my career I'd learned too many hard lessons about the necessity of "star appeal" to sell magazines. So, I was a little worried about the all-news, no puff *Advocate* I was to be running.

The president of our company is a connoisseur of high art, finance, and the news. He is so bright, he reminds me of my late friends, the Mitchell twins, in that his intellect literally hums if you stand too close to him. He also believes *The Advocate* is in competition with *Newsweek* and *Time*—and not in a figurative way—literally. In fact, when either of those magazines publishes a feature story that *The Advocate* is prepping, we must immediately tear ours down and devise something new. We can never be seen as following other newsmagazines! On the one hand, it's admirable and lifts our sense of competition in the newsgathering business to the highest level. On the other, it's nuts. *The Advocate* has a small editorial budget, five editors, one art director, and one photo editor; so you can only imagine my surprise the day I visit the *eleven* floors of *Newsweek* offices in New York City. "Editors who have been dead for years still have offices here!" Sarah Pettit will tell me after becoming a senior editor at *Newsweek*.

Trying to out-think major mainstream newsmagazines while fighting for respect from an all-male senior staff was so challenging, every morning I literally willed myself to sit on my front steps and meditate: "Just show up for a year—don't quit." So many people gave me this advice, it was astonishing: associates, best friends, publicists, readers, parents, celebrities, writers, and heads of gay organizations. They called or wrote letters, sent emails and notes, all telling me what it meant to them that a woman was finally at the helm of this prestigious magazine. I had no idea it meant so much to so many. So I listened. No matter how hard it got, no matter how inadequate I felt, no matter how disappointed I was in myself for not knowing more than I did, I couldn't quit. *Everything always changes*. I told myself. *This will change too.*

Because of my strong background in the entertainment business, initially I was seen as an editor who knew nothing about politics, LGBT issues, HIV, or anything heavyweight. It would seem my bosses forgot that I lived through more than one social movement, or that I, too, had been reading *Time*, *Newsweek*, and *The Advocate* for years, digesting information about leaders and legends, getting to know the heads of gay organizations, and teaching myself what I didn't know by following the best: dedicated activists like Urvashi Vaid, Kate Clinton and Michelangelo Signorile, as well as diehard newsmen like the magazine's own correspondents John Gallagher and Chris Bull. But when people see you a certain way, it's hard for them to accept or trust that you can shine in another.

Well, money changes everything. It's vulgar and it's depressing, but there it is. The hard-news *Advocate* was a reaction to the celebrity-driven *Advocate*, and neither were what readers wanted. So, one evening after work hours, I approached the president in his office. We were facing each other across his desk, and he was completely accessible. Uncharacteristically subdued, he measured me thoughtfully, even curiously. And in that split second, I felt my wings pop open and stretch. A year of *Advocate* magazines lay all along the cabinets under his office windows. We walked over and started looking at them. We talked for a long time about the bold and newsy cover stories. All were timely. None reached their sales potential.

"We need to balance our covers," I said, casually. "We should keep doing this," I pointed to editorial that illuminated how the Far Right was twisting the phrase "Gay Rights" into "Special Rights." But we'd better follow it with a sexy celebrity."

He winced. "Is that your vision for the magazine?"

"We need *calculated* balance," I repeated. "Unless it's a breaking news story that we have first, we very purposely vary our covers: hard news, then celebrity. And sometimes more people might wind up reading a great news story if they buy the issue for a celebrity, and stumble on the deep stuff."

I continued, determined not to squander this opportunity with him, even mentioning my favorite cause, getting more female voices into the magazine

"Camille quit her column because of you, not me!" he jumped in.

It's true. Camille Paglia quit her *Advocate* column in a rage at me. "But it wasn't about her column," I protested. "Camille quit because she was furious at me for sending in another writer to interview Dennis Rodman after she left the interview because Dennis had kept her waiting too long." He stared at me, remembering. "And aren't you glad we didn't lose that interview?

"Very!" he said, recalling the sales.

"Did you see that *Time* magazine cover with a publicity photo of Brad Pitt from his new film *Seven Years In Tibet*? The cover line said: "America's Fascination With Buddhism."

He laughed in spite of himself: "So the editorial was about the state of Buddhism in America?"

"Yeah," I chuckled, "*Time* used a movie star to sell its editorial package about religion. We can do that kind of thing too!" I reminded him of our cover-story interview with Bob Paris talking about his break-up with Rod Jackson. It sold well, but now it was clear we missed an opportunity to do an "Update On Civil Unions," with Paris on the cover and the cover line, "Civil-Union *Divorces*: How They Work." I could have used the news department to highlight where civil unions stood legally, state by state, and put sexy Bob on the cover to sell it.

He agreed, then reached past me to lift several *Advocates* off the counter. All three were recent and featured real lesbians with real stories to tell. He waved them at me like they were all my fault.

"I know! I know!" I sighed. "I don't understand lesbian readers either. I thought they'd buy those in a frenzy. The stories are all about their lives." While we reviewed the sales figures, my eyes strayed to the Year-In-Review issue with Melissa Etheridge on the cover.

"Look how well Melissa sold!" I cheered.

"She's an anomaly," he responded, correctly.

All my jostling to present Melissa as a sexy "dangerous lesbian" with great photos and bold, intrusive questions, paid off. Habitually reticent women readers went bonkers. Male readers liked her too. For a while, Melissa sold *The Advocate* as well as any gay man.

Still, we remained frustrated with the sales that inevitably resulted whenever a non-celebrity lesbian, tied to an authentic news event, made it to cover. At the newsstand, male readers pretty much took a pass; and the women didn't fill in the numbers. Why? After my first year at the magazine, women subscribers had risen from 3% to 27%. With that in mind, I'd been hustling and nudging lesbians onto *Advocate* covers, believing "if you build it, they will come."

Well, they certainly did not.

Then a truly titanic opportunity stepped forward. After a multitude of cover stories on AIDS for special *Advocate* Health Issues, I'd been lying in wait for a chance to bring "lesbians and breast cancer" to cover. The question was: are lesbians any different from straight women when it comes to breast cancer health? As it turned out, the answer was yes. Even in 1997, enough lesbians were in the closet to cause a decent percentage of them to resist seeing a gynecologist—where a woman's breasts are usually checked. *Bingo!* That could certainly cause a higher breast cancer death rate for lesbians.

Thankfully, the president became my passionate co-pilot with this story after a tragedy in his own family ignited his interest. So, before I could completely believe it, *The Advocate* was reaching for a very unfamiliar brass ring. But what cover image would we use?

When the art director sent through a colorful likeness of a woman's breast that took up over half of the cover, all I could think was, *Wait until lesbian readers see this on the newsstands!* At long last they would know that the magazine was listening, and risking its core readership to deliver this vital information. I was so overly confident; I never saw the "perky breast" complaints coming.

In retrospect, I should have been relieved that readers didn't tear up the cover and mail it back to us in pieces. That had happened before. Once we made Madonna "Sissy of The Year," and it caused a shit storm that shut down our offices. After that catastrophe, we stopped doing "Sissy Of The Year"—an *Advocate* special "honoring" the year's most homophobic people or actions, and rethought the whole concept, which harkened back to a younger, angrier, shoot-from-the hip *Advocate*. What *is* a "sissy," anyway? Slander referencing females and gay men to describe a person's spineless behavior? In Madonna's case, it was an excuse to put her on the cover and editorialize our disappointment over her need to give a mainstream interview clarifying, "I am not a lesbian." Madonna is ambitious, but she's not a coward. She's done a massive amount of good for the gay community, so the whole thing was a ferocious mistake.

Newsstand buyers didn't send the breast cancer cover back to us because they didn't buy it in the first place. Why? Too in your face? Maybe. According to the ladies who contacted me, they couldn't get past the cover image. They never read the feature at all. Just seeing a breast on the newsstand upset them. The image we selected was offensive, simply "too cute and perky" for them to pick up and read our health issue. Can you imagine? Lesbians are difficult. I know. I am one.

Thwarted, I reached out to every lesbian with a phone, including my strongest and most generous colleagues at the time: Elizabeth Birch, the former executive director of the Human Rights Campaign, and Lorri Jean, the executive director of the Los Angeles Gay & Lesbian Center. Both shed tears when I relayed the "perky breast" chronicle. Like me, they cried with disbelief, laughter, and disappointment. Unlike me, their experiences with their own organizations were satiated with overly supportive gay men and encouraging women. For them it was LGBTs against inequality, not each other. Seeing me without this support, fired up their compassionate natures. Several ladies-who-lunch outings followed. Both women—separately—came to the conclusion that the hurly-burly, competitive world of journalism, combined with this full-tilt juncture in LGBT growth, had created a decidedly different petri dish for me to work in. Best of all, they decided to help.

Soon Elizabeth and Lorri were pushing open their formidable doors for me to walk through. With their ongoing assistance, my transformation into a confident editor in chief began. During the HRC's annual Washington D.C. dinner, for example, Suzanne and I were seated at Elizabeth's table directly across from Ellen DeGeneres and Anne Heche. Everything in Ellen's personal and professional life was blowing sky high thanks to the barn-burning moment she and her sitcom character created by coming out. Her "handlers" were only allowing mainstream journalists anywhere near her—which was code for "no gay press." So, for me to be strategically placed across from her, was a ginormous gift. Additionally, the dinner was the very first time a sitting U.S. President (Bill Clinton) ever addressed an LGBT organization. His presence and supportive speech bedazzled us all. As we feasted on history being made—while trying to digest mere chicken—the normal walls separating people vanished; soon everyone was laughing and swapping opinions like old friends. So many introductions were made for me that night, I ran out of business cards before dessert. These connections led to crucial *Advocate* interviews and career-long relationships. Elizabeth's generosity was so consequential, she forever demolished the bewildering "perky breast" glee club in my head. I was reenergized and back on the court, ready for the next confounding volley of LGBT queerness—and, yes, there would be plenty of it.

I didn't blame the company for being disappointed in the breast cancer issue's sales. I too felt let down. On the bright side, everyone seemed to be aboard the "calculated balance" mission; so two weeks later we were on the newsstands with a behind-the-scenes cover story on the film *In & Out*, including an interview with the elusive Tom Selleck, who usually avoids gay publications because too many of them insist he's gay, despite his happy 26-year marriage to a woman.

This, in fact, is an *Advocate* quandary I try to put some boundaries around. All those famous celebrities, and you know who they are, whom gays insist are gay—despite their public denials and lawsuits—should be left alone. Why give them ink? *Forgetaboutum.* If they're really gay and lying, how sad for them. No closet's going to be big enough. And if they're not gay, and we're insisting they are—how sad for us.

Besides, what about experimentation? Many of us have experimented with heterosexuality for boundless valid reasons: we're not sure; we're afraid and hope we're not gay; we're bisexual enough to be attracted to both sexes; we want children the old-fashioned way; the times were once so forbidding we entered into heterosexual marriages that ultimately didn't work, etc. Shouldn't we want "straights" to try a same-sex encounter or romance without the threat of being labeled or outed? Doesn't this potentially open people to a deeper understanding of all sexualities, no matter where they ultimately wind up?

Random Events Tend To Cluster

* * *

Denise Brown has just begun drawing in full, deep breaths. It's taken a couple of years to become someone even she has a hard time recognizing. Always a handsome woman, who, before June 12, 1994, described herself as "just a mom from Laguna Beach," these days Denise has streamlined herself into a confident, one-woman crusader.

At first, the journey was only about finding retribution for her youngest sibling, Nicole Brown Simpson. For Denise, Nicole's murder would have been sufficiently devastating on its own; but discovering that her sister had managed to keep a dangerous secret from her for so long—was the deeper wound. Buried in the harrowing closet of domestic violence, Nicole Brown Simpson was living a half-life, "walking on eggs," hiding her bruises and cuts, all alone, and telling no one but her unread diaries and unsent letters.

Now that she knows, restoring justice for Nicole has become a life-changing commitment for Denise: somehow, she must use what she's learned to help raise public awareness about domestic violence—a crime she's discovered kills four women every day in the United States. Although she'd trade her enlightenment to have Nicole back, the puzzling reality is, the year she lost her sister is the year Denise began to find real backbone and strength of character in herself.

When she discovered the letters Nicole wrote to her husband, begging him not to treat her like a punching bag, Denise promised herself she would make sure the letters saw the light of day. No matter what it took, Nicole's voice would never be beaten down again.

* * *

9 Matthew and Nicole

There's no way for me to continue writing about my time at *The Advocate*—and later *Out*, *The OutTraveler*, and *HIVPlus* magazines—without describing my relationship with the publisher, Joe Landry.

Ours is a kinship not a lot of people would've put money on in Vegas, not even me. On the exterior, we appear so dissimilar and incompatible—from our 20-year age difference to the usual incomprehensible gay-boy-girl interests. Yet, out of so many possible others, ours is the attachment that bloomed past the supportive, creative partnership it evolved into within the company, to the ongoing, thriving one it will become years after I leave. When the success and adversity that clutters life, clears, it turns out Joe understands something truly elegant: loyalty.

The events ricocheting between '93 and '98 sent *The Advocate* spinning in a myriad of growthful ways, including Joe pushing hard to take the infamous sex ads out of the publication in order to make way for national advertisers. These changes rattled through our editorial and executive offices, erupting regularly in the kind of territorial battles most mainstream magazines were used to. We were not.

After closeted Republican Arizona Rep, Jim Kolbe, voted for the Defense of Marriage Act (DOMA) in 1996, *The Advocate*, along with the *Washington Blade*, pressured him to either come out, or be outed by the publications. As easy as this might have been a few short years earlier, behind closed doors, it caused mayhem. Joe was dealing with national advertisers who were appalled at outing and uninterested in understanding any political reasons for doing it. They were opposed to controversy, so just being in a gay publication was controversial enough. If *The Advocate* outed Kolbe, they would pull their ads. Predictably, I found both Joe and the company president hyperventilating in my office and insisting, "Pull your writer back. Don't out Kolbe." At the same time, activists and writers were on my phone demanding, "What the hell does the magazine stand for: advertisers? news? activism?" while I sensed the days of shooting down the bad guys were over. Fortunately, in the end, Kolbe jumped everybody's guns, and came out of the closet on his own—blaming *The Advocate* for pressuring him. It was after that, for our own sanity, we wrote up *The Advocate*'s long overdue "no outing" policy.

* * *

Denise Brown and Fred Goldman—father of Ron Goldman, the young waiter who was also murdered on that fatal night—are resolute that the deaths of their loved ones shall not end with the ludicrous criminal verdict of the O.J. trial. Together they've discovered that civil trials are different from criminal trials in several crucial ways that are worth exploring:

In a criminal trial, you must prove a person "guilty beyond a reasonable doubt." That's tough to do. In a civil trial, you must prove that the preponderance of evidence supports the claim. That's easier. In a civil trial, you can call the defendant as a witness and question and cross-examine his statements. That could be a game-changer with the right lawyer. Furthermore, in addition to all the original evidence that was ignored in the criminal trial, fresh evidence that includes 30 photographs of O.J. wearing the infamous Bruno Magli shoes size 12 that left bloody footprints at the crime scene, have now been located.

This basic evidence, unadorned and available to anyone all this time, is breathtaking to Daniel Petrocelli—a not-at-this-point-famous attorney hired by the Goldman family for the civil case. Even though O.J.'s criminal lawyers had been able to make twelve jurors disregard this same evidence, Petrocelli is

9 Matthew and Nicole

confident that he can convince twelve other jurors it is indisputable. Indeed, he's ready to bet his entire legal career on it.

* * *

Late one evening, the VP of Editorial rushed into my office, breathless. "Write something short and quick about Catherine Deneuve, right now!"

"What? Now? Why?"

"I just posted your interview with Deneuve on our new website, *Advocate.com*. I need you to write something extra about her, something special, something only you know, an introduction, anything!"

So, I did. But, when I saw it later at home, I didn't like it; so, I called the VP and said I'd been unprepared and wasn't happy about what I'd written on La Deneuve. He stopped my complaining with, "No problem. I'll take it down in the morning. It'll be gone. Instead we'll post something on her that you do like. Write it now, and give it to me in the morning. Good night."

To be honest, that gave me brain spasms all night. This was really what we could do now? Be a radio in writing? Zip, plop, there it is. Oh, you don't like it? Zap! Gone. Neither Joe nor I could ever imagine during those early years, that *Advocate.com*, like all online news sites, would one day eclipse its print counterpart.

After years of being the scrappy voice for thousands of disenfranchised gays and lesbians, *The Advocate* had now entered adulthood. But with adulthood, came adult problems. We were courting "straight" advertisers who—under Joe's staff's guidance—were tiptoeing into our niche publication with little or no education about our issues or identity. Suddenly we had outside eyes and agendas swooping down on us to make sure that their national ad pages weren't opposite editorial that might distract from their products, like, oh, almost every single unsettling news story in *The Advocate*.

"Who can think about partying or driving a new car with *that* bummer in your face?"—one rep scolded me, holding up his beer ad opposite an editorial page on gay suicide. *And snap!* It's clash of the titans, with Joe and Judy left on the battlefield to make it work. And most of the time, we did.

It's not that hard if you're both champions of the magazine. As I grew more sure-footed in my role, I became like a ferocious lioness-in-chief about the publication's content, while Joe took on the role of cunning hunter for the brand's essential ad nourishment.

What's more, if an advertiser had a problem with *Advocate* editorial (sex, violence, strong commentary), facing their ad page, Joe and I would stare at the pagination until we were lightheaded, usually finding a way to move either the ad or the editorial to another place in the issue.

[A startling burst of applause fills the Ballroom of the Century Plaza Hotel and snaps me into the present.] I look down, past the blinding spotlights, and see Suzanne, Joe, the V.P. and his partner, the president and his partner, in fact, "tout les gros fromages" on their feet, clapping and elated. My speech is over, though I hardly remember making it.

Walking offstage, I encounter comedian/actress Tracey Ullman, who received the Rand Schrader Distinguished Achievement Award earlier in the evening. "You're funny!" she says, hugging me. "That 'perky breast' stuff? Absolutely ingenious and hilarious. How did you ever think that up? What a sense of humor you have!"

If only.

✻ ✻ ✻

9 Matthew and Nicole

These days, the subject of domestic violence not only steers Denise's single-minded journey, it also becomes the stake Petrocelli plans to drive into the heart of the '94 murders. The canny lawyer knows that if he can get a jury to believe O.J. Simpson could repeatedly beat his wife and lie about it, he can also get them to believe he killed her—and is lying about that. What's more, Petrocelli plans to put the real O.J. on the stand—not the charming, cunning one. And so, he devours the defendant like a predator, studying his every move. The most crucial decision Petrocelli makes is to never, ever call the defendant O.J. "'O.J.' was a celebrity," Petrocelli insists. And remembering how that roguishly seductive man ran through airports, hopping over cars and winking at grandmothers, Petrocelli resolved there would be no "O.J." in his courtroom.

So, when the time finally comes to question the person Petrocelli is certain killed Nicole and Ron, the lawyer enters the courtroom hell-bent on controlling a man who's never let anyone do that. Standing before the judge, Petrocelli uses his most discourteous voice, and barks, "We call to the stand the defendant, Orenthal James Simpson."

* * *

Of course it would be totally misleading to imply that Elizabeth sat me across from Ellen DeGeneres and, presto, that HRC dinner turned into a chute down which *The Advocate* slid into an interview with the most sought-after gay celebrity in LGBT history. As I said, Ellen's publicists are having none of us. They've picked *Time*, Diane Sawyer, and Oprah. My many letters to Pat Kingsley, Ellen's publicist, fall on blind eyes. What's more, *Out* magazine, our fierce competition during this time, is helmed by another very determined lesbian EIC who "wants her!" In fact:

"I was in the shower this morning, and suddenly I thought to myself: Judy Wieder!" Sarah Pettit unexpectedly says on the phone to me one morning at work. "I'm going to be in L.A. next week, and I assume you aren't getting Ellen either, so let's double the pressure."

I am so stunned that she's calling me and admitting that she is getting nowhere with an Ellen interview, and needs help, my help, I can't reply. So she goes right on:

"I think you and I should climb up to the Hollywood Sign together, the two of us, sit there, and hold a big press conference!"

"What?" I finally react.

"Ellen is the biggest coming-out in our movement's history; and her handlers are not including the gay press," Sarah goes on, accurately. "That's a little homophobic, don't you agree?"

"Yes, but, is it about that, or...?"

"Of course it is!" she blows down the rest of my sentence. "We are too gay for Ellen."

"I don't know, Sarah," I stall, "Even if you're right, I don't think sitting in front of the Hollywood sign and calling her handlers homophobic is going to get us our interviews."

She sighs loudly, annoyed. "I *have* to *do* something!"

"Oh, well, we do too," I shoot back. "*The Advocate*'s a newsmagazine. She is news. This is happening. We have to write about her—with or without her participation, which I hate."

Now I'm ringing Sarah's competition bell.

"Well, we're *already* doing something on her!"

"Oh?" I say, worried. "Without her, naturally," I poke around.

"Nothing from her, no." She says, crestfallen; then finishes off our conversation: "Well, it was an idea, anyway."

9 Matthew and Nicole

"Yes, yes, and thank you for thinking of me for your Hollywood Sign plan," I trail off awkwardly.

A week later, *Out* appears on the stands with a cartoon of Ellen on the cover, sticking her toe in the water with the cover line: "Come On Out Ellen, The Water's Just Fine—an editorial by Sarah Pettit."

The Advocate takes an altogether different approach. At first, I admit, it drives me bats! But without help from Ellen, there is nothing I can do: Because of our over 70% male readership, the president and those he shares council with, hit on the idea that even though this may be a great time for lesbian stars who are coming out (Ellen, Melissa Etheridge, k.d. lang, Janis Ian, Amanda Bearse, Martina Navratilova, etc.), what about male stars? And there it is: the perfect *Advocate* cover story, accompanied by a large cover photo of a headless man's buffed-up torso. Newsstand candy. The cover lines read: "Lesbian celebrities are leading the way out of the show business closet…so where are the men?"

Crazy! Instead of celebrating this amazing vogue of gutsy lesbian closet-busters, culminating in an interview with Lady Ellen, *The Advocate* is going on the newsstands asking why it is a bigger risk for gay male celebrities to come out than for lesbians. It's antagonistic, controversial, thought-provoking, very *Advocate*, and the best we can do without the star herself. Everybody is regurgitating Ellen's quotes and editorializing about her historic move. We can't do that. *The Advocate* has to lead, and we can't lead without Ellen. So, we look at a different side of the phenomenon, and it works because in our society it's easier to condemn sex between men than between women. Aside from the prevalent use of "girl-on-girl porn" to turn straight men on, the less apparent reason for reviling male-male sex is because that sex act is misunderstood to mean one man is being used "as a woman"—and, well, we all know how lowly women are! An openly gay actor risks being seen as more female, and is thus aligned with the "weaker sex." It just interrupts too many movie-goers' fantasy lives.

Still, I continue to insist that an in-depth interview with Ellen is essential for *The Advocate*'s history. I don't care how many Diane Sawyer or Oprah talks she does! What she will tell the gay press—her family, so to speak—will be newsworthy and totally different from her mainstream interviews. And so I keep the team focused.

More letters are mailed to publicists, more *Advocate* issues sent to "her people." Then one day, Ellen signals back. As her television show progresses, the plot line turns to finding "Ellen Morgan" a girlfriend. One night during an episode, a main character turns to a girl Ellen is interested in, and says, "Are you an advocate of *The Advocate*?"

"OMG!" I jump up. "They're using *The Advocate* to determine if this girl is gay and a potential partner for Ellen," which, incidentally, is something a lot of people actually do. Men and women, who are uncomfortable saying they're gay, often tell me, "Oh, I'm a longtime reader of *The Advocate*."

Naturally, I want to believe this means Ellen is opening to the idea of being interviewed by *The Advocate*, so I jot off still another note, thanking her for including the magazine in her show. A few weeks later, I am invited to be *in* an episode of *Ellen*, selling *Advocate* magazines at a women's music festival. At this point, I'd be a rhino on skates selling popsicles if that's what it takes to get her to talk to us. At the taping, Ellen comes over and chit-chats with me, thanking me for being in the episode. I do what I can to show her I'm just another human being, not out to take anything from her. And I don't bring up the interview.

Then, in the midst of her very closely run press carnival, Ellen appears on *Oprah* with actress Anne ("straight-before-I-met-Ellen") Heche, and watches, stunned, as her girlfriend sets off a twister that shoots the whole show to Oz. DeGeneres' normal control over the discussion is obliterated when the focus switches to Anne's "terrifying remarks about sexual fluidity." With haiku-like brevity, Anne freaks out both Oprah and America with her poetically precise, "I didn't all of a sudden feel, *Oh, I'm gay*. I just all of a sudden felt, *Oh, I love!*"

Well, you could hear people kicking their TVs over from coast to coast. Suddenly LGBTs weren't in their defined boxes, and that scared all the box people. Poor Oprah had to call an "emergency follow-up show with experts on the subject of LGBT sexuality." When my phone rings with an invitation to appear alongside such heavyweights as Dr. Dean Hammer, Charles LePresto, and Chandler Burr, I know *The Advocate* has to quickly pull together a cover story on this hot-button topic—and have it ready for me to wave around on the *Oprah* show. Timing is everything, and over three million people will watch this episode of *Oprah*; so our ability to capture what this moment in LGBT visibility means, is a huge opportunity for the magazine. After several heavy-duty brainstorming sessions with the staff, we hit on, "Beyond Bisexuality," with Anne Heche on the cover, naturally.

* * *

Approximately 35 miles away, in Santa Monica, CA, the jurors for Orenthal James Simpson's civil trial interrupt their deliberations to request that certain passages of the trial, notated by the official court reporter, be re-read to them. The first passage involves the chauffeur for Town and Country Limousine, Allan Park, who's direct testimony about waiting to pick up the defendant, contradicts O.J.'s testimony that he was home taking a nap at the time his wife was murdered. The reporter reads to the jury:

Question by Mr. Petrocelli: Sir, about what time was it when you approached 360 Rockingham?

Allen Park: That would have been just around 10:23, 10:24.

Q: And you were supposed to be at Mr. Simpson's at what time to pick him up?

A: 10:45.

Q: And had you been told what time the flight was going to depart LAX?

A: I knew it was around 11:30.

Q: Now, did you see that car [White Bronco] parked there at 10:23, 10:24, when you drove by 360?

A: No I didn't.

Q: Is there any doubt in your mind?

A: No.

Q: Now, could you tell the jury what happened after you pulled up to the Ashford Street gate?

A: After I pulled up to the gate, I got out of the vehicle, left the door open, went to the call box, and there's an intercom in there with a button. I rang the buzzer. I repeated pushing the button two or three times before I got back into the limousine and—

Q: Did you make any observations about lights being on or off in the house?

A: I noticed that there were no lights on downstairs. I only noticed one light on upstairs...

Q: Now, I direct your attention to the first entry in the cell phone records. Does that represent the time when you called the limo owner, Mr. Dale St. John's, pager?

A: Yes.

Q: And so what time, based on the entry of 10:43 and 44 seconds, do you think it was when you first buzzed into the Simpson residence and got no answer?

A: 10:40 to 10:43.

Q: Okay. And what happened after you hung up your cell phone upon paging Dale?

A: I got back out of the car and I proceeded to ring the buzzer a few more times.

Q: And your next call to Dale began at 10:46 and 30 seconds, right? So, you buzzed into the Simpson residence between 10:44 and 10:46; is that what you're saying?

A: Correct.

Q: What did you do next?

A: As I was standing next to the buzzer, waiting for an answer from somebody, I heard the phone ringing inside the car, and grabbed the phone. And it was Dale.

Q: Relate your conversation with Dale.

A: I told Dale that I didn't think anybody was home. I told him there's no lights on in there. And somewhere in the conversation, that's when I saw the blond, white male (Kato) come out from behind the back of the house.

Q: In this last 30 seconds in your telephone call with Dale, when you first saw this blond-haired person, did you then see anyone else come into this area over here?

A: Yes. I saw somebody come from the driveway area and go into the house.

Q: And can you tell us what the person looked like that you saw go from the driveway area into the house?

A: Six foot, 200 pounds, and all black clothing.

Q: When you say all black clothing, what do you mean by that?

A: Well, dark pants, dark top.

Q: What happened next?

A: What happened was, that person went into the house. I finished up my phone call with Dale when the person went into the house…

Q: Let me stop you right there. First of all, can you tell whether the person that went into the house was Caucasian, African-American or another race?

A: Afro-American.

By studying chauffeur Allan Park's detailed answers along with his cellphone company's well-documented records for that night, the jury can finally be clear about a heretofore disputed fact: At the time Nicole and Ron were being stabbed to death (between 10:15 PM and 10:40 PM), O.J. was *not* asleep at home in his bed. This observable and crucial timeline was ignored at the first O.J. trial.

* * *

I thought that it wouldn't be hard to get accurate information and a great picture of an up-and-coming young actress like Anne Heche at this juncture in her career, but her publicist (with whom I will have a great relationship later), refuses to let *The Advocate* speak with or photograph Anne, and insists he has no art work on her.

Obviously, if we aren't allowed to conduct our own photo shoot of Heche, then we must find a photo somewhere else, which we do; it's an old picture that nobody likes, but that's what happens when you have no choice. Somehow the "Beyond Bisexuality" issue survives its poor cover image on both Oprah's show and the newsstand. People are enthralled with the subject matter. Nevertheless, when Anne sees her cover photo on *The Advocate*, she is so irate, she "punishes" us by giving her first gay-press interview to *Out*. Additionally, a split-second after she welcomes *Out* into her home, her publicist calls me, screaming, "How dare you use that dated picture of Anne on your cover! She looks terrible. Why didn't you come to me?"

Taking stock, I see clearly that we now have *both* Anne and Ellen upset with the magazine. Is it time to throw in the towel…and washcloth and soap dish? For weeks, I give up, realize I can't do that, and try again to find a way to land an interview with Ellen. Then Joe gets an idea: The magazine should sponsor a reading for Ellen's mother, Betty DeGeneres's book. He insists I show up. "You have to be there. *This* is what you do," he tells me just when I need to hear it. "You and Ellen just need to talk, person to person."

And that's what happens. Betty does her reading, and afterward Ellen and I talk, and talk. Ellen tells me that she is producing three short films for HBO called *If These Walls Could Talk*. There are terrific writers and stars attached to it, and she's looking for a great place to talk about everything—like, hey, what about *The Advocate*?

I pretend to think about it for a minute. "Hmmm…Let me see. Would that work?" Then we both laugh, relieved to have finally found a way. And when the cover story interview comes out, to say that Ellen is pleased with her first gay media appearance, simply would not be giving her enough kudos. The experience makes her wildly enthusiastic about coming out all over again. Because she and Sharon Stone co-star as lovers in *If These Walls Could Talk,* we put them both on *The Advocate* cover. What's more, Ellen's exhilaration fires up Sharon's to the extent that Sharon is really disappointed when I tell her that the building-high mural of *If These Walls Could Talk* on Sunset Blvd featuring Sharon and Ellen isn't an ad for *The Advocate* interview. It's for their HBO show.

"Well, it should have been!" Sharon tells me at a function for the show's premiere. "It should have been a poster for Ellen's interview."

* * *

COURT CLERK: You do solemnly swear that the testimony you may give in the cause now pending before this court shall be the truth, the whole truth, and nothing but the truth, so help you God?

ORENTHAL JAMES SIMPSON: I do.

DIRECT EXAMINATION BY MR. PETROCELLI: You and Nicole lived together for about five years, until you married in February 1985, true?

A: That's correct.

Q: And in January 1992, Nicole told you she wanted to leave you, right?

A. She wanted to separate, yes.

Q: And the two of you then separated, correct

A: Yes.

Q: And Nicole filed for divorce shortly thereafter, right?

A: Yes.

Q: And the divorce was final October 15 of that year, correct?

A: Yeah, about that time.

Q: And the following year, 1993, the two of you attempted a period of reconciliation, right?

A: Yes.

Q: And that lasted about one year?

A: I believe exactly one year.

Q: And it ended in May 1994, true? Weeks before her death on June 12, 1994, correct?

A: Almost exactly a month.

Q: And you were together, then, with Nicole about 17 years; is that right?

A: Most of 17 years, yes.

Q: And during that period of time, Mr. Simpson, there were some good times and some bad times?

A: Mostly good, yes.

9 Matthew and Nicole

Q: And there were bad times, right?
A: A few, yes.
Q: More than a few, right?
A: Well, like any long relationship, there were a few bad times, yes.
Q: We're only talking about your relationship, sir, not other relationships, okay?
A: Yes.
Q: And it was a problem relationship for you throughout much of that time, true?
A: Not true.
Q: Did you not say to Detectives Lange and Vannatter, who interviewed you on June 13, 1994, hours after Nicole's death, "I always have problems with her; you know, our relationship has been a problem relationship." Did you say that?
A: Yes…Yes, we'd had a physical altercation.
Q: Well, there was more than one physical altercation, true?
A: I think you'd have to define that. There was one very physical altercation, and there were other times when they were not so physical.
Q: What do you mean by "not so physical," Mr. Simpson?
A: Well, Nicole hit me a few times, and I didn't consider that too physical.
Q: So the altercations with Nicole that were not so physical are the times when you say Nicole hit you, true?
A: Yes. And one time I grabbed her at a door and pushed her outside the door. That —if you call that physical, that's physical, yes.
Q: And how many times, Mr. Simpson, in the course of these physical altercations, did you hit Nicole?
A: Never.
Q: How many times did you strike Nicole?

A: Never.

Q: How many times did you slap Nicole?

A: Never.

Q: How many times did you kick Nicole?

A: Never.

Q: How many times did you beat her?

A: Never.

Q: And are you aware that Nicole has written down in writings that you did hit her?

A: Yes.

Q: And your view is all that is false?

A: True, yes.

Q: Let's talk about 1989. That was an angry, intense, physical confrontation, true?

A: Correct.

Q: And you hit her that day, didn't you, sir?

A: No.

Q: Did your hand make contact with her face at all to cause injuries on her face?

A: I don't know.

Q: Remember I took your deposition over a number of days and Mr. Brewer also asked you questions? You said in the deposition, you remember exactly what you did, true?

A: Yes.

Q: You caused all those injuries, did you not?

A: I feel totally responsible for every injury she had then, yes.

Q: Sir, I'm not asking you about your feelings of responsibility. Do you understand?

A: Yes. I feel responsible for every injury she had.

Q: Move to strike as non responsive.

THE COURT: Stricken. Jury is to disregard that answer.

Q: Please answer the question.

9 Matthew and Nicole

A: I don't know. I don't know that I caused every injury.

[Petrocelli puts up Exhibit 3, pictures of Nicole's battered face after this altercation.]

Q: By the way, you say that some of the marks on this photograph are caused by Nicole picking her face that night, true?

A: No, I told you when she cleans her face.

Q: You said in your deposition, sir, did you not, that that night she was picking at her blemishes, and that caused marks on her chin and on her cheek, true?

A: I don't know.

Q: Tell the jury right now, did Nicole cause any of those marks to herself that night by picking at her face?

A: I don't know; as I told you in the deposition, in wrestling her, maybe my hand hit—hit or was on her face. I certainly didn't punch her or slap her.

Q: You say your hand was on her face. Did you strike her at any time?

A: As I told you, I had her in a head lock at one point, in trying to get her out of the door, so I would assume that my hand was somewhere around her—her face.

Q: And when you said you grabbed her, you put your right hand into a fist—

A: Quite possibly when I grabbed her arm, quite possibly I did.

Q: When you did that just now, you put both hands into a fist. When you did it that night, did you punch her in the face with your hands?

A: No. No.

Q: Did you put your fingers and hands on her throat and leave marks on her throat, sir?

A: I don't recall doing that at all. I assume the injuries occurred during this event, but I didn't see—you know, when you're doing things, you don't see exactly, you know, see when

— 429 —

they happen. I just saw the next day or later on that she had them, and I—I felt I was responsible for them.

Q: Now, after this incident, sir, you wrote this letter to Nicole, did you not? *[Exhibit 13, OJ's letter.]*

A: Yes.

Q: And this is one of the letters where you expressed how wrong you were for hurting Nicole, true? You also said in this letter that you had gone crazy; you got crazy, true?

A: Yes.

Q: And when you said to Nicole in that letter that you got crazy, sir, you were not merely talking about defending yourself, were you?

A: No.

* * *

It's a dismal October day in New York City, and I'm sitting 20 floors up in Rockefeller Plaza, looking out the windows of Warner Brothers publicist Liz Rosenberg's eccentric office. Liz, by reputation, one of the most imposing figures in celebrity PR, isn't looking at me. She's on the phone and staring at a monitor full of questions we've been writing together. If all goes according to our plan—and it won't—Rupert Everett will soon be posing these questions to his co-star, Liz's longtime friend and client, Madonna. Although Liz can rip the heart out of any media person that harms one of her pack, when she's off-duty, Liz is one of the smartest and funniest people in the business. Today, it's clear that the superstar on the phone with her isn't cooperating. She listens attentively, sighing heavily at intervals.

Finally Liz glances my way, wearing a strange smile. She's off the phone and I sense something regrettable coming: "What would you think if we had someone else answer Rupert's questions for Madonna?"

9 Matthew and Nicole

What could she be talking about? The Advocate is planning a big cover story with Madonna, ostensibly because of her upcoming movie, *The Next Best Thing,* with her openly gay costar, British actor, Rupert Everett.

"How can she not be in the interview?" I ask. "It's *her* interview."

"Oh, I know, I know. She'd be in it…" Liz fumbles around trying to come up with a way to dodge the disaster only she knows is headed straight for us.

"Madonna has to answer the questions," I say as calmly and authoritatively as I can. "What's more, Rupert needs to ask them. That's what we're promising readers." Inside I'm panic-stricken. We are very late with this interview. It's to be our first cover story for next year and I've come to New York specifically to find out why things have broken down. Now I'm trying to listen to Liz, but my alarm bells are drowning her out.

"Yes, of course. Forget it. I was just trying to figure out a way…"

"Liz, what's wrong? What's going on?"

Liz sits up straight, takes a breath, and goes for it: "Madonna's not leaving England," she says bluntly. I stare at her as if I don't understand English. She says it a different way: "She has cancelled her American publicity tour. She's in love. She's making a movie with him. She doesn't want to leave him now. She's…"

"No!"

"Yes."

"Ugh…Liz!" I whine. "What about our cover story? Can't she at least do *The Advocate*?" I plead. Then I drop my head into my hands, thinking: *Of course not! We called her a sissy! And now look at the excrement she's left us in!*

Riding down the 20 floors to 51st Street, my entire last month passes before me. What a stupid waste of time and energy. I love Liz and learn from her any time we are together. But I have bigger problems now: The dreaded vacant cover affliction. All I can do is take comfort from something an editor told me years ago when I was running around the offices in a cover-story panic: "Judy, calm down. In 25 years of publishing, *The Advocate* has never yet gone to press without a cover!"

Manhattan's fidgety streets are the perfect match for my mood as I try to walk myself toward a brighter side of the day. After all, big stars cancel interviews all the time. If I'm mad at anyone, I'm mad at myself for choosing to plow down a road of such obvious resistance. It's just that so many times I have been able to set my determination against a disintegrating interview, and win. I just haven't learned when to let go in order to make way for something better. (And I'm guessing that's a bigger lesson than just magazine covers!)

It's complicated because you never know where today's work will lead. You never know if or when the seeds you've planted will suddenly burst out of your grueling groundwork. Only two weeks ago, I was on a beach in Venice, CA with George Michael, watching him film a video for his single, "Outside." Our meeting was the culmination of years of obstinacy on my part, urging and teasing possibilities out of thin air until we were finally talking, first casually on the beach, then seriously for hours at his Beverly Hills home four days later. I don't know why I wouldn't give up on George. I honestly don't. I just knew he had a fascinating story to tell, one that no gay man had told us before. Talk about "Where Are The Men?" Here he was, a huge pop star for over a decade with young girls throwing their undies at him onstage. What was *that* like for him? How did he live like that? What did he give up to present that image? What made him change? And why did the "infamous bathroom incident" have to occur for him to escape his closet? His answers would lead thousands out of theirs.

9 Matthew and Nicole

So yes, even this current Madonna dead end will detour into a freshly paved opportunity in eight years when Liz and I get her onto the cover of *Out* magazine for a lively interview. But *The Advocate*'s Madonna interview was doomed long before I cried "uncle." And once I let go, I could finally hear Destiny screaming at me to pay close attention. For the cover Madonna is vacating will soon showcase a very different kind of "madonna," one whose child was mistaken for a scarecrow as he hung dying on a fence in the broken heart of America.

The senseless death of Matthew Wayne Shepard on October 12, 1998 in the small town of Laramie, Wyoming was a slingshot event for LGBT and straight Americans. We flew forward.

Crucial elements involved in Matthew's death transformed his tragedy into a nation-wide benchmark, mowing down both straight and LGBT assumptions about homosexuality. For gays, any illusions we had about being able to live in a "post gay" world, where non-straight people are equal and safe, died with every blow Matthew suffered at the hands of Russell Henderson and Aaron McKinney, the men who pistol-whipped and beat him to death.

For straight America, the 21-year-old's demise literally brought them face-to-face with one of their oldest fears—"queers"—and they blinked! What the heartland saw was something unexpectedly familiar: a boyish, approachable, college kid, just living out his not-so-perfect life. Even Matthew's lovely, middle-class parents, Judy and Dennis, looked like everyone's parents, and could have been. Astonishingly, the usual indoctrinated distaste that stops many "regular," caring, human beings from including gays in their compassion, seemed to dissolve over Matthew: Politicians made spontaneous speeches surprising themselves and their constituents, proclaiming Matthew could be one of their own sons. Even the Fred Phelps Westboro Baptist Church lunatic fringe ran into trouble when they tried to disrupt Matthew's funeral. "The angels" (Matthew's fellow students and friends dressed in white) were there as well to literally spread their wings and protect the mourners from Phelps' wall of hate. There was just something about Matthew. Unthreatening and vulnerable, he did not come across as "the other."

While it's true that the particulars of Matthew's brutal murder are appalling, the crime of gay bashing ("Let's physically damage and annihilate what we're afraid of, and afraid we might be"), is timeless. But after the October 7th Shepard attack, it seemed as if all the invisible victims swirled together like ancient dust particles, taking shape in this one alluring boy. We cried for all of them.

Many factors drove Matthew's murder deep into America's conscience. To begin with, he lay unconscious for five days in a hospital bed with his family around him until he died. That's a long time. This crucial interval gave the country a chance to think, pray, discuss, stand vigil, identify, and ultimately invest emotionally in Matthew and what killed him. When he finally passed away, everyone had lost a son, brother, lover, and friend. Everyone grieved.

Additionally, Matthew's murder collided with a leap in our communication skills. Because of the Internet, there was extensive and graphic coverage of the physical condition Matthew was left in, tied to the Wyoming fence all night. No one could ignore or forget the cruelty. The amount of information available so quickly to people was *unfamiliar*. This was three years before 9/11! And we weren't used to it. The repeated emphasis on the hideous beating of the boy who "could have been my son," pulled a stitch loose from the moral fabric of America's behavior code. Something came unspooled. The deed itself was too awful and it was done to someone we now felt we "knew."

9 Matthew and Nicole

And, despite the fact that Matthew's youthful and guileless demeanor made him sexually less threatening to a general public that might have otherwise been "uncomfortable," he was still gay and out to his own community. The simple fact that his attackers knew Matthew was gay, was said to have "set them off." Obviously, his batterers were really set off by their *own sexuality*. Why were Henderson and McKinney in a gay bar? Why did they do it? Any true understanding of *homophobia*—and the hate crimes it triggers—must acknowledge that at its heart sits that nasty little bugger *misogyny*: the hatred and fear of females. *(That man is acting like a girl! Ick, kill him!)* The defendants even tried to use the "Homosexual Panic" defense in court, but the judge threw it out.

But why dump all the guilt on the two "evil doers?" The criminals are a natural outcome of the homophobic teachings and attitudes existing in their immediate area, as well as the entire country. *They didn't do this alone.* They were born and bred to do it. America helped McKinney and Henderson kill Matthew Shepard, therefore America must change. Surely when we stand amazed at the progress in LGBT equal rights over the next 15 years, a timeline can be drawn back to Matthew's murder and the world's empathetic response. Even the gift of gay marriage—where most partners relate to each other as equals because they don't have to create gender roles to fit together—owes something to the compassion that came spilling out in the wake of Matthew's murder.

* * *

All the verdicts for the Civil Trial are in and unanimous: Guilty on all counts. Nicole Brown's family did not sue for wrongful death or seek compensatory damages. They were after something else; something that would benefit others, especially women in extreme danger. Misogyny, untreated, kills. Because the jury found Simpson guilty of battery against Nicole, and because that battery was committed with oppression and malice, which means extreme cruelty, the conclusion was: Nicole's death was the logical last step in the escalating physical and emotional abuse she was enduring at the hands of her husband. That's what Denise and her family wanted out in the open for the public to contemplate and understand. For within that learning curve, lay a solid warning for others currently suffering behind closed doors: Without help and intervention, you will die.

✳   ✳   ✳

When I return to L.A. from New York on Monday morning, I pass art director, Craig Edwards at his desk, and sense some ordeal poised to strike before I can even make it into my office. Craig's heard about the Madonna fiasco, as has everyone. In fact, racing past several open doors while in my own cocoon of concerns, I clock a weird excitement surging in editorial. Worried, I turn back and approach Craig's office door. He doesn't even wait for me to ask.

"*Thank God you lost Madonna!*" he shouts.

"Well, I didn't exactly do it all by myself," I sigh, defensively.

"It doesn't matter. Something incredible is happening. Go see Jon and Bruce."

All I want to do at this point is put the heavy bits and pieces of my New York work spree down on my desk. Both the executive editor, Bruce Steele, and the associate news editor, Jon Barrett, have heard Craig's announcement about Madonna and are waving me ahead to Bruce's office.

"Judy Shepard is willing to talk to certain press!" Jon erupts as I get close. What if we could get her for an interview for your missing cover story?" he continues excitedly.

9 Matthew and Nicole

For a moment I can't even respond I'm so stunned.

Jon tells me Judy Shepard has a website called *MatthewsPlace.com*, and that he's been in touch with someone named Lee Thomson who works with Judy. According to Lee, Judy and Dennis are launching a foundation in Matthew's name at the beginning of the year.

"Yes! Yes!" I say, "Will she talk to us?"

"There's more," Jon, stops me as I try to go on. "Judy and Dennis are probably going to do *Dateline* with Katie Couric and one mainstream magazine."

"Wow," I step back. "How can they bear so much attention so soon? It's only been a month. I mean, aren't they numb?"

"That's how they're getting through it." Bruce surmises.

My assistant finds me in Bruce's office. "There you are! Welcome home," Georgette says happily. Georgette's general cheeriness in the midst of any crisis is a source of wonder to me. Things can be coming at me at a projectile pace from within and without, and she's unflappable.

"You have a call from Nathan Lane's publicist," she tells me now.

"Tell him I'll call him later," I say, distractedly.

"No," Bruce interrupts. "You've got to schmooze him. We need him to move Nathan's cover story up an issue."

"Up? To where? Wait, a cover?"

"To the empty Madonna cover issue."

"What? I thought you just said that we're getting Judy Shepard," I'm starting to feel my jetlag.

"I don't think we can possibly rush Judy Shepard into that issue," Bruce insists. Jon is nodding his head furiously.

"But Nathan Lane instead of Madonna? He's not even out."

"Yes! He is finally coming out in this interview with us," Bruce defends.

"That's a problem," I argue. "I think he's waited too long; I mean, maybe not too long for his timetable, but for this magazine's readership. Readers will write letters saying: 'So what? Who doesn't know he's gay?' When Nathan was really hot after *Birdcage*, that's when people wanted him to come out, and he wouldn't do it. So why now? What changed his mind?"

"Matthew Shepard," Bruce says.

"*What?*"

"Nathan is completely blown away by Matthew Shepard's murder, and feels he has to do something, to stand up and be counted in some way," Bruce says.

"You are kidding! Well, that's great, ok, give him the cover," I say cavalierly. Predictably, Nathan's coming-out interview winds up being exactly the double-edge sword we feared, with slews of *Advocate* readers emailing "Duh" to the "revelation" of his sexual orientation. Worse yet, we always have to print one or two reader letters in the next issue, which Nathan then reads and is heartbroken. And of course, *Voila*! His publicist is on me like an assassin for embarrassing Nathan.

"There are some other problems." Bruce stops me again from leaving, and signals Jon.

On cue, Jon begins: "Lee says this interview, if it happens, isn't going to happen over the phone. Judy has to see my eyes."

"Your eyes?"

"Yes, she's not going to talk on the phone to a reporter about her murdered son. It's too intimate. I have to fly to Wyoming and meet with her. Do we have the budget?" he asks.

"Let me get this straight," I say, scooping up my debris. "I need to go in there and talk Nathan Lane's publicist—who's hung up on me by now—into kick-starting Nathan's coming-out story and photo session, so we can jet him onto the first cover of the year. Then I have to march into our new president's office—after my expensive business trip—and tell him to come up with...how much?"

"I'm not sure. We want to make any plane arrangements we can on short notice if Judy says yes, and, of course we need to take a photographer."

"Oh, of course," I say, "So that's two people round-trip and a hotel?"

"Yep, and one other thing," now Jon is smiling.

"After you get the money approved, *you* are going to have to talk Judy Shepard into doing the interview. I mean, you are going to have to talk her into seeing me."

"You mean your eyes?"

"Yeah."

"I wonder if I was actually further along with Madonna?" I mumble.

"*WHAT?*" they all bark.

"Kidding."

When the next day arrives, I'm staring at a little yellow piece of paper with a phone number on it. If I dial it, Judy Shepard will answer. To me, she is the most important person in the world. No movie or music star has ever had me so anxious. I try meditating; nothing formal, just a few breaths to remind myself that I must be truthful and clear in order to give Judy confidence; to give credence to my own conviction that we are the right magazine and Jon is the right person to trust with her important story. She hasn't said yes. She hasn't said no. "It's all on you," Jon whispered nervously when he handed me the phone number yesterday. He meant to make me feel important. But having just lost an interview, all I could hear was, "If she doesn't wind up talking to me in Wyoming, your magic wasn't big enough."

I dial Judy. Her phone is ringing; the minute I hear Judy's sad but strong voice, I know there's hope. Unlike so many situations involving national news events or celebrities coming out for the first time, Judy Shepard, a mother with precious little background in gay issues, instinctively knows *The Advocate* should be included in her communications. The magazine mattered to her murdered son, and that matters to her. Yes, she and her husband are doing two mainstream media outlets, but she understands that isn't enough.

"I'll talk to *The Advocate*," she decides. "But not on the phone."

"I know, you need to see his eyes," I repeat.

"I do. I need to see who he is before I talk about Matthew to this magazine."

"This magazine" represents all Matthew's gay brothers and sisters to Judy. "I used to see it in his room," she half-whispers.

"So, then," I continue, a little worried about my next move. "I need to have one promise from you, Judy."

"What's that?" she asks, without attitude.

"If we fly Jon out there for several days and put him up in a hotel, along with a photographer, will you promise me— once you see his eyes, of course—that you'll receive him?"

There's warm, throaty laughter rolling at me from the Wyoming side of the call. I almost can't believe her astonishing humanity at such a time. "Yes," she says. "Once I see his eyes, I will most certainly take Jon in and do the interview and photo shoot."

"Fantastic! Then I'll work everything out. Just let us know when you want him to come," I say, relieved. "I'm so grateful you talked to me, Judy. And you did it without seeing my eyes!"

Then Judy says the most wonderful thing: "I didn't need to see your eyes. I knew the minute I heard your voice that you were okay."

In the remarkable way that a cover story can work when it's right, Jon and a photographer fly to Casper, Wyoming, where Judy so loves Jon's eyes that the two become emotionally and professionally bonded. *The Advocate*'s cover story is a heat-seeking bull's-eye critically and commercially and it gives this Editor in Chief just the swift kick she needs to fight on for what truly belongs on its pages.

∗ ∗ ∗

10

Aloha Technology!

I am enjoying a sunset dinner with Suzanne at Huggo's on the Big Island of Hawai'i. Established in the '60s on a lone dirt road that once encircled the entire island, this 1960s gathering place for local fisherman is now Kailua-Kona's most popular oceanfront dining spot. I inhale my South Pacific sanctuary while studying a fisherman and his son clinging to slippery lava rocks nearby. It's the summer of 1999, and everything feels like it's exactly where it belongs. Then my cellphone rings.

It's Jim, our company's new president, and he sounds very excited. "What are you doing?" he hazards, knowing I'm on vacation. "Something big has come up," he says, "And I need you to start thinking about it."

"O-okay…" I say, staring at the giant piece of mud pie in front of me.

"Get ahold of yourself," he continues, "our company is going to buy *Out* magazine!"

With that, Hawai'i disappears. Kite surfers fall out of the waves. Turtles slip back into the sea. Dolphins vanish into the sunset. Trade winds are sucked back into the sky, taking with them a ghostly whiff of tropical sugar plantations and sultry rainforests. My bliss, my utopia, my temporary respite: *poof*.

"*We're going to buy Out magazine!*" I blurt, for Suzanne's benefit.

"Yes! So, in your spare time in Hawai'i," he laughs, "I'd like you to put on your thinking cap about editorial."

"Doesn't *Out* have its own editorial staff?"

"Yes, but we need to think about the bigger picture."

"But, Jim, I'm the editor in chief of *The Advocate…*"

"That's something we're going to talk about," he stops me.

"We are? *That* sounds ominous."

He laughs again. *I definitely don't have enough facts.* "Jim, *Out*'s always been *The Advocate*'s biggest competition. That keeps both magazines on their toes. I think we need separate staffs."

"Maybe, but editorial needs to change. You're moving up."

"What?"

"I need an editorial director *now*. So, it's time for you to move on from *The Advocate*," he concludes decisively."

"Leave *The Advocate?*" I stifle a gasp, feeling like I'm being shoved out of an airplane naked.

"Yes, I need your help. We have to decide which *Out* employees to hire and which not to hire." I hear him take a breath. "And *you're* going to do this!"

"*Me?*" I squawk full volume, causing Suzanne to order a Mai Tai.

"We'll all help you," he soothes, "but you'll be the face of it. So, start thinking about an editor in chief."

"For which magazine?" I ask, softly.

"Ultimately? For both magazines. But today, think about an editor in chief for *Out*," then he adds, "So, go ahead, relax. Enjoy what's left of your vacation. You'll need it." *Click.*

Suzanne stares into my wide eyes, waiting.

"What?" she says.

"Well, you heard the part about buying *Out*, but what you missed is he wants me to become the editorial director of the company. Of both magazines…"

"OMG! That's awesome!" she lifts her glass in a toast. "Honey, congratulations. Be happy. You'll have time to worry later. Right now, eat your pie and celebrate."

I'm so dazed I don't know how to do that. I pick up my fork, only to put it back down.

"What?" Suzanne asks again, laughing.

"There's too much on my plate."

"Get used to it, baby."

The flight from Hawai'i to Los Angeles is one I am becoming more and more used to. The ride back seems to reverse all the enchanted feelings I embrace on the flight there when I literally float above the Pacific, high on my excitement about the Polynesian delights I will soon revel in.

In my eyes, the Hawaiian archipelago is lot more than one-palm-tree-away from a greeting card. Yes, there *are* serene beaches, but there are also *pali* (cliffs), rivers, pastures, waterfalls, forests, plantations, deserts, valleys, volcanos, and the highest mountains on earth. With 137 (not eight!) islands, Hawai'i's *mana* (spirit) can be unlocked with one tender word: *Aloha*. And despite the word being coopted as jargon to drive tourism, "aloha" really means something. More than a greeting, it's a way of living life in empathy, love, and peace. I've seen for myself how aloha functions every single day as an invisible adhesive that allows so many dissimilar heritages to exist together in one place.

Hawaiians believe their gods take the form of plants and animals, and that these plants and animals are part of their *ohana* (family). If your gods are your family manifested in nature, it's easy to see how your relationship with nature is transformed. That's why the aloha spirit includes a love of *aina* (land and sea). The land's destiny is your destiny. We are simply not complete without our aina, our place.

Unfortunately, the bliss I've been devouring on my brief vacation is now seeping out of me. Taxiing to our gate, my cellphone barfs up all sorts of missed voicemails about work. By the time I listen through everything, I'm standing at the Wailing Wall of my job, utterly aloha-less.

The *Out* acquisition goes well. Still, take-overs are painful. And, no matter what side you're on, being "the face of it" isn't pretty. Instead of the community reacting with pride and support over an LGBT company revitalizing *Out*—thus owning and running the two most popular gay magazines in America—readers go batty. Somehow the leap they make is that we—and me in particular—are going to homogenize all the gay voices and distill LGBT publishing down to one bland format.

"To what purpose?" Sarah Pettit laughs over the phone, when I call her ranting about the hate mail I'm getting. "It's the opposite of what makes you successful," she says, adding how happy she is to be at *Newsweek* now, where this unique brand of jealous, eat-our-own, in-fighting doesn't rule. "There are other challenges here," she confides, "but it's a relief to be away from *that*!"

This whole soul-rotting malaise about Liberation Publications, Inc. *[LPI, our parent company]* being on a mission to own and destroy the movement's individuality, vaults another loopy level when *The Advocate* becomes a sponsor of the Millennium March on Washington in the spring of 2000. We create a special *Advocate* edition celebrating both the March and the Human Rights Foundation's Equality Rocks Concert, taking place the night before. Well, holy outrage! The amount of time I spend trying to soothe irate readers, by explaining, "This is a *special* issue of *The Advocate*; our *regular* biweekly *Advocate* issue is also on the stands," is ridiculous.

I'm so surprised by the community's reaction I decide to visit Jann Wenner in NYC. Creator and editor of *The Rolling Stone,* Jann's always been generous with his advice and mentoring, although I never succeed in getting him to come out in *The Advocate*. "Growth and change doesn't necessarily make folks happy," he tells me after I whine about the anger we've aroused for buying *Out*. "You dared to stick your head up, Judy. And while you thought they'd applaud your hard work and success; that's not what happens, is it? Instead, *they shoot at you!*"

* * *

Joe, Suzanne, Jim, me, and about 50,000 euphoric people are on our feet screaming at the top of our lungs, whipped into a frenzy after George Michael throws an arm around Garth Brooks for the finale of their "Freedom" duet. The moment is truly the zenith of the Equality Rocks Concert at RFK Stadium. Absorbing this imposing warm-up to tomorrow's LGBT Millennium March on Washington, I'm truly stunned to have facilitated what George's manager said couldn't be done: getting the notoriously difficult pop star up and onto that stage. After saying "no" his customary number of times, George finally gave me the two conditions under which he'd perform. One of them we are currently witnessing: "I want to sing a duet with Garth Brooks!" The other was his desire to make—and present during the concert—a film about the terrors endured by LGBT youths whose parents force them into phony clinics where they are brutalized into rejecting their same-sex urges.

"*You are kidding me!*" Elizabeth (Birch, also an Equality Rocks producer) said over the phone when I told her about George's demands. "And exactly how are we going to make all this happen?" I told her I had absolutely no idea, but had already said, yes. "OMG," she sighed, but agreed we had to get him into the line-up.

Although we spent months trying to meet George's stipulations, in the end, none of us could. But instead of pulling out of the show, George used his own money to make the documentary himself. Unfortunately, the film doesn't find a good home at a concert drunk on celebrating the first LGBT stadium rock festival. Attendees are stupefied by the documentary. Amid cheering and partying, this "dark bummer" lands, rendering dancing and singing the wrong response. George multiplies the resistance by screaming, "How the fuck is this going on in America? Your children are being imprisoned and tortured on a daily basis!"—As if it's all *our* fault. This, I confess, is the George I know and love.

His duet request was no picnic to pull off either. Fortunately, Lisa Sanderson, who worked with Garth regularly, understood the symbolism of an out and edgy pop star like George sharing the stage with America's favorite country boy. Garth, whose sister is a lesbian, was one of the first to sign on to the concert, but getting him to harmonize with George was the wall we had to climb. It took Lisa weeks to get that "yes."

The Equality Rocks/Millennium March gives me an unexpected gift: a new perspective on some of the purists attacking *Out* and *The Advocate* for being owned by the same company. Apparently, the minute the HRC launched its plans for a March on Washington, certain grassroots advocates along with elected San Francisco and New York gay officials, issued joint statements saying they would not attend the March, and urged their constituents to boycott the event.

"*Now* I know what you've been talking about!" Elizabeth called to commiserate. "We are being attacked from every side. Why do we do this to each other?"

It's a great question. We have real enemies in this world. Why "eat our own?" The March and concert are immeasurably uplifting to the three hundred thousand who attend! Every hotel in DC is sold out. Hordes of LGBTs fill the nation's capital, and lots of them are young and don't know or care about the things we once marched for. That's the trick about the past: *it's not everybody's.*

* * *

There was such trepidation around the turn of the millennium, with people predicting our computers and electronics would implode, when no major events happened, we figured: *All clear.* Now, nine months into 2001, we can finally let our guard down.

That's when it happens! They get us with our own planes! Islamic Fundamentalist terrorists hijack four United States commercial airliners and slam two of them into the World Trade Center towers in New York City, one into the Pentagon in Arlington, Virginia, and miss their fourth target—purportedly the White House or Capitol building. All totaled nearly 3000 people die in a vicious suicide mission coordinated by a militant jihadist. A permanently darker world is born on September 12, 2001.

While exhausted firemen are pushing through the ashes of fallen buildings, *The Advocate* staff gathers in my office to discuss what in the world we're going to do. Every mainstream news outlet can put the flaming towers on their screens, home pages, and covers and have an up-to-date story; but what is the national LGBT newsmagazine of record going to come up with? Is there a legitimate LGBT story somewhere amid this horror? It feels like our whole reason to be is suddenly in question.

Hours go by while we fling ideas around, frantically seeking a story that's on subject and true to our news niche. I do my damnedest to keep the trim but combustible team from bursting into flames, while every discussion keeps circling back to the question, "How many gay people died on 9/11?" It's an interesting question, but why would we ask it? Isn't it disrespectful to all the other people who died? Why single out LGBT deaths? Why not African Americans or Hispanics? Still, it intrigues us, and soon we take it another step by wondering whether we could actually *find* LGBT people who died on 9/11 and tell their stories. What would that look like? At least it's something no other news service will be doing. Still, I worry about the blatant narcissism of just making one segment of humanity seem special or different in this massive tragedy.

Then it hits me. *That's* the point! LGBTs *aren't* any different in this death count, are they? They're *equal* to all the other human beings who died in this terrorist attack. So why is it so obvious that we are equal in death, but not in life? Singling out LGBTs who died on 9/11 and telling their stories, might make some people mad, and question, "what difference does it make that these people were gay?" But that's our point too. We agree. They were just like everyone else; they were "equal people." When Ronald Gamboa, Dan Brandhorst, and their 3-year-old son, David, disintegrated into the ashes of the South Tower of the World Trade Center along with their hijacked airliner, it's hard to argue that they weren't equally vulnerable, equally unlucky, equally frightened, and equally human. So, we ask: *why*, when these people died, is it obvious that they're equal to everyone else? But had they lived, they'd still be fighting for the same rights their heterosexual co-passengers had.

Now the story was starting to feel like a fresh and timely approach to our ongoing coverage of equal rights. All we had to do was find all the LGBTs who perished on 9/11! An investigative nightmare! Calling grieving friends and relatives of the 9/11 victims we *suspected* were LGBT; trying to confirm the sexual orientation of the people they lost? I can still see columnist Liz Smith holding up this *Advocate* issue in her favorite Tex-Mex restaurant, yelling at me, "*How did you do this?*" I have never been prouder of *The Advocate* editorial team, or the cover feature we delivered in a week and a half.

Unsurprisingly, all the challenges LGBTs are struggling with, emerge in one casualty's story or another: We learn about gay partners who had to immediately get into their deceased lover's apartment in order to "de-gay" it before the grieving parents discovered their son or daughter's closeted orientation. The Victim's Compensation Fund—payouts from the US government of between $250,000 and $1.8 million given to the "straight" spouses and families of those who perished on 9/11—have a whole different set of rules for openly gay or lesbian partners. Decisions affecting whether these people receive money are made on a case-by-case basis. Such things taken into consideration include cooperation from the victim's biological family, which might easily turn sour if the biological family rejects the victim's partner. We found cases in which surviving partners weren't on good terms with their deceased partner's family. Motivated by greed and homophobia, some families turned their backs on—thus stole from—the very people their deceased children chose to love.

The Advocate's 9/11 cover story is rich in lessons, pain, and heroics. We unearth Mark Bingham, a gay businessman from San Francisco who was aboard Flight 93 and joined other courageous passengers in pushing a service cart through the locked pilots' door in order to wrestle the controls from the terrorists and down the plane in Shanksville, PA. *The New York Times* writes a supportive piece about our cover story, understanding what we did and why it had to be done.

And we, *The Advocate* staff, close the issue fully appreciating the importance of any legal contracts LGBT partners can put in place—including, of course, the essential package that will one day come with marriage equality.

* * *

The initial orders given to the Fire Department of New York (FDNY) after the planes struck, were to get into the Twin Towers, assist people who were trapped, and evacuate all floors of both Towers. Rescue operation bases had been set up *inside* the WTC. Incredibly, no one realized that radio communications, due to the impact of the planes, were failing. FDNY commanders were losing contact with the very firefighters they were sending into the Towers. As a result, firemen could not report back about their progress; and worse—from within the flaming structures, firefighters couldn't hear their evacuation orders.

The final curse came when firemen couldn't communicate with the NYPD. The two departments always used different radio frequencies. But on 9/11, because the NYPD had helicopters flying around the Twin Towers and could *see* the towers would fall, they could warn their people inside. With the FDNY using a different frequency, they never heard these life-saving warnings.

* * *

Throughout 2002, the trauma of an unexpected attack on American soil burrows inward, unhinging our feelings of well-being. At work, most of our manager meetings oscillate between reports of lower magazine sales (due to 9/11's impact on the economy), and exhilarating plans to launch a new high-end LGBT travel magazine, *The OutTraveler (TOT)*. Joe reports that travel ads are up in both *Out* and *The Advocate*, indicating that one of the ways gays are coping with continuous exposure to the world's most volatile elements—is to go out and see more of it!

Every day I arrive with a jam-packed calendar and a frequently changing vision for the company's future: "What about an *Advocate* Casino and Resort in Vegas, where top gay performers headline, and the rooms, gambling chips, paraphernalia, and decor feature LGBT celebrities from Liberace to Ellen DeGeneres?" Or how about an *Advocate* news radio partnership?

Apparently, Showtime and MTV have also gotten the frantic post-9/11 memo. The two companies announce plans for a gay-oriented cable channel. This possibility galvanizes me because I've always wanted *The Advocate* to have its own *60 Minutes* TV news show. So, I shadow the three men involved in forming the gay cable channel until I worm my way onto a conference panel with them. While the audience listens to plans for what will become the LOGO channel, I use my speaking time to pitch program ideas to the executives. After several post conference lunches, LOGO agrees to launch *The Advocate Newsmagazine* with Rachel Maddow as one of the hosts, *The OutTraveler* with Chad Allen, and at least one *Out 100 Special*.

✳ ✳ ✳

On November 2, 2002, a young mother named Pulau is shaken off her feet when a 7.3 magnitude earthquake erupts off the island of Simeulue, Indonesia. Only three people die. Pulau knows why so few people are killed. On her island, it's common folklore that a mammoth earthquake and tsunami hit in 1907, killing most of its inhabitants. They died because they ran to the beaches after seeing the water recede, never guessing it would rush back in and swallow them all. Over time, survivors spread this tragic story to all new Simeulue inhabitants, turning an oral history into the saving grace of this seismically active region.

The '02 quake does not trigger a tsunami, but hindsight will reveal it is, in fact, a *foreshock* to the worst tsunami disaster in recorded history: the '04 Indian Ocean quake. It is a warning. Unfortunately, without the technology to decipher what it's saying, it's useless.

✳   ✳   ✳

It's the spring of 2003, and I'm in New York City, staying at my favorite home away from home: the W Hotel on 39th and Lexington. Normally, my amazing suite would not fit my travel budget; but one evening years ago, when I was staying in their smallest room, I ran into the hotel's manager in a mini market. He recognized me from the photo that accompanies my *Advocate* Editor in Chief column, and introduced himself. He told me that a particular EIC column I'd written changed his life. It had convinced him to come out to his family, and in doing so he'd been transformed. Naturally, encounters like this are the highlight of my job; I thanked him, and we talked for a bit until he realized I was staying at his hotel. He asked what room I was in, and when I gave him the number, he laughed.

I returned the next evening to find the hotel had moved all my belongings into a beautiful corner suite facing the Chrysler Building and East River. I rushed to the front desk and explained to the manager that I didn't have the budget for that gorgeous suite. It was then he told me, "From now on, *that suite* is your room; and the price is the same as the small room you were in."

So, tonight, I'm standing in this stunning suite when the phone rings and my assistant sounds the way he sounds when a high-powered publicist has frightened him. "Judy," he chokes out, "Rosie and Kelli are sending a car for you!"

"Why?"

"I don't know, but it should already be there." Having learned in recent years that the "road of least resistance" is the one to walk, I throw on some jeans and a sweater, take the elevator downstairs, and walk obediently past the hotel doorman and into the waiting town car.

The chauffeur looks at me in his mirror. "We're going to Nyack, New Jersey," he announces.

"I thought so," I reply. Rosie O'Donnell, her current wife, Kelli, and their four children, live in Nyack, New York, right on the Hudson River.

"I'm taking you to their favorite restaurant in Nyack: Casa del Sol," the driver offers.

Oy! I can't eat spicy food! But I smile. "Sounds like fun."

When we finally arrive, Kelli waves me over to a large table she's sharing with Rosie and two men I've never seen before: Gregg Kaminsky and his partner, Dan McDonald. The first thing I notice, because I'm famished, is that everyone has already eaten. They're clearly raring to launch into something I am totally unprepared for:

"Do you know what Gregg used to do?" Rosie asks me with characteristic directness. I'm still not sure which one is Gregg, so I just shake my head "no."

"Gregg used to be the Vice President of Atlantis Events, the biggest gay cruise ship company!"

"Oh, wow," I say, still baffled.

"And Daniel is Rosie's business partner," Kelli adds, studying me for a moment. "Did you eat dinner?" she asks, always the caretaker. My face must have brightened, because Kelli quickly pulls over a tray of chips and guacamole, which I mindlessly dive into before the spicy avocado registers.

"Oh, shit!" I blurt, and grab someone's water.

"It's not *hot*," they all respond.

Why do people who love spicy food always say that?!

Tears flash flood out of my eyes while I blow my nose and try not to leave the table. Kelli pulls a waiter aside and orders several bland items for me. Then Rosie, who can't stand it another second, lets loose:

"Look, Judy, we've invited you here for a reason! This is the beginning of something *huge*, and we want you to be a part of the launch and—if you're interested— maybe do a magazine with us!"

"What are you talking about?" I sniffle, my sinuses burning.

"Gregg and I are going to start a vacation cruise ship business for LGBT families," Kelli begins. "It's going to be called *r family vacations*. Rosie is going to help get it going, but Gregg and I are going to run it."

"*OMG!* That's amazing!" I yell through my napkin. "What a great idea. Like *Olivia Cruises* is for lesbians?"

"Exactly," Rosie says. "Just imagine what this will mean for children being raised in gay families! Where do these kids get a chance to meet other kids who share their life experiences?"

"Soon the kids of gay parents can go on a vacation cruise like ours and meet hundreds of others like them," Kelli adds.

"And the magazine you want to do?" I venture.

"Ah...!" Rosie points at me. "Do you think the world is ready for a gay family magazine?"

I think about the ones that already exist, and worry. "Well, I doubt that it would be easy. But if *you* were involved, it would be worth exploring."

"Oh, I'll be involved. It'll be you and me at the top!" she proclaims, and gives me a thumbs-up.

I thumbs-up her back, while wondering what Jim and Joe will think. Jim will probably like the idea of an LGBT family magazine because he loves family and he's open to new ideas. Joe is a different story. I can already hear him asking, "What about advertisers? What'll we sell in the magazine?" So, I turn the question on Rosie. "What ads could we get?"

"We can go after the same advertisers who advertised in *Rosie* magazine," she says, referring to her now defunct publication. "Or maybe consider ads that are in *Martha Stewart Kids*."

"Ro, I'm sorry," I say nervously, "but companies like Procter & Gamble advertised in *Rosie*."

"Right!" she concurs, wondering what my point is.

"These companies advertise in mainstream magazines. They do not want to sell their wares 'in a gay environment,'" I say.

"What are you saying?" she challenges. "Gays don't use toothpaste to brush their teeth? Or...?"

"Yes, of course they—we—do," I stop her. "But these companies have other outlets—mainstream magazines with huge circulation numbers, or highly-rated television shows—where they can sell their products *to us* without exposing themselves to any controversy."

"What controversy?"

"Ro, *we* are the controversy: gays. A company that advertises in a gay magazine receives hate mail from homophobes who find their ads in our publications. They go after these companies, and boycott them. They launch hate letter-writing campaigns. It's a mistake to think the same companies that go into *Parents Monthly* would go into *r family*."

Rosie thinks for a minute. "Well, how gay do we have to

be? I mean, can't our magazine be for alternative families? Maybe a bit gay-er, but not totally gay. Like real life, populated with all kinds of families," she explains.

"I think we have to define our niche, Ro," I say, "At least where things stand today, magazines need to be clear about who they're appealing to. Besides, getting vague about the gay thing isn't going to fool advertisers."

Rosie offers to create an *r family* prototype with some ex-*Rosie* editors and get back to me. Then she disappears with her own ideas until the first *r family vacations* cruise. She decides to test her family magazine onboard, using some of the passengers as a focus group. A question and answer sheet is given out with copies of the prototype, and a research report is assembled from their responses. Later Rosie sends me the final report, along with a personal note that says, "You were right. They didn't understand the magazine. They said they were confused by it, said it needed to be more gay..." Then adds, "I don't want to do an all-gay family magazine. It's just not my world."

I completely understand Rosie's decision. Additionally, it's getting impossible to ignore the fact that something massive is already sweeping in and overhauling the media: The kinds of readers that most advertisers want are young people who don't have to invent or understand the Internet to love it. They no more question surfing the web than we asked, "Where does the electricity go when nothing's plugged into the socket?" We're all born accepting the science that came before us. Advertisers are going online because more and more "eyeballs" are there— especially young ones.

So, while editors and executives argue over what stories, typefaces, colors, or logos may be turning off print magazine buyers, we're really just rearranging furniture on the Titanic! Online publications don't need furniture. The heavy costs of printing, color tests, re-runs, paper, postage, delivery trucks, circulation, newsstand fees, etc. all disappear with web publications. And it's not that I don't see this bigger picture; I'm just too close to it to see that I should be a part of it—*right now*.

*   *   *

A few seconds before 1 A.M. on the day after Christmas 2004, it happens again. Pieces of the Indian Ocean floor pop straight up and displace thousands of tons of water. Within minutes, this water is elevated to the height and speed of three tsunamis, all racing toward the landmasses around them.

If this same 9.2 earthquake had happened in the Pacific Ocean, the Pacific Tsunami Warning Center, in 'Ewa Beach, Hawai'i, would be issuing warnings to all the vulnerable coastal areas. Following a 1946 tsunami that killed 165 people in Hawai'i, a technological system was put into place that measures the tides in all areas of the earthquake. Although the technology exists in '04, it will not be installed in the Indian Ocean for another year—prompted by the incomprehensible death toll of 230,000 humans and God knows how many animals that may have had adequate time to find safety had they known what was coming.

While Pulau is herding her family away from the waterless beaches around her, on distant Khao Lak, Thailand, locals stroll outside clueless. Fishermen and shell collectors rush onto the uncovered sea beds, grabbing fish and other treasures. The exposed sea bottom creates little pools too irresistible for children not to play in.

An hour later, the scavengers look up to see the horizon is blocked by a rapidly growing blue wall. A blink of an eye later, and the blue mountain is moving at the speed of 150 mph into the cove and over everyone. There will be no outrunning the 80-foot tsunami. And this is only the first swell.

10 Aloha Technology!

The few who survive, run back into the receding tide to help those gagging on gallons of salt water. But the second and deadliest of the three waves comes swiftly, sweeping hotels, cars, busses, buildings, trees, power lines, and people miles inland, breaking them to pieces in a whirlpool of deadly debris.

Miraculously—even though they're located a stone's throw from the epicenter—every single Simuelue villager escapes the *two-mile-high tsunami* that crashes through their village. Safe with other survivors, Pulau is devastated to learn how many people did not know her lifesaving information. Thinking back to the tsunami that wiped out Simuelue in 1907, she wonders, *does everyone have to go through the same tragedy?* What if Pulau had possessed a few tools to distribute this simple lesson (run *away* from—not *into*—the sea)? Information means nothing if it can't be shared.

* * *

Rather than continuing the upstream fight to keep *Out* co-gender like *The Advocate*, a business decision is made in '03 to turn the magazine into a publication for gay men. Knowing that one of *Out*'s original founders, Sarah Pettit, (who, tragically, passed away in January, 2003) left *Out* over disagreements about balancing *Out*'s content so that lesbian readers weren't shortchanged, I feel like a failure. For her sake, should I have fought harder? But, to what end?—as Sarah herself might have said. I would just be one more lesbian editor who didn't "get it." ("It" being the fact that gay men buy stuff and lesbians don't.) What's more, it's probably a smart decision. By positioning the magazine as the spirit, fashion, and culture of gay male life, *Out* is finally free to be what it's destined to be: successful!

Coincidentally, I find myself falling in love with the fashion industry. My mother, the model, must be laughing down the runways of the hereafter to see her unfashionable daughter cherishing the Milan and New York fashion shows. Both a mirror of—and a window into—our restless world, what's coming down the runways, can be a sharp commentary on the times.

In addition to making *Out* a publication for gay men, we decide to stop delivering our magazines in those white plastic bags that hide *The Advocate* and *Out* from a nosey neighbor or housemate. Naturally, there are readers from more hostile communities who balk and cancel their subscriptions. We don't blame them. Still, we decide to stop colluding with those who would make someone feel shame or fear over receiving an LGBT publication.

Unfortunately, none of our transformations hide the fact that magazine circulations are trending downward throughout the print industry. The best way to get our content to today's readers, is to get it on web browsers, smartphones, tablets and in time, watches, cars, and eyeglasses.

I try very hard to feel the excitement of this inevitable publishing revision. After all, so many things will be easier. *The Advocate* can no longer be an up-to-date newsmagazine if it's only coming out every two weeks.

※ ※ ※

The Indian Ocean tragedy does not end when the water settles back down. Disease and starvation rise in its wake. Who is going to clean up the beaches piled high with bloated bodies being washed out to sea and returned with each tide? Who can help with all this loss?

Defeat and loss is not foreign to Adam Wilson. His own life slid into a deep depression after seeing so much devastation out his Manhattan window on September 11th. The shock drove him into a grief he did not understand. He walked the streets afraid to look up, terrified he would see a passenger plane heading for a nearby building.

Then, on December 26, 2004, Adam turned on his television and saw the Thailand death toll climbing higher and higher. Soon he found himself shouting at the TV footage, "Why isn't everyone rushing over there to help?" That's when he wondered why he wasn't going. Although he'd been planning a trip to Rome, Adam decided to switch his ticket to Thailand.

Today, looking across the shores of Khao Lak, the wreckage is worse than the WTC. Yet, here amidst this rubble, his spirit is lifting. Because he suffered so much after 9/11, Adam can empathize with the tsunami victims.

But truthfully, it's the Thai survivors who are helping him. There isn't a family in Khao Lak that hasn't lost at least one family member. Yet everyone's outside, assisting someone. So, Adam tosses his return ticket into the sea. He even decides to attend the 100 Days Tsunami Memorial ceremony. There he learns why grieving for lost souls must end after 100 days. Following 100 days, the soul passes on to its next life. This feels perfect to Adam.

※ ※ ※

My 60th birthday started on my 59th, when I asked my friends Linda, Helen, Carol, and Sue not to give me presents. Instead I requested they save their money for plane tickets to Hawai'i the next year. Suzanne agreed to take care of setting up the perfect *hale* [house] on Kealakekua Bay, where the Kona winds are so divine they sound like they have their own woodwind section.

I'd already learned to surf the year before in Kauai—or at least to stand up and scream for joy until I fell. So, when the actual morning of my birth arrives, I decide that surfing at 60 is just the sort of fist shaking at age I need to do. No one disagrees. In fact, as we prepare for the outing, Linda decides she too wants to surf.

We zero in on a surf school in Keauhou, a nearby town. Soon we are each given heavy longboards we can barely move, a pair of worn out reef walkers, and faded long sleeve tops to prevent "board burns." Linda pays extra for a photographer, and Suzanne, Carol, and Sue leave us to climb a large lava hill above the beach. There they set up chairs, towels, and binoculars, ready to cheer us on. After they depart, Linda and I find ourselves face-to-face with an island born surfing instructor named Kalani. Looking bored already, Kalani leads us to a nearby busy street; there he insists we lay our boards on the sidewalk and practice "popping up" as if we are surfing, while he makes personal cellphone calls.

Here? I protest. This method of leaping straight up from a lying down position is very different from how I learned on Kauai; but when I mention this, Kalani covers his cellphone and yells: "Again!"

Finally, Kalani motions for us to follow him down to the beach. But before we begin the steep climb balancing our hulking boards on our heads, he points to an area on the sandless shoreline below where there are large boulders of lava and coral poking up out of the ocean. Indicating the rocks, Kalani says, "If you *do* happen to catch a wave and stand up long enough to get to this rocky beachfront, jump off your boards before you hit that lava." *What?!!*

I let Kalani drop my surfboard into the shallow, rocky, water. Then he pushes me down on it, sliding my body around until I can paddle with my arms while keeping my feet out of the water in back. "Now you are on your sweet spot," he grins, and does the same thing with Linda. Giving both our boards a shove with his foot, Kalani slips onto his and sails by us, his strong arms propelling him over the incoming waves. I, on the other hand, smack into every one, flipping backward, and restarting my journey each time. When I finally join the rest of the class, Kalani has everyone lined up, waiting for the right wave to crest. The moment it does, he gives us each a push down the front of it. This isn't unusual for beginning surfers who haven't yet learned how to paddle into place. As the wave is lifting, Kalani grabs our boards and shoves us hard toward the beach, screaming "Paddle, paddle, paddle! *Stand up!*"

And when you *do* finally stand up, your eyes on the shoreline, your board steady as the floor beneath your feet, your posture getting straighter by the second, your smile getting bigger and wider until you can almost swallow your head—it is unfreakingbelievable.

After what seems like a long time in the water, I'm exhausted. What's more, the waves are getting burlier; something has shifted in the currents. I signal to Kalani that I'm getting out, but he misunderstands and starts dragging me back in.

Once behind the breakers, I sit up on my board and let my legs dangle in the water to rest, hoping to spot Suzanne. When I see her, she waves. What I *don't* see is the breakers rolling directly into the rocky shoreline below her—the one we're supposed to avoid. I'm not the only oblivious one either. Kalani is turning my board squarely into this waiting calamity, grunting, "Paddle, paddle...*Stand up!*"

I am absolutely nowhere near my "sweet spot" when a jerky shove sends me soaring off my board. I am so unprepared for anything but soft, sandy, salt water, I don't stick my hands out to protect my head. Then I hit a submerged mass of lava and coral, face first. Although I don't lose consciousness, I'm in a world of pain. My face is gashed open from my right cheek to my right eye; my nose is broken; there's a deep abrasion on my left temple and several slashes above my upper lip. When I come up, I am stunned, and bleeding like a fountain. I hold onto my board with one hand, while I explore my torn face with the other. A surfer glides up to me, alarmed. "Are you all right?" When he sees my face, he gasps, and begins pulling me toward the shore, yelling for help.

"How do I look?" I ask him naïvely. He refuses to answer.

Watching from shore, Carol can see me in her binoculars and knows instantly I'm hurt. Her girlfriend, Sue, leaps into action and gives a two-fingers-in-the-mouth whistle. Suzanne nearly kills herself climbing straight down the face of the lava cliff trying to get to me.

Even though I'm a bleeding mess, while everyone is trying to reach me, my own thoughts turn surprisingly calm. With no one willing to tell me how I look, and no mirror to look in, I wonder if my days of worrying about aging are over. Like most, I ponder every new line and wrinkle that drags me further from the youth parade. Will this accident change all that? Will my ragged face mean I am so badly scarred that age is unrecognizable? Is this my *Vanilla Sky*? Will anyone love me?

All the screaming and whistling from the cliff finally gets Linda's attention. When she sees all the red on my face, she paddles towards me thinking I have a bloody nose. Kalani follows her until they both get close enough to freak out. Propelled by guilt, Kalani has me back on shore in 12 heartbeats. Carol greets me by pulling off her white t-shirt, filling it with cold salt water, and dabbing my face. All I can manage is, "How bad is it?" and all Carol can say is, "Now, now..."

My exchange with a white-faced Suzanne is even less heartening. When she races up in our rented Mustang to rush me to the Kona emergency hospital, I ask her, "Honey, don't you think I should look at my face?" Keeping her eyes glued to the map she's studying, she insists, "Not now."

Before leaving, the girls make Kalani empty all the ice from his beer cooler, which is promptly put in Carol's t-shirt and held against my face. Kalani howls, "Stay calm, girls," before he and the photographer jump into a nearby Jeep. Linda yells to them about the photos she paid for, wondering if they could be used as evidence of negligence. (She's undoubtedly right because he and the photographer flee the scene with the film.)

For those of us who have waited long hours in large city emergency rooms, I can't say enough about what it's like to be badly injured in an isolated place, and have nurses and doctors literally waiting outside to greet you when you arrive. "Someone called ahead," one nurse tells me, as she makes me comfortable on a stretcher and wheels me in.

I have CAT scans, X-rays, physical examinations, and my wounds dressed. The doctor on duty tells us about some very scary things that could have—but *didn't*—happen, though only by millimeters. We shed tears of relief, although even in my twilight state I can tell that today's surf ride through near-tragedy will leave an indelible imprint on all six of us.

Outside my hospital room a discussion ensues about stitching up my face. It's noon when the attending physician comes in and offers to do it himself. There's a moment of silence before Suzanne asks to speak with him privately. Outside a major hoo-haw follows, when suddenly I hear Suzanne yell, "It's her *face*!" The next thing I know my future wife is back in the room explaining how "we're all going to be spending your birthday in the hospital." Apparently the very best plastic surgeon on the island is currently in Hilo—on the other side of the island. He won't get here until 7 p.m. tonight.

"I don't want to wait all day," I moan deliriously. Everyone looks at me appalled. "Do you want another CAT scan?" Suzanne threatens.

Later in the evening, while the plastic surgeon stitches my face back together, he chats with me as if we're playing cards: "You know this makes you an official 'warrior of the waves.'"

I look up at him loopy. *Is he talking to me?* No one else is in the room.

"That's what ancient Hawaiians called people who 'rode the charging blue monsters of the sea,'" he continues. When I say nothing, he tries a different tack. "I hear it's your birthday today. Are you going to go out later and celebrate?"

I still can't quite believe he's asking me questions, especially after instructing me to hold very still. Anesthetized and in some sort of nebulous fugue state, I natter about canceling all birthday plans because I've put everyone through too much grief with this accident.

He looks at me with stirring intelligence, and says, *"Aloha, Judy!* This could have been a fatal accident. Of course, you must celebrate. You not only lived *until* 60, you lived *through* 60!"

* * *

Ivor van Heerden, a hurricane expert at Louisiana State University, is tired of being ignored, so he calls a press conference and delivers an alarming prediction that shows how a major hurricane could flood and destroy the city of New Orleans.

Using all the technology at his disposal, Ivor demonstrates how raging storm waters will become toxic, picking up dangerous chemicals leaking from so many things smashing apart. Folks with the least resources will be stranded on their roofs because the water that floods the city won't leave. Survivors will need skilled medical help; many will need detoxification because putrefaction and fermentation will set in at temperatures of 100 degrees Fahrenheit. Finally, Ivor shows how these contaminated waters will flow into New Orleans where at least 300,000 people will *not* have evacuated on time.

Ivor talks about the importance of *advanced* preparation. "Where will the city rescue its people to: Tents? Stadiums? Auditoriums? Louisiana can't handle this. This is something that requires the full resources of the U.S. government."

Surely the Federal Emergency Management Agency (FEMA) knows this, and knows he isn't talking about the future. Ivor's talking about a storm that's right on the horizon.

On August 29th, 2005, Hurricane Katrina makes landfall on the Gulf Coast as a Category 3 storm with winds of 140 mph. Hundreds of thousands of people in Louisiana, Mississippi and Alabama are homeless, injured, and ill. U.S. government officials, including President Bush, take days to provide emergency help and seem confused about how bad things are. Those stranded and starving blame the Army Corps of Engineers for the bad decisions that led to the failures of the levees, yet Ivor himself was ridiculed by FEMA for predicting the levees would fail.

Thankfully, amid the worst screw-ups in emergency history, some agencies and individuals respond heroically. The Coast Guard rescues 34,000 stranded survivors. The Humane Society and other animal groups save more than 15,000 animals left behind by evacuees who thought they'd only be gone for a day.

From the ashes of government failures, new technologies for better crisis response are created. Emergency websites, maps, blogs, chat rooms, and help lines are posted and updated—all creating one online disaster community that will facilitate the rescue of so many people caught in 2017's Hurricane Harvey and buried in the 2010 Haiti and 2015 Nepal earthquakes.

Random Events Tend To Cluster

* * *

As tech becomes the story of the new millennium, for me it becomes a good door through which to leave my work of nearly 15 years. An LGBT Internet company buys LPI Media. As with most online media, the "editorial wall" standing between content and advertising, blows over completely. Everywhere I look this once paramount wall is replaced by some mercurial gibberish ushered in by computers, the Internet, cellphones, tablets, and social media. The "highway of information" as the Internet was once called, is now a shifty piece of work snapping up sound bites of things that have already taken place. For a nanosecond we think we know something; we even pass it along to others who are grateful because now they think they know something. But, really, we're all just echoes. What does it mean if we don't understand it? And how can we understand it without context, backstory, investigation, questioning, and real analysis by professionals who know something to begin with and are willing to study to find out more? Without the connections that surround each breaking-news event, awareness goes on a very undernourished saga. Uncontextualized content is a moody, excitable thing that will leave us anxious and starving.

Incredibly, my departure comes at the exact moment Suzanne and I sign a deal to tear down our funky Venice bungalow and build a modern two-story house on the same lot. We already have fully-approved plans from one of the city's up and coming architects; and the endless permit chase is finally over. But finding yourself without a salary when your architect initiates the launch with the toast: "I hope you girls are ready to start hemorrhaging money," is daunting. After all, I'm still the daughter of Jack and Paula, the parents who interrupted me regularly when I used their phone to ask, "Is that a local call?"

In their worldview—or that of any number of sane people—this would not be the right instant to take out a large bank loan for the first time in my life, or hand over long hoarded sums of cash. But I have Suzanne, and her worldview adds a lot of shades to what the Wieders would see only in black & white.

Naturally during construction, we must live elsewhere; so we pack up our dog and cats and move into two rooms above Carol and Sue's garage. This means most everything goes into storage. Notwithstanding some tough challenges that occur during the year and a half we live this way (I'm mourning the loss of nearly 15 years with my *Advocate* and *Out* family; our beloved cat, "Piano," gets ill and dies; both Suzanne and I suffer serious pneumonia bouts; and Carol has a pancreatic cancer scare), the experience of living so close to friends under demanding circumstances changes my priorities. It's a cliché, but life happens and your reaction is everything. Having *ohana* ready to rush you to the hospital in the middle of the night because you're so dehydrated you're talking gobbledygook, is pretty fierce. With three out of four of us taking a turn on that emergency-room caravan, we become a very deep-rooted team.

* * *

When Barack Obama wins the 2008 presidential election, the big story is his race. But there's an equally ground-breaking story to be told: Obama's *presidential* race. It's a triumph of the candidate's techno-demographic command. Simply put, he wins because he's able to use online social networking sites to connect directly with American voters. His is the first political campaign to harness the power of social media and make everyone feel like they're in on the conversation.

Best of all, the web technology Obama masters brings him more than a political base. He creates a database: the names of millions of supporters he can reach whenever he needs them. Obama uses technology to win the presidency, and as President, he uses it to govern. He did it first, but every political campaign to follow will build on the use of this technology—even to the detriment of the country, when it is corrupted in eight years.

* * *

Suzanne and I are legally married on August 24th, 2008; a few months after the California Supreme Court put the kibosh on banning same-sex couples from marrying. Of course, we know California's Prop 8 is a threat, but with momentum growing for Obama, we are certain we are on the verge of a brave new world, and just don't believe it will pass.

When it does, I'm so upset, I don't see the blessing in disguise: Previously complacent young LGBTs wake up from feeling that activism is uncool, and realize that a lot of people think they're second-class citizens. Prop 8 lands this nasty message so hard, a new movement is born;

"No more Mr. Nice Gay!" and "No H8!" become battle cries heard across the state. After Prop. 8, marriage is *the* most important Equal Right to have in America. Bash-back tactics echoing the angry outing techniques of the AIDS epidemic, are used by gay activists—but now they have better tools: Online Prop 8 donation lists are stolen and published on popular websites, resulting in boycotts and public humiliations.

Fortunately, the right to be legally married becomes especially important for one 82-year-old widow, Edie Windsor. With class and courage, she takes her case against the Defense of Marriage Act (DOMA) to the U.S. Supreme Court, and sets the course of fair-mindedness for generations to come.

10 Aloha Technology!

* * *

I am trying to enjoy a late lunch at Huggo's On The Rocks in Kailua-Kona. Unfortunately, I am so nervous I'm tossing the beets and organic lettuce of my Ono Bay Salad from one end of the plate to the other. Suzanne and our realtor, Lori—who's been speeding us from house to house for four blurry days—are my table mates, and they too are dazed and playing with their food. We are all waiting for the arrival (by stand-up paddle board) of our new friend Eric Von Platen Luder, who, along with his soon-to-be husband, Scott Dodd, runs and owns a number of popular restaurants on the Big Island, including Huggo's. Even though I am flying blind, I sense we need to talk to a reliable lifetime Big Islander about what we plan to do next:

When my father passed away a year ago in the spring of 2011, my brother and I sold the family home in Rustic Canyon. I knew instantly what I wanted to do with my share of the money. Although many people advised me to sock it away for my uncertain future, all I could see was my dream: a second home in Hawai'i where my wife, friends, and relatives could always come and soak up aloha.

Suzanne and I have scared ourselves to death considering horse property and coffee farms, but finally today, the last day of our house-hunting trip, Lori drove us to a property that looked out over the city of Kailua-Kona and the entire Kona Bay. Huge palm trees lined the winding driveway, and when the automatic gate opened, we saw not one, but two *hales*. One needed total renovation; and one was gorgeous as is. When I walked out on the *lanai* and saw the sweeping ocean views, I said to Suzanne, "OMG, *this* is the house." So, we snapped phone pictures of everything and raced to Huggo's to figure out if we should make an offer.

"There's Eric!" I say, pointing to a tall, muscular man who is pulling his paddleboard out of the ocean and making his way into the restaurant. I bring up the subject of our house hunting, and Eric asks if we've seen anything we like. Naturally we talk about the last hale. When he asks where it's located, Lori tells him.

"That's the gate right next to *our* home!" he laughs enthusiastically. "That property is an amazing buy!" Knowing that Eric and Scott will be close by, and that the area is as special as it looks, kicks us into action. The second Eric leaves the table, Lori points a finger at us and insists, "You've got to make an offer tonight!"

Of course, that's exactly what we do.

※ ※ ※

Afterword

One night I dream I'm dancing around a mysterious beach fire. When I look above it, I see my silhouette reaching into the dark heavens. And there, behind my own spirit, I finally behold the full, boundless mana of Hawai'i. When I awake, I know this *aina*, this paradise we call *"Hale Mana'o"* [House of Intuitions] is truly ours to care for.

My niece Sarah decides to use her summer break from teaching to visit and help me with this new home. Somewhere between lining shelves and daily surfing excursions, a big aloha kernel falls in her heart. By the end of her second visit to the island, Sarah announces, "I'm moving to Kona. I love it here!"

This is a sign from heaven. Sarah moves to the Big Island, gets a teaching job at the local high school, makes a load of new friends, falls in love with a fantastic man and marries him! The *mana* of this is head spinning because at the end of my father's life, all he kept telling me was how much he wanted his granddaughters to be "settled and happy." Well, my beloved niece, Rachel, who once told me that her friends called her the "homo police" because she objected to derogatory LGBT slurs, is married, and working in Brooklyn, the place Dad was born and raised. So, there you go, Dad, all "settled and happy." Rest in peace.

But I must say, unless you're dead, it's not all that easy to rest in peace. I've always been described as a "doer," so closing my eyes and letting the gracious island winds clean out my to-do lists is practically impossible. Even in this beautiful place, there's always something to build, fix, plant, organize, observe, or write.

Looking back as I have with this book, I can see that even though I've helped others along the way, my work in music, and journalism, and LGBT rights has primarily benefited *me*. I think a lot about the altruistic things some people do and the joy they say that comes to them when they do it. I had no models for this in my family. They were good at other things, like humor, education, saving money, and being cautious. These qualities are good to have, but there is so much more to life.

Maybe this journey really began back in 1992 during my first Big Island visit. I remember getting up to leave a public beach when something caught my eye in a nearby palm grove. At first I couldn't believe what I was seeing: hundreds of feral cats and kittens scattered about in the shade scavenging for food. Who did they belong to? Why so many? How did they get there? Who took care of them?

Nearly 25 years ago when I first saw those cats, I had no one to ask. Now, because my friend Scott serves on the Hawai'i Island Humane Society [HIHS] board of directors, I am learning a lot. One cat and her kittens can produce 420,000 offspring in seven years. So, the hundreds of feral cats I saw that were left to fend for themselves on the Big Island in '92, are now the feral millions!

The impact of these feral cats on their environment is shattering. Life for certain indigenous island creatures—including birds—is being threatened because of these starving cats. Beleaguered cat activists and volunteers trap, fix, and release as many cats as possible to try and stop their proliferation. One day, I watched hundreds of cats climb down a hillside to be fed by a "cat lady" they trusted. It cracked my heart open and gave me a glimpse of what it means to be human in a world of disadvantaged animals.

Afterword

All this made me wonder if volunteering at a shelter was anything I'd have the nerve to do. On the mainland, just walking into a shelter made me feel like I had two choices: take them *all* home immediately; or turn and run like hell. I did a lot of running.

Surprisingly in this new setting, I felt something in me shift. So, I decided to visit Kona's HIHS, one small building with some trailers, built in the 60s on barely an acre of land and located next to the Kona Police Station and the dump. Not ideal at all. I spent the morning going through the requisite training with my remarkable teacher, Bebe Ackerman. Then, after lunch, I pushed open a door to a small, cramped area that housed the kitten cages, and saw…"Maxine." With her black and off-center white markings, she huddled frightened and shaking in the back of her cage. I couldn't take my eyes off of her.

Maxine had been at the HIHS a week. I read her chart carefully before opening the door to the cage she shared with a hyper animated tabby kitten that catapulted himself into my arms the minute he saw the opening. I petted him, leaning my head down so I could see Maxine better. She was clearly pretending I wasn't there. Her head was dropped down like a heavy rock on her folded, minuscule body. Definitely not "thriving." So, I began to speak softly in her direction. My penchant for talking to animals as if they understand every word I say kicked in. I do this with my own four-legged family regularly. Other volunteers drifted into the kitten area, wondered why I was talking to myself, and left quickly.

Finally, Maxine gave up and looked at me. The little tabby had conked out in my arms, so I slipped him onto a towel, and in one swoop dropped off tabby and lifted out Maxine. Her little blue eyes got as big as her entire head. *What just happened?* I chattered on casually. After some time, I put Maxine down on my lap, petting her but no longer restraining her, and talked at length about the merits of love. ("You'll like it, Maxine. It grows on you. Oh, you're purring; you agree?") At one point, she turned her whole head around and looked up at me like, *Wow! Nice.*

Encouraged, I did the same thing the following day. And by the third day, something had changed. When I walked through the door, Maxine was at the *front* of her cage. A stranger was hovering around the kitten cages checking out who was available for adoption, and Maxine *wasn't* hiding. She was reaching her little black and white paw through the cage trying to touch the young woman. I held my breath, but the lady picked another kitty. When she walked away, Maxine saw me, and meowed. I grabbed her up, and kissed her purring head into mush.

When I returned after the weekend, Maxine's chart was missing. I got worried and made my way to the front desk calling for Roxy, the Kona Shelter Manager, "What does it mean when their charts are gone?"

Roxy smiled at me and announced proudly, "Maxine got adopted Saturday. She's scheduled for surgery [spaying] at the end of the week, and then her new owner will pick her up."

"*She got adopted!*" I bellowed at her, ecstatic.

"Yes," Roxy laughed. Then remembering my play dates with Maxine, she turned and said pointedly, "*You* did that for her! You made a people connection for her."

Nothing like that had ever happened to me before. I understood all about falling in love with a shelter animal and wanting to rescue her for *myself, my* pet, *mine*, like a child, an extension of *me*. But volunteering and doing something to help an animal that wasn't mine have a better life, *without me?* That was a new experience in giving. And I'd never felt better in my life.

When I told Scott, he drove me out to see 12 exquisite acres of land located in the cool uplands of Keauhou *mauka*

Afterword

[mountains]. As we stood amidst several large trees and scattered buildings with winding trails and grassy valleys as far as we could see, Scott told me that thanks to a generous donor, all this would be the new home of the HIHS.

It will be called the Animal Community Center because it's much bigger than anyone's past idea of an animal shelter. There will be exercise parks and dog runs, event areas, and a central adoption region where benches, trees, and flowers will surround the animals and interested adopters.

I didn't know whether to applaud or cry as I was led past a huge barn with a tree in the center of it. "This will house all the cats," Scott beamed. All around are structures that will become education buildings, a state of the art veterinary center, an equine park and stable for the horses, a children's education center, and an administration building—everything they don't have today. And local community members will be invited to come and bring their own pets as well.

Executive Director, Donna Whitaker, tells me they want to become a genuine community center; encouraging at-risk youth as well as *kupuna* [elderly] to mingle with the animals in special spaces designated for just that purpose. "That way seniors and teenagers, who might be experiencing some isolation or depression, can care for an animal and receive much needed affection."

So, my life–changing experience with Maxine is going to happen to lots of people in this gorgeous place where so many more at-risk animals and people need help. How perfect that the progression of animal shelters—to officially include therapeutic interactions between animals and people—is taking such a big leap in Hawai'i, the place that's both behind and ahead of everywhere else.

Similar thoughts come to me often about this extraordinary place. The first legal battle for "gay marriage" was fought and lost in Hawai'i. Authentic Hawaiian culture has always held that every human being has a complete collection of male and female characteristics. How these traits manifest is unique to each person. In fact, ancient Hawaiians *celebrated* the transgendered members of their community. That's a lot nicer than what happened when the missionaries arrived. Their attitude was that Hawai'i was paradise if only they could get rid of the Hawaiians. In so many ways, a microcosm of America today, a country in crisis.

So, really, what else can we do but pry open all the jammed windows we can find, so the fresh air that truth brings rushes in and makes us all a bit healthier? There is one thing I have certainty about: people should be allowed to be all the extraordinary things they are. Then the clustering random events will finally make sense. They're our lives.

Mahalo and aloha.

Acknowledgments

Judy would like to thank: **Lisa Hagan**, publisher of Lisa Hagan Books, for signing this unusual journey because she feels "it's a real game-changer in memoir writing;" her attorney, **Tony Amendola**, for his careful vetting and unwavering support of this defiant tome; and **Frank Rich**, for his early but crucial enthusiasm for the project.

No book gets born without the dedicated labor of several "in-process readers." Right from the beginning, I got lucky. For their keen eyes, minds, and opinions, I am forever grateful to: **Linda Villarosa, Carol Cole, Linda Laisure, Helen Alland, Joe Landry, Sharon Landa, Christine Russell, Nikki Trumbo, Karen Fite, Ruth Scovill, Tim C. Johnson, Lenore Buirgy, Jana Welch, Jason Watford**, and, of course, **Suzanne Buirgy**, for watching over every page and never letting me abandon the challenging road to *Random Events Tend To Cluster*.

Made in the USA
San Bernardino, CA
04 October 2017